Teaching, Learning, and Motivation in a Multicultural Context

A volume in
Research in Multicultural Education and International Perspectives

Teaching, Learning, and Motivation in a Multicultural Context

Edited by
Farideh Salili
and
Rumjahn Hoosain

INFORMATION AGE
PUBLISHING

80 Mason Street • Greenwich, Connecticut 06830 • www.infoagepub.com

Library of Congress Cataloging-in-Publication Data

Teaching, learning, and motivation in a multicultural context / edited
by Farideh Salili and Rumjahn Hoosain.
    p. cm. – (Research in multicultural education and international
perspectives ; v. 3)
  ISBN 1-931576-94-7 (pbk.) – ISBN 1-931576-95-5 (hardcover)
  1. Multicultural education–Cross-cultural studies. 2. Motivation in
education–Cross-cultural studies. I. Salili, Farideh. II. Hoosain, R.
(Rumjahn) III. Series.
  LC1099.T423 2003
  370.117–dc21

2003000043

Printed in the United States of America

LIST OF CONTRIBUTORS

Hector Betancourt	Loma Linda University, California
Monique Boekaerts	Center for the study of Education and Instruction, Leiden University, Leiden, The Netherlands
Belle Derks	Departments of Psychology and Education, Leiden University, The Netherlands
Aurora Elizondo	Universidad Pedagogica Nacional, Ausco
Márta Fülöp	Institute for Psychology, Hungarian Academy of Sciences Budapest, Hungary
Sandra Graham	Department of Education, UCLA.
Ratna Ghosh	Faculty of Education, McGill University
Kit-Tai Hau	Faculty of Education, The Chinese University of Hong Kong
Rumjahn Hoosain	Department of psychology, The University of Hong Kong
Marian Jazvac	Department of Educational and Counseling Psychology, McGill University
Chi-Kwong Kong	Faculty of Education, The Chinese University of Hong Kong
Benjamine Leung	Department of Sociology, The University of Hong Kong
Herbert W. Marsh	Self-concept Enhancement & Learning Facilitation (SELF) Research Centre, University of Western Sydney, NSW
Ference Marton	Department of Education, Gothenburg University, Sweden
Kevin McGuire	John A. Brashear High School, Pittsburgh PA

Valentina McInerney   School of Psychology, University of Western Sydney, Australia

Dennis McInerney   School of Psychology, University of Western Sydney, Australia

Paul Pintrich   Combined Program in Education and Psychology, University of Michigan

Farideh Salili   Department of Psychology, The University of Hong Kong

Alenoush Saroyan   Department of Educational and Counseling Psychology, McGill University

Norma Tarrow   California State University

April Z. Taylor   Department of Education, UCLA

Oliver C.S. Tzeng   Osgood Laboratory for Cross-cultural Research Department of Psychology, Indiana University-Purdue University at Indianapolis

David Watkins   Department of Education, The University of Hong Kong

Takashi Yamauchi   Psychology Department, Texas A&M University

Gangaw Zaw   Loma Linda University

Akane Zusho   Combined Program in Education and Psychology, The University of Michigan

CONTENTS

PREFACE

In the past two decades or so, several important developments throughout the world has made multicultural education a necessity in the developed world. They include demographic changes in nations' population as a result of increased mobility, globalization of the economy, ever advancing technological developments, and increased demand for skilled workers.

The schools and educational institutions are faced with the challenging task of preparing students to compete in the global economy which is increasingly knowledge oriented and complex. Many students in our schools are from diverse ethnic, racial, and religious backgrounds, and educational reforms should address this diversity. Appropriate multicultural education is needed to help these students attain skills necessary for them to be productive members of their societies.

Multicultural education reforms that are designed to transform the schools in ways that promote educational equality, critical thinking, and justice for all groups would teach students the life skills necessary to be members of free and democratic societies. It teaches them to transcend beyond their cultural boundaries and acquire the knowledge, skills and attitudes needed to participate in discourse with people whose view points differ, and engage in civic actions for the good of the society (Bank & Bank, 1997). Thus, multicultural education is an imperative for the survival of pluralistic and democratic nations of the twenty-first century.

As Volumes 1 and 3 show, multicultural education programs are being experimented in many parts of the world. It is, however, important to realize that we are still at the start of this important enterprise. Despite the many interesting ideas presented by scholars such as James Bank (see Bank &

Teaching, Learning, and Motivation in a Multicultural Context, pages ix–x
Copyright © 2003 by Information Age Publishing
All rights of reproduction in any form reserved.

Bank, 1997) on the mission and goals of multicultural education, there are still many unresolved issues. There are large gaps between the underlying ideas and assumptions of multicultural education and the actual practice in schools. The purpose of this book series is to provide a forum for research and discussions addressing issues related to multicultural education.

Volume 3 of this series is designed to present educators with current research and emerging issues in teaching, learning and motivation in a multicultural context. The book is separated into four sections. In the introduction section we have outlined some of the current issues and recent thoughts about the nature of learning, teaching, and school reforms from a multicultural perspective.

Part II focuses on theoretical and methodological issues and applications in multicultural settings. Chapters 2 and 3 argue for different conceptualization or approaches in theorizing and research for better understanding of cultural differences in student motivation in the context of a classroom. Chapters 4 examines usefulness of attribution processes for conflict resolution in multicutural educational settings, while Chapter 5 presents a study in which attribution theory was applied to conduct an intervention on at risk youths. Chapter 6 presented a study exploring the applicability of self-concept theory and measures in the Chinese context. Finally, Chapter 7 compares how students from different cultures perceive and understand knowledge.

Part III focuses on perspectives on teaching and teacher education. Chapters 8 and 9 deal with value education for teachers, and teachers' attitudes towards aspects of multicultural education. Chapter 10 addresses the need to improve the quality and the value placed on teaching in post-secondary institutions worldwide. In chapter 11 the relevance of Western theorizing and research to teacher thinking and the effectiveness of Western teaching innovations for a Chinese educational context is examined.

Finally, in Part IV Chapters 12 and 13 explore the factors that affect success and failure in the multicultural classroom, while the last two chapters (14 and 15) deal with issues of disidentification and labeling in multicultural educational settings.

ACKNOWLEDGMENTS

We are deeply grateful to the scholars who contributed to this book by assisting us in reviewing the chapters and for their valuable comments that helped improve the quality of the book. We would also like to acknowledge with thanks the contribution of our son Amir Hoosain who acted as our editorial assistant.

part I

INTRODUCTION

CHAPTER 1

RECENT DEVELOPMENTS IN MULTICULTURAL EDUCATION

Issues and Ideas

Farideh Salili and Rumjahn Hoosain

Multicultural education is defined as a process whereby a person develops competencies of perceiving, believing, evaluating, and doing things in multiple ways (Bank, 1981). The definition implies that the multicultural person is a dynamic, fluid and changing individual (Banks, 1981; Nieto, 1992 cited in Ford, 1999). Multicultural education is a reform movement, with the goal of democratizing education so that individuals with diverse backgrounds could have equal opportunity to achieve academically in schools. In order to promote educational equality among students of diverse groups, it is necessary to change each major aspect of the school, "such as its culture, power relationships, the curriculum and materials, and the attitudes and beliefs of the staff" (Banks & Banks, 1997, p. 1). It is also important for educators to learn about students' cultural values and beliefs that influence their learning and motivational characteristics.

ISSUES RELATED TO CURRENT PRACTICES

The view of multicultural education which calls for process-oriented and inclusive education has not gone far beyond the rhetorics. The application of

Teaching, Learning, and Motivation in a Multicultural Context, pages 3–9
Copyright © 2003 by Information Age Publishing
All rights of reproduction in any form reserved.

multiculturalism in the classroom is mainly through product oriented, objectified and packaged sets of skills which focus on "static features of generalized groups of people rather than on the people themselves" (Ford, 1999, p. 5).

Ford has pointed out to a number of problems associated with product oriented curricula. These include *global approach* to learning various subjects. For example, in social studies the global approach focuses on individual differences and cultural diversity by having students identify and label the content of various cultures such as food, dress, dance, and so on. By focusing on the objects from the culture rather than intentions, actions and achievement of people, the individuals who form that culture also become objects, thus marginalizing the people that the dominant culture wants to understand.

A second problem concerned with product-oriented application of multicultural education is *objectifying the learning styles.* The idea of individual differences and diversity is packaged by some educators into learning style inventories and strategies (Dunn & Dunn, 1978). Teachers are encouraged to buy these ready made packages and assess and match their own teaching styles with individual students. This is presumed to help them find out the potential sources of misunderstanding and to adjust teaching styles to accommodate learner differences. For example, Longstreet (1978, cited in Ford, 1999) has provided a guideline in which five aspects of ethnicity are identified to help pinpoint potential sources of misunderstanding: (1) verbal communication (e.g., grammar), (2) nonverbal communication (e.g., signs and symbols), (3) orientation modes (e.g., attention modes), (4) social value patterns (e.g., hard work), and (5) intellectual modes (e.g., preferred modes of learning).

There are problems with objectifying the learning styles. First, there is a risk of over generalizing cultural characteristics which may lead to stereotyping of students and their cultures. For example, the image of the Asian student being diligent and good at math assumes that every Asian student behaves the same way and has the same attributes, rather than an individual with his/her own characteristics. Stereotyping not only marginalize individuals of different cultural backgrounds but also lead to a self-fulfilling prophecy in which teachers may perceive some differences that does not exist (Brown, 1988).

The prescriptive interpretation of cultural differences may hinder communication as the teachers may believe that they already know the reason for students' behaviors and there is no need for them to try and find out by speaking to them. Furthermore, when students' behaviors are different from those of the dominant culture, differences are often interpreted as deficiencies and targeted for change (Gilmore, 1985).

Knowledge about cultural differences without an opportunity for interaction is not enough for developing a multicultural perspective and may lead to stereotyping and misinterpretation of students' intents and pressure for students to conform with mainstream norms of the society (Ford, 1999).

Another strategy used recently to implement multicultural education in schools has focused on *recruiting ethnically diverse undergraduate students* into the field of education to become teachers in North America. It is thought that by being ethnically different these teachers who also have experience with the dominant culture have already learned how to cope in European American dominated schools. This system can be flawed as it assumes that these individuals can transfer their own experiences to a social understanding of other students. It also suggests that every teacher regardless of their ethnicity, religion or race will "think, act, believe, and respond in manners similar to others of that same race" (Ford, 1999, p. 7).

DEVELOPING MULTICULTURAL PERSPECTIVE

These efforts to introduce multicultural education into the classrooms oversimplify the personal meaning construction of knowledge in the process of learning. Knowledge is not objective, but rather constructed as a result of transaction between the person and what is to be known. Teachers and students bring their own personal meaning construction to the learning context. These meanings are influenced by their intellectual, social and emotional histories. Being a multicultural person does not necessarily mean that the individual is ethnically different from the dominant European American culture. How does one become a multicultural person? According to Ford's (1999) model, in order to become multicultural one must engage in critical self-reflection through which the individual becomes more conscious of him/herself and develop understanding of how others operate in the world. The process of becoming a multicultural person involves a sequence of four phases of self-development in which the self grounded on direct experiences becomes multicultural through self reflection (past remembrance), critical self-reflection (questioning), social consciousness (perceiving the self in relation to others), and critical social consciousness (understanding the self in relation to in-group others and the self in relation to out-group others). Critical social consciousness encourages individuals to see themselves as part of a larger community, going beyond their ethnic identity and culture, and developing a sense of responsibility and belonging to all humanity. This is when multicultural perspective is achieved.

IMPLICATION OF MULTICULTURAL EDUCATION FOR SCHOOLS

Multicultural education is closely linked to critical pedagogy (Nieto, 1995). Both multicultural education and critical pedagogy challenge and question the acceptance of the interpretation of knowledge by dominant main-stream culture and empowers students and teachers to bring about social change (Sleeter, 1995). The mission of multicultural education is to instill in students a sense of responsibility and commitment to bring about social justice and democracy (Maning & Baruth, 1996).

Translated into teaching practices, the mission of multicultural education suggests that the teachers should encourage students to engage in critical self-reflection and to question their own self-concept in relation to social reality and to others. They should be encouraged to debate conflicting and different interpretations of knowledge, create their own interpretation, and discover their own position (Bank, 1996). They should be encouraged to be critical thinkers and taught the values of social justice, equal opportunity as well as moral and ethical values, so that people of diverse ethnic, religious and racial backgrounds can live and work together harmoniously in civil and democratic societies. The mission of multicultural education is important in today's pluralistic societies. How does one instill these values in students and teachers especially when they may be in conflict with the values instilled in some students and teachers through being members of their own culture? Ratna Ghosh, Norma Tarrow, and Aurora Elizondo (in Chapter 8) suggested that these values cannot simply be taught through instruction, because values are acquired, not given. The authors proposed that "teachers must create the conditions that encourage the development of these values through the school curriculum and program of studies, the organizational culture, the processes of decision making, critical thinking, and communication in the classroom as well as in the larger school environment. Because teachers are crucial in this process, attention or lack of attention to values in pre-service programs which produce teachers are of great significance."

Despite the many efforts in promoting multicultural education, there are still many unresolved issues. One of the major challenges faced by teachers in multicultural classrooms is how to motivate students of diverse backgrounds to learn and to succeed academically, which is the topic of this book. Few educators and scholars would argue with the contention that we know very little about how students with different ethnic, religious and racial backgrounds learn, what motivates them and how they cope with the new learning environment. We know, for example, from the research findings (see, e.g., Stevenson & Stigler, 1992) that some ethnic groups tend to outperform others in academic achievement, while others often underperform or fail to succeed in schools. Culturally responsive education goes a long way in improving the education for students whose cultures have been marginalized, or omitted from the school curricular. It provides insight and understanding why students from some cultural backgrounds succeed in schools and why others fail to achieve, but by itself it cannot guarantee that all students will learn. School reforms and changes in school policies can positively influence student learning, but there is no simple cause-effect relationship between these reforms and student learning. These changes may improve educational outcomes for many students who are not achieving academic success, but taken in isolation they fail to reflect the complex nature of student learning. "A comprehensive view of student learning that takes into account the many internal and external influences on achievement may help explain why some students succeed academically while others do not" (Nieto, 1997, p. 387).

Nieto (1997) proposed five conditions that are necessary to promote student achievement within a multicultural perspective.

1. *School reform should be antiracist and anti-biased.* Multicultural education does not automatically take care of racism. In fact, without an explicit anti-racist focus it may perpetuate racism through stereotyping and focusing on superficial aspects of culture. To be anti-racist means paying attention to all areas in which some groups are favored over others. These include school policies (which reflect institu tional power to develop harmful policies), curriculum, choice of materials, attitudes and behavior of the staff, their interactions with each other, with students and with the communities (Nieto, 1997). For example, the schools need to examine how the curriculum may perpetuate distorted, negative or incomplete accounts about some groups while exalting others as the makers of history.

2. *Understanding and acceptance of all students as having talents and strengths that can enhance their education.* Rather than viewing some ethnically different groups as having deficits (e.g., by not knowing English) or coming from deprived background, which is not very helpful, the schools should consider the students and their families as having important talents that can help them achieve in school if they are considered. For example, the teachers could consider whether parents could use their native language to help their children at home rather than convincing them to learn English. The schools should also consider whether the students should learn English only, or in conjunction with their own language. Their native language is also necessary to maintain the important connection with their own communities and their loving relationship with their families.

3. *School reform should be considered within the parameters of critical pedagogy.* The link between multicultural education and critical pedagogy is an important one. Critical pedagogy is an approach that encourages students and teachers to view the learning material critically. It is essential to expose students to a wide range of view points,

to help them develop critical judgment and decision making skills. This is needed if they are to be productive members of a democratic society. "A critical perspective does not simply operate on the principle of substituting one truth for another; instead, students are expected to reflect on multiple and contradictory perspectives to understand reality more fully" (Giroux, 1983; Shor, 1992 cited in Nieto, 1997, p. 396).

4. *Teaching and learning need to be meaningfully involved in school reform.*   Research findings have shown that involvement by parents, students, and teachers in decision making on education reform and implementing them dramatically improve student learning (Abi-Nader, 1993; Henderson & Berla, 1995, cited in Nieto, 1997). Yet the people who are most affected are often excluded from policy discussions and decision making about the reform and its implementation. Participation of teachers and students provide important and insightful perspectives about student learning and the realities of the classroom in school-based reform (Thorn, 1994).

5. *School reform needs to be based on high expectations and rigorous standards.*   Many students who come from low socioeconomic background or from under-privilege minority groups are automatically considered at risk of academic failure, and too often the teachers have low expectations of these students because of their background. These low expectations become self-fulfilling prophecies and teacher expectancy research generally supports this contention.

We have outlined some of the basic ideas, issues, and recent thoughts on multicultural education to provide a framework for the chapters that follows. However, readers should note, as James Bank so aptly stated, that " Multicultural education is a continuing process because the idealized goals it tries to actualize—such as educational equality and the eradication of all forms of discrimination—can never be fully achieved in a human society" (1997, p. 26). We can only hope that efforts towards multicultural education and research in this area would lead to more effective learning and the possibility that schools can become places of hope for students of all backgrounds.

REFERENCES

Abi-Nader, J. (1993). Meeting the needs of multicultural classroom: Family values and the motivation of minority students. In M. J. O'Hair and S. Odell (Eds.), *Diversity and teaching: Teacher education year book* (pp. 212–236). Fort Worth: Harcourt Brace Jovanovich.

Banks, J. A., & Banks, C. A. M. (Eds.), (1997). *Multicultural education: Issues and perspectives.* CITY: PUBLISHER.

Banks, J. A. (1981). *Multiethnic education: Theory and practice.* Boston: Allyn & Bacon.

Brown, E. B. (1988). African-American women's quilting: A framework for conceptualizing and teaching African American women's history. In .R. Malson, E. Mudimbe-Boyi, J. F. O'Barr, & M. Weyer (Eds.), *Black women in Africa: Social science perspectives* (pp. 9–180). Chicago: University of Chicago Press.

Dunn, K., & Dunn, R. (1978). *Learning style inventory.* Lawrence, KS: Price Systems.

Ford, T. (1999). *Becoming multicultural: Personal and social construction through critical teaching.* New York: Falmer Press.

Gilmore, P. (1985). Gimme room: School resistance, attitudes, and access to literacy. *Journal of Education, 167,* 111–128.

Giroux, H. A. (1983). *Theory and resistance in Education: A pedagogy for the opposition.* South Hadley, MA: Bergin & Garvey.

Henderson, A. T., & Berla, N. (1995). *A new generation of evidence: The family is crucial to student achievement.* Washington, DC: Center for Law and Education.

Longstreet, W. (1978). *Aspects of ethnicity: Understanding differences in pluralistic classrooms,* New York: Teaches College Press.

Maning, M. L., & Baruth, L.G. (1996). *Multicultural education of children and adolescents.* Boston: Allyn & Bacon.

Nieto, S. (1992). *Affirming diversity: The sociopolitical context of multicultural education.* New York: Longman.

Nieto, S. (1995). From Brown heroes and holidays to assimilationist agenda: Reconsidering the critics of multicultural education. In C. E. Sleeter & P. L. McLaren (Eds.), *Multicultural education, critical pedagogy, and the politics of difference.* Albany: State University New York Press.

Shor, I. (1992). *Empowering education: Critical teaching for social change.* Chicago: University of Chicago Press.

Sleeter, C. E., & McLaren, INITIAL. (1995). *Multicultural education, critical pedagogy, and the politics of difference.* Albany: State University New York Press.

Stevenson, H. W., & Stigler, J. (1992). *The learning gap: Why our schools are failing and what can we learn from Japanese and Chinese Education.* New York: Summet Books.

Thorne, J. (1994). Living with the pendulum: The complex world of teaching. *Harvard Educational Review, 64*(2), 195–208.

part II

THEORETICAL AND METHODOLOGICAL PERSPECTIVES: ISSUES AND APPLICATIONS IN MULTICULTURAL EDUCATION

CHAPTER 2

HOW DO STUDENTS FROM DIFFERENT CULTURES MOTIVATE THEMSELVES FOR ACADEMIC LEARNING?

Monique Boekaerts

Over the last few decades, many articles have been written to explain the nature of motivation and its effect on student learning in the classroom. Many researchers argued convincingly that learning and achievement goals cannot be understood when isolated from the motivation processes that guide the pursuit of these goals. Yet, at the beginning of the twenty-first century, teachers and educators still find it hard to apply the principles of motivation theory in the live classroom situation. Why is that so? When educators skim the psychological literature in an attempt to find general motivation principles, they are struck by the fact that there is not just one, or maybe two, main theories of motivation but dozens of theories that consist of overlapping and non-overlapping constructs and conflicting hypotheses. They lose their way in the morass of motivational beliefs, such as self-efficacy, value, and expectation, and wonder how these beliefs differ from motivation strategies, including attributions, coping strategies, goal-setting and goal-striving. Moreover, there are abundant intervention programs that promise to boost students' self-efficacy, self-esteem, intrinsic motivation, and the like. The alert observer notes that these interventions are wrapped

Teaching, Learning, and Motivation in a Multicultural Context, pages 13–31
Copyright © 2003 by Information Age Publishing
All rights of reproduction in any form reserved.

in fragmented layers of empirical support. This state of affairs leads to the conclusion that the field of motivation is plagued by lack of consensus about fundamental issues. In my opinion, our attempts to build up cumulative wisdom are hindered by the fact that our conceptual frameworks harbor many misconceptions and are still incomplete. In the next sections I will argue that Western theories of motivation are incomplete and should be redesigned to include the principles that hold for students from other cultures. I will also refer to a widespread misconception, namely that lower quality learning strategies are associated with low motivation.

MOTIVATION, CULTURE, AND LEARNING

Accumulating evidence points to the effect of culture on motivation. It seems that the effort students are prepared to invest (goal-setting) and actually invest (goal-striving) in curricular activities and extracurricular tasks is culture-dependent. Researchers and teachers agree that students from different cultures are apt to hold different views of what constitutes optimal learning settings and that this conception has a strong impact on the effort they are prepared to invest. Watkins (2000) examined the relationship between the learning environment and the approach to learning students adopt in different cultures. His database included at least 8000 subjects from eight Western and eight non-Western countries. Results indicated that higher quality learning strategies are associated with higher student self-esteem and internal locus of control across a number of very different cultures and at both school and university level. However, higher quality learning strategies were not always reflected in higher academic grades in both Western and non-Western samples. Many researchers (e.g., Scouller, 1998) commented on these disappointingly low correlations by referring to the assessment system. They argued that students are getting wise. They adopt superficial learning strategies when they learn that teachers are encouraging them to use deep learning strategies, whilst assessing the quality of their learning with multiple-choice questions. This is a clear example of self-regulation. Why should one adopt time consuming deep learning strategies when the assessment system prefers quantity to quality?

At this point in the discussion, motivation becomes a salient explanatory construct. Watkins examined this construct in a cultural perspective. He wrote:

> …Western dichotomies that do not seem to travel to the Orient are related to the construct of motivation. Western psychology books treat intrinsic and extrinsic motivation as a bi-polar construct. The intrinsic end is considered the more desirable by Western educators (Watkins, p. 166).

They consider intrinsic motivation to be a precursor of the desired deep learning strategies. This conception is in conflict with data reported on Chinese students, who seem to adopt deep strategies out of personal ambition, family face, peer support and material reward. Interestingly, Ramburuth and McCormick (2001) reported that, contrary to results found in Western countries, Asian students combine surface strategies with intrinsic, or deep, motivation whereas Australian students combined extrinsic, or surface, motivation with deep strategies. This finding suggests that Australian students need to be inspired by their teachers or parents to use deep-level strategies and they expect to be valued, or even rewarded for using these strategies. Much is still to be learned about the reasons why students select deep- or surface-level strategies. For example, why do Asian students, who are motivated to learn, deliberately select surface-level strategies? Purdie and Hattie (1996) shed some light on this phenomenon. They compared the study strategies, will power, and cheating behavior of Australian, Japanese, and Japanese-Australian high school students and concluded as follows:

> Memorization was the strategy rated by the Japanese students as being the most important in learning. Furthermore, the Japanese students maintained the importance of memorization as a learning behavior even after experiencing the Australian classroom learning context in which memorization is not encouraged as a strategy for learning....there were no differences among Japanese high, medium, and low achievers in their use of memorization strategies. In agreement with the findings of Stevenson and Stigler (1992), therefore, the emphasis on memorization appears not to be detrimental to academic achievement of Japanese students (p. 861).

In this chapter, I will argue that a more complete understanding of student motivation in the context of the classroom will require a conceptual framework that casts student behavior as more than just a product of preferential learning styles and motivational traits. A potential avenue for moving beyond these traditional frameworks is offered by two recent conceptualizations of goal-directed behavior, namely appraisal models and goal theory. The first line of research is generally referred to by the term "context-sensitive motivation" because students' motivation is measured in situ during actual goal pursuit (for review see, Volet & Jarvela, 2001). The second line of research is known as "goal theory." It explains student functioning in terms of across-episode patterns of cognition, emotion, self-monitoring, and reflection that accompany the pursuit of desired end-states and avoidance of undesired end-states (e.g., Boekaerts, 1999, in press; Carver & Scheier, 2000; Emmons, 1997; Ford, 1992; Karoly, 1998). Recognition of the dynamic aspects of motivation as well as the self-regulatory or goal-directed nature of student behavior is, in my view, essential to a full understanding of motivated learning in different cultures and in multi-culture classrooms.

In order to explore the divergent meanings behind the construct of "motivated learning" in the context of the classroom, I will pursue three main objectives. First, I will give a brief overview of prominent conceptualizations of cultural differences in student motivation. Second, I will explore whether context-sensitive appraisal models have the potential to provide insight into cultural differences in motivation, and thirdly I will offer a goal-based model of self-regulation that can account for cultural differences in motivation.

CULTURAL DIFFERENCES IN MOTIVATION

In the last decade, researchers have become more concerned with cultural variation in motivation (Kitayama & Markus, 1999; Markus & Kitayama, 1991; Graham, 1994; Salili, 1994). It has been argued convincingly that students from different cultures have different ways to motivate themselves for achievement, because they have been exposed to different child rearing practices, different teaching methods, and to different motivational practices in the family and at school. These different exposures led to different values being attached to academic goals, different expectancies, conceptualizations of achievement, and attributions.

A prominent line of investigation has shown that divergent motivational practices exist between East and West. Although these researchers admit that there is a great deal of cross-cultural overlap and that there is also variability within cultures, they mainly focus on typical student characteristics, while simultaneously pointing to motivational practices that are widely accepted within a culture. For example, Markus and Kitayama (1991) and Kitayama and Markus (1999) argued that in most Western cultures, students are viewed as autonomous persons with distinctive characteristics that largely determine what they think, feel, and do in a school context. Examples of these characteristics are attribution to ability, self-esteem, self-efficacy, optimism, and helplessness. In order to boost students' self-esteem, they are encouraged by their parents and teachers to be optimistic, focus on their strengths, believe in themselves, and increase their confidence. This positive focus is believed to raise students' self-efficacy, and through it their school achievement, well being, and self-esteem. Kitayama and Markus (1999) argued that this culturally accepted way of boosting self-esteem gives rise to a conceptualization of achievement that is called "self-enhancement." As I explained elsewhere (Boekaerts, 1998), such a conceptualization implies that students focus on their strengths and are motivated to invest effort, demonstrating self-efficacious behavior. Self-criticism is not encouraged and weaknesses are played down. These motivational practices are in line with an entity view of intelligence, that is, a belief that the Self is quite stable and consists of a relatively fixed and consistent set of attributes that is largely unchangeable (Dweck, 1996). In short, most teachers and parents in Western cultures make attempts to raise students' school achievement and school satisfaction by creating a mindset that prompts selective awareness and monitoring of positive characteristics of the Self. These motivational practices also allow attenuation, and even neglect, of negative characteristics, and contrast with those practiced in Eastern cultures.

Kitayama and Markus demonstrated that in Asian cultures, students are not viewed as autonomous persons with distinctive characteristics. They have a fixed position within a hierarchical set of social structures and this position is embodied in their specific role (e.g., I am a first daughter and also a high school student). The Self is viewed as fluid and should be improved in accordance with one's fixed role. Understanding one's social identity and fixed role implies that one acquires the action programs and scripts that are necessary to fulfill that role to perfection. This is the responsibility of every individual, and striving towards these goals is valued by parents, teachers, and peers. In other words, in Asian countries students have to live up to their role as "a student," meaning that they have to adjust to the context of the school, improve their academic and social skills, and avoid embarrassing their family. In order to live up to their student role, students are encouraged by their parents and teachers, but also by their peers, to invest effort, to be self-critical and pay attention to weaknesses and imperfection. In the classroom, the focus is on constructive criticism, investing effort, and learning in partnership (see Hatano & Inagaki, 1996). It is believed that this culturally accepted way to enhance role perfection raises students' self-discipline and through it, their school achievement (Chiu, Hong, & Dweck, 1997; Su, Chiu, Hong, Leung, Peng, & Morris, 1999). These motivational practices are in line with an incremental view of intelligence, that is, a belief that the Self is quite malleable and can be improved (Dweck, 1996). It is easy to see that these motivational practices create a mindset that prompts selective awareness of and monitoring of imperfections.

These observations and descriptions have inspired many researchers to compare and contrast motivational practices and teaching methods in different cultures and minority groups. Yet, these conceptions have their limitations. Indeed, attention is typically restricted to identifying differences in relatively fixed student characteristics (e.g., attribution to ability versus attribution to effort; or focus on self-esteem versus focus on self-discipline) or to culturally determined motivational practices used by parents and teachers. Such an approach places a strong emphasis on personal and environmental factors and is well suited to studying the direct effects, as well as the moderating effects, of these factors on student achievement. The strength of this approach is that it can identify prominent culture-dependent determinants of student achievement, self-esteem, motivation, and well being (e.g., Stevenson, Chen, & Lee, 1993; Hatano & Inagaki, 1996). The weakness of this approach is that it highlights (dis)similarities between different cultures along a set of motivational constructs, without illuminating why individual students, as opposed to the average student, are intrinsically (extrinsically) motivated, persist longer after failure, are interested in the subject matter, or make choices in favor of or counter to the use of deep learning. When within-group variation is ignored or played down we lose the possibility of penetrating to the depths of the students' goal structure and gaining insight into their appraisal and self-regulation processes. My conclusion is that despite there being general agreement that students of different cultures have different conceptualizations and concerns about achievement and accomplish achievement goals by different means, there are few studies that have examined cultural differences in goal-setting and goal-striving processes in actual unfolding accomplishment situations. Yet, insight into these goal processes is essential to determine unequivocally whether or not the same motivation model underlies the observed disparity in behavior.

FAVORABLE AND UNFAVORABLE APPRAISALS OF ACADEMIC TASKS

Motivation: Choice and Decision Making

My point of view is that in order to describe and explain motivated learning in the classroom, researchers should do more than give an indication of where students are located along a dimension ranging from ego-oriented to task-oriented, or along the extrinsic-intrinsic dimension. Several researchers have cautioned against generalizations based on "dispositional" motivational characteristics and counseled against proclaiming some traits as favorable and other traits as unfavorable. It has indeed become clear that neither ego orientation nor extrinsic motivation is negative for all students. For example, Pintrich and Garcia (1991) provided evidence that extrinsic motivation showed a positive association with deep-level processing, provided students were low on intrinsic motivation. Interestingly, these researchers also found that students who were low on extrinsic motivation showed a positive association between deep-level processing and intrinsic motivation. I interpret these results as demonstrating that regularities in student behavior, defined in terms of stable motivational characteristics, should not be confused with students' tendency to react favorably or unfavorably in relation to tasks and assignments in a domain of study. Therefore, it is more informative to describe students' motivation in terms of the *commitment pathways* that take shape in the context of real-life classroom situations. Indeed, an important question that begs answering is whether goal-setting and goal-striving processes are fundamentally different in Eastern and Western cultures? In order to examine this question, it is necessary to define these constructs first. Goal-setting refers to the perception of choice between alternative actions, followed by decision making. It is characterized by conscious or subconscious deliberations over options to enactment and concluded with a decision to act or not to act (behavioral intention). Goal-striving begins when contemplation ends and refers to the students' ability to initiate actions, and inhibit counter-intentional impulses till the task is completed. Several researchers have used the term "volition" to refer to the self-regulatory processes that protect behavioral intentions from competing action tendencies, once they have been formed (cf. Kuhl & Gosche, 1994).

Gollwitzer and Rohloff (1999) compared and contrasted the types of information processing that people use in the deliberative mindset and the implementation mindset. They observed that ... "very simple plans that link suitable anticipated situations (good opportunities) to appropriate goal-directed actions are powerful self-regulatory tools when it comes to getting started." ... "Such plans, called implementation intentions, automate action initiation and thus guarantee that goal-directed actions will be elicited even when the individual is distracted by performing other tasks, is caught up in ruminating thoughts, or is simply tired" (p. 148). In other words, students must not only create a favorable mindset about a task or assignment, specifying their intention to learn (goal-setting), they must also be equipped with the necessary scripts and be willing to use them in the service of their behavioral intentions (goal-striving).

Our question can now be re-phased as: "Are behavioral intentions and implementation intentions formed in the same way in different cultures?" Or, even more concretely, "Does goal-setting, defined as choice and decision making about the pursuit of a learning target mean the same thing in different cultures?"

Goal-setting: Creating Positive Scenarios That Guide the Selection of Cognitive Strategies

Setting a learning goal refers to the students' deliberations over options to enactment of a learning task, leading to a low, medium, or high learning intention. Students appraise some learning task in a split second and decide quasi automatically to put in effort or not. Alternatively, their appraisal can take the form of a long-winding cost-benefit analysis, or be located anywhere in between. Recent years have seen the emergence of on-line measures of motivation that register students' appraisal processes and the effect of these appraisals on intended and actual effort. Studies conducted with the on-line motivation questionnaire (see Boekaerts, 2001, for review) revealed that students' appraisal of a learning task concentrates on three main types of judgments. First, students appraise task demands in relation to their own resources to meet these demands (subjective competence). Second, students appraise task attraction. Third, they judge the relevance and importance of the task (perceived utility). These three appraisals mediate the relation between activated domain-specific motivational beliefs and learning intention. It seems that students, who attach value to a learning task (i.e., find it important, personally relevant, or attractive), are prepared to invest more effort than students who do not value the task. There is no direct effect of subjective competence on learning intention. This effect is mediated by task attraction, meaning that students who think they are not capable of doing a task, because they view this demand-capacity ratio as being too high, express low liking for the task and this leads to a low learning intention. Alternatively, students who express confidence in their ability to do the task and like it therefore experience causality pleasure and are motivated to invest effort. Our results also showed (see Boekaerts, 1999) that students' appraisals of math tasks originate in domain-specific motivational beliefs about mathematics. Scores on perceived utility and task attraction had their roots in task orientation for mathematics, interest in math, pleasure in math, and need for achievement and they *mediated* the effect between these positive motivational beliefs and learning intention.

Interestingly, scores on subjective competence had their roots in different domain-specific motivational beliefs, namely in attribution to ability, self-concept of ability, and avoidance ego-orientation (wanting to hide mistakes and failure). Again, there was no direct effect of these motivational beliefs on learning intention. The effect was *mediated* by the students' subjective competence in combination with task attraction. Two major commitment pathways were discerned: a value pathway and a demand-capacity pathway. It is assumed that high activity in the latter pathway, triggered by unfavorable motivational beliefs (attribution of failure to ability, low self-concept, avoidance ego orientation) creates a negative mindset. This scenario directs students' attention towards cues in the task environment that signal high demands, low resources to meet these demands, low perceived support, and high costs. In other words, the perceived demand-capacity ratio is out of balance and students experience low liking. In a dissimilar vein, it is assumed that high activity in the value pathway is fed by task orientation, interest in mathematics, and pleasure in math. Activation of these motivational beliefs creates a positive mindset. This scenario directs students' attention towards relevant cues in the task environment that help the meaning-generating process (attach value to the task), and away from irrelevant cues that impede goal-setting and goal-striving. Remarkably, attribution to effort did not show significant relations with any of the appraisals.

These and similar findings have convinced teachers and educators that they can influence students' appraisals in several ways. They can encourage them to attach value to curricular tasks by explaining why tasks are important, showing how the tasks relate to previously learned material, and what the purpose is of learning new skills. They can also invite students to pay attention to cues in the task and the social environment that inspire learning. For example, they can direct students' attention to the effort that other students are investing in the task, urging them to ignore cues that distract them from learning, or cues that can be interpreted as signals of low capacity.

It is noteworthy that no statistical association was found between learning intention and affective state, after controlling for domain-specific motivational beliefs and appraisals in the situation. This finding confirmed our hypothesis that there are two independent processing paths, a learning or mastery path and a well-being or ego-protective path (see also Boekaerts, 2002). It was also observed that two of the domain-specific motivational beliefs, namely avoidance ego-orientation and fear of failure, were directly linked to adolescents' affective state, but not to their learning intention. In other words, the effect of encoded information about negative experiences with math tasks in the past on affective state was not mediated by the appraisals. This implies that having to complete a math task that triggers a mindset characterized by fear of failure or avoidance ego-orientation (wanting to hide mistakes and failure) has direct access to a student's feeling state but not to his learning intention. Hence, it seems that whether or not students are prepared to embark on a learning task depends on their perception of the value of the task (attraction and relevance) and on the degree of causality pleasure they expect, and not on their affective state. Indeed, our results suggest that students who are invited to complete math tasks may express negative emotions (I feel tense, irritated, sad) but they nevertheless agree to do the task. They may also express positive emotions (I feel happy, pleasant) but choose not to invest effort into the task.

The proposed appraisal model is invariant across gender, time and domains (math, history, native and foreign language learning, and various courses in vocational school and at university). Unfortunately, these data are restricted to Western countries. Hence, we do not know whether the appraisal model is culturally invariant. In the absence of studies that shed some light on students' appraisal processes in Asian cultures, we can only speculate on the links between domain-specific motivational beliefs and Asian students' appraisals, and between their appraisals and learning intention. My guess is that, similar to what was found in Western cultures, appraisals mediate the relation between domain-specific motivational beliefs and learning intention. However, the commitment pathways may be different. A hypothesis that needs to be tested is whether direct links ought to be permitted between motivational beliefs and learning intention. Based on conceptual reviews of cultural differences (quoted previously), it is assumed that Asian students have fewer deliberations over options to enactment. Indeed, my guess is that they have established direct links between motivational beliefs, particularly attribution to effort, and intended and actual effort. In other words, there may be a direct triggering mechanism, very much like the one described between avoidance ego-orientation and fear of failure on the one hand, and affective state on the other. Preliminary evidence for such a link comes from the study conducted by Purdie and Hattie (1996) and from a recent study conduced by Heine, Kitayama, Lehman, Takata, Leung, and Masumoto (2001). Purdie and Hattie's study suggests that Japanese students conceptualize "willpower" in a different way from Australian students. Japanese students use willpower as a regulation strategy that is in line with their cultural emphasis on commitment to schoolwork and the ability to persevere. They seem to engage in self-talk or self-instructions to try harder.

Heine and his team of cross-cultural researchers also showed that Japanese undergraduates persisted longer after failure than North American students. These researchers also reported that students' lay theory of effort was reflected in their persistence score. More concretely, Japanese students, who failed on a task, persisted more on a follow-up task than those who succeeded, and this pattern was reversed in North American students. Interestingly, Japanese students viewed performance on a creativity test to be due to incremental abilities more than did American undergraduates.

More research is needed to provide insight into the direct and indirect effects of motivational beliefs on learning intention and affective state in Asian countries. My hypothesis is that all students, whether they live in Asian or Western cultures, have established habitual commitment pathways but that the nature of these pathways differs. Clearly, a more complete understanding of goal-setting and goal-striving processes in a cultural perspective will require a conceptual framework that takes account of the thoughts and feelings that individual students *generate* in the service of goal attainment.

PURSUIT OF PERSONAL GOALS

Personal Goals as Organizers of Behavior

In my opinion, a successful motivational account of cross-cultural differences in student motivation and the way they adapt to multiple learning environments must also take account of the students' personal goals. How are these goals connected to their ideal Self and to the many scripts that they have available in their repertoire? Austin and Vancouver (1996) showed that people's thoughts, feelings and actions in a given situation are determined jointly by their personal goals and their appraisal of contextual factors. Several other researchers (e.g., Baumeister, 1989; Ford, 1992; McGregor & Little, 1998) have demonstrated that personal goals give meaning to people's life and that progression towards these goals enhances performance and well being (see also, Bandura, 1989; Carver & Scheier, 2000; Emmons, 1986). It is easy to understand that the content of students' personal goals is highly informative when it comes to explaining and predicting their behavior in concrete learning situations, for, having information about students' personal goals penetrates deep into their Self structure and taps their unique wishes, interests, and concerns.

Goal theorists describe the Self as a coherent system of principles. For example, Carver and Scheier (2000) describe a goal hierarchy with abstract principles or higher order goals located high up in the hierarchy. An example is "I want to be successful in life" (see Figure 2.1). This "I want to be goal," or simply "be goal," gives meaning to a person's life and specifies the quality of all the personal goals that are attached to it. Personal goals are personally meaningful objectives that individuals pursue in their daily lives (Elliot & Sheldon, 1998). These goals are more concrete than the higher order goals they are attached to, specifying the actions a person preferentially performs to achieve these meaningful targets. Personal goals are also referred to as "do goals," or "action programs" in the pursuit of desired consequences (approach goals) or in avoidance of undesired ones (avoidance goals). An example of an approach goal is "I want to get through finals", and example of an avoidance goal is "I want to avoid being a nerd." Attached to personal goals are cognitively represented behavioral sequences of actions, called scripts that specify how to reach these goals. For example, if I want to avoid being a nerd, I should never work for school on week-ends, I should go to all birthday parties, and I should not admit to the teacher in public that I spent many hours preparing for the math exam. In short, scripts make personal goals more concrete by fitting them to the local conditions.

Examination of the links between scripts and personal goals and between personal goals and higher order goals reveals a network of goals

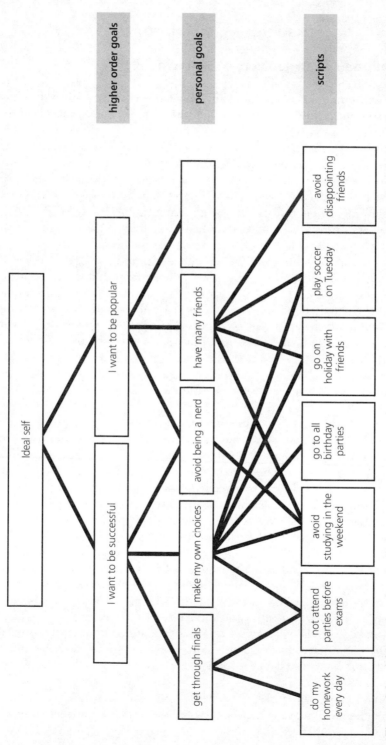

Figure 2.1. A hierarchy of goals. *Note:* Lines indicate how lower level goals are connected to "personal goals" and "higher order goals."

that is unique to an individual student (see Figure 2.1). The theory of Self that is presented here maps onto theories of motivation and self-regulation. Indeed, personal goals can be viewed as a person's tools to organize his or her goal structure. They are also the most salient energizers of behavior, since they determine the content, direction, and strength of a person's motivation.

Balance and Imbalance in the Goal Structure

Now that I have outlined the structure of the goal system and described some of the goal processes, let us return to the question that we set out to answer: "Does goal-setting and goal-striving mean the same thing to students from different cultures?" Recall that goal-setting refers to the perception of choice between alternative actions, followed by decision making. It is easy to imagine that goals that students deem important need less deliberation before a behavioral intention is formed. Important goals have been accessed frequently and have been encoded in a highly accessible knowledge structure (Bargh & Gollwitzer, 1994). In other words, these goals have become central to a person's Self and are therefore more resistant to change (Petty & Krosnick, 1995). There is growing agreement (e.g., Forgas, 1995; Bargh & Gollwitzer, 1994) that goal importance and goal frequency are important criteria for inclusion in the structure of Self (goal internalization). A direct link has been established between the salient goal and the situations in which it is pursued, on the one hand, and the scripts that have been effective in satisfying this goal in the past on the other hand. Little cognitive effort is required to initiate these goals, mainly because they have been proceduralized well (direct access processing). As was mentioned previously, Gollwitzer and Rohloff (1999) viewed these links as implementation intentions that trigger "automated action initiation and thus guarantee that goal-directed actions will be elicited even when the individual is distracted by performing other tasks, is caught up in ruminating thoughts, or is simply tired"(p. 148).

Taken to the classroom, these conceptualizations imply that academic goals, which are set by the teacher, may be perceived by the students as in agreement with, or as alien to, their goal structure. Goals that are perceived as congruent have a better chance of being proceduralized and being linked to one or more personal goals. Evidence in support of this hypothesis comes from a study by Barth and Parke (1993). These researchers found that students are more committed to attaining parent-valued goals and are more willing to take responsibility for achieving them, when these goals hold personal value for them. Other researchers showed that students, who consider the goals set by their parents or teachers as alien to

the Self, use various forms of self-protective strategies to avoid these undesirable end-states. Examples are self-handicapping (Covington, 1992),
effort avoidance (Rollett, 2001) and disidentification with school (Van
Laar, 2001).

In Western cultures, teachers and parents often complain that students
do not diligently pursue academic goals. They report many conflicts of
interest that lead to frustration in both students and teachers. For example, teachers want their students to use deep-level strategies while students
give preference to less-time-consuming, surface-level strategies. These com-
plaints illustrate the fact that in Western cultures it is no longer expected
that students spend their days studying to the exclusion of other salient
personal goals. Students in Western countries are very much part of the
consumer society. They follow their own interests and determine for themselves how they resolve conflicts between goals. Parents and teachers grant
them freedom of action and this frequently leads to academic goals being
put on hold till other salient goals are achieved (social, artistic, romantic,
or materialistic goals). The tolerance pattern thus noted is not paralleled
in Asian cultures. As Asian researchers explained, Asian students are
allowed less freedom of action. Their world is well structured and protects
their academic goals. It is argued that Asian students perceive their student
role and what they have to do to fulfill that role as part of their Self. This
implies that academic goals are personal goals that have been encoded in
highly accessible knowledge structures with direct links to: (1) the learning
situations organized by teachers (in school) and parents (in so-called
"cram schools" or in the home) and (2) to scripts that are characterized by
expending effort.

My hypothesis is that students from Western or Asian cultures, who view
learning tasks set by their teachers as congruent with their own goals have a
double advantage. First, the scripts that have been linked to their personal
goal "I want to be a successful student" form a framework for goal-setting
and goal-striving. Second, these goals have multiple connections in their
goal hierarchy, thus increasing their motivational significance. Ford (1992)
explained that personal goals that have multiple connections in the goal
hierarchy are better practiced, implying more efficiency and higher motivation, because the person has more than one reason for engaging in the
course of action. Isolated personal goals or goals that are in conflict with
other personal goals cause frustration and uncertainty. In this respect the
pioneering work of Phelan, Yu, and Davidson (1994) is informative. These
researchers maintained that the meanings and understandings, which students derive from the different worlds to which they belong, combine to
affect the quality of their engagement with school. They reasoned that contemporary students live in many different worlds (family, school, peer
groups) and derive different meanings from these worlds. Conflicts may

arise when some personal goals find their origin in one of these worlds while other personal goals stem from another world.

For example, Phelan et al. (1994) reported that 90% of the students, who indicated that there was no conflict between the values, beliefs, and expectations in their family, peer group and school, reported that maintaining high grades and doing well on standardized tests was their most salient personal goal. However, they also reported that they were under tremendous pressure to achieve academically. These students had a long-term time perspective and equated worrying about a test with worrying about their future. Phelan et al. (1994) noted that these students were preoccupied with grades and scored low on intrinsic motivation. They also competed with their friends and this created conflicting thoughts about interpersonal relationships.

Phelan et al. (1994) also examined what happened when students noted conflicts between the values, beliefs and expectation in their different worlds. Some students managed the transitions between the different worlds successfully, others reported that changeovers were troublesome, and still others resisted transitions. Students, who managed the transitions successfully, felt pressure both to do well academically and to "fit in." These students, who were often the only minority students in their high-track classes, expressed discomfort in school because they felt isolated. Students who reported that the changeovers were troublesome also expressed fear of being isolated. However, these students were often found in regular or remedial tracks where there were many same-culture students. Their frustrations had a different origin: they found the material boring, worried about not understanding content material, and not getting sufficient help from the teacher. Notably, these students continued to struggle, often adopting maladaptive means of coping with their frustrations (copying their friend's work, being passive or aggressive in class). Finally, students who resisted crossing the borders between their different worlds were at risk of dropping out. These students worried about an uncertain future, they expressed helplessness, and low social support from teachers, mainly for reasons of ethnicity and because they held different values.

CONCLUSIONS

I began this article by stating that researchers who are not familiar with motivation research, educators, and teachers lose their way in the morass of motivational beliefs. I also stated that there are, at present, many intervention programs that promise to boost students' self-efficacy, self-esteem, intrinsic motivation, and the like, but that the alert observer notes that these interventions are wrapped in fragmented layers of empirical support.

I pointed to the effect of culture on motivation and summarized some of the main conceptualizations of cultural differences in motivation. From the perspective of this paper, a focus on goal-setting and goal-striving processes is considered to be particularly useful to this line of investigation. It was argued that such an approach serves as a common basis for integrating the diverse treatments of motivation in the psychological literature. Two lines of development are of particular importance because they have the potential to provide insight into cultural differences in motivation.

The first line of development, usually referred to as context-sensitive appraisal models, can help clarify and develop the appraisal concept in cross-cultural research on motivation. It was argued that future work needs to include students' appraisals in order to gain insight into the types of judgments that students from different cultures make about concrete learning assignments. An interesting question raised in this chapter was whether student appraisals mediate the effect of motivational beliefs on learning intention in the same way in different cultures. In the absence of empirical evidence it was speculated that Asian students deliberate less about options for action. More concretely, it was hypothesized that these students have established direct links between motivational beliefs, particularly between attribution to effort and intended and actual effort investment.

The second line of development is to investigate how personal goals are linked to higher order goals and to the many scripts that specify how personal goals can be attained. What can be learned about cultural differences in personal goals? How are they connected to scripts that have been successful in the past? It was hypothesized that both Western and Eastern students list "I want to be successful" as a salient higher order goal. However, it is expected that there are significant cultural differences in the content of personal goals and the type of scripts that are linked to this higher order goal. Asian students perceive their student role and what they have to do to fulfill that role as part of their Self. This perception implies that academic goals (set by teachers and by school entrance examinations) are established as salient personal goals from an early age. The consequence is that academic goals are well integrated in the students' goal structure as important, frequently accessed knowledge structures with direct links to: (1) the learning situations organized by teachers (in school) and parents (cram schools) and (2) to scripts that have been successful in the past. In Western cultures, the content of personal goals may vary from student to student and goal salience, as well as goal-setting and striving, is largely determined in the actual learning situation.

In conclusion, it is evident that our attempts to build up cumulative wisdom about motivation are hindered by the continuing underdevelopment of the role of the students' on-line self-regulatory processes, including their goal-setting and goal-striving processes. Future work needs to include greater differentiation between goal-setting and goal-striving processes as a main key to understanding why students from different cultures are prepared to invest effort and why they persist in the face of failure.

REFERENCES

Austin, J. T., & Vancouver, J. B. (1996). Goal constructs in psychology: Structure, process, and content. *Psychological Bulletin, 20*, 338–375.

Bandura, A. (1989). Self-regulation of motivation and action through interval standards and goal systems. In L. A. Pervin (Ed.), *Goal concepts in personality and social psychology* (pp. 19–85). Hillsdale: Lawrence Erlbaum.

Bargh, J. A., & Gollwitzer, P. M. (1994). Environmental control of goal-directed action: Automatic and strategic contingencies between situations and behavior. In W. Spaulding (Ed.), *Nebraska symposium on motivation* (pp. 71–124). Lincoln: University of Nebraska Press.

Barth, J. M., & Parke, R. D. (1993). Parent-child relationships influences on children's transitions to school. *Merrill-Palmer Quarterly, 39*, 173–195.

Baumeister, R. F. (1989). The problem of life's meaning. In D. M. Buss & N. Cantor (Eds.), *Personality psychology: Recent trends and emerging directions* (pp. 138–148). New York: Springer Verlag.

Boekaerts, M. (1998). Do culturally rooted self-construals affect students' conceptualization of control over learning? *Educational Psychologist, 33*(2/3), 87–108.

Boekaerts, M. (1999). Motivated learning: The study of student * situation transactional units. *European Journal of Psychology of Education, 14*(1), 41–55.

Boekaerts, M. (1999). Coping in context: Goal frustration and goal ambivalence in relation to academic and interpersonal goals. In E. Frydenberg (Ed.), *Learning to cope: Developing as a person in complex societies* (pp. 175–197). Oxford: Oxford University Press.

Boekaerts, M. (2002). The on-line motivation questionnaire: A self-report instrument to assess students' context sensitivity. In P. R. Pintrich & M. L. Maehr (Eds.), *Advances in motivation and achievement, Volume 12: New directions in measures and methods* (pp. 77–120). Stamford, CT: JAI Press.

Boekaerts, M. (2002, April). *Student appraisals and emotions within classroom context.* Paper presented at the annual meeting of the American Educational Research Association, New Orleans, LA.

Boekaerts, M. (2002). Bringing about change in the classroom: Strengths and weaknesses of the self-regulated learning approach. *Learning and instruction, 12*(6), 589–604.

Carver, C. S., & Scheier, M. (2000). On the structure of behavioral self-regulation. In M. Boekaerts, P. R. Pintrich, & M. Zeidner (Eds.), *Handbook of self-regulation.* San Diego, CA: Academic Press.

Chiu, C., Hong, Y., & Dweck, C. S. (1997). Lay dispositionism and implicit theories of personality. *Journal of Personality and Social Psychology, 73*, 19–30.

Covington, M. V. (1992). *Making the grade: A self-worth perspective on motivation and school reform.* New York: Cambridge University Press.

Dweck, C. S. (1996). Implicit theories as organizers of goals and behavior. In P. M. Gollwitzer & J. A. Bargh (Eds.), *The psychology of action* (pp. 69–90). New York: Guilford Press.

Elliot, A. J., & Sheldon, K. M. (1998). Avoidance personal goals and the personality-illness relationship. *Journal of Personality and Social Psychology, 76,* 628–644.

Emmons, R. A. (1986). Personal strivings: An approach to personality and subjective wellbeing. *Journal of Personality and Social Psychology, 51,* 1058–1068.

Emmons, R. A. (1991). Personal strivings, daily life events, and psychological and physical wellbeing. *Journal of Personality, 59,* 453–472.

Emmons, R. A. (1997). Motives and life goals. In R. Hogan, J. Johnson, & S. Briggs (Eds.), *Handbook of personality psychology* (pp. 485–512). San Diego: Academic Press.

Ford, M. E. (1992). *Motivating humans: Goals, emotions, and personal agency beliefs.* London: Sage.

Forgas, J. P. (1995). Mood and Judgment: The affect infusion model (AIM). *Psychological Bulletin, 117*(1), 39–66.

Gollwitzer, P. M., & Rohloff, U. B. (1999). The speed of goal pursuit. In R. S. Wyer, Jr. (Ed.), *Perspectives on behavioral self-regulation* (pp. 147–160). Mahwah, NJ: Lawrence Erlbaum.

Graham, S. (1994). Motivation in African Americans. *Review of Educational Research, 64*(1), 55–117.

Hatano, G., & Inagaki, K. (1996). *Cultural context of schooling revisited: A review of the learning gap from a cultural psychology perspective.* Paper presented at the University of Michigan.

Heine, S. J., Kitayama, S., Lehman, D. R., Takata, T., Leung, C., & Matsumoto, H. (2001). Divergent consequences of success and failure in Japan and North America: An investigation of self-improving motivations and malleable selves. *Journal of Personality and Social Psychology, 81*(4), 599–615.

Karoly, P. (1998). *Intentional mindsets: Goal framing in seven dimensions.* Address presented at the 10th Annual Convention of the American Psychological Society, Washington, D.C.

Kitayama, S., & Markus, H. R. (1999). Yin and Yang of the Japanese self: The cultural psychology of personality coherence. In D. Cervone & Y. Shoda (Eds.), *The coherence of personality* (pp. 242–302). New York: Guilford.

Kuhl, J., & Goschke, T. (1994). A theory of action control. In J. Kuhl & J. Beckmann (Eds.), *Volition and personality: Action versus state orientation* (pp. 93–134). Göttingen: Hogrefe & Huber.

Markus, H., & Kitayama, S. (1991). Culture and the self: Implications for cognition, emotion, and motivation. *Psychological Review, 98,* 224–253.

McGregor, I., & Little, B. R. (1998). Personal projects, happiness, and meaning: On doing well and being yourself. *Journal of Personal and Social Psychology, 74,* 494–512.

Petty, R. E., & Krosnick, J. A. (1995). (Eds.) *Attitude strength: Antecedents and consequences.* Hillsdale, NJ: Lawrence Erlbaum.

Phelan, P., Yu, H. C., & Davidson, A. L. (1994). Navigating the psychological pressures of adolescence: The voices and experiences of high school youth. *American Educational Research Journal, 31*(2), 415–447.

Pintrich, P. R., & Garcia, T. (1991). Student goal orientation and self-regulation in the college classroom. In M. L. Maehr & P. R. Pintrich (Eds.), *Advances in motivation and achievement: Goals and self-regulatory processes* (pp. 371–402). Greenwich, CT: JAI Press.

Purdie, N., & Hattie, J. (1996). Cultural Differences in the use of strategies for self-regulated learning. *American Educational Research Journal, 33*(4), 845–872.

Ramburuth, P., & McCormick, J. (2001). Learning diversity in higher education: A comparative study of Asian international and Australian students. *Higher Education, 42*(3), 333–350.

Rollett, W. (2001). *Effort avoidance motivation in achievement situations.* Paper presented at the 9th Conference of the European Association of Learning and Instruction, Fribourg, Switzerland.

Salili, F. (1994). Age, sex, and cultural differences in the meaning and dimensions of achievement. *Personality and Social Psychology Bulletin, 20*, 635–648.

Scouller, K. (1998). The effect of assessment method on students' learning approaches: Multiple choice question examination versus assignment essay. *Higher Education, 35*, 453–472.

Stevenson, H. W., Chen, C. H., & Lee, S. Y. (1993). Mathematics achievement of Chinese, Japanese, and American children: Ten years later. *Science, 259*, 53–58.

Su, S. K., Chiu, C. Y., Hong, Y., Leung, K., Peng, K., & Morris, M. W. (1999). Self organization and social organization: American and Chinese constructions. In T. R. Tyler, R. Kramer, & R. L. John (Eds.), *The psychology of social self* (pp. 193–222). Mahwah, NJ: Erlbaum.

Van Laar, C. (2001). Understanding the impact of disadvantage on academic achievement. In F. Salili & R. Hoosain (Eds.), *Multicultural education: Issues, policies and practices.* Greenwich, CT: Information Age Publishing.

Volet, S., & Järvelä, S. (Eds.) (2001). *Motivation in Learning Contexts. Theoretical Advances and Methodological Implications.* New York: Pergamon.

Watkins, D. (2000). Learning and Teaching: A cross-cultural perspective. *School Leadership & Management, 20*(2), 161–173.

CHAPTER 3

A PROCESS-ORIENTED APPROACH TO CULTURE

Theoretical and Methodological Issues in the Study of Culture and Motivation

Akane Zusho and Paul R. Pintrich

Over the past several decades, we have come to understand a great deal about the role of motivation in students' learning and achievement. At least among motivational theorists, it has become common knowledge that students' perceptions of their academic competence can have a profound impact on their achievement behavior including choice, effort, persistence, cognitive engagement, and performance (Bandura, 1997; Eccles, 1983; Eccles, Wigfield, & Schiefele, 1998). We have also come to understand the role of task value, interest, and goals in influencing students' motivational trajectories and various achievement outcomes (Dweck & Leggett, 1988; Eccles et al., 1998; Pintrich, 1999; 2000). Yet, as we develop our models of motivation, we must nevertheless consider the manner in which our generalizations about the role of these two general aspects of motivation are applicable to populations other than white, middle-class, Anglo American students who represent, more often than not, the prototypical sample for motivational research. Second, there is a need to extend our understanding of how cultural factors relate more generally to basic

Teaching, Learning, and Motivation in a Multicultural Context, pages 33–65
Copyright © 2003 by Information Age Publishing
All rights of reproduction in any form reserved.

motivational processes regarding efficacy and values, interest, and goals. These two concerns are the focus of this chapter.

We frame our discussion of these concerns in terms of a dynamic process-oriented conceptualization of culture. We first define what we mean by a process-oriented perspective on culture. Second, given this view of culture, we discuss the implications for future research including an examination of how general cultural processes might be related to basic motivational processes and achievement regarding efficacy as well as values, interest, and goals. We also include a discussion of acculturative processes such as ethnic identity, which is relevant to the generalization of motivational findings to different ethnic groups. Finally, given our view of culture and its potential effects on motivational processes, we conclude with a discussion of some methodological concerns when conducting research in this area.

CULTURE AS A PROCESS

Although the role of culture in basic psychological processes can be traced back to the eighteenth and nineteenth centuries with the work of scholars such as Herder and Wundt, research emphasizing the link between culture and psyche was not really a focus of most psychological research until the 1980s and 1990s, when work in this area enjoyed a renewed resurgence (Schweder, Goodnow, Hatano, Levine, Markus, & Miller, 1998). At the same time, given psychology's general focus on the individual and this relatively recent interest in cultural processes, it is not surprising that psychology's conception of "culture" has been rather simplistic with most definitions focused on either patterns of behavior (i.e., behavioral aspect of culture) *or* shared beliefs (i.e., symbolic aspects of culture). In addition, much of the research on culture has conflated ethnicity with culture, or has treated culture as an independent variable. In other words, there is still a tendency within psychology to treat culture as an antecedent of psychological phenomena, rather than an integral part of it, as represented by much of the cross-cultural work of the last two decades. Research in motivation is no exception to this general trend in psychological research on culture.

However, recent work in cultural psychology has lead to a reconsideration of this more simplistic approach to culture. The theory and research from this perspective advocate treating "culture as a process" (Greenfield, 1997; Schweder et al., 1998; Miller, 1997, 2002). This view, also called the "system view" of culture (e.g., Kitayama, 2002), maintains that culture is constituted of both shared practices *and* shared mentalities as represented by the "custom complex" (Schweder et al., 1998; Whiting & Child, 1953) or cultural "selfways" (Markus, Mullally, & Kitayama, 1997), and that these two aspects continually interact with one another. This process-oriented view of culture combines previous conceptualizations of culture by examining the symbolic or belief system aspects concomitantly with the behavioral aspects of culture. In short, it is assumed that culture and psyche complement one another and that it is difficult to extricate one from the other, as they are mutually constitutive. It is also believed that the custom complex is passed on from generation to generation.

Figure 3.1 displays this relationship. Briefly, the cultural side of the custom complex is represented by macro-level cultural practices, such as child rearing, educational system, language, and religious beliefs. The psychological side is represented by cultural mentalities, which can be broadly defined in terms of what an individual actually knows, thinks, wants, feels, and values. The interaction between these two aspects of culture can be thought of in the following manner. An individual is born into a culture with predefined set of meanings and practices that have been shaped and sustained over time from generation to generation. In an attempt to become a full-fledged member of that society, the individual participates in practices that are promoted within said culture, be it language, political system, or religion. These practices, however, have evolved over time to perpetuate a certain worldview. Thus, as a result of participating in these cultural practices, that individual not only learns how to integrate this worldview into their own psyche but also learns how to coordinate their responses with those norms and ideals that are promoted within their culture. In short, psychological functioning is established through the synchronization of individual responses with cultural practices and meanings (Kitayama & Markus, 1999). In addition, this method of attuning psycho-

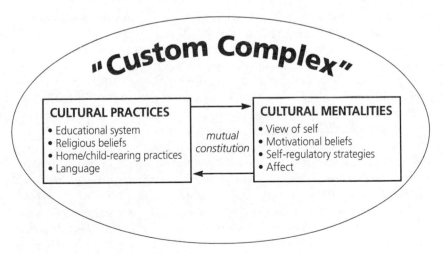

Figure 3.1.   The Custom Complex.

logical and cultural processes becomes habitual and automatic over time, thus resulting in the reproduction of the original set of cultural practices and meanings.

The process view of culture is predicated on a number of assumptions about the relation of culture to basic psychological processes. It is these assumptions that distinguish this approach to culture from traditional conceptualizations and that have implications for motivational research. In addition, it should be duly noted that the process view of culture as forwarded by cultural psychologists shares features with a select number of other cultural approaches, including symbolic action theory, social constructionism and socio-cultural approaches in the Vygotskian tradition (Miller, 1997), as well as Bandura's (1976, 1986) reciprocal determinism. Given space constraints, we are unable to provide a comprehensive discussion of these approaches. Accordingly, we direct readers interested in such a discussion to other sources (e.g., Cole, 1996; Miller, 1997).

First, cultural psychologists generally eschew what Kitayama (2002) calls the "entity view" of culture, which assumes that culture is a static causal antecedent of behavior or a specific psychological characteristic. For example, an entity view of culture might lead to motivational research that attributes mean level differences in the motivational processes of certain ethnic groups to "culture." On the other hand, a process perspective on culture might suggest that it is not "culture" per se that explains these differences but rather an interaction between the meanings and practices individuals in these groups hold and engage in which, in turn, leads to the mean level differences. In addition, a process perspective would attempt to examine and understand the interaction between the shared beliefs and cultural practices that seem to generate the mean level differences.

Second, and related to the first assumption, is the notion that culture is not a simple omnibus independent variable that distinguishes between different cultures at a global level. In other words, individuals who belong to a specific culture do not always behave in a similar manner nor do they always hold the same beliefs. Thus, there can be individual variation by members within a culture. Again, what accounts for cultural differences is the extent to which the individuals in these cultures participate in those everyday activities that encourage the instantiation of those beliefs or promote those behaviors. A process-oriented approach to cultural research would then attempt to investigate and understand these potential individual differences within cultural groups and how they are developed and maintained over time.

Third, cultural psychologists believe that the influence of culture on psychological processes is heavily dependent upon context. Once more, this idea is based on the premise that culture is complex and not always stable over time. A good example of this assumption is represented in the work on culture and cognition, such as the research on Brazilian children's understanding of mathematical concepts in out-of-school and in-school contexts (Nunes, Schliemann, & Carraher, 1993). In this type of research it is axiomatic that children's cognition and learning is dependent on various cultural cues, features, and practices and that it is difficult, if not impossible, to separate out children's cognition from the cultural practices (see Figure 3.1). Although this situated perspective is fairly common in research on cognition, it has not been used as often in motivational research, although there is emerging interest in situated motivational research (e.g., see Volet & Järvelä, 2001).

Finally, research in the tradition of cultural psychology is not motivated solely by a quest to uncover universal truths, nor is it guided by a concern to validate existing psychological theories in varied cultural settings. In this way, the field of cultural psychology distinguishes itself from cross-cultural psychology. Rather, the general aim of research in cultural psychology is as Miller (2002) states, "to identify new constructs and theories that capture aspects of psychological functioning not accounted for within existing psychological approaches" (p. 99), although she is quick to note that this does not mean that cultural psychologists should then seek to establish new theories, or that no universals can be found. However, she suggests that even universals can benefit from research attending to cultural practices and meanings (Miller, 1997). For example, when researchers focus their attention on examining the motivational processes of a specific ethnic group, they can be rewarded with uncovering important constructs that may be particular to that ethnic group. Specifically, the phenomenon known as "acting white" has been implicated as a potential reason behind African American students' low academic performance (Fordham & Ogbu, 1986). This construct of "acting white" clearly has important implications for African American students' motivational processes; however, its role in explaining the motivational processes of other groups is probably not very large. To this end, a process-oriented perspective would attempt to investigate how different cultural practices and mentalities might create or foster different cognitive or motivational pathways for achievement.

While we would not go so far as to suggest that there is little value in conducting cross-cultural comparisons, we nevertheless believe that if we are to deepen our understanding of cultural influences on psychological functioning, including motivation, we need to consider these assumptions and their implications for our theories and research. Accordingly, we suggest that motivational research might have much to gain by adopting a more nuanced process-oriented approach to culture as an overarching framework for how cultural processes might be related to motivation. At the same time, we realize that this process perspective on culture, given its complexity, presents a number of challenges to the study of motivation. In the remainder of this chapter we discuss the implications of this process-oriented perspective on culture for future research on motivation and achievement.

THEORETICAL ISSUES CONCERNING THE STUDY OF CULTURE AND MOTIVATION

In this section, we discuss implications of the "culture as process" perspective for the study of motivation. In order to ground this approach to culture in terminology more familiar to motivational theorists, we borrow a concrete example from Kitayama and his colleagues (Heine, Kitayama, Lehman, Takata, Ide, Leung, & Matsumoto, 2001; Heine, Lehman, Markus, & Kitayama, 1999; Kitayama & Markus, 1998, 1999; Kitayama, Markus, Matsumoto, & Norasakkunkit, 1997) of an American custom complex and a Japanese custom complex and its relation to a specific motivational construct, namely self-esteem. We then propose a theoretical model outlining how cultural and motivational processes might relate to each other. We conclude this section with a discussion of the implications of this process-oriented perspective for specific motivational theories of efficacy and goals.

Self-esteem and Hansei

The self-esteem movement in American schools can be considered a prototypical example of the American custom complex. The number of programs, both formal and informal, targeted at enhancing American children's self-esteem is remarkable. In general, American schools have been found to promote self-esteem in the following ways: (1) personal development training, including sensitivity training, (2) enactment of formal curricula aimed specifically to increase students' self-esteem, and (3) making school level structural changes to empower students by placing more emphasis on community involvement and student collaboration/cooperation (Beane, 1991). These programs targeted at enhancing children's self-esteem represent the "practice" or behavioral component of the complex while the symbolic portion can be characterized by the ideas that guide such a practice, namely the view of the self as an independent, autonomous entity (Kitayama, 2002; Markus & Kitayama, 1991) Figure 3.2a displays this relationship. In addition, as part of this relationship, a general self-enhancement strategy emerges whereby both the cultural practices and the individuals are assumed to be focused on enhancing individual self-esteem, which should result in relatively high levels of self-esteem for most individuals in this culture. Moreover, there is evidence to suggest that Anglo-Americans rate their self-esteem higher than Japanese individuals (Heine et al., 1999, 2001)

We can contrast this American custom complex with the Japanese custom complex (see Figure 3.2b). The predominant practice within educational settings in Japan is not to increase children's self-esteem, but rather to promote self-criticism or "*hansei.*" (Heine et al., 2001; Lewis, 1995). *Hansei* is a common practice within the Japanese educational system whereby individuals reflect back upon their conduct in hopes of identifying areas for self-improvement. *Hansei* takes on many forms; for example, it is not uncommon to find Japanese teachers exhorting their students to focus on their mistakes so that they could improve upon them in the future, or ending each school day with a shared discussion of some of the day's oversights. Thus, the practice of *hansei* comprises the behavioral portion of the Japanese custom complex. The ideological component is represented by a view of self as shared and/or interdependent (Kitayama, 2002; Markus & Kitayama, 1991). This custom complex leads to a general strategy of self-improvement through both the cultural practices as well as the individual mentalities. At the same time, given the focus on self-criticism and improvement, general self-esteem ratings may be lower for Japanese groups (Heine et al., 1999, 2001).

In both cases, one can see how the behavioral and psychological components of the custom complex interact with each other. In the case of Japan, a populous country known for its geographical confines and agrarian roots, values such as group harmony and cooperation displaced over time values emphasizing individual goals and pursuits, thereby instilling within Japanese individuals a shared sense of self (Azuma, 1998; Kitayama &

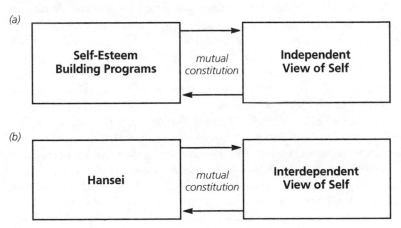

Figure 3.2.   (a) An example of the American Custom Complex.
(b) An example of the Japanese Custom Complex.

Markus, 1999). This mentality, in turn, prompted the emergence of practices, such as *hansei*, that aided in propagating that interdependent view of self. At the same time, participation in such practices also helped to further cement those ideologies within the Japanese psyche. The same general process can be used to explain the American custom complex. In this case, given religious, cultural, and historical ideologies such as Protestantism, Cartesian philosophy, and the Declaration of Independence, it is not difficult to see how values such as autonomy and self-determination became firmly entrenched within the American mentality (Markus, Mullally, & Kitayama, 1997). Moreover, given this mentality, one can see how self-esteem programs help to promulgate such values; these programs teach children to view themselves as unique and special, values that are consonant with an independent view of self.

In terms of how this relates specifically to motivation, there is recent empirical evidence that supports the general hypothesis that as a consequence of the independent self-view, Anglo Americans typically operate under a self-enhancing motivational strategy. In contrast, Japanese individuals who endorse an interdependent self-view would be more likely to be motivated toward self-improvement rather than self-enhancement (e.g., Heine et al., 1999, 2001; Kitayama et al., 1997). For example, in one study, participants were presented with a number of common social situations found in both American and Japanese cultures, and were asked to indicate for which situations their own self-esteem would be affected, either positively or negatively. These situations were previously determined to represent either a failure situation (a situation where self-esteem would decrease) or a success situation (a situation where self-esteem would normally increase). Japanese respondents were much more likely to select failure situations as being relevant to their self-esteem while the American participants were found to select more success situations as being relevant to their feelings of self-esteem (Kitayama et al., 1997). Another more recent study found that Japanese individuals were much more likely to persist on a second task if they were told that they had performed poorly on a similar initial task. In contrast, Americans were found to persist longer on the second task if they were initially told that they had succeeded on the first task (Heine et al., 2001). Heine and his colleagues thus concluded that these studies lend support for the hypothesis that Americans are more motivated in those situations that make salient the positive aspects of the self (i.e., self-enhancement) while Japanese are more motivated in situations that not only underscore their shortcomings but also provide an opportunity to improve upon their faults (i.e., self-improvement).

The important point from a process-oriented view of culture is that any potential differences in the mean level of self-esteem between American and Japanese students can in part be attributed to the custom complexes of the two cultures. In one culture, both the practices and mentalities support a general self-enhancement strategy that can lead to higher ratings of self-esteem. In contrast, in the other culture practices and mentalities lead to a general self-improvement strategy which may lead to lower ratings of self-esteem. The key issue from a process-oriented perspective is to understand the interactions between the cultural practices and mentalities that generate these different strategies, not demonstrating the general mean level differences in self-esteem. At the same time, keeping in mind the second general assumption about the need to understand individual differences within a culture, it would be important to investigate how and why some individuals in these different cultures do not use the modal self-enhancement or self-improvement strategies.

Culture and Motivation

We can summarize the relationship between culture, motivation, and achievement in the following manner. First, a culture affords an individual opportunities to engage in certain cultural practices. These opportunities are generally in place to help advance a specific mentality (e.g., view of self). When an individual takes advantage of those opportunities and engages in those cultural practices, the mentality underlying these cultural practices becomes increasingly the dominant mentality within the person. This interaction between cultural practices and mentalities (e.g., the custom complex) should then lead individuals within that culture to develop certain situational preferences as well as sensitivities toward certain kinds of information. Optimal adaptation ensues when these preferences are met, thus leading to better outcomes, which then leads to the further instantiation of those cultural ideals and practices. This optimal adaptation also could lead to more optimal motivation as the individual has the various mentalities and strategies to be successful in that specific culture, in contrast to a different culture which does not provide the same type of affordances for the more dominant mentalities and may not offer the same opportunities for success.

To refer back to our previous example of Japan and the United States, in the case of the United States, American culture provides more opportunities for self-enhancement (e.g., self-esteem programs, tracking, awards ceremonies). Such practices coupled with a view of self as independent leads Americans to become more sensitive to information indicating their strengths. Given such a proclivity, Americans are much more likely to become motivated in situations that help to reaffirm their positive characteristics (Heine et al., 2001). Placing individuals in those self-enhancing situations should then lead to adaptive motivational outcomes, including increased levels of interest and persistence.

The Japanese culture, on the other hand, provides its citizens with more opportunities for self-improvement (e.g., hansei). These cultural affordances along with the predominant view of the self as interdependent should then lead Japanese individuals to become more sensitive to negative aspects of themselves that are seen as improvable (Heine et al., 2001). This tendency toward self-criticism in turn should lead the Japanese to prefer more those situations that make salient these negative, improvable aspects of the self. Placing Japanese individuals in such a setting should lead them to the most adaptive outcomes, including higher levels of interest and persistence.

The conceptual model proposed here reflects some of the ideas already present in the dialogue among researchers investigating the role of context and motivation (see Volet & Järvelä, 2001); in particular it highlights the fit between the person and his or her environment (Eccles et al., 1993). This is perhaps not surprising given that one of the primary assumptions of cultural psychology underscores the contextual dependence of cultural processes. For example, in her multidimensional model of the person-by-context interaction, Volet (2001) introduces the notion of a match/mismatch between a learner's "effectivities" (i.e., the individual's general learning-related cognitions, motivation, and affect) and the affordances provided by the context. In addition, she places the learner's effectivities on a continuum from more stable cognitions, motivations, and affect (i.e., inclinations) to those that are more readily influenced by the context (i.e., appraisals). In terms of context, Volet also distinguishes between (a) more distal macro-level societal dimensions such as the belief systems that govern a community, (b) the immediate learning environment including field of study, and (c) the experiential domain which represents the academic task the student is currently engaged in.

To support her model, Volet cites research she has conducted on Singaporean students attending university in Australia. She argues that when these students attend their home university in Singapore, in general, their effectivities match the cultural context. She notes that in response to the heavy emphasis placed on testing in the Singaporean educational system, students in that country have developed a strategy called cue-seeking, whereby they systematically seek any information related to upcoming exams and assignments from their peers and teachers. However, when these same students study abroad in Australia, they often find that their strategies, in this case cue-seeking, are not nearly as effective and often engender feelings of frustration and anxiety among students and their Australian professors. According to Volet, the students believe that cue-seeking is an appropriate strategy; however their professors, who are accustomed to encouraging independent thought and self-direction, do not.

Volet's example serves well to support our general claim regarding how the cultural process shapes and prompts the emergence of certain contextual preferences and sensitivities as well as the idea of optimal adaptation and motivation when there is a fit between the culture and the person. For example, the assessment-focused nature of the Singaporean educational system (cultural practice) could be explained in part as an attempt to facilitate an interdependent view of self (cultural mentality) to the extent that it fosters, as Volet notes, a reliance on the teacher's input and guidance. Given such a custom complex, it would not be hard to imagine that these students might then feel more comfortable in those situations that mirror the learning environment back home (e.g., test-taking situations) and in turn, develop a certain motivational mentality. In their home culture, their mentality and strategies represent a good "fit" to the testing and cultural context and they generally do well and are motivated. In contrast, in the Australian context, their mentality and strategies are not a good match to the cultural norms and expectations, leading to less success and less adaptive motivational beliefs and affect.

While Volet's model is helpful in elucidating the relation between motivational processes and context, it does leave us with a number of questions concerning how we have defined cultural processes and how they relate specifically to motivation. The first concerns the definition of effectivities and mentalities. As mentioned before, mentalities can be broadly defined in terms of what an individual knows, thinks, feels, wants, and values. As such, there seems to be a conceptual overlap with Volet's definition of effectivities, which include an individual's cognitions, motivation, and affect. At the same time, however, we have offered self-construals (e.g., interdependent view of self) as an example of a mentality. To that end, effectivities and mentalities may be considered to be somewhat different from one another since the self is usually not thought of as a part of an individual's effectivities, although it is certainly believed to have implications for an individual's cognitions, motivation and affect, as we have demonstrated throughout this paper. In addition, Volet's definition of the most distal level of context, what she calls the macrosocio-cultural societal dimensions, seems to also overlap somewhat with our definition of cultural mentality as she focuses on the values and belief systems present in a community. These questions underscore the need for theorists to clarify what we mean exactly by mentalities, what we mean by context, and what we mean by culture. While we are far from fully comprehending the complex interaction between culture, context, and motivation, increased attention to these issues should nevertheless help to refine our understanding of not only situated motivation but how cultural processes also fit into this picture.

Implications for Motivational Theory

Clearly, the "culture as process" perspective has a number of important implications for the study of motivation. First and foremost, as stated earlier, this view suggests that culture should not be treated as a mere static antecedent of psychological phenomena but rather a dynamic, integral part of the motivational process. Unfortunately, the majority of studies devoted to the study of cultural differences in motivation to date have for the most part treated culture as an independent variable, usually categorizing individuals into one cultural group and comparing their scores with individuals in other cultural groups. For example, one common practice within the field of psychology is to dummy code ethnicity as a proxy for culture.

There are a number of theoretical as well as methodological problems with this approach. In terms of theory, one problem is that this approach does not capture the complex and reciprocal relation of cultural processes to motivation. As we have noted in our analysis of self-esteem, the cultural practices and mentalities may mutually support the use of different self-enhancement or self-improvement strategies.

Second, to confound ethnicity with culture is problematic. While it may be logical to assume that persons who share a similar ethnic makeup may also espouse similar values, this is not always the case, and it may be misleading to collapse all individuals into one ethnic category. In other words, ethnicity does not define one's culture. One example of this would be the line of research examining acculturative processes such as ethnic identity. This body of work makes clear the importance of taking into account the extent to which an individual actually feels a part of their ethnic group and engages in their group's cultural practices (Phinney, 1990, 1996). In terms of the role of the custom complex, to the extent that an individual does not take part in the practices of their cultural heritage, be that language, educational practices, or celebration of cultural holidays, the likelihood of that individual feeling a kinship with his or her own ethnic group would be lessened. Therefore, while physically, an individual may appear to be a part of a certain ethnic group, and may perhaps even identify him or herself as belonging to that ethnic group in response to a close-ended ethnicity question on a survey, one cannot be entirely certain whether or not that individual is actually functioning as a member of that ethnic group without taking into consideration constructs such as ethnic identity or acculturation. Therefore, we would argue that researchers interested in cultural differences must consider ethnic identity as an important variable of interest, especially when examining the motivation of individuals with more than one identity.

This brings us to another important issue; that is the study of motivational processes of ethnic minority groups. Much of the work supporting the "culture as process" perspective thus far has been conducted on two specific cross-national samples, namely Anglo-Americans and the Japanese. Therefore, more work needs to be done on the motivational processes of other groups, if we are to extend our understanding of the link between culture and motivation. Specifically, we believe that research examining the motivation of ethnic minority students framed within the "culture as process" paradigm is sorely needed. Ethnic minority groups such as Asian Americans are often exposed to more than one culture, (1) the culture of their ethnic background, in this case their Asian heritage, and (2) the culture of the society at large. In a sense, these individuals are "biculturals." In terms of our theoretical model, biculturals generally have participated in more than one cultural institution. For example, in terms of educational system, many Asian American students attend Chinese school or Japanese school on the weekends in an effort to maintain their Asian heritage. Similarly, these students may speak more than one language at home. Therefore, these practices may result in biculturals espousing more than one view of self.

Research on biculturals is still fairly new and has primarily been devoted to the link between culture and cognition; however, the results so far have been quite interesting. For example, researchers have demonstrated that it is possible for biculturals to switch between various "cultural frames of reference" in response to corresponding social cues (Hong, Morris, Chiu, & Benet-Martinez, 2000). Moreover, it has been found that the response styles of biculturals are influenced by which culture is brought to the fore. For example, it has been previously suggested that the fundamental attribution error, or the tendency for individuals to underestimate situational influences and overestimate dispositional influences in explaining the behaviors of others, may be a North American phenomenon (Markus & Kitayama, 1991; Morris & Peng, 1994; Ross, 1977). Morris and Peng (1994) found their Chinese participants to accord more weight to the social context than their American participants when explaining an individual's behavior. However, Hong and her colleagues (2000) demonstrated that Chinese biculturals also commit the fundamental attribution error when placed in a context that makes the American culture more salient.

Hong et al. (2000) thus conclude that their findings support what they call a "dynamic constructivist approach to culture and cognition." Their approach is consistent with the approach to culture we have proposed in this chapter. In fact their results serve to further support the notion of cultural mentalities as ever changing and sensitive to contextual cues. In addition, their findings underscore the need for researchers to consider within-group variability and to consider the role of cultural cues in influencing the motivational processes of ethnic minority students. For example, in terms of the relation between culture and motivation, their findings suggest that Asian-American students' motivational processes would depend upon which view of self (i.e., cultural frame) is made salient. Therefore, it would be erroneous to assume that just because Asian Americans share a common Asian heritage, and that most Asian cultures espouse an interdependent view of self, that Asian Americans would also always operate under that mode.

This also brings us to the tendency among psychologists to rely heavily on the distinction between independent/interdependent selves in explaining cultural differences. To be sure, this framework has guided a great many publications within the field of psychology (e.g., Oyserman, Coon, & Kemmelmeier, 2002) and will most likely continue to do so in the future as it clearly has implications for motivational theory. We, too, have used self-construals as an example within this chapter. While its simplicity adds to its appeal, and studies addressing this dichotomy have certainly provoked deeper thinking about the generalizability of our constructs to other groups, we should be wary of labeling cultures as individualistic/collectivistic or individuals as espousing an independent/interdependent self. For one, researchers should recognize that individualism and collectivism (and by its relation, interdependent and independent selves) do not necessarily lie on a continuum. In other words, it is possible for individuals to possess varying degrees of both individualistic and/or collectivistic tendencies, as documented by the research on biculturals (Singelis, 1994).

Second, we believe that the independent/interdependent distinction seems useful in accounting for differences between Asians and Anglos in particular but are unsure of its explanatory power for the motivational processes of other ethnic groups, for example, African American students, although there has been some limited conjectures on African selfways (Markus, Mullally, & Kitayama, 1998). Rather than self-construals, Graham, Taylor, and Hudley (1998) have proposed that cultural values may help to better explain the motivational processes of African American students. Nevertheless, this notion of investigating what individuals know, feel, think, want, and value (i.e., cultural mentality) and how this relates to practices in which they engage should allow researchers to ground their theoretical models within a specific cultural context.

Finally, in terms of investigating cultural differences on specific motivational constructs, the emphasis should be placed not on whether there are mean-level differences between cultural groups but rather on the processes that underlie those differences. For example, we have argued in this paper that one cultural mentality that can influence motivational processes is an individual's view of self. To that end, we might expect there to be differences between Asians and Anglos in their average level of endorsement of those motivational constructs that are based on an independent view of self, for example expectancy constructs such as self-efficacy. Indeed, a number of researchers have uncovered such mean-level differences between these two groups (Eaton & Dembo, 1997; Stigler, Smith, & Mao, 1985; Whang & Hancock, 1994).

Stigler, Smith, and Mao (1985) were among the first researchers to examine Asian students' self-perceptions of competence. Specifically, the researchers investigated possible mean level differences in Taiwanese and American students' levels of perceived competence as well as cultural differences in how students' competence perceptions in various domains (i.e., academic, social, physical) relate to one another. The researchers assessed Chinese and American fifth grade students' perceptions of competence using Harter's Perceived Competence Scale for Children (PCSC) and reported nearly identical factor structures across the two groups. In line with the research on attributional biases, the authors also noted a trend among the Taiwanese participants to display self-effacing tendencies, especially in the ratings of their perceptions of academic competence. In contrast, the American children were found to show more positive self-evaluations of cognitive competence. The authors argued that such findings were inconsistent with the general assertion that higher achievement should be linked with higher perceptions of competence considering research findings that demonstrate Chinese students' comparatively higher levels of academic performance. Such arguments notwithstanding, however, the authors also report a significant and positive correlation between Chinese students' school grades and their ratings of perceived academic competence.

Similarly, Eaton and Dembo (1997) assessed Asian-American students' perceptions of their self-efficacy for a novel reading achievement task and reported lower levels of situational self-efficacy beliefs among Asian-American students than among non-Asian American students. Whang & Hancock (1994), too, described Asian-American students in their sample as having lower self-concepts of their academic ability in comparison to non-Asian students. In both studies, the authors accounted for such findings by arguing that motivational variables like self-efficacy are rooted in theories of achievement motivation that are based in individualism. Thus, the authors posited that for Asian students and other members of collectivistic societies, such constructs might not be as valid.

However, from a process-oriented approach, there may be difficulties with this conclusion. The results may merely reflect a problem with calibration, that is, the extent to which students' ratings of their motivational beliefs such as self-efficacy accurately reflect their true level of motivation and achievement as measured by some external, objective standard. Given Anglo Americans' proclivity toward self-enhancement and Asians' tendency toward self-criticism, one could argue that Anglo American students merely overestimate how well they think they will perform on future tasks, while Asian students generally underestimate their abilities.

But, perhaps more importantly, it is not enough to merely attribute it to cultural differences in individualism and/or collectivism at such an abstract level. This is especially true when doing research on biculturals such as Asian Americans, where they may have access to both types of mentalities. We must determine for whom and under what conditions these differences emerge and we must investigate more closely the etiology of these differences. One way to do this would be to examine the cultural practices, such as the educational system, language, and interactions with parents, which these students engage in, to determine whether level of engagement in these practices has any effect on motivation. To paraphrase Kitayama (2002), culture is, after all, not just "in the head" but also "out there" in the form of collective patterns of behaviors.

In addition, more work needs to be done on investigating how individuals in various cultures actually define specific motivational constructs. In other words, we need more research on the meanings individuals in these cultures attach to motivational terminology. For example, Maehr and his colleagues (Maehr & Nicholls 1980; Fyans, Salili, Maehr, & Desai, 1983) conducted a number of studies on how cultures around the world define "achievement" and "success." They reasoned that the goals driving achievement-related behavior might differ between cultures based on how individuals in these cultures viewed success and failure. For example, they noted that in India, "success" was defined primarily in terms of power motivation and political success while Western cultures placed more emphasis on concepts such as ability and effort (Maehr & Nicholls, 1980). The notion that these concepts might potentially vary between cultures as well as by individuals within cultures is a good one that deserves further attention. We believe that one area of motivation that might benefit from such an inquiry is achievement goal theory.

A second major approach to motivation, besides efficacy, concerns the role of achievement goals. Achievement goal theory was developed within a social-cognitive framework and focuses on explaining how goal orientations influence how individuals approach, engage in, and respond to achievement situations (Ames, 1992). Much of the research framed within the achievement goal tradition identifies two primary achievement goals, namely mastery and performance goals, as being important determinants of students' motivation and learning. Endorsement of a mastery goal, or the goal to develop competence and task mastery, has been found to be positively related to various learning and motivational indices. In contrast, adoption of a performance goal, or the goal to validate one's competence in relation to others, is generally thought to have a negative effect on students' achievement motivation and academic performance (Dweck and Leggett 1988), although some recent findings concerning a particular dimension of performance goals (i.e., performance-approach goals) seems to suggest that when students are focused on besting others, they may be rewarded with higher achievement although perhaps at a cost of avoidance behaviors or other academically detrimental outcomes (Midgley, Middleton, & Kaplan, 2001).

Despite the recent popularity of the goal orientation framework in the field of achievement motivation, there has been very little research specifically examining how cultural processes influence students' adoption of either a mastery and/or performance goal. Holloway (1988), for example, did not directly assess Asian students' goal orientations. However, through an analysis of practices displayed by teachers at school and by parents at home, she concluded that the Japanese school and home environments foster Japanese students to adopt a mastery (or what she called a task-involvement) orientation. In particular, she pointed to the emphasis placed on cooperation by Japanese teachers and parents, a feature normally associated with mastery-oriented settings. In terms of the classroom context, she noted the use of cooperative reward structures and cooperative group instruction. She also cited Japanese teachers' frequent exhortations to effort and perseverance. In correspondence to such findings, researchers have found Japanese students to prefer cooperative group activities while American children have been found to favor competitive or individual pursuits (Weisz, Rothbaum, & Blackburn, 1984). Such trends have been observed not only with Japanese students but with Chinese students as well; studies have shown Chinese students to be more cooperative under both competitive and cooperative reward structures, especially among older students (Hau & Salili, 1996).

Based on such claims, Whang and Hancock (1994) hypothesized that Asian students may indeed be more mastery-oriented than non-Asian students and suggested that their mastery-oriented nature might explain, in part, their academic accomplishments. Similar to the research on self-efficacy, we believe that there is not, at present, enough evidence to support such a claim. For one, the limited goal theory findings on this population have been, for the most part, inconsistent (cf. Zusho, Pintrich, & Schnabel, 2002). Moreover, studies that merely compare the relative endorsement of mastery and/or performance goals among Asians (or any other ethnic group for that matter) to another group of students generally do little to explain *why* those differences exist in the first place. However, phenomenological research examining the meanings these groups associate with mastery and performance goals might reveal some insight into the processes underlying the motivation of these groups.

For example, we have presented some nascent evidence suggesting that the Japanese might be more motivated toward self-improvement (Heine et al., 2001). However, there is a need to clarify what exactly "self-improvement" entails. Intuitively speaking, one might argue that this notion of self-improvement might be closely related to mastery-goal orientation. However, at the same time, Kitayama and his colleagues (Heine et al., 1999, 2001; Kitayama & Marcus, 1999) suggest that this Japanese proclivity toward self-improvement actually stems from their self-critical nature as a result of an interdependent view of self. Consequently, they refer to this as "relational self-improvement," emphasizing how this notion of self-improvement is embedded firmly within a social context (Kitayama & Marcus, 1999). It would follow then, that relational self-improvement is different from mastery goal orientation to the extent that there is some element of social comparison in relational self-improvement, which is absent in the traditional conceptualization of mastery goals.

Similarly, further research examining the definition of competition might help to clarify how performance goals might be conceptualized differently among Japanese individuals. For example, Heine et al. (2001) have argued that among those who espouse an interdependent view of self, competition can been framed not as a focus on outperforming others per se, but rather as a focus on living up to socially shared standards of excellence.

Thus, given such considerations, it may not be enough for researchers to rely solely on factor analytic techniques to establish whether or not our theories are applicable to other cultures. For example, while it is interesting that similar factor structures can be uncovered for diverse cultural groups, this does not mean that these structures actually capture the motivational processes of these groups. We have suggested that for Asian cultures in particular, one must consider how these processes are dependent upon context and/or one's relationship with others. Therefore, to the extent that the items used in factor analyses do not explicate these contextual factors, one cannot argue that these structures are truly identical and capture the day-to-day experiences of these cultural groups.

METHODOLOGICAL ISSUES CONCERNING THE STUDY OF CULTURE AND MOTIVATION

Appropriate research methods form the basis of any scientific inquiry. Without appropriate methods with which to investigate hypotheses, data cannot be integrated and interpreted in an intelligible form. In this section, we discuss various methodological issues associated with the study of cultural differences in motivation, organized under the four assumptions detailed in the first section of this chapter. More specifically, we examine specific culturally informed methods that would be more appropriate for the study of motivational differences, given the process-oriented perspective of culture.

Assumption 1: Culture as a Non-entity

As stated earlier, one of the basic tenets of cultural psychology is that culture should be conceptualized as a process, rather than a mere antecedent of psychological phenomena. From this assumption, we can draw several conclusions about the appropriateness of certain common methodologies within the field of psychology.

The first concerns the relatively widespread practice within psychology of using close-ended ethnicity questions as a measure of "culture." A common practice investigators use when conducting research on more than one ethnic population is to have a participant identity to which ethnic group they belong. Oftentimes, this takes the form of a single-item, self-report assessment in which a respondent is asked to differentiate him or herself from various ethnic groups (e.g., Caucasian American, African American, Hispanic/Latino, Asian/Pacific Islander). Although a researcher might supplement this question with other measures (e.g., language they speak at home, generational status), more often that not, researchers classify the respondent as Asian American or African American based on this single item response.

Although this is quick and efficient, it may create some difficulties from a process-oriented perspective. From the participant's perspective, a response to this question might take on a completely different meaning. For example, in answering such a question, a participant might classify him or herself as Asian American simply because the respondent believes that he or she possesses physical markers or features that are characteristic of Asian persons. Alternatively, a participant might have arrived at their response as a result of a process of elimination (i.e., I'm not Caucasian, I'm not African American, I'm not Hispanic, so I must be Asian American).

Thus, self-identification procedures tell us very little about how that individual actually feels about being Asian or Asian American, or the extent to which that respondent actually identifies with their ethnic group, or whether or not that individual actually takes part in some of the cultural practices of that group. In short, to rely on this single item as an index of culture could be misleading as it substitutes ethnic group membership for culture. If the important process is the cultural complex defined by the cultural practices and mentalities, then it is important to measure those aspects, not just simply ethnic group membership.

An example of this notion that might resonate with motivational theorists is the work conducted by Eccles and her colleagues (e.g., Eccles et al., 1998) on gender differences. Like culture, psychologists have often treated gender as an entity that precedes psychological phenomena. For example, researchers have contended for many years that males and females possess varied academic strengths; that males and females differ in mathematical and verbal skills and that these different capabilities, in turn, partially account for the disparities in achievement levels between the sexes in certain academic domains (Maccoby & Jacklin, 1974). Similarly, researchers have noted mean level differences between boys and girls in their ratings of self-efficacy, particularly in domains such as science and mathematics. Such findings have led some researchers to conclude that it is gender that causes these achievement and motivational differences.

However, Eccles and her colleagues have clarified that it is not gender, per se, that accounts for these differences (Eccles et al., 1998). Rather, they stress how these differences vary depending on the extent to which boys and girls actually endorse cultural values regarding gender-related superiority in these domains. In short, the work of Eccles suggests that it is not really gender that is directing these differences, but whether or not these girls and boys actually are raised in an environment that promotes gender socialization and stereotyping. Correspondingly, Harter, Waters, and Whitesell (1997) underscore the need for researchers to consider gender orientation, rather than actual gender, when examining gender differences in psychological constructs, in this case the phenomenon known as loss of voice, or the tendency to inhibit one's thoughts and feelings. Thus, these findings suggest that relying solely on a dichotomous measure of gender may not fully capture the processes that are actually driving these differences to emerge.

Accordingly, the same could be said for research examining ethnic differences to the extent that whatever mean level differences in motivation that have been noted between certain ethnic groups can probably be accounted by the custom complex, or this interaction between cultural mentalities and practices. Of course, the logical question would then be, what would be considered "appropriate" research methods when evaluating the motivational processes of various ethnic groups. Perhaps the most important thing would be for the researcher to avoid categorizing individuals into specific groups based solely on a single close-ended ethnicity question. Instead, if one must categorize individuals into groups, then it should be based on other criteria, including ethnic identity and other acculturative measures.

Assumption 2: Culture is Not an Omnibus Global Variable

Similar to the first assumption, the second assumption recognizes that variation within a culture is possible. In short, it acknowledges within-group differences. As such, the process perspective would encourage the investigation of individual differences within groups. For example, the model minority stereotype of Asian American students has recently come under attack. Hsia and Peng (1998) note that on average "Asian American" students outperform other ethnic minority populations in terms of academic attainment and achievement. At the same time, however, they stress that such comparisons ignore the enormous variation within Asian American population and that not all Asian sub-groups are performing at such high levels. Thus their findings call into question the practice of lumping specific subgroups of Asian American students, as most published reports on this group have done to date. In doing so, we mask potential problems and educational needs of some subgroups and perhaps more importantly, it does little to further our understanding of the nature of this group's achievement motivation.

In terms of specific methodologies, one method that can be used to investigate within-group differences is priming (Hong et al., 2000). For example, Hong et al. (2002) used cultural icons as primes. In this particular instance, the authors used cultural icons as their primes to investigate potential variation in Chinese biculturals' cognitive attributions. For the American prime, the authors collected pictures of American symbols such as the American flag, iconic heroes such as Abraham Lincoln, and landmarks, such as the Capitol building. They collected similar pictures for the Chinese culture condition (e.g., Chinese dragon, the Great Wall of China). While Hong et al were concerned with cultural differences in attributional biases, we believe that priming techniques can also be used to investigate potential variation in motivational processes among biculturals. For example, researchers interested in investigating the motivational processes of Asian American biculturals can place these participants in either an American and/or Asian condition to see if their motivational patterns are influenced by their cultural frame of reference. Such a study would allow insight into not only how motivation might vary within the Asian American population but may also extend our understanding of the contextual dependence of motivational processes.

At the same time, however, we would caution against the indiscriminate use of primes and would advocate for extensive testing of primes on numerous samples to ensure that the primes are actually priming what is intended. For example, cultural icons have been shown to effectively influence the cognitive attributions of Chinese American biculturals. However, it is unclear what features of Chinese or American culture were primed when they used these icons. Thus, one cannot decisively determine which aspect of culture was influential in bringing about these differences. Did these icons help biculturals access their view of self or did they make specific cultural practices more salient? In addition, the meanings attached to specific cultural icons can change over time. For instance, after the horrific events of September 11th, one could easily argue that the American flag is perhaps a better symbol of patriotism, rather than ideals such as life, liberty, and the pursuit of happiness. Thus, it is important for researchers to be cautious in not only using certain primes but also in the interpretation of their findings.

Nevertheless, the general premise underlying this particular methodology is a good one and should be explored further. For one, as noted above, it can be used to recognize intra-group variability. It is important to note, however, that the technique of priming in and of itself does not ensure that one's research is in accordance with a process-oriented approach to culture. Priming, after all, can and has been used, especially within social psychology, for purposes other than demonstrating intra- or even intercultural variability. However, the key point is that when it is used appropriately with the express purpose of investigating within-group differences, it can help to further our understanding of cultural processes. In addition, we should also stress that researchers who use priming in relation to cultural differences are making an assumption about the level at which cultural processes operate. Specifically, these investigators assume that cultural processes operate at a primarily subconscious level. This may be especially true for biculturals who have grown accustomed to "living in two cultures. It is not likely that biculturals are fully cognizant at all times of what cultural frame of reference they are in, after all. Rather, biculturals most likely determine this through cues in the environment, for example what language they are speaking. To this end, priming may be considered a rather authentic way of investigating cultural processes.

Assumption 3: Cultural Processes are Dependent Upon Context

The third assumption acknowledges the role of context on cultural processes. For example, Kitayama and Marcus (1999) discuss how Japanese individuals' motivational patterns might differ depending upon whether the official (outside the home) or private (inside the home) frame of reference is in operation. Thus, some researchers have advocated the use of "on-line" studies (Kitayama, 2002), or studies that examine an individual's spontaneous motivation or cognition in actual social settings (*not* internet-based studies). An example of an on-line study as it pertains to the study of motivation is that of Heine et al. (2001). In this study, the authors randomly assigned Japanese and Anglo American participants into one of two conditions, success or failure. In the success condition, participants were given feedback that they had performed well on an initial anagram task, while participants who were assigned to the failure condition were told that they had performed poorly on this initial task. Then, participants were given the opportunity to work on a second similar task. The researchers then measured how long individuals persisted on this second task as a behavioral measure of motivation. This study is considered to be on-line because it recorded participants' spontaneous motivation (i.e., persistence) as a result of an actual social setting (i.e., success/failure condition). Another example of an on-line study would be one conducted by Salili and her colleagues examining the effects of extrinsic rewards (i.e., evaluation) on Iranian students' continuing motivation (Salili, Maehr, Sorensen, & Fyans, 1976). The important point is that the motivational processes are measured in the situation (on-line) and allows for some assessment of the dynamics of the processes as they unfold over time in context.

Assumption 4: Research on Cultural Processes Should not be Guided Solely by a Quest to Validate Existing Theories

As stated earlier, with this assumption, cultural psychology parts ways with cross-cultural psychology such that research in the cultural psychological tradition is generally not guided by a desire to test the universality of existing theoretical frameworks. As such, a cultural psychologist probably would not be concerned with proving that achievement goal theory or expectancy-value theory is relevant or applicable to different ethnic minority populations or cultures around the world. To that end, one could extrapolate that cultural psychologists generally would not focus on research that compares the motivational processes of one group to another, a notion that presents challenges for conventional psychological research.

In a similar fashion, there is a movement even within the field of motivation that calls for a decreased emphasis on what Graham refers to as "race-comparative" as opposed to "race-homogeneous" studies (Graham, 1994; Yu & Wolters, 2002). Race-comparative studies can generally be defined as those studies that examine between-group variability while race-homogeneous studies can be described as studies that are conducted on a single ethnic group. There is some debate in the field of psychology regarding the merit of race-comparative research. Most often, critics of this approach voice the complaint that race-comparative studies do little more than identify areas in which the values, attitudes, and beliefs of ethnic minority members, such as Asian American or African American students, contrast with the values, attitudes, and beliefs of members of the majority culture—typically, Caucasian American students (Graham, 1994). In the presence of more sophisticated research based on contemporary psychological frameworks, simple race-comparative studies whose sole aim is to identify mean level differences is less useful, as such research typically does not address why these differences exist in the first place.

Moreover, we should acknowledge that excessive reliance on this methodology can have some unfortunate consequences, such as promoting a trend of ignoring within-group differences. Another issue concerns the selection of the comparison groups. As mentioned previously, the majority of comparative studies use Caucasian students as their comparison groups. More problematic is the practice of collapsing Caucasian students with other ethnic minority students. For example, some researchers have chosen to compare the motivational beliefs of Asian and/or Asian-American students to those of what they call "non-Asian" students, who include not only Caucasian students but Latino and African American students as well. Clearly, this is problematic, as researchers have shown that the motivational patterns of these other minority students differ distinctly from Caucasian American students (Graham, 1994).

We contend, however, that there is still value in conducting comparative research. Moreover, we believe that it is not a question of whether or not one should or should not conduct comparative studies but *how* those studies are actually conducted, as illustrated by those studies conducted by Heine et al. (2001). Their work clearly highlights differences between Anglo Americans and the Japanese; however, rather than merely documenting these differences, they tried to understand the processes underlying these differences by examining the relation of self-improvement to the relational self for the Japanese and self-enhancement to the autonomous self for Americans and how these relations between self and motivation in turn resulted in differential patterns of motivation and achievement.

Nevertheless, there are specific issues related to the instruments investigators use that one should bear in mind when comparing the psychological processes of one group to another. More specifically, researchers who do cross-cultural research or research on ethnic minority populations must take into consideration the "cultural appropriateness" of assessment instruments. In the area of cultural psychology, researchers often distinguish between two "types" of constructs: constructs that are considered to be "universal" (etic) and those that are considered to be specific to a particular culture (emic). It has been argued by some that studies on multiple populations should, in fact, include both types of constructs so as to provide a more detailed analysis of the particular groups under examination (Tanaka, Ebreo, Linn, & Morera, 1998). In terms of motivation, many of the self-report instruments can be considered to be "etic" measures while qualitative ethnographic approaches would be more likely to be classified as "emic" to the extent that they focus on documenting certain aspects of a culture without concern of how that culture compares to another in terms of a specific motivational construct. For example, to administer a self-report instrument with questions that are targeted at measuring an individual's goal orientation would be considered to be an etic approach. In contrast, open-ended descriptive methodologies may be considered to be more emic in nature.

Researchers must also contend with the issue of using instruments that have been standardized on non-Anglo populations. This can pose a potential bias as a researcher might very well find that such instruments measure different things in other cultures which, in turn, might influence some of the psychometric properties of the instrument. For example, one might encounter problems associated with the construct validity of an instrument, including low reliabilities. This problem was noted quite well in the recent meta-analysis of studies examining individualism and collectivism conducted by Oyserman and her colleagues (Oyserman et al., 2002). More specifically, if an instrument's reliability varies greatly from culture to culture, then it suggests that that instrument may not be measuring well the intended underlying construct for those cultures exhibiting low reliability. Thus, using such faulty scales might lead researchers to make false conclusions. For example, Oyserman et al. (2002) noted that researchers who used low reliability collectivism measures found no difference between U.S. and Japanese respondents' level of collectivism. However, investigators who used high reliability measures found that Americans were higher in collectivism than their Japanese counterparts. It is also important to note that this particular issue of using culturally insensitive measures is not limited to only those who do comparative research. Researchers interested in conducting non-comparative research should also be aware of this problem, especially if they choose to use measures that have been normed on samples other than the culture they are investigating.

Additionally, researchers should take into account the measurement equivalence of instruments that have been translated. In cross-cultural studies, and in studies where respondents do not speak English, it is often necessary to use translated instruments. While a number of researchers have voiced concerns over such practices (e.g., Stevenson & Lee, 1990) other investigators have proposed some guidelines for achieving cultural equivalence: (1) translation by two or more bilingual speakers independently, and (2) back translation (i.e., translation of the instrument into English to another language and then "back-translate" that same instrument into English) (Tanaka et al., 1998).

In addition to the methodological issues presented above, researchers must also face another set of issues related to response bias. Research on African American and Hispanic students has demonstrated their tendencies toward exhibiting extreme response styles, especially when answering Likert scale items (Padilla & Lindholm, 1995; Tanaka et al., 1998). Analogously, researchers have noted among Asians or Asian-Americans a trend to avoid the extreme ends of a scale (e.g., ones and fives on a five-point Likert scale), perhaps as a result of their self-effacing tendencies (Stevenson & Lee, 1990). At the same time, researchers have observed that the ratings these ethnic minority students provide on self-report assessments are often discrepant with actual behavior. In the case of African American students, researchers have found that despite higher ratings of self-esteem and self-efficacy, these students often obtain lower achievement scores. Similarly, Asian-Americans have been found to provide lower ratings of their efficacy, despite higher achievement levels. While the reason underlying such response styles is unclear, these discrepancies certainly pose a validity problem.

Thus, based on such findings, one may conclude that perhaps it may be inappropriate to use self-report instruments on ethnic minority students. The question, then, is what kinds of instruments are "appropriate." In addition to the aforementioned priming and on-line studies, one alternative, as proposed by Peng, Nisbett, and Wong (1997) is the use of vignettes. They argue that in comparison to other research methodologies (e.g., ranking, attitude scales), the use of what they call the scenario method yields the most reasonable criterion validity to the extent that these scenarios measure individuals' attitudes in a specific context, thereby lessening the likelihood of an individual imposing his or her own value judgments on the interpretation of a question. Likewise, Heine et al. (2001) note the problems associated with reference group effects when using Likert-scale measures. When answering such items, the participant is often asked to base their response in comparison to others. But, who are the "others?" The reference group respondents base their answers on undoubtedly varies from group to group (e.g., Americans would compare themselves to other Americans, not Japanese), thereby confounding such comparisons. To deal with such issues, the authors recommend the use of a forced-choice format, whereby participants are asked to choose between two options that vary in the attitude under consideration. For example, in their study examining Japanese and American students' beliefs about incremental intelligence, participants were given a short description of a student who had performed well on an exam and were asked to estimate the percentage of this student's performance that can be attributed to innate intelligence and effort respectively (Heine et al., 2001).

There are still other approaches that have been developed by cross-cultural psychologists that may be especially useful in uncovering phenomenological differences across cultures. One is the semantic differential technique, a method that allows investigators to determine the level of divergence and/or convergence in the meaning of a construct, for example achievement, across a wide number of cultures (Fyans et al., 1983). Salili (1994) notes, however, that the semantic differential technique may yield results that are either too broad or too vague, which hinders the interpretation of such findings. Instead, Salili advocates for the repertory grid technique. This technique is based on Kelly's personal construct theory and follows the form of a structured interview. Through this interview, respondents are asked to generate situations concerning a specific construct and asked to compare how similar and dissimilar these situations are to each other (Salili, 1994). For example, Salili (1994) used a specialized type of grid, namely the rating grid, to investigate Hong Kong students' conceptions of success. She first asked students to generate four situations in which they were successful, four situations in which they would have liked to be successful, and four situations in which they were unsuccessful. For each set of four situations, respondents were asked to rank-order each situation in order of importance. Participants were then asked to compare these situations to one another and determine on which dimensions (i.e., construct) these situations were similar or dissimilar to one another. Finally, subjects were asked to rate each of the 12 generated success situations with each construct, using a 7-point scale (Salili, 1994).

Finally, as mentioned before, there is probably a need to go beyond quantitative methodologies and incorporate more qualitative techniques in our analyses of culture and motivation. For example, rather than relying solely on self-report measures, we should consider asking more open-ended questions or conducting more in-depth interviews with participants so that we can conduct a more fine-grained analysis of the extent of participation in cultural practices as well as their cultural ideologies.

CONCLUSION

We have proposed, in this chapter, a more dynamic approach to the study of culture and motivation. More specifically, we suggest that future research in the area of motivation should adopt a process-oriented approach to culture. This vision of culture suggests that the relation between culture and psychological processes are closely entwined—that cultural practices and cultural ideologies (i.e., the custom complex) are mutually constituted. The key issues for future research concern developing our theoretical models for understanding this relation and developing our methodologies to generate reliable and valid empirical data on this process.

In terms of our theoretical models, we can build on more traditional research on classic motivational constructs such as efficacy, values, interest, and goals. These constructs can and do play a role in individual motivation across cultures as part of different cultural mentalities. However, a process-oriented approach suggests that the function of these constructs may be different between cultures and different for various individuals within cultures. Future research needs to understand how these constructs function in these cultures and how they are constituted by and through different cultural practices. Moreover, a process-oriented approach suggests that there may be other constructs that are not part of our normative psychological motivational models that may play an important role in certain cultural groups. A process-oriented approach would be open to finding and examining these constructs in contrast to a traditional approach that focuses on testing the cross-cultural generalizability of motivational theories such as self-efficacy theory or achievement goal theory.

Research on the role of contextual factors in current motivational research (see Volet & Jarvela, 2001) can serve as a guide to understanding how cultural practices and cultural mentalities are mutually constituted. Although this research does not advocate an explicit cultural psychological perspective, it does stress the importance of understanding how student motivation within classrooms is shaped and constituted by classroom practices and cultures. This work highlights how both the context and the individual student can contribute to the motivation of students in classrooms. Although this research has far to go in developing integrative and clearly defined conceptual models regarding both cultural practices and mentalities, it does offer some findings and models that can guide future process-oriented research. In particular, it offers a way of conceptualizing classroom cultures that may be applicable to more general cultural processes and practices. In addition, it helps us understand the classroom culture itself as one context where student motivation plays out, regardless of whether it is in the United States, Japan, or elsewhere and how classroom cultures can afford or shape student motivation of all students, regardless of cultural background or ethnicity.

This work on classroom contexts and situated motivation also offers some methodological tools that may be useful, including more ethnographic methods and methods that integrate traditional quantitative survey measures with other more qualitative measures. Of course, there are methodological challenges in this more contextual work. These include defining a proper unit of analysis and establishing not only culturally-informed measures but also instruments that are culturally valid. We have suggested that priming and on-line studies represent a very promising approach to the study of motivational and cultural processes. However, in all of this work with new methods, the proof of utility will be in the actual results and understandings that are generated. Findings, even with new process-oriented or qualitative methods, that simply replicate the main generalizations of traditional motivational theories do not take us very far in our understanding of motivation and culture. For example, some of the findings from the situated or contextual perspective on student classroom motivation (see Volet & Järvelä, 2001) just replicate, albeit at a much more micro-level and situated classroom level, what has already been documented in more traditional motivational studies. To that end, it is not clear how much these studies have added in actually deepening our understanding of students' motivational processes.

However, it may be that a combination of these more diverse and innovative methods with a more process-oriented perspective on motivation and culture will result in better theory and understanding of motivational processes. The field of motivational research has progressed quite far in understanding student motivation and it is now ready to take on the challenge of understanding culture and motivation. We have shared some models and methods that should help us in this goal and we look forward to more theory and research in this area that will help us understand student motivation as well as develop cultures and contexts that support the development of adaptive student motivation.

AKNOWLEDGMENTS

We would like to thank our colleagues at Michigan, Stuart Karabenick, Yi-Guang Lin, Bill McKeachie, Christina Rhee, and Brian Sims, as well as the editors, Farideh Salili and Rumjahn Hoosain for very helpful comments on an earlier draft.

REFERENCES

Ames, C. (1992). Classrooms: Goals, structures, and student motivation. *Journal of Educational Psychology, 84,* 261–271.

Azuma, H. (1998). Japanese collectivism and education. In S.G. Paris (Ed.), *Global prospects for education: Development, culture, and schooling* (pp. 291–307). Washington, DC: American Psychological Association.

Bandura, A. (1978). The self system in reciprocal determinism. *American Psychologist, 33,* 344–358.

Bandura, A. (1986). *The foundations of social thought and action.* Englewood Cliffs, NJ: Erlbaum.

Bandura, A. (1997). *Self-efficacy: The exercise of control.* New York: W.H Freeman.

Barron, K., & Harackiewicz, J. (2001). Achievement goals and optimal motivation: Testing multiple goal models. *Journal of Personality and Social Psychology, 80,* 706–722.

Beane, J. A. (1991). Sorting out the self-esteem controversy. *Educational Leadership, 49,* 25–30.

Cole, M. (1996). *Cultural psychology: A once and future discipline.* Cambridge, MA: Harvard University Press.

Dweck, C. S., & Leggett, E. L. (1988). A social-cognitive approach to motivation and personality. *Psychological Review, 95,* 256–273.

Eaton, M. J., & Dembo, M. H. (1997). Differences in the motivational beliefs of Asian American and Non-Asian students. *Journal of Educational Psychology, 89*(3), 433–440.

Eccles, J. (1983). Expectancies, values, and academic behaviors. In J. T. Spence (Ed.), *Achievement and achievement motives* (pp. 75–146). San Francisco: Freeman.

Eccles, J.S., Midgely, C., Wigfield, A., Buchanan, C., Reuman, D., Flanagan, C., & Mac Iver, D. (1993). Development during adolescence: The impact of stage-environment fit on young adolescents' experiences in schools and families. *American Psychologist, 48,* 90–101.

Eccles, J. S., Wigfield, A., & Schiefele, U. (1998). Motivation to succeed. In W. Damon & N. Eisenberg (Eds.), *Handbook of child psychology: Vol. 3. Social, emotional, and personality development* (5th ed., pp. 1017–1095). New York: Wiley.

Fordham, S., & Ogbu, J. U. (1986). Black students' school success: Coping with the "burden of acting White." *Urban Review, 18,* 176–206.

Fyans, L. J., Salili, F., Maehr, M. L., & Desai, K. A. (1983). A cross-cultural exploration into the meaning of achievement. *Journal of Personality and Social Psychology, 44,* 1000–1013.

Graham, S. (1994). Motivation in African Americans. *Review of Educational Research, 64*(1), 55–117.

Graham, S., Taylor, A. Z., & Hudley, C. (1998). Exploring achievement values among ethnic minority early adolescents. *Journal of Educational Psychology, 90,* 606–620.

Greenfield, P. M. (1997). Culture as process: Empirical methods for cultural psychology. In J. W. Berry, Y. H. Poortinga, & J. Pandey (Eds.), *Handbook of Cross-cultural psychology: Theory and methods* (Vol. 1, pp. 301–346). Needham Heights, MA: Allyn & Bacon.

Harackiewicz, J. M., Barron, K. E., & Elliot, A. J. (1998). Rethinking achievement goals: When are they adaptive for college students and why? *Educational Psychologist, 33,* 1–21.

Harter, S., Waters, P. L., & Whitesell, N. R. (1997). Lack of voice as a manifestation of false self-behavior among adolescents: The school setting as a stage upon which the drama of authenticity is enacted. *Educational Psychologist, 32,* 153–173.

Hau, K., & Salili, F. (1996). Achievement goals and causal attributions of Chinese students. In S. Lau (Ed.), *Growing up the Chinese way: Chinese child and adolescent development.* Hong Kong: The Chinese University Press.

Heine, S. J., Kitayama, S., Lehman, D. R., Takata, T., Ide, E., Leung, C., Matsumoto, H. (2001). Divergent consequences of success and failure in Japan and North America: An investigation of self-improving motivations and malleable selves. *Journal of Personality and Social Psychology, 81,* 599–615.

Heine, S. J., Lehman, D. R., Markus, H. R., & Kitayama, S. (1999). Is there a universal need for positive self-regard? *Psychological Review, 106,* 766–794.

Holloway, S. D. (1988). Concepts of ability and effort in Japan and the United States. *Review of Educational Research, 58*(3), 327–345.

Hong, Y., Morris, M. W., Chiu, C., & Benet-Martinez, V. (2000). Multicultural minds: A dynamic constructivist approach to culture and cognition. *American Psychologist, 55,* 709–720.

Hsia, J., & Peng, S. S. (1998). Academic achievement and performance. In L. C. Lee & N. W. S. Zane (Eds.), *Handbook of Asian American psychology.* Thousand Oaks, CA: Sage.

Kitayama, S. (2002). Culture and basic psychological processes—toward a system view of culture: Comment on Oyserman et al (2002). *Psychological Bulletin, 128,* 89–96.

Kitayama, S., & Markus, H. R. (1998). The cultural psychology of personality. *Journal of Cross-Cultural Psychology, 29,* 63–87.

Kitayama, S., & Markus, H. R. (1999). Yin and yang of the Japanese self: The cultural psychology of personality coherence. In D. Cervone & Y. Shoda (Eds.), *The coherence of personality: Social-cognitive bases of consistency, variability, and organization* (pp. 242–302). New York: Guilford.

Kitayama, S., Markus, H. R., Matsumoto, & H., Norasakkunkit, V. (1997). Individual and collective processes in the construction of the self: Self-enhancement in the United States and self-criticism in Japan. *Journal of Personality and Social Psychology, 72,* 1245–1267.

Lewis, C. C. (1995). *Educating hearts and minds: Reflections on Japanese preschool and elementary education.* New York: Cambridge University Press.

Maccoby, E. E., & Jacklin, C. N. (1974). *The psychology of sex differences.* Stanford, CA: Stanford University Press.

Maehr, M. L., & Nicholls, J.G. (1980). Culture and achievement motivation: A second look. In N. Warren (Ed.), *Studies in cross-cultural psychology* (Vol. 3). New York: Academic Press.

Markus, H. R., & Kitayama, S. (1991). Culture and the self: Implications for cognition, emotion, and motivation. *Psychological Review, 98*(2), 224–253.

Markus, H. R., Mullally, P. R., & Kitayama, S. (1997). Selfways: Diversity in modes of cultural participation, *The conceptual self in context: Culture, experience, and self-understanding* (pp. 13–61). New York: Cambridge University Press.

Midgley, C., Kaplan, A., & Middleton, M. (2001). Performance-approach goals: Good for what, for whom, under what circumstances, and at what cost? *Journal of Educational Psychology, 93,* 77–86.

Miller, J.G. (1997). Theoretical issues in cultural psychology. In J.W. Berry, Y.H. Poortinga, & J. Pandey (Eds.), *Handbook of cross-cultural psychology: Theory and methods* (Vol. 1, pp. 85–128). Needham Heights, MA: Allyn & Bacon.

Miller, J. G. (2002). Bringing culture to basic psychological theory—beyond individualism and collectivism: Comment on Oyserman et al. (2002). *Psychological Bulletin, 128,* 97–109.

Morris, M. W., & Peng, K. (1994). Culture and cause: American and Chinese attributions for social physical events. *Journal of Personality and Social Psychology, 67,* 949–971.

Nunes, T., Schliemann, A. D., & Carraher, D. W. (1993). *Street mathematics and school mathematics.* New York: Cambridge University Press.

Oyserman, D., Coon, H. M., Kemmelmeier, M. (2002). Rethinking individualism and collectivism: Evaluation of theoretical assumptions and meta-analyses. *Psychological Bulletin, 128*, 3–72.

Padilla, A. M., & Lindholm, K. J. (1995). Quantitative educational research with ethnic minorities. In J. A. Banks & C. A. MacGee-Banks (Eds.), *Handbook of research on multicultural education* (pp. 97–113). New York: Macmillan.

Peng, K., Nisbett, R. E., & Wong, N. Y. C. (1997). Validity problems comparing values across cultures and possible solutions. *Psychological Methods, 2*(4), 329–344.

Phinney, J. S. (1990). Ethnic identity in adolescence and adulthood: A review of research. *Psychological Bulletin, 108*, 499–514.

Phinney, J. S. (1996). When we talk about American ethnic groups, what do we mean? *American Psychologist, 51*, 918–927.

Pintrich, P. R. (1999). The role of motivation in promoting and sustaining self-regulated learning. *International Journal of Educational Research, 31*, 459–470.

Pintrich, P. R. (2000). Multiple goals, multiple pathways: The role of goal orientation in learning and achievement. *Journal of Educational Psychology, 92*, 544–555.

Ross, L.D. (1977). The intuitive psychologist and his shortcomings: Distortions in the attribution process. In L. Berkowitz (Ed.), *Advances in experimental social psychology* (Vol. 10). New York: Academic Press.

Salili, F. (1994). Age, sex, and cultural differences in the meaning and dimensions of achievement. *Personality and Social Psychology Bulletin, 20*, 635–648.

Salili, F., Maehr, M. L., Sorenson, R. L., & Fyans, L. J. (1976). A further consideration of the effects of evaluation on motivation. *American Educational Research Journal, 13*, 85–102.

Schweder, R. A., Goodnow, J., Hatano, G., LeVine, R. A., Markus, H., & Miller, P. (1998). The cultural psychology of development: One mind, many mentalities. In W. Damon & R. M. Lerner (Eds.), *Handbook of child psychology: Vol. 1. Theoretical models of human development* (5th ed., pp. 865–937). New York: John Wiley & Sons.

Singelis, T. M. (1994). The measurement of independent and interdependent self construals. *Personality and Social Psychology Bulletin, 20*, 580–591.

Stevenson, H. W., & Lee, S.Y. (1990). Contexts of achievement. *Monographs of the Society for Research in Child Development, 55*. Chicago: The University of Chicago Press.

Stigler, J. W., Smith, S., & Mao, L. W. (1985). The self-perception of competence by Chinese children. *Child Development, 56*, 1259–1270.

Tanaka, J. S., Ebreo, A., Linn, N., & Morera, O. F. (1998). Research methods: The construct validity of self-identity and its psychological implications. In L. C. Lee & N. W. S. Zane (Eds.), *Handbook of Asian American psychology* (pp. 21–79). Thousand Oaks, CA: Sage Publications.

Volet, S. (2001). Understanding learning and motivation in context: A multi-dimensional and multi-level cognitive-situative perspective. In S. Volet & S. Järvelä (Eds.), *Motivation in learning contexts: Theoretical advances and methodological implications* (pp. 57–84). Oxford: Elsevier Science.

Volet, S., & Järvelä, S. (Eds.) (2001). *Motivation in learning contexts: Theoretical advances and methodological implications*. Oxford: Elsevier Science.

Weisz, J. R., Rothbaum, F. M., & Blackburn, T. C. (1984). Standing out and standing in: the psychology of control in America and Japan. *American Psychologist, 39*(9), 955–969.

Whang, P. A., & Hancock, G. R. (1994). Motivation and mathematics achievement: Comparisons between Asian American and Non-Asian students. *Contemporary Educational Psychology,* 19, 302–322.

Whiting, J. W. M., & Child, I. (1953). *Child training and personality.* New Haven, CT: Yale University Press.

Yu, S. L., & Wolters, C. A. (2002). Issues in the assessment of motivation in students from ethnic minority populations. In P. Pintrich & M. Maehr (Eds.), *New directions in measures and methods* (Vol 12, pp. 349–380). New York: Elsevier.

Zusho, A., Pintrich, P. R., & Schnabel, K. (2002). *Motives, goals, and adaptive patterns of performance in Asian American and Anglo American students.* Unpublished manuscript.

CHAPTER 4

CULTURE, ATTRIBUTION PROCESS, AND CONFLICT IN MULTICULTURAL EDUCATIONAL SETTINGS

Hector Betancourt and Gangaw Zaw

Conflict can be defined as the objection of one individual to the actions of another; whether these actions may or may not have been intended (Isenberg & Raines, 1991). It can occur in any setting, especially in learning and educational environments, essentially because it is a natural part of human interaction. Although conflict is inevitable in educational settings, from pre-school through the 12th grade, the sources of these conflicts evolve as the children become older. In the case of preschool children, the primary cause of conflict involves possession disputes and access or denial of play into a group (Isenberg & Raines, 1991). Typically, children dispute over classroom toys and materials when there is scarcity of play materials. Conflict can also arise when a child attempts to enter a group of children engaged in play and the group meets the child with resistance.

As children become older, the nature of these conflicts changes from concrete struggles over possessions to conflicts over roles (Isenberg & Raines, 1991). When studying disputes over roles, it is essential to have an understanding of the group interactions as well as culturally based factors, such as the values, beliefs, and expectations of a group. This is the case

Teaching, Learning, and Motivation in a Multicultural Context, pages 67–89
Copyright © 2003 by Information Age Publishing
All rights of reproduction in any form reserved.

particularly in the increasingly multicultural environment of learning institutions in the United States, where the nature of disputes over roles involves who possesses the dominant role. In order to understand these disputes it is essential to highlight the way in which conflict emerges and how the conflict may escalate or de-escalate. In fact, these interpersonal and cultural factors may influence whether conflict is handled constructively or destructively.

Although the increasing ethnic and cultural diversity of the population is a reality across the nation, this is particularly notorious in some regions of the country. In some states it is no longer an ethnic majority versus ethnic minority groups, but rather a dominant ethnic group, which no longer represents the majority of the population, and the non-dominant ones, which together are or are soon going to be the majority. For example in California, according to estimates from the 2000 U.S. Census Bureau, the mainstream Anglo American population (non-Latino Whites) represent 49.9% of the 33.9 million residents. Latino Americans (of any racial background) follow at 31.6%, Asian Americans at 11.4%, African Americans 6.7%, and Native Americans less than 1% of the population (Richardson, 2001). In major cities, such as Los Angeles, the "minority" groups already total the numerical "majority." This increase in ethnic and cultural diversity is even more apparent in educational settings and can present new challenges to understanding conflict, its resolution, and its impact in education and social relations. However, oftentimes educators do not recognize the role of culture in psychological processes relevant to interpersonal and group processes as well as the impact these have on teaching, learning, motivation, and education in general.

Historically, educators have viewed squabbles among school children as negative and undesirable. Many teachers and administrators sought out strategies to avoid or prevent any conflict. However, approaches based on the cognitive-developmental and socio-cultural perspectives found that this traditional method of dealing with school conflict did not resolve much and could actually have a negative impact on the punished participants. In addition, schools often failed to prepare children to deal with conflict and the realities of a multicultural society. In the meanwhile, researchers in this area learned that when conflict is handled properly, it has the potential to stimulate children's social, cognitive, and moral functioning (Isenberg & Raines, 1991). Essentially, preventing conflict in school is less significant than understanding the process. The latter may allow conflict to be organized in ways that make positive contributions to the social system as well as to the parties involved (see Woehrle & Coy, 2000). Moreover, the understanding that conflict is a normal aspect of daily life may result in approaches that emphasize non-violent conflict resolution (see Arnow, 2001).

The objective of this chapter is to examine some of the psychological processes and related cultural factors relevant to the understanding of conflict in multicultural educational settings. First, some of the historical approaches to conflict and the mediation programs that emerged as a way to offset the traditional punishing methods for dealing with disputes in schools will be briefly reviewed. In general, these programs lacked a foundation in the psychological principles relevant to conflict and its resolution. In addition, they fell short of accounting for the influence of cultural factors relevant to conflict and the psychological processes involved. Second, in order to illustrate the role of culture and related psychological processes, the collectivism and individualism value orientations will be examined in relation to psychological processes relevant to the understanding of conflict and its resolution. Specifically, cognitive (attribution) processes and emotions theoretically relevant to interpersonal and group processes associated with conflict and violence will be analyzed. The role of value orientations, such as collectivism and individualism, in attribution processes as well as in conflict resolution are used to illustrate the various ways in which culture plays a role in both psychological process and related social behavior in schools. Finally, various implications for future research and interventions dealing with conflict in multicultural educational settings will be discussed in light of the analysis of these cultural and psychological factors.

CONFLICT RESOLUTION PROGRAMS IN SCHOOLS

Traditional methods of handling conflicts in school included a rather polarized approach in which one student was seen as being right while the other was considered to be wrong. The consequences for the "bad" student included detention, suspension, or expulsion (Webster, 1991). More recently, reformers began to see that the traditional methods of dealing with school-based conflicts were arbitrary and fostered a competitive environment. Since the implementation of the school-based conflict resolution programs that came about in the 1960s and 1970s, traditional means of punishing students have become less common. According to Webster (1991) there were several assumptions behind these school-based conflict resolution programs. First, children in conflict situations were thought to have the wisdom to resolve the dispute and the will to choose to do so once it was clear that mutual interests could be satisfied by a non-violent resolution. Second, conflict was seen as an unavoidable circumstance and, therefore a prime opportunity for student learning and growth. Third, because conflict was seen as unavoidable, teaching conflict resolution skills can be an educational experience that can be applied to other areas. In addition, it was assumed that encouraging disputing students to collaboratively resolve the current conflict is more effective in preventing future conflict than the administration of punishment.

There were two critical movements that triggered the development of these school-based conflict resolution programs. The first movement came from the outbreak of mediation centers in different communities. This outbreak was a reaction to the overwhelming amount of lawsuits that would have to be dealt with without arbitration. Law professors began to train community members in mediation, so they could serve as facilitators in the resolution of interpersonal conflicts that ranged from quarrels between two persons to disputes involving the entire neighborhood (Webster, 1991). The objectives of the centers were clear: To resolve the conflicts without going to court. This operation of mediation began to be seen as a powerful tool. Given the incidence of conflict in schools, educators and other individuals involved in mediation realized that the skills taught in mediation training should be transferred to the schools.

The other critical movement resulted from the socially responsible ideals of particular religious groups. Peace-minded religious groups, in their efforts to reduce violence, contributed to the introduction of conflict resolution teaching in schools. During the early 1970s the Quakers in New York City believed that children who learned conflict resolution skills at an early age would grow up to be less violent. Based on these beliefs they developed a program currently called Children's Creative Response to Conflict (CCRC) that emphasized cooperation and communication through music and structured tasks (Webster, 1991).

Over the years, the developments of various mediation programs in public school settings have been expansive as a result of these two movements. Currently there are hundreds of school-based mediation programs throughout the United States. The main focus of these programs is to teach cooperation, problem solving, and empathy-building strategies. These programs train teachers and administrators to use collaborative problem solving strategies in handling conflicts between students (Messing, 1991). By using teachers as mediators, students have been allowed to verbalize their concerns and find alternative solutions to their conflicts. Students were provided the opportunity to build empathic skills by listening to each other's concerns in order to find solutions that were agreeable to both parties. For instance, some studies show that when kindergartners were trained in conflict resolution skills, these children demonstrated the ability to retain the conflict resolution procedures as well as the willingness and ability to use the procedures in future conflicts (Stevahn, Johnson, Johnson, Oberle, & Wahl, 2000).

These programs may have been successful in the days when quarrels among school children resulted in fistfights, bloody noses, and damaged property. In the wake of the incidents of violence in Columbine and other notorious cases of school violence, destructive conflicts between students have reached a new height and have taken much more violent forms. The traditional foundations for mediation programs do not seem to be sufficient to address this growing problem.

Many schools today appear to have more and more students who feel neglected and rejected by peers, groups, the school, or society in general. These students are often perceived as the "outsiders" and "different" from mainstream groups (Weintraub, Hall, & Pynoos, 2001). They are taunted, teased, and shunned by classmates from the mainstream crowds. The harassment toward the misfitting student is as old as history. However, the chance of the outcasted students to respond with extreme forms of violence or guns is much higher than in the past. According to Arnow (2001), high numbers of children are weaned on violent video games, toys, and media programming that teaches them how to conquer the "bad guys" through violence and aggression. In effect, these children have become desensitized to violence more than ever before.

Arnow (2001) has suggested that the fear of attack breeds more violence and that this fear of violence in the schools has major emotional and behavioral consequences for the students. These children experience more depression, anxiety, a sense of meaninglessness and emptiness, loss of self-esteem, and humiliation. There is also a sense of impotence from the perceived loss of control over certain aspects of life, psychic numbing, and emotional exhaustion in addition to sleep disturbances, irritability, and excessive aggression. Too many of these students spend too much of their energy on survival, energy that otherwise could be spent on academics.

Some programs, such as the Friends Council on Education (McHenry, 2000), have attempted to understand and prevent atrocities like those of Columbine by explaining the role of moral education. This team of researchers believe that moral growth means teaching children and adolescents to emphasize the necessity of attachments to the group (i.e., the value of community) across the human life span and to create communities that cultivate responsibility to their environment (McHenry, 2000). They thought that conflict in schools was a fertile ground to teach moral growth and to make individuals aware of their own attachments to the community. They reasoned that without this attachment, violence against the community (i.e., schools) becomes inevitable.

Another program called Attribution, Behavior, Life-skills Education (ABLE) aimed at improving students' self- concept (Hay, Byrne, & Butler, 2000). These authors defined self-concept as the descriptive and evaluative aspect of the self. They proposed that a positive self-concept is related to motivation, achievement and improved social relationships that include conflict resolution and problem solving. Research (Hay et al., 2000), has demonstrated that low self-concept appears to be related to decreased cooperation, persistence on a difficult task, and expectations for future schooling, as well as to an overall negative attitude toward school. These researchers found that programs such as ABLE encouraged students to practice effective conflict resolution strategies, which improved their self-concept as well as their relationships to others around them (Hay, Byrne, & Butler, 2000). The improved self-concept of these children may be derived from identification with a social group. Later in this chapter we discuss how the sense of self in relation to a group influences positive and or negative ideas about oneself and others, based on social identity theory.

Conflict Resolution and Learning

Although the previous programs have merits, they were not founded on psychological knowledge and principles relevant to the understanding of human interaction and conflict. Isenberg and Raines (1991) analyzed the theories of Piaget and Vygotsky dealing with how children construct knowledge of their social world based on their interactions in the environment. They hold that the social interactions and the understanding children get through these interactions have implications for the child's intellectual development, less egocentric thinking, and cooperation and reciprocity with others. Essentially, knowledge derived from social interactions enable children to construct and act on their own understandings of acceptable social behaviors with peers and adults. These authors observed that children who had limited interactions were more likely to employ inappropriate social skills when dealing with a dispute.

Learning to manage conflict is a developmental task in which children become less egocentric and learn perspective taking as well as empathy to arrive at a collaborative way of solving their conflicts. Cooperation is one type of social interaction that includes conflict resolution and mutual respect and allows children to operate in terms of the other's needs and desires. According to Piaget (1965) children gradually move away from egocentric thinking and begin to consider another's points of view through the process of cooperation (Isenberg & Raines, 1991).

The Consequences of Destructive Conflict in Schools

The failure to develop skillful conflict resolution skills may lead to many negative consequences in learning and education. First, the conflict situation can escalate to a level of extreme violence such as that illustrated by recent incidents of school violence in the United States. Other consequences may be less atrocious, but still create problems in the schools. In the early 1990s approximately 282,000 students were attacked each year.

These were mostly victims of bullying and gang violence (Isenberg & Raines, 1991). According to statistics from sources such as the U.S. Departments of Justice and the Bureau of Justice Statistics (Fisher & Kettl, 2001), in 1995 gangs contributed to 28.0% of the delinquency in schools. That same year, there were 190,000 reported fights without weapons, 115,000 cases of theft, 98,000 incidents of vandalism, 11,000 physical attacks with a weapon, 7,000 robberies, and 4,000 cases of rape or sexual battery in school settings.

These problems continue to exist today, in addition to troubled teens slaughtering their classmates with bombs and machine guns. Two years after the tragedy at Columbine, more teenagers who feel isolated have identified themselves with the killers and yearn for the attention they received (Weintraub, Hall, & Pynoos, 2001). Since then, approximately 20 other schools have been plagued with new violent attacks (some foiled others not).

Psychological Processes and Conflict

It is beyond the scope of this chapter to explain all of the psychological processes operating in the minds of these youthful killers. It is, however, important to understand that there are several relevant psychological factors that contribute to the escalation of destructive conflict (other than poor self-concept or lack of group-belonging) that may sometimes lead to various problems in school. The rest of this chapter will deal with some of these psychological processes and related cultural factors as a way of illustrating how these influence conflict and can serve to prevent violence. Specifically, it deals with the role of cognitive (attribution) processes and related interpersonal emotion, and how cultural values (e.g., collectivism and individualism) influence these psychological processes and the development and resolution of conflict. Of course, there are many other psychological and cultural variables that are pertinent to these phenomena and the proposed factors are not necessarily the most relevant to conflict and violence in educational settings. These variables represent the interests and expertise of the authors and are intended to illustrate how such factors may be relevant to the understanding and prevention of destructive conflict and its resolution in multicultural educational settings.

Cognitive processes such as attributional thinking and related interpersonal emotions (e.g., anger and empathic feelings) have been found to influence pro-social behavior (for a review see Weiner, 1995; 1996). These processes have also been identified in response to provocation in conflict environment (Betancourt, 1991, 1997; Betancourt & Blair, 1992). In general, it has been observed that the attributions one makes about another person's actions, its causes and outcomes influence one's decision to help or how to respond to that other person. For instance, when one attributes a needy person's behavioral outcome to something uncontrollable, one might be more likely to help the person in need than if the outcome was attributed to something more controllable. The willingness to help, according to Betancourt (1990), is mediated by empathic emotions. Hence, in the previous case, attributing the behavioral outcome to less controllable causes elicits higher levels of empathic emotions and lower levels of anger than attributing it to more controllable causes, which in turn mediates the higher probability of helping. According to this approach (see Betancourt 1991, 1997; Betancourt & Blair, 1992), the intentionality ascribed to a person's negative or frustrating action (e.g., bulling, offending, or attacking someone), and the perceived controllability of its cause influence violence of responses directly and through mediating interpersonal emotions. Individuals who perceive the actions of the individual as unintentional and its causes as uncontrollable are expected to respond with less violence.

Since these attribution processes are subject to the influence of cultural factors (see Betancourt, Hardin, & Manzi, 1992; Betancourt & Lopez, 1993; Betancourt & Weiner, 1982), the role of culture is thought to be particularly relevant in understanding conflict and violence in multicultural settings. This becomes essential especially in school environments with increasingly diverse student populations.

Multiculturalism and Conflict

The United States is one of the largest multicultural countries in the world. For instance Arnow (2001) reported that by the middle of the twenty-first-century, Anglo Americans will be the numerical minority, and the "average" American will be able to trace his or her origins to Africa, Asia, and Latin America—anywhere but Europe. Moreover Asian Americans make up about half of all new immigrants. In 25 of the largest school systems, students from current minority (non-dominant) ethnic groups are expected to become the majority. Currently, children from non-dominant ethnic groups make up about 30% of the youths under age 18.

Regardless of whether we recognize it or not, these changes in demographics are real and accelerating (Arnow, 2001). As ethnic and cultural diversity increases, various group identities become more salient and these groups tend to split. As they divide, there is the potential for them to come into competitive conflicts with each other. However, it is possible for such diverse groups to realize that cooperation and interdependence are essential to peaceful society. Hence, learning about conflict and how to deal with it is ever more critical for schools in diverse settings. Teaching these skills must begin as children enter the schools. In order for the learning environment to keep up with changes, educators bear the responsibility to acknowledge the increase in diversity and incorporate an understanding of it in dealing with conflict as well as with pedagogical techniques in the classrooms (see Arnow, 2001).

Past studies (e.g., Isenberg & Raines, 1991, Webster, 1991) emphasizing the positive effects of conflict on learning have failed to consider the vital role of cultural factors relevant to conflict environments. There is harm in ignoring cultural factors because of the growing multicultural nature of interactions in educational settings. Of course, this by itself can result in misunderstanding or igniting disagreements among teachers, students or groups. However, even more critical than this is the influence that cultural factors may have in psychological processes that are relevant to the origin and resolution of conflict. Such psychological processes and related cultural factors are relevant not only to the understanding of conflict in educational settings but also to social learning, motivation, and education in general.

An important consideration in the study of culture in relation to psychological processes and behavior, such as in the case of conflict in educational settings, is that cultural differences do not only exist among different ethnic groups. In fact, according to authors in this area (e.g., Betancourt & Lopez, 1993), often there are more cultural differences within than between ethnic groups. Cultural variations are not only associated with ethnic groups but also other grouping factors, such as gender, religion, and political ideology, all of which have demonstrated to play a role in major destructive conflicts around the world.

The case of Andy Williams, from Santee, California, exemplifies the transition from a more traditional and rural culture in Maryland to a large school, within the context of the notoriously individualistic Anglo American suburban culture of Southern California. Williams was repeatedly rejected, ridiculed and bullied by classmates while ignored by other schoolmates and teachers. Another instance is the case of Columbine. It has been reported that prior to the disaster, there were conflicts between different social groups that helped create a tense climate at the high school (Weintraub et al., 2001). The conflicts occurred between those who were a part of the mainstream "popular" crowds and those who were cast off as the "outsiders" or the "culturally different". If these differences are present even within the dominant culture, it becomes even more imperative to understand how cultural factors that originate from various SES and ethnic groups become mixed into the already existing multicultural environment. Each culture, particularly mainstream culture, carries within it the values, norms and expectations concerning interpersonal and group behaviors associated with conflict. These norms and conceptions oftentimes dictate the way in which conflict is to be handled. The method one adopts to resolve a conflict can at times be taken offensively by members of non-dominant cultural groups.

The Biases of the "Invisible" Dominate Culture

So far, the discussions regarding conflict and its resolution mostly come from articles written by authors influenced by perspectives based on the dominant mainstream (Anglo-American) culture. Often, individuals from dominant cultures tend to be particularly ethnocentric and ignore the fact that their views and ways of approaching phenomena such as social relations is heavily determined by their cultural background. This reality, which naturally results in cultural bias, can be exacerbated by the low level of exposure to non-dominant cultures observed among many researchers and policy-making individuals in education. For instance, the current mainstream dominant individualistic views in the United States regard conflict positively and it is considered an opportunity to renegotiate or to improve currently existing relationships. It is also viewed as "the greatest potential for learning" (McHenry, 2000, p. 223). In essence, conflict is welcomed and individuals on average confront or attempt to find constructive ways to face the conflict situation.

Other cultures, however, view conflict quite differently. Conflict in other cultures is considered a disruption to the natural harmony that exists among people. Individuals from this type of cultural background often use avoidance tactics in order to prevent conflict situations. An example of this is found in the research on simpatia as a cultural script for Latino Americans (Triandis, Lisansky, Marín, & Betancourt, 1984). These authors observed that in contrast to Anglos, Latinos valued and expected individuals and groups to minimize disagreements and negative feedback, and emphasized certain levels of conformity and respect in interpersonal relations.

These varying views about conflict and the approaches taken to handle the problem can lead to escalation of disputes between people from different cultures and or ethnic groups. The cooperative or competitive inclinations in dealing with conflict often arise from differences in cultural value orientations (Janssen & van de Vliert, 1996). In essence the same interpersonal or group responses may have quite different meaning and could result in eliciting opposite reactions from people of different value orientations.

When teaching conflict resolution skills, educators must be sensitive to the varying views on interpersonal behaviors and approaches for handling conflicts that different cultures prescribe. However, since clashes in a fast growing multicultural society are inevitable, the most sensible approach to conflict is to develop and teach culturally based constructive methods for dealing with conflict. The prime time to begin training these skills is in the schools. According to some authors (e.g., Tatum, 2000), if educational institutions bring together students from various ethnic and racial backgrounds, they have the opportunity to disrupt the cycle of lifetime segregation that threatens the fabric of our pluralistic democracy.

The next section of this chapter will address how the individualism and collectivism value orientations serve to illustrate the role of cultural variations in conflict and social behavior in general. Then the role of cognitive (attribution) processes and emotions that have been found to mediate the effects of culture on conflict and conflict resolution will be discussed. The purpose is to provide an illustration of the relationships between culture and psychological factors as determinants of conflict resolution and its consequences for individuals and education in multicultural settings.

Culture and Social Behavior: The Case of Collectivism-Individualism in Conflict and Violence

Betancourt and Lopez (1993) argued that the study of culture has been largely ignored in mainstream psychology and is often relegated to the domain of cross-cultural psychologists. Commonly, mainstream psychological theories do not include cultural variables and the results or findings in their studies are thought to apply to individuals of any cultural background. In effect, this suggests that psychological knowledge developed in the United States by Anglo-American scholars, using Anglo-subjects, is universal. On the other hand, cross-cultural researchers, normally segregated from mainstream psychology, have focused on comparative studies of culture without much regard for the specific measurement of the cultural variables and its implications for mainstream theory. Often they attribute to "culture" the differences observed between ethnic or racial groups, without measuring, testing, or even specifying the cultural factor that might be responsible for the differences. When culture is involved, it is not sufficient to compare ethnic groups and attribute to ethnicity the observed behavioral differences. According to Betancourt and Lopez (1993), it is important to define and actually measure the specific cultural elements that are predicted to account for changes in behavior. Moreover it is important to actually test whether the well-defined and measured cultural variables in fact account for variations in the corresponding psychological processes or behaviors.

A number of dimensions of cultural variation have been identified. A good example of cultural factors relevant to psychological processes associated with social learning, motivation, and interpersonal phenomena is the collectivism-individualism value orientation. This is perhaps one of the dimensions of cultural variation that has received more attention than any other cultural factor from researchers in psychology during the last few years. In addition, the collectivism value orientation is one of the most distinctive cultural characteristics of Asian and Latino American immigrants, the fastest growing ethnic groups in the United States. Since this is also an important cultural antecedent of how individuals deal with conflict and its resolution, it serves well to illustrate the importance of culture in understanding and preventing destructive conflict and violence in multicultural educational settings. The following section briefly reviews the literature on individualism and collectivism, followed by an illustration of how this cultural variable influences conflict resolution.

Individualism and Collectivism

According to authors such as (Triandis et al., 1993) generally, collectivism stemmed from agricultural societies. Common features of the construct include conformity, interdependence within a group, sacrificing individual goals for the collective good, and maintaining social harmony. Persons of this orientation tend to accept the rules and authority of the in-group without question. In-groups are "sets of individuals with whom a person feels similar" (Triandis, 1994, p. 43). In collectivist cultures, in-groups are ascribed and individuals are bounded to it by factors such as kinship, tribe, or religion. There is a strong maintenance of cohesive "in-groups." This perpetuates in-group favoritism and ethnocentrism. The strong emphasis on in-group loyalty often fosters out-group derogation and competition with the out-group. The firm group boundaries that sustain the in-group allow fluid boundaries between individuals to flow freely. There is an implicit understanding that individuals are to be concerned for the needs of others in the group as well as what they think or feel, without them having to openly express those needs. The characteristics of an individualist society are in general converse to those of the collectivist one.

According to Triandis and colleagues (1993) the essential features of individualistic cultures are rooted in societies that developed around economic activities such as fishing and hunting. Although cooperation was necessary among these groups, survival was not entirely dependent on other group members. The aspect of individualistic cultures that are particularly distinctive is the separation from the ascribed in-groups. Individualist in-groups are bounded together by factors such as similar beliefs, attitudes, values, action programs and occupation (Triandis, 1994). The thread that binds them is changeable and allows individuals to move from one in-group to another. Normally individuals tend to be detached from family, relatives, and the community. They are encouraged to express their ideas freely and to assert their own needs over those of others.

The individualism and collectivism variables are not necessarily the opposite poles of the same dimension. Instead, each construct is unidimensional and aspects of one can coexist with the other. Even though it may sound contradictory, individualism can still be exhibited in a collectivist culture, and collectivism can be demonstrated in individualist cultures. For example, in an individualist culture like the United States, there may be a collective of people who share common interests, backgrounds, and beliefs. They may gather because they have similar needs. The members of these groups become interdependent on each other and behave more like collectivists. To clarify, Triandis and colleagues (1993) have used different terms to describe the within and between group variations. Corresponding to collectivism is allocentrism, whereby the individual defines himself in relation to others. Allocentrics are more likely to downplay their personal goals in relation to the goals of the collective. Concerning individualism, the corresponding construct is idiocentrism. This is the tendency of one individual to define oneself in terms of self-attributes rather than in terms of the attributes of the group.

Collectivism-Individualism and Models of Conflict and Its Resolution

When explaining conflict resolution strategies, various authors have focused on two models. The first model is the dual concern model (Pearson & Stephan, 1998; Janssen & van de Vliert, 1996). Two axes depict this model (see Figure 4.1). The first axis is *self-concern*, while the second axis depicts *other-concern*. *Self-concern* places importance on one's own interests while *other-concern* places an emphasis on the interests of others. The

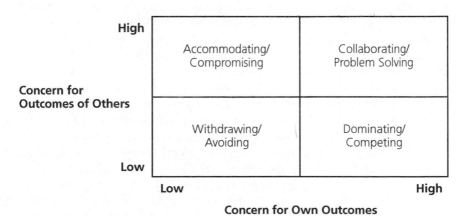

Figure 4.1.   Dual concern model of negotiation. *Source:* Adapted from Pearson & Stephan, 1998.

dimensions of self and other concerns are determinants of conflict resolution behaviors and not necessarily the components of the behavior itself. According to Pruitt and Rubin (1986), the combination of these two can range from indifference (low concern for self or other) to very great concern (high concern for self or other). This model predicts four styles of conflict resolution, each of which can be located within these two axes: Accommodating, compromising, avoiding, and forcing.

Another model of conflict resolution involves the Cooperative-Competitive dimension (see Deutsch, 2000). This model focuses on the behavior or approach of individuals to the conflict. Specifically, while a cooperative style means that the individual has a concern for the welfare of their opponent, the competitive style reflects the individual's interest in doing better than the other does as well as doing well for him or herself. What these two models have in common is that the resolution tactics of conflict are manifold and can range from tactics that are totally self-centered to being very mindful of one's social environment.

The individualistic and collectivistic values fostered in cultures are likely to influence social interaction and behaviors such as conflict resolution. In most Western cultures, most of which tend to be individualistic, conflict is accepted as a useful process in which almost anything is negotiable. Concern for others is not necessarily a major consideration when dealing with conflict and individuals are more likely to engage in competitive than cooperative strategies. Characteristics of the competitive strategies include the use of threats and coercion, downplaying the intentions and behaviors of others, asserting opposing interests, and enhancing rather than diminishing power differences between the parties (Janssen & van de Vliert, 1996). Whereas individualistic societies allow for negotiations in conflict situations, a competitive style for dealing with conflict tends to be practiced even though it may not always be most adaptive.

In collectivist societies, conflict tends to be perceived as a disturbance to the natural harmony within the group. Members in a collectivist community are expected to adjust to the system, more than in the case of an individualist society. These are highly interdependent cultures that demand more conformity so that differences and conflicts tend to be minimized (Pruitt & Rubin, 1986). Since individuals must yield to traditional patterns, negotiations can at times be difficult. There is a strong focus on concern for others and this motivation usually results in more cooperative strategies in handling conflicts. The cooperative tactics involve an emphasis on common interests, the exchange of information to solve the problem or to meet each other's goals, being helpful in the exploration of the conflict issues, showing trust in the intentions and capabilities of others, searching for solutions that are mindful of the needs and interests of both parties (Janssen & van de Vliert, 1996). Although this may seem ideal in handling conflict, collectivists engage in this type of conflict resolution tactics more with members of their own in-groups than with others. It appears that the group boundary that ties collectivists encourages the members of the in-group to maintain harmony among them, while behaving more competitively and aggressively toward members of out-groups.

Research evidence (Itoi, Ohbuchi, & Fukuno, 1996) indicates that collectivists use more mitigating and less competitive styles when dealing with an individual perceived to be a member of an in-group. For example, Itoi and his associates (1996) observed that that Japanese subjects preferred to make apologies rather than to provide a justification to assert their side. However, when these same collectivist students had to deal with solutions to a conflict involving people belonging to an "out-group," they showed a tendency to avoid it altogether, which was an indication of their lack of concern for behaving cooperatively. In contrast, the individualistic students showed no significant differences in tactics used based on perceptions of individuals as being in-group versus out-group members. Similar results by Pearson and Stephan (1998) found that individualist students were less likely to discriminate between perceived "in-group" versus "out-group" members. More specifically, the study showed that when Brazilians had to negotiate with members from an in-group, they made more accommodations or avoided the conflict to preserve the relationship with the individual. However, when they had to make decisions concerning out-group members, such as in the case of dealing with a stranger in a business transaction, they were more likely to behave competitively and act in their own self-interest.

Collectivism-Individualism and Attribution Processes in Conflict and Violence

Thus far, we have focused on the influence of culture (e.g., value orientations) on conflict and its resolution. However, the direct relationship between culture and conflict is only one piece of the puzzle in understanding the role of culture in conflict environments. Interpersonal and intergroup phenomena, such as conflict and its resolution, have also been found to be at least in part a function of psychological processes, such as social cognition and related emotions. For example, Betancourt and colleagues (e.g., Betancourt, 1991, 1997; Betancourt & Blair, 1992) have documented the role of cognitive processes, such as attributional thinking, and related interpersonal emotions as determinants of violent behavior in conflict environments. In addition, a number of studies (see Betancourt, Harding, & Manzi, 1992; Betancourt & Lopez, 1993; Betancourt & Weiner, 1982) have found that these same attribution processes, which play an important role in conflict and violence, are in part a function of cultural factors such as cultural believes and value orientation. Moreover, as observed in the section on collectivism-individualism and styles of conflict resolution, research evidence (e.g., Guthrie & Betancourt, 2001) indicates that, at least in the case of competition in intergroup environments, attributions of controllability and intentionality are influenced by the in-group versus out-group identity of the perpetrator. Hence, intergroup biases appear to be a factor to consider in understanding conflict and its resolution not only in relation to its influence in the way collectivists and individualists relate to their in-groups and out-groups, but also as a direct influence on attributional thinking itself.

Psychological Processes and Conflict: The Case of Attributions

Concerning the role of attribution processes in conflict environments, a number of studies (e.g., Betancourt & Blair, 1992), have examined the way in which attribution processes influence violence in conflict situations. Specifically, attributions concerning the intentionality of a frustrating or instigating action and controllability of its cause were found to influence violence of responding both directly and through mediating anger and empathic emotions. When the actions of a person were perceived as controllable and intentional, subjects experienced higher degrees of anger and lower degrees of empathic feelings than when the action was perceived as unintentional and its cause as uncontrollable. Higher degrees of anger and lower degrees of empathic emotions were in turn associated with a higher probability of violent responding, such as retaliation and punishment. Essentially, according to these findings, attributional thinking concerning intentionality of an action and controllability of its cause influence violence in conflict environments, both directly and through empathic emotions.

Culture and Attribution Processes: The Case of Collectivism-individualism

More recently, a number of studies by Betancourt and his associates (e.g., Campbell & Betancourt, 2001; Zaw & Betancourt, 2002) have examined the role of cultural factors as determinants of the attribution processes relevant to the understanding of conflict and violence. For instance, one of these studies (Zaw & Betancourt, 2002), found that the individualist value orientation was associated with attributing the opponent's behavior to more controllable circumstances which, consistent with previous research and theory in this area, is associated with lower levels of empathic feelings and preference for a more dominating approach to the resolution of a conflict. A plausible explanation for these results is that the individualist emphasis on the self influences the attributions individuals make (e.g., "I am in control of my life, therefore the other is also in control of her life"). This may influence the preference for dealing with conflict more dominantly.

In the case of collectivism, these authors observed that subjects who scored higher on collectivism tended to engage in more compromising style of responding. However, given the fact that collectivists have been observed to approach conflict differently when dealing with in-group versus out-group members, in this case the relationship appears to be more complex. This complexity is consistent with previous research suggesting that attributions of controllability and intentionality are at least in part a function of the in-group versus out-group status of the perpetrator. The brief description of social identity and the formation of groups in general that follows is intended to provide a basis for a brief discussion of its importance in understanding conflict and its resolution in multicultural group environments from a cultural (collectivism-individualism) as well as a psychological (attribution processes and emotions) perspective.

The In-group/Out-group Distinction

Social identity is conceived of as the element of an individual's self-concept that is developed from knowledge of membership in a social group and the values and emotional significance attached to that membership (Cook-Huffman, 2000). Essentially, it refers to a sense of self in relation to the social environment, by which the individual defines himself or herself in relation to the group. Conceptually, individuals that come from a collectivist culture have developed strong ties to their social system based on family membership, religion, or community. Whereas in collectivist cultures individuals have little choice in deciding the groups they belong to, in individualistic cultures a person can easily shift from one social group to another. Group membership in individualist cultures is based on beliefs, attitudes, action programs, or occupation, and any individual can change his/her mind and leave the group without major direct consequences.

The In-group/Out-group Distinction and the Attribution Process

The mere in-group versus out-group distinction appears to influence the attribution of intentionality and controllability. So appears to do the collectivist versus individualist cultural value orientation. Hence, to understand the attributional thinking of collectivists concerning conflict and its resolution, one needs to understand social identity formation, the way in which individuals of different cultural backgrounds relate to groups, and the influences these factors have in psychological functioning and social behavior. In this section we first illustrate how the in-group versus out-group distinction influences attribution processes in conflict situations.

Research in this area (see Betancourt, 1997) suggests that the role of attribution processes operating in conflict situations is influenced by the in-group/out-group distinction. For example, in a study conducted by Guthrie and Betancourt (2001), it was observed that when children of 3rd and 6th grade had to make judgments about the violent actions of other children, the in-group versus out-group identity of the perpetrator influenced their judgment. They made more intentional and controllable attributions for the frustrating aggressive behavior of out-group members than for in-group members. At the same time, consistent with previous research and theory in this area, they reported higher levels of anger and lower levels of empathic feelings toward the out-group than toward the in-group perpetrator. Also consistent with theory, judgments of retaliation and punishment were a function of perceived intentionality and controllability, both directly and through the influence of these attributional variables on anger and empathic emotions.

The In-group/Out-group Distinction and Attribution Processes Among Collectivists and Individualists

Since collectivists, compared to individualists, have stronger ties to their groups (in-groups), it is understandable that they show differences in the way they approach conflict with the in-group versus the out-group. Based on these and other features that differentiate collectivists from individualists, it is reasonable to expect that it may also influence their attributions of controllability and intentionality for in-group versus out-group members. In fact, there is evidence (Menon, Morris, Chiu, & Hong, 1999) that when compared to individualists, collectivists tend to make more situational (external) attributions than individualists. Although these studies did not clarify the particular social situation or to which group (in-group or out-group) the attributions were being made, the influence of value orientation in the attribution process is clearly demonstrated. Also, as reported above, the research of Itoi, Ohbuchi, and Fukuno (1996) demonstrated that collectivists tend to use more mitigating and cooperative ways of responding to conflict when dealing with in-group member, while using more competitive strategies when dealing with the out-group. In sum, it appears that the in-group/out-group distinction may play a significant but complex role in the attributions collectivist individuals make in multicultural/intergroup conflict environments.

Implications for Multicultural Educational Settings

Groups have a high need for a positive self-image and generally strive to maintain this positive social identity by comparing with other social groups (e.g., Cook-Huffman, 2000). Making these comparisons allows for social categorizations to be made, which are the "consensual constructions that characterize and delineate boundaries of group membership" (p. 116). In every social system, there is always the dominant or mainstream group that holds the power, which is what makes a pluralistic society (Pruitt & Rubin, 1986). Schools, particularly those within a multicultural society, are no exception to this. To be a member of the high status group provides individuals with positive self-concept and high self-esteem. However, for one reason or another, not everybody is part of the mainstream group. As a result the social system divides itself into separate groups in which the separated groups hold less power. Membership in these low-status groups is often associated with less positive and even negative self-concept (Cook-Huffman, 2000).

These social categorizations and the desire to maintain positive group distinctiveness can be a cause of many inter-group conflicts. Schools provide an excellent illustration of settings where group comparisons and categorizations are made. For example, in the case of Andy Williams, from Santana High School, the mainstream groups cast him off as different and relegated him into a lower status group, leaving him to feel unwanted and isolated. This experience was in stark contrast to his experience at his previous high school, where he felt accepted, within the context of a culture (the community) he felt part of. A similar case can be made about Eric Harris and Dylan Klebold from Columbine High School. Before the massacre, there were rising conflicts between the different social groups in the high school that helped create a tense environment among the students (Weintraub et. al., 2001). Harris and Dylan were categorized as "outsiders" who did not belong to any desirable social groups. Their feelings of rejection and isolation, and the anger normally associated with such frustrating situations, may have been related to the realization of their low-status categorization in comparison to the more mainstream social groups. Also, it may have been the case that much of their anger was driven not only by their own isolation, but by the attributions of intentionality concerning the behaviors of their peers, controllability of the causes they attribute such behaviors to, and the responsibility they attributed to the teachers and the system in general. Of course, there are many conditions that may influence the occurrence of conflicts and whether or not these result in violence. The background of the individual, the cultural context, and the psychological processes involved represent only part of the picture—an important part though given the multicultural nature of schools settings in most of the United States today.

There is a broad literature dealing with the factors that have been identified as important conditions for the emergence of conflict in general. For example, according to some authors (e.g., Woehrle & Coy, 2001) there are four specific conditions that must be minimally met for social conflicts to emerge. First, the parties must identify themselves as separate from one another. Then one or more of the parties must have a grievance. Third one or more of the parties must develop goals to change the other party in order to reduce their grievance. Finally, the distressed party must believe that they can be successful in changing the other party (Woehrle & Coy, 2001). Although this may be observed in society at large, it is particularly so in schools.

In order to be effective, the prevention of destructive conflict in multicultural educational settings requires a good understanding and consideration of the role of culture and relevant psychological processes. Specifically, rejected, excluded, or victimized students may recognize their separation from the mainstream groups. They are also likely to have grievances toward mainstream groups or kids they see as abusive. Of course, most of these students may find constructive methods to reduce their grievances, particularly when there is support from teachers, the school, home, or the social environment outside school. However, there may be other students who will find more destructive and violent ways to deal with such reality. What makes the difference between the former and the latter, may be the psychological processes, such as attributional thinking concerning why rejection, stigmatization, bullying, or any similar frustrating situation might have occurred. The attributions they make concerning the intentionality of those seen as responsible for their situation and negative outcomes, as well as attributional thinking concerning the privilege of others, the attitudes of peers, and the way teachers and the school deals with such situations, are likely to influence the degree of anger-related emotions, which will in turn influence the way they respond and cope. These thinking processes may in fact make the difference between choosing a constructive or destructive course of action.

From the perspective of the cultural diversity that is characteristic of multi ethnic and pluralistic societies, a full understanding of these psychological processes as well as the way individuals are likely to deal with such situations requires that we consider the cultural background of all students involved. Although there is little research on the role of ethnicity and culture specifically dealing with conflict and violence in multicultural educational settings, there are preliminary studies that have identified how value orientations, such as collectivism and individualism, and other cultural factors influence conflict and its resolution, both directly and though its influence on psychological processes such as attributional thinking and related emotions.

Cognitive processes such as attributional thinking concerning intentionality of actions and controllability of their causes are thought to account at least in part for the emotions relevant to destructive conflict and violence, from anger and frustration to pity and empathic feelings (see Betancourt, 1991, 1997; Betancourt & Blair, 1992; Weiner, 1991, 1996). In addition, the fact that these processes, as well as the way individuals deal with conflict and its resolution, are influenced by culture makes the study of these factors an absolute priority for the study of conflict and intervention in multicultural educational settings.

As indicated earlier in this chapter, the focus on psychological processes was intended to illustrate the role of psychological factors such as social cognition and emotion in conflict and violence. Similarly, collectivism and individualism were conceived as examples of the role of cultural factors such as value orientation in relation to both, conflict and the psychological processes it involves. In addition, given the multi-group environment of schools, biases associated with social identity and intergroup phenomena, as well as the ways in which these relate to culture and psychological processes, served to illustrate the complexities associated with understanding and dealing with conflict in multicultural settings. Of course, in no way do we intend to suggest that these are the main determinants of conflict. In fact, there is a large literature demonstrating the importance of other psychological factors. However, the role of culture in conflict and its resolution, both directly and through the influence on relevant psychological factors, has not received enough attention. This influential role is more critical when dealing with multicultural educational settings both at the national as well as international levels.

The emergence of conflict is especially inevitable when there are differences in culture (i.e., values and beliefs), power inequalities, resource distribution, lack of communication, and a strong sense of a collective identity. In an ever-increasing multicultural society, there is a stronger potential than ever for misunderstanding and mishandling conflict. The emergence of various in-groups creates a larger potential for segregated collectives to form and influence interpersonal relations, including but not limited to conflict. Just as an example, the formation of different groups in the competitive environment that dominate schools, makes in-group favoritism and out-group derogation more likely to occur and to have unpredictable consequences. Although the formation of in-groups can be used to promote socially positive outcomes, such as the creation of positive images, self-esteem, and a sense of community, it can also promote in-group favoritism, out-group derogation, and destructive conflict and violence. From the perspective of this chapter, awareness and understanding of the role of cognitive processes and cultural factors, which are amenable to change, are particularly likely to contribute to the control and prevention of destructive conflict and violence in the multicultural environments that are more and more characteristic of teaching and educational settings in the United States.

REFERENCES

Arnow, J. (2001). The school in multicultural society: Teaching tolerance and conflict resolution. In M. Shafii & S. L. Shafii (Eds.), *School violence: Assessment, management, and prevention* (pp. 291–302). Washington, DC: American Psychiatric Publishing.

Betancourt, H. (1990). An attribution-empathy model of helping behavior: Behavioral intentions and judgments of help giving. *Personality and Social Psychology Bulletin, 16,* 573–591.

Betancourt, H. (1991). An attribution approach to intergroup and international conflict. In S. Graham & V. Folks (Eds.), *Attribution Theory: Applications to achievement, mental health, and conflict.* Hillsdale, NJ: Lawrence Erlbaum.

Betancourt, H. (1997). An attribution model of social conflict and violence: From psychological to intergroup phenomena. *Psykhe, 6* (2), 3–12.

Betancourt, H., & Blair, I. (1992). A cognition (attribution)-emotion model of violence in conflict situations. *Personality and Social Psychology Bulletin, 18,* 33–350.

Betancourt, H., Hardin, C., & Manzi, J. (1992). Beliefs, value orientation, and culture in attribution processes and helping behavior. *Journal of Cross-Cultural Psychology, 23,* 179–195.

Betancourt, H., & Lopez, S. R. (1993). The study of culture, ethnicity, and race in American psychology. *American Psychologist, 48,* 629–637.

Betancourt, H., & Weiner, B. (1982). Attributions for achievement-related events expectancy, and sentiments: A study of success and failure in Chile and the United States. *Journal of Cross-Cultural Psychology, 13,* 362–374.

Campbell, R. (1997). *Service providers' perceptions of sexual assault.* Unpublished master's thesis, Loma Linda University, Loma Linda, CA.

Cook-Huffman, C. (2000). Who do they say we are? Framing social identity and gender in church conflict. In P. G. Coy, & L. M. Woehrle (Eds.), *Social conflicts and collective identities* (pp. 115–129). Lanham, MD: Rowman & Littlefield Publishers.

Deutsch, M., Coleman, P.T. (2000). *The handbook of conflict resolution: Theory and practice* (Eds.). San Francisco, CA: Jossey-Bass, Inc.

Fisher, K. M., & Kettl, P. (2001). Trends in school violence: Are our schools safe? In M. Shafii & S. L. Shafii (Eds.), *School violence: Assessment, management, and prevention* (pp. 291–302) Washington, DC: American Psychiatric Publishing.

Guthrie, V., & Betancourt, H. (2001). *Examination of an attribution-emotion model of reactions to violence in children.* Manuscript submitted for publication.

Hay, I., Bryne, M., & Butler, C. (2000, Feb). Evaluation of a conflict-resolution and problem-solving programme to enhance adolescents' self-concept. *British Journal of Guidance & Counseling, 28,* 101–114.

Isenberg, J. P., & Raines, S. C. (1991). Peer conflict and conflict resolution among pre-school children. In L. S. Bowen & J. B. Gittler (Eds), *The annual review of conflict knowledge and conflict resolution,* Vol. 3 (pp. 21–42). New York: Garland Publishing.

Itoi, R. Ohbuchi, K. I., & Fukuno, M., (1996). A cross-cultural study of preference of accounts: Relationship closeness, harm severity, and motives of account making. *Journal of Applied Social Psychology, 26,* (10), 913–934.

Janssen, O., & van de Vliert, E. (1996). Concern for the other's goals: Key to (de-) escalation of conflict. *The International Journal of Conflict Management, 7,* 2 (April), 99–120.

Menon, T., Morris, M., Chiu, C., & Hong, Y. (1999). Culture and the construal of agency: Attribution to individual versus group dispositions. *Journal of Personality and Social Psychology, 76* (5), 701–717.

Messing, J. K. (1991). Conflict resolution on the elementary school level. In L. S. Bowen & J. B. Gittler (Eds), *The annual review of conflict knowledge and conflict resolution, 3* (pp. 21–42). New York: Garland Publishing.

McHenry, I. (2000). Conflict in schools. *Phi Delta Kappan, 82,* (3), 223–228.

Pearson, V. M. S., & Stephan, W. G. (1998). Preferences for styles of negotiation: A comparison of Brazil and the U.S. *International Journal, 22* (1) 67–83.

Piaget, J. (1965). The moral judgment of the child. New York: Free Press.

Pruitt, D. G., & Rubin, J. Z. (1986). *Social conflict: Escalation, stalemate, and settlement.* New York: Random House.

Richardson, L. (2001, January 10). When demographics change faster than terms. *The L.A. Times* (On-line). Available: www.latimes.com.

Stevahn, L., Johnson, D. W., Johnson, R. T., Oberle, K., & Wahl, L. (2000). Effects of conflict resolution training integrated into a kindergarten curriculum. *Child Development, 71* (3) 772–784.

Tatum, B. D. (2000). The ABC approach to creating climates of engagement on diverse campuses. *Liberal Education, 86,* (4), 22–30.

Triandis, H. C. (1994). Theoretical and Methodological Approaches to the study of collectivism and Indivdualism. In U. Kim, H. C. Triandis, C. Kagitcibasi, S. C. Choi, & G. Yoon. *Individualism and collectivism: Theory, method, and applications* (pp. 19–40). Thousand Oaks, CA: Sage.

Triandis, H. C., Lisansky, J. Marín, G., & Betancourt, H. (1984). Simpatía as a cultural script of Hispanics. *Journal of Personality and Social Psychology, 47* (6) 1363–1375.

Triandis, H. C., Betancourt, H., Iwao, S., Leung, K., Salazar, J. M., Setiadi, B., Sinha, J. B. P., Touzard, H., & Zaleski, Z. (1993). An etic-emic analysis of individualism and collectivism. *Journal of cross-cultural psychology, 24* (3) 366–383.

Webster, L. (1991). Conflict mediation in the secondary school. In L. S. Bowen & J. B. Gittler (Eds), *The annual review of conflict knowledge and conflict resolution, 3,* (pp. 113–134). New York: Garland Publishing.

Weiner, B. (1991). On perceiving the other as responsible. In R. A. Dienstbeir (Ed), *Perspectives on motivation. Current theory and research on motivation.* Lincoln, NE, U.S.

Weiner, B. (1995). *Judgments of responsibilty. A foundation for atheory of social conduct.* New York: Guilford Press.

Weiner, B. (1996). Cohort and prejudice: White's attitudes towards blacks, Hispanics, Jews, and Asians. *Public Opinion Quarterly, 60,* 253–327.

Weintraub, P., Hall, H. L, & Pynoos, R. (2001). Columbine High School shootings: Community Response. In M. Shafii & S. L. Shafii (Eds.), *School violence: Assessment, management, and prevention* (pp. 291–302). Washington, DC: American Psychiatric Publishing.

Woehrle, L. M., & Coy, P. G. (2000). Collective identities and the development of conflict analysis. In P. G. Coy, & L. M. Woehrle (Eds.), *Social conflicts and collective identities* (pp. 1–15). Lanham, MD: Rowman & Littlefield Publishers.

Zaw, G. (2002). *Collectivism/individualism, psychological processes, and styles of conflict resolution.* Unpublished master's thesis, Loma Linda University, Loma Linda, CA.

CHAPTER 5

A MOTIVATION INTERVENTION FOR AT-RISK YOUTH

Sandra Graham, April Z. Taylor, and Collette Dolland

Children who become alienated from school at any early age often have histories of dysfunctional relationships with peers, characterized by aggression against others even in the absence of legitimate provocation; and of poor academic performance, characterized by failing grades and chronic truancy (see review in Coie & Dodge, 1998). Thus, two sources of motivation—*aggression* (the desire to go against others) and *achievement* (the desire to do well)—are interrelated precursors of school disengagement. Change efforts might therefore focus on *decreasing* the motivation to aggress and *increasing* the motivation to achieve as pathways to improving social and academic outcomes.

In this chapter we describe a promising new school-based intervention for at-risk youth that was based on motivational change. As motivation researchers who study attributional processes, we utilized causal constructs as a theoretical framework for organizing the intervention. Attribution theorists are concerned with the "why" of behavior (see Weiner, 1986, 1995). For example, a student might ask: "Why do other kids in my class pick on me?" or "Why did I fail the exam?" Such "why" questions indicate that we make causal attributions about other people's behavior as well as our own. Attribution theory has provided a useful model for understanding aca-

Teaching, Learning, and Motivation in a Multicultural Context, pages 91–115
Copyright © 2003 by Information Age Publishing
All rights of reproduction in any form reserved.

demic and social motivation not only in the general population, but in multicultural educational settings as well. Because the theory is concerned with the relationships between causal beliefs and core psychological constructs like self-esteem, perceptions of control, and expectations for success, it has been particularly influential in studies of coping and adaptation in African American youth (see Graham, 1994, 1997). Psychologists who study ethnic minority groups are turning to attribution theory because of their interests in how members of stigmatized groups feel about themselves, cope with uncontrollable events, and adjust their expectations in relation to perceived barriers to success.

The organizing attributional theme for our intervention is the causal construct of perceived responsibility—in both other people and the self. We consider whether peers are perceived as responsible for negative events, which has implications for reducing the motivation to aggress against those peers; and we examine the degree to which individuals perceive themselves as responsible for their academic outcomes, which has implications for increasing their own motivation to achieve.

We begin with a brief overview of the goals and content of our intervention, focusing on its theoretical grounding in attributional analyses. Next we describe early findings of the intervention when implemented with a sample of ethnic minority 3rd–5th grade boys who were both labeled as aggressive and judged to be at risk for academic disengagement. Our sample was limited to boys because aggression is much more prevalent in males than in females at all stages of the life course. The choice to study minorities—in this case, African American and Latino boys—grows out of our longstanding commitment to better understand the social and academic trajectories of ethnic minority youth (see Graham, Taylor, & Hudley, 1998; Graham & Taylor, 2002). As members of economically marginalized ethnic groups in the United States, African American and Latino boys are particularly at risk for antisocial behavior and chronic school failure (e.g., Jencks & Phillips, 1998; Suarez-Oroczo & Suarez-Orozco, 1995). By intervening to counteract the effects of poor relationships with peers and low achievement strivings, our goal was to reduce the risk that ethnic minority boys would continue on a trajectory of cumulative social and academic maladjustment. After describing the effects of the intervention, we conclude with a discussion of the implications of our findings for school-based interventions.

OVERVIEW OF THE INTERVENTION

The intervention that we developed, titled *Best Foot Forward*, consists of a thirty-two-lesson curriculum with two separate but interrelated components. The *social skills* component focused on teaching participants how to make accurate judgments about the causes of other people's behavior, particularly the degree to which others are perceived as responsible for negative outcomes. Accurate beliefs about others' responsibility should then lead to better anger management and aggression control. The *academic motivation* component focused on training participants to assume self-responsibility for school learning. Strategies were taught that encouraged participants to choose tasks of intermediate difficulty, be realistic goal setters, be strategic help seekers, and attribute academic failure to lack of effort rather than to factors that are not within their control. All of these strategies derive from principles of motivation that are known to "work"— that is, to increase academic motivation (see review in Graham & Weiner, 1996). Table 5.1 presents an overview of the *Best Foot Forward* curriculum.

Social Skills Training

The social skills component of the curriculum is divided into two sections. The first section addressed account giving. Accounts are explanations or reasons for social transgressions and they include apology (confession), excuses, justifications, and denials (Scott & Lyman, 1968). Effective account giving is an important social skill because accounts help us manage the impressions that others have of us—they influence a receiver's judgments about responsibility as well as their emotional reactions to the account giver (e.g., anger versus forgiveness; see Weiner, 1995). We know that aggressive boys show less understanding of the consequences of some accounts (i.e., excuses) and we have hypothesized that they may be less willing to extend forgiveness to peers who offer other accounts (Graham, Weiner, & Benesh-Weiner, 1995). This phase of the intervention taught participants to understand the characteristics of different kinds of accounts, and what they imply about personal responsibility. Our goal was for participants to learn to display greater forgiveness when others apologize for their misdeeds, a strategy that should promote better peer relations. We also wanted them to learn the adaptiveness of accepting responsibility for their own misdeeds, as when they apologize.

The second social component addressed attributional bias or inferring hostile intent in others. One robust finding in the peer aggression literature is that aggressive children have a tendency (bias) to over attribute hostile intent to peers, particularly in ambiguous situations (Coie & Dodge, 1998). Imagine, for example, that you are standing in line and unexpectedly receive a push from the person behind you, but it is unclear whether the person intended the push or not. Aggressive youngsters are more likely to infer that the push was instigated "on purpose" (i.e., the person is

Table 5.1. Curriculum Overview

Topic	Primary Goals/ Objectives	How Achieved
Intro. (1)	• introduce program • develop group guidelines • introduce us to students	as a group decide on guidelines for the program complete student questionnaire
Intermediate Risk (4)	• encourage intermediate risk taking	identifying *their* intermediate level and practicing monitoring their own progress
Account Giving (7)	• recognize the use of various accounts and their emotional and interpersonal consequences	generating accounts, analyzing their emotional responses, considering the pros and cons of various accounts, practicing using and honoring through role play and modeling throughout program
Inferring Intent (8)	• accurately infer intentionality/ responsibility in others	recognizing different intents, analyzing stories/video scenes for intent, recognizing various intent "cues," role playing adaptive behavioral responses to provocation
Help Seeking (3)	• be effective help-seekers (demonstrating effort)	analyzing stories, role playing good and bad help-seeking, practicing help-seeking with challenging tasks
Goal Setting (4)	• learn to set realistic proximal goals	defining and breaking down own goals, look at the pros and cons of decisions that effect your goals, learn how to gather more information before making a decision
Attribution Retraining (5)	• recognize their control in effecting change and the role of effort in achieving change • attribute outcomes to effort	determine areas requiring effort in order to achieve goals for themselves and others, identify reasons for failure and the adaptiveness of focusing on effort, practicing persistence

responsible) and to respond with anger and aggression (e.g., Graham & Hudley, 1994).

Being quick to assign blame following a negative outcome often is an impulsive reaction that can be modified with training in how to more accurately infer another's intentions and in recognizing the difference between intended and accidental behavior. In an earlier intervention, we documented that training aggressive boys to infer non-hostile intent in ambiguous situations resulted in reductions in antisocial behavior as rated by classroom teachers (Hudley & Graham, 1993). We elaborated on those findings in this component of *Best Foot Forward*. Hypothetical stories were used to demonstrate different intentions, after which students looked for examples of such situations in their own lives. Students practiced discerning another person's intention by reading non-verbal cues (tone of voice, facial expression, body language), through matching faces to appropriate feeling labels, pantomiming in small groups, and role play exercises.

In sum, our responsibility perspective leads to very specific ideas about what to include in a social skills-oriented aggression change program. By altering inferences about the responsibility of individuals and understanding accounts, we believe that our intervention has the potential to influence the aggressive child's tendency to engage in antisocial behavior.

Academic Motivation Training

The academic motivation component of the curriculum was divided into four sections that focused on risk taking, help seeking, goal setting, and attribution retraining. The section on risk taking taught students how to determine what makes a problem easy, medium, or hard and to recognize the motivational benefits of intermediate difficulty (see Atkinson, 1964). For example, boys participated in a weekly spelling game where they chose words that were easy, medium, or hard. Although more points (exchangeable for prizes) could be earned by correctly spelling more difficult words, participants learned that the best strategy (more points) over the long run was to concentrate on intermediate difficulty words.

The help seeking section demonstrated when it was most useful to seek help from others. Participants learned that the most successful help seekers were those who had shown that they had already exerted effort and that they had genuinely reached an impasse. Those lessons also stressed the importance of persistence in the face of a challenging task.

Lessons on goal setting taught participants about the importance of setting proximal or short-term goals rather than (in addition to) distal or long-term goals. Bandura (1997) has argued for the motivational significance of proximal goals. Such goals help the individual to monitor how much effort is needed to accomplish particular tasks. Using concrete everyday examples where goal setting is likely to be instrumental to success, we taught intervention boys how to set their sights on more immediate attainments that lead to longer-term successes. They also learned strategies for monitoring their behavior directed towards achieving those goals and for revising their goals in response to success or failure. For example, while playing a competitive game of ring toss, intervention boys were taught to adjust their goals upward after success and downward after failure. In this way, they learned about the motivational advantages of continuously revising their goals and level of aspiration in the direction of intermediate difficulty.

Finally, lessons in the attribution retraining section were designed to promote adaptive explanations for achievement failure. By reading hypothetical failure scenarios and working on several achievement tasks, participants learned to attribute academic setbacks to factors within their control, such as lack of effort, and to avoid the endorsement of factors outside of their control, such as low ability and external causes (e.g., poor teaching, bad luck). Many successful attribution-based interventions have documented that when students are trained to attribute failure to causes within their control, they show greater persistence in the face of failure, more confidence, and more positive attitudes toward school work (see Graham & Weiner, 1996).

In sum, our self-responsibility perspective also leads to specific ideas about what to include in an achievement change program. By teaching self-responsibility in risk taking, goal setting, help seeking, and attributions for failure, and by highlighting the interpersonal consequences of taking responsibility for achievement, we believe that we can provide aggressive boys with a set of motivational skills that are generalizable and adaptive across a variety of achievement contexts.

CURRICULUM INTERVENTION

Because of the breath of the curriculum and number of lessons (32 sessions, plus pre-testing and post-testing), the decision was made to implement the intervention as an after-school program. Participants attended the intervention three days a week for 12 weeks in sessions that lasted approximately one hour. One strength of the intervention is that it provides a structured activity for at-risk youngsters during a portion of the after-school hours. A considerable amount of recent research has documented that the hours between 3 p.m. and 7 p.m. are critical because those are the times when most delinquent activity is likely to take place (i.e., the prime hours when adult supervision is minimal) (Flannery, Williams, & Vazsonyi, 1999).

Selecting Participants

Participants were selected from a K–5 elementary school located in an economically depressed community in Los Angeles, California. The ethnic composition of the school was about evenly divided between African American and Latino students. Parent permission forms describing the study were sent home with each child in the 3rd, 4th, and 5th grade. Only students who returned signed consent forms participated in the screening phase of the study. About 500 3rd–5th graders distributed across 25 classrooms participated in that phase.

Using well-established methods in the peer aggression literature, we relied on a combination of both teacher ratings and peer nominations to select eligible participants. We selected boys who were identified by their peers and teachers as most aggressive and by their teachers as having serious motivational problems. Students were identified as eligible for the intervention if they satisfied three selection criteria: (1) they were in the top 40th percentile of those nominated as aggressive by peers; (2) their teacher ratings on the aggression measure were above the class mean; and (3) their teacher rating on the motivation question was below the class mean. These are conservative selection criteria, so that no more than 10% of boys in any classroom are identified as sufficiently at risk to be eligible for the intervention. We are confident that we identified boys who, in the absence of intervention, are most at risk for disengaging from school and becoming involved in the kinds of antisocial activities that often lead to adolescent delinquency.

We recruited 66 3rd–5th grade boys who met the eligibility criteria and whose custodial parent(s) or guardian provided informed consent. Thirty-one boys were randomly assigned to the intervention and 35 were assigned to a no-treatment control group (a few parents only agreed to allow their son to participate if he was a control subject).

Sample Attrition

As one might well imagine, subject attrition can be a problem is studies such as this. Participation was voluntary and required sustained after-school attendance, which meant that we did not have the "captive" audience that would have been available had the intervention been run during regular school hours. Recognizing these constraints, we attempted to build in incentives for sustained participation. These included creating a warm and supportive atmosphere, nutritious snacks at each session, small prizes (e.g., UCLA pencils, movie tickets) for regular attendance and good behavior, and the promise of a chance to win a larger prize (e.g., a CD player) for successful completion of the intervention.

Over the course of the intervention, we lost 9 of 31 intervention boys: 1 had an extended hospital stay, 1 was asked to leave the program because of his continued disruptive behavior, and 7 were dropped due to irregular attendance. Among the controls, 10 of the initial 35 did not complete both pre-testing and post-testing: 1 boy moved away, 2 were expelled from school, 3 voluntarily dropped out of the project, and 4 were chronically absent from school during the post-testing. Thus the final sample consisted of 47 3rd to 5th grade African American and Latino boys: there were 22 youth in the intervention and 25 in the control group.

Outcome Measures

We included a variety of outcome measures, both attitudinal and behavioral, and that relied on multiple informants (self-report, behavioral observations, teacher report, and searches of school records). This also is a strength of our intervention approach. The outcome measures assessed improvements in both social skills and academic motivation. For social outcomes, we assessed changes in children's reactions to ambiguous peer provocation and their understanding of accounts. Teacher ratings of children's social behavior before and after the intervention also were examined. Among the academic outcomes, we examined changes in students' goal setting and attributions for achievement failure. We also examined students' cumulative folders for their semester grade equivalents and teacher comments about academic progress. Finally, both intervention and control group boys participated in a laboratory maze task that both simulated ambiguous peer provocation and measured intermediate risk taking. A subset of those outcome measures will be discussed in greater detail in the next section.

RESULTS OF THE INTERVENTION

Data on most measures were gathered at the pretest phase, 1–2 weeks before intervention implementation, and again at the posttest phase, within 2–3 weeks after the intervention ended. For each of those measures, we conducted a 2×2 (treatment group $\times$ time of measurement) ANOVA with repeated measures on the second factor (i.e., pre-test and post-test scores). Meaningful effects of the intervention would be indicated by a significant Treatment Group $\times$ Time interaction. Such an interaction would document changes (improvement) in the variables of interest from pretest to posttest, but only for those aggressive boys who participated in the intervention.

Social Skills: What Did Intervention Boys Learn About Effective Account Giving?

The account giving lessons focused on two social skills. The first skill to be learned was that some accounts for wrongdoing are more effective than others. Specifically, when you offend a peer, they are likely to be more accepting and forgiving if you confess or apologize for the transgression that if you deny wrongdoing or express indifference. Legitimate excuses or justifications may be appropriate in some cases, but we mainly wanted our intervention boys to recognize the value of apology as an adaptive impression management strategy. The second skill was directed toward learning to honor or accept the accounts of others. For example, we wanted intervention boys to acknowledge the apologies of their peers as indicators of remorse and the desire to make amends for their wrongdoing. Together, the use of adaptive accounts when you are the wrongdoer and the honoring of appropriate accounts of others who are wrongdoers should lead to better peer relations and to less interpersonal conflict.

Using Accounts

To measure the use of accounts, participants read a set of hypothetical stories where they imagined that they transgressed against a peer (e.g., bumped into them, did not return a borrowed possession on time). We gave them a set of four possible responses ("things you could say") that included *apology* ("I'm sorry"), *legitimate excuse* ("excuse me, but…"), *denial* ("I didn't do it"), and *indifference* ("so what"). Boys were told to choose the account "that they would say first". If the intervention had its desired effect, we would expect intervention boys to show a relative increase from pretest to posttest in choosing an apology as their preferred account and a relative decrease in choosing denial or indifference. No such changes in adaptive account giving were predicted for control group boys.

Each respondent's selected account at pretest and posttest received a weighted score reflecting the adaptiveness of their first choice. That is, choosing the apology option received a score of +4, excuse received a score of +2, denial a score of –1, and indifference a score of –2. These weighted scores were based on the assumption that the most adaptive first choice would be to offer an apology with remorse, and the least adaptive strategy would be to acknowledge the transgression but with indifference and no remorse. The hypothesized Group × Time interaction approached significance ($p = .10$). That interaction is depicted in Figure 5.1.

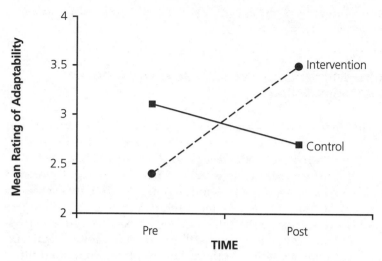

Figure 5.1.   Adaptability of accounts for intervention and control group boys at pretest and posttest.

Intervention boys showed a significant increase in the endorsement of adaptive accounts from pre- to post-test. For control group boys, there were no significant changes in the pattern of account giving from pre- to post-test. Those results suggest that aggressive boys who participated in the intervention showed an increase in their understanding of accounts like apology as a positive strategy to manage the impressions of others following social transgression.

Honoring Accounts

Did treatment boys learn to accept the apologies of peers who transgressed against them? To address that goal of the intervention, we had participants read hypothetical vignettes describing a provoking peer who offered one of the four account types (apology, excuse, denial, indifference). Following each account, boys rated on 6-point scales how *sorry* they believed the peer to be and whether or not they would *forgive* him. These stories were presented at both pretest and posttest sessions.

We were mainly interested in whether intervention boys more systematically used the account cues from pretest to posttest to make inferences about the hypothetical peer provocateur. The relevant data are shown in Figure 5.2. Before the intervention, the top two graphs in Figure 5.2 reveal that intervention boys were relatively undifferentiated in their reports of believing the peer to be sorry and willingness to forgive him. In other words, there was not much variance in their judgments as a function of the account given. After the intervention, however, these boys used the

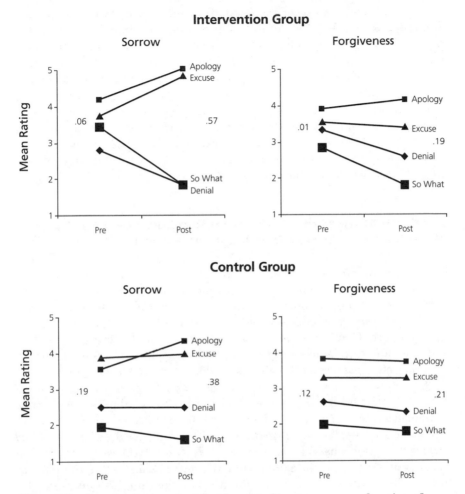

Figure 5.2.   Perceived sorrow and forgiveness of transgressor as a function of
account type for intervention and control group boys at pretest and posttest.

account cues very systematically and in accord with what we would expect if
the curriculum was successful. For example, intervention boys believed the
peer felt more sorrow when he apologized than when he denied wrongdoing, and they were more willing to forgive a repentant peer than a denying
or indifferent one. For control group boys, however, the bottom two
graphs of Figure 5.2 show very little change from pretest to posttest in the
pattern of their inferences.

Included in Figure 5.2 is the omega-square statistic which reports the
variance accounted for in judgments of perceived sorrow and forgiveness
as a function of the presented account. This statistic, which ranges from 0

to 1, provides a measure of the strength of the effect. What is evident in Figure 5.2 is that the effect of different types of accounts from pre-test to post-test is stronger (explains more variance) among intervention boys than control boys (e.g., from 6% of the variance in perceived sorrow to 57% for the treatment group, compared to 19% and 38% for controls).

To summarize thus far, the social skills component of the intervention was successful in changing the way aggressive boys thought about the function of accounts and about the intentions of peers who might have provoked them. They learned about the importance of apologizing for one's wrongdoing as a way to maintain good peer relations and they learned what it means to honor the apologies of others.

Academic Motivation: Did Intervention Boys Learn to Make More Adaptive Attributions for Achievement Failure?

Now we turn from inferring responsibility in others and social skills, to self-responsibility for achievement and motivation skills. The goal of the attribution re-training component of the intervention was to teach participants to attribute academic setbacks to factors within their control, such as lack of effort. That was viewed as more adaptive than believing that failure is due to uncontrollable *internal* factors like low ability, or to uncontrollable *external* factors such as a difficult task, bad luck or poor teaching.

At both the pre-test and post-test, we asked participants to recall the last time that they did poorly on a test and to rate five attributions as possible explanations for their failure. These attributions were *low ability* ("you are not smart enough"), *lack of effort* ("you did not try hard enough"), *a bad teacher* ("you don't have a good teacher"), *bad luck* ("you were unlucky; the teacher asked things you hadn't studied") and *task difficulty* ("the test was too hard for everyone"). Each attribution was rated on a 7-point scale (1 = *definitely not a reason* and 7 = *definitely a reason*). Because the bad luck, bad teaching, and task difficulty causal ratings were highly correlated, we combined them into a single external attribution variable.

Figure 5.3 displays the pattern of failure attributions at pre-test and post-test for intervention and control group boys. There were no significant treatment group or time effects for either of the internal attributions. All participants tended to report that their last failure *was* due to lack of effort and was *not* caused by low ability, and this was true at both the pretest and the posttest. For external attributions, however, there was a significant Group × Time interaction ($p < .001$). As hypothesized, intervention boys were less likely to endorse external and uncontrollable causes for recalled failure after participating in the intervention. For the control group, in contrast, there was no significant change across time for external attribu-

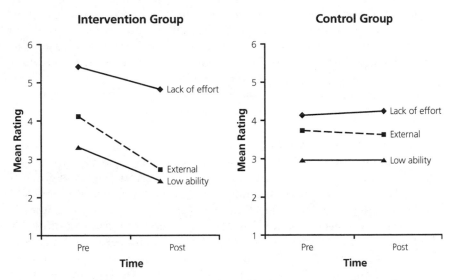

Figure 5.3.   Attributions for failure endorsed by intervention and control group boys at pretest and posttest.

tions. Note that at the posttest for intervention boys, the general attributional pattern for failure was particularly adaptive: high endorsement of lack of effort, a controllable cause of failure, and low endorsement of lack of ability and external factors, both of which are generally perceived as uncontrollable.

Laboratory Analogue Task: Practicing Social Skills and Academic Motivation Skills

Thus far our outcome measures have focused on children's self-reports largely in response to hypothetical social or academic dilemmas. Since this was a real intervention, we would hope that its effects might generalize to situations of actual behavior. Obviously we could not create the kinds of social dilemmas depicted in the hypothetical vignettes and we did not have the resources to be present in classrooms to observe the practice of motivational skills such as intermediate risk-taking or realistic goal setting. Nor could we mount a large scale observation study of naturally occurring peer provocation. Our compromise was to create a laboratory analog task that would: (1) simulate ambiguous provocation, and (2) provide opportunities for boys to display adaptive motivational strategies.

About one month after the intervention ended, all boys participated in a maze task that supposedly was unrelated to the intervention. The task required the boy to communicate with an unseen peer who was seated on the other side of a barrier. Using simple grid maps, the unseen peer was to give directions to the participant so that he could complete a maze, with the goal of winning a prize. In fact, however, the task was designed to block goal attainment. Unbeknownst to either child, the peer's map was different from the participant's. Thus incorrect solutions were necessarily given, the maze was not completed, and no prize was awarded.

Attributions to Hostile Peer Intent

After the first trial, when it was clear that the participant had not completed the maze, he was asked to rate on 7-point scales the unseen peer's intent ("Do you think your partner meant to give you bad directions?") and his feelings of anger toward that peer. Consistent with our hypotheses, aggressive boys who participated in the intervention inferred significantly less hostile intent ($M = 2.1$) on the part of the unseen peer than did boys in the control group ($M = 3.35$). The group differences for anger, however, were not significant. All boys reported relatively low levels of anger toward the unseen peer ($M = 1.8$ for intervention boys and $M = 2.2$ for control group boys).

Risk Taking Before Failure

Before the first trial, the participant was given the opportunity to choose the maze he would like to attempt from among ten possible choices that ranged in difficulty. Mazes 1–3 were described as easy ("Everyone solves them correctly and they are a bit boring"). Mazes 4–7 were portrayed as of medium difficulty ("You can solve them, but you will have to think and try"). And Mazes 8–10 were described as hard ("Hardly anyone gets these right, not even big kids in high school"). In addition, it was explained that success on more difficult puzzles would be rewarded with a more valuable prize, thus making the trade-off between difficult and intermediate risk more consistent with what we had stressed in the intervention (e.g., the spelling game).

Adaptive choices (intermediate risk taking) would be indicated if participants initially chose one of the mazes described as moderately difficult. The number and percentage of boys in each group who initially selected an easy (1–3), medium (4–7), or difficult maze (8–10) are shown in the top panel of Table 5.2. It is evident that intervention boys were more likely to choose a maze of intermediate difficulty than were control group boys. Eighteen of 22 intervention boys (82%) were intermediate risk takers compared to 4% who were low risk takers and 14% who were high risk takers. Among control boys, in contrast, less than half (11 of 25 boys, or 44%) chose a maze of intermediate difficulty, compared to 28% who were low and 28% who were high risk takers. In fact, the controls were fairly evenly distributed across the three difficulty levels.

Table 5.2. Risk Taking Before "Failure" and Goal Setting After "Failure" on the Laboratory Task for Intervention and Control Group Boys

	Treatment Group	
	Intervention n = 22	Control n = 25
	% n	% n
Risk Taking (before "failure")		
Easy Task	4 (1)	28 (7)
Medium Task	82 (18)	44 (11)
Difficult Task	14 (3)	28 (7)
Goal Setting (after "failure")		
Unrealistically low	18 (4)	24 (6)
Realistic	64 (14)	32 (8)
Unrealistically high	18 (4)	44 (11)

Note: The data are presented as percentages within each treatment group. Numbers in parentheses are frequencies.

Goal Setting After Failure

Next we examined how participants' level of aspiration changed after their "failure" to successfully complete the first maze. Adaptive goal setting would be indicated by choosing a relatively easier puzzle. Participants who shifted downward to a less difficult maze that was within three levels of their first choice were classified as *realistic* goal setters. Those who selected more difficult mazes were classified as *unrealistically high* goal setters, while those who chose puzzles more than three levels easier than their first choice were classified as *unrealistically low* goal setters.

The bottom panel of Table 5.2 displays the goal setting patterns of the two groups of boys. Almost two-thirds (64%) of intervention boys, compared to only one-third (32%) of control group boys, chose a maze that was of intermediate difficulty *for them* in light of their prior failure. For the control group, there were higher percentages of boys who showed unrealistically low (24%) or unrealistically high (44%) shifts in their level of aspiration.

Verbal Behavior During the Maze Task

The final category of variable examined in the laboratory maze task allowed us to examine both social skills and academic motivation. While participants were working their way through the first trial where failure was manipulated, everything that they said was recorded by a female observer who was unobtrusively positioned close to the participant. Those verbatim

statements were analyzed and coded into one of the following four mutually exclusive categories:

- *Task focused:* references to what needed to be done to complete the
  maze (e.g., "I can't go up six blocks because there's nothing there; I
  need another route")
- *Negative comments about the task or self:* (e.g., "this is stupid"; "this is boring"; I don't know what to do")
- *Criticizing:* negative remarks to the unseen peer about his performance (e.g., "Are you deaf?" "Cheater!")
- *Irrelevant:* comments not focused on the task or the unseen peer
  (e.g., "I'm going to my friend's house after school")

If boys in the intervention inferred less hostile intent on the part of the
peer and showed adaptive motivational patterns in terms of their risk taking and goal setting, then they should report fewer comments that criticized the peer and more comments that indicated a task focus. The data
presented in Figure 5.4 show that this was indeed the case. Intervention
boys reported a total of 104 codeable comments compared to 70 on the
part of boys in the control group. Two-thirds (67%) of the intervention
boys' recorded statements were focused on the task, compared to 14% that
were negative comments, 16% that criticized the peer, and only 2% that
could be classified as irrelevant. For control group boys, in contrast, the
preference for task focus was not nearly as strong. While 40% of these boys'
comments were directed toward the task, 33% were classified as negative,
21% were critical of the peer, and 6% were irrelevant.

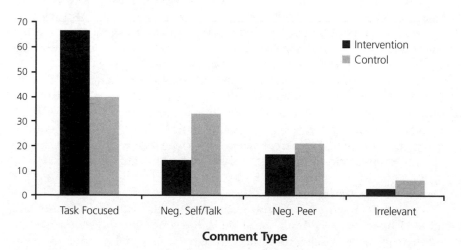

Figure 5.4.   Percentage frequency of each comment type for intervention and
control group boys on the laboratory maze task.

Did Teacher Ratings of Social Behavior and Academic Motivation Change for Boys Who Participated in the Intervention?

So far we have only examined *participants'* self-report and behavioral data. But this multi-informant intervention study also gathered relevant data from the boys' homeroom teachers (who were blind to the random assignment of students). Students' social behavior and school motivation were measured with items selected from the Social Skills Rating System for Teachers (Gresham & Elliot, 1990). Teachers rated each participating boy in their homeroom on items that comprised a *negative social behavior* subscale (e.g., fights with others, has temper tantrums) and a *cooperation/motivation* subscale (e.g., produces correct schoolwork, ignores peer distractions when doing schoolwork). We also created three new items that tapped other specific motivation skills included in the intervention (i.e., gives up easily in schoolwork, asks for help without trying, and prefers to review work they already know). We considered these items to be a measure of teacher-rated *persistence*.

Figure 5.5 shows the teacher ratings of negative social behavior, cooperation/motivation, and persistence at pre-test and post-test for intervention and control group boys. There were no effects of the intervention on teacher ratings of their students' negative social behavior (left panel of Figure 5.5), although boys in the control group showed a non-significant decrease in rated negative behavior. On the other hand, for cooperation/motivation, the predicted Group × Time interaction was found ($p < .01$). The middle panel of Figure 5.5 shows that teacher ratings of cooperation/

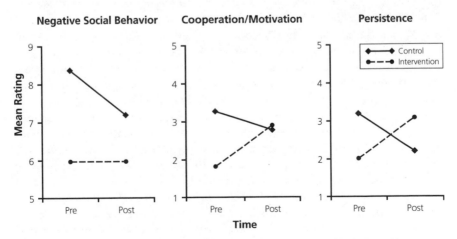

Figure 5.5.   Teacher ratings of social behavior and academic behavior of intervention and control group boys at pretest and posttest.

motivation increased significantly from pretest to posttest for intervention boys, whereas there were no changes in ratings for control group boys. Finally, the Group × Time for persistence also was significant ($p < .001$, right panel). Intervention boys were rated higher in persistence from pretest to post-test, whereas ratings for boys in the control group actually declined.

Searching Archival Data: Is There Evidence of Social Skills or Academic Motivation Change in the Cumulative Folders of Intervention Boys?

The final outcome measure involved a search of participants' end of semester cumulative folders for both grade equivalents and teacher comments about progress during that term. Teachers at the participating elementary school evaluate a number of skill areas according to three criteria: area of strength, shows growth, or needs improvement. We calculated a grade equivalent in math and language arts for each participant, yielding a score that could range from 0 to 16 for each subject area. The analysis revealed no difference between intervention and control group boys in semester grade equivalents for either language arts ($Ms = 7.35$ vs. 7.59) or Math ($Ms = 5.80$ vs 6.36).

Then we examined the open-ended comments that teachers wrote about the progress of their students at the end of the semester. We created ratings for these comments that varied along a 5-point scale ranging from +2 to −2. A score of +2 was given to comments that suggested significant improvement in both social behavior and study skills over the term immediately following the intervention. A score of +1 revealed improvement in one of these areas. A score of "O" was assigned to neutral comments, −1 to deteriorating performance in either the social or academic domain, and −2 to declines in both areas. Two raters blind to the treatment group of students independently read participants' folders and assigned scores to teacher comments. Inter-rater agreement reached 95%.

Table 5.3 shows the frequency of each comment type for the two groups of boys. What stands out most clearly here is the different pattern of responses in the two groups for very positive (+2) and very negative (−2) comments. Eight of 20 intervention boys (40%) received the most positive teacher comments, while no control group boys achieved this level of teacher evaluation. In contrast, 9 of 23 control boys (41%) had comments classified as most negative, whereas such disparaging remarks were detected in only one intervention boy's cumulative folder. Thus by the end of the term following the intervention, significantly more treatment group boys were judged by their homeroom teachers to have shown improvements in both social and academic skill areas, whereas significantly more control group boys were judged to have displayed deteriorating behavior.

Table 5.3. Percentage of Intervention and Control Boys with Positive, Neutral, and Negative Written Teacher Comments in their Cumulative Folders.

		Group	
		Intervention	*Control*
Comment Type		*% n*	*% n*
+2	Positive Social and Study Skills	40 (8)	0 (0)
+1	Positive in one area	20 (4)	27 (6)
0	Neutral	10 (2)	9 (2)
−1	Negative in one area	25 (5)	23 (5)
−2	Negative in both Social and Study Skills	5 (1)	41 (9)

Note: $n = 20$ in the intervention group and $n = 22$ in the control group

SUMMARY OF INTERVENTION EFFECTS

Although our sample sizes were small and the effects therefore modest, the intervention yielded encouraging results. First, boys in the intervention learned the social skills of strategic account giving, honoring the accounts of others, and assuming non-hostile peer intent in ambiguous situations. Second, they learned the academic motivation skills of intermediate risk taking, realistic goal setting, task focus, and attributions for failure to factors within their control. Third, intervention boys used these social and academic motivation skills in the laboratory maze task that simulated ambiguous provocation and provided opportunities for intermediate risk taking and realistic goal setting. And fourth, boys in the intervention were rated by their teachers as showing more cooperation and persistence than control group boys. They were also judged as having improved more in the social and academic domain based on end-of-the semester written comments by teachers.

As currently designed and implemented, *Best Foot Forward* was a pilot intervention and we recognize that there are many things that we need to do better. The intervention was generally more successful with *increasing competencies* (pro-social skills, motivation) than with *decreasing problem behavior* (e.g., teacher-rated negative social behavior). In the language of risk research, that means that we were more successful at enhancing protective factors that buffer against future negative events than we were at reducing current risk. If the target is present risk, then we should consider strategies for increasing the immediate impact of the intervention on antisocial behavior. For example, there could be more lessons on behavior management and anger control in the social skills component. We also need to measure a range of anti-social and problem behavior outcomes, such as school truancy and disciplinary actions, to better test for treatment effects. In addition, we need to work on procedures for studying intervention effects in naturally occurring school contexts (e.g., playground, cafeteria, classroom academic time).

It will be important to develop more effective and creative strategies for reducing participant attrition in an after-school program. Although we lost only about 25% of our intervention boys to sample attrition, this is significant when the size of the group was small to begin with. Our incentives for regular attendance were successful, but we still faced the competition of other after-school activities, including free time for play. It may be that we need to work more closely with parents to help us sustain their child's commitment to the intervention.

Inclusion of a follow-up component also is a task for the future. We do not know whether the intervention had any lasting effects beyond the end of the school semester following implementation. That is particularly important given our interests in the effect of the intervention on more general outcomes such as academic performance and attitudes about school. We suspect that these outcomes are part of more cumulative intervention effects that unfold gradually over time.

Finally, we need to develop strategies for monitoring intervention fidelity. By fidelity we mean how thoroughly and consistently the curriculum was carried out. We know that some lessons worked better than others, just as some outcomes proved more amenable to change. We need a system for documenting both the extent to which teacher-trainers remained faithful to the intervention and the variations in implementation (e.g., number of activities and lessons taught).

IMPLICATIONS FOR INTERVENTION DESIGN

School-based programs are a natural context for aggression and violence prevention because children spend the bulk of their week days at school (hence, the captive audience). Not surprisingly, school-based violence prevention programs have proliferated in the past two decades at an enormous rate and astronomical cost. In the United States, for example, the Safe and Drug-Free Schools and Communities Act has allowed the government to appropriate over $500 million annually to school districts for prevention programs. However, programs supported by these tax dollars remain largely unevaluated, and they are often created by professional curriculum developers rather than experts in the science of prevention/intervention research. Furthermore, the large-scale evaluations that do exist have yielded disappointing results (see review in Gottfredsson, 2001).

We believe that our intervention approach (including its strengths and limitations) can serve as a springboard for discussion about how school-based programs for violence prevention can better conform to the guidelines of good prevention science. We therefore conclude this chapter by outlining six principles for the effective design and implementation of school-based interventions.

Interventions Need to be Theory Guided

Unless an interventionist has a clear theory about what causes aggression, youth violence or other problem behaviors, it is difficult to avoid what has come to be called a "laundry list" approach—in other words, a curriculum that includes a little bit of everything and not much of anything specific to the targeted behavior. Our intervention was informed by a particular theoretical perspective on the cognitions, emotions, and behaviors that are precursors to social competence and academic motivation. That perspective guided the choice of both curriculum activities and outcome measures. Thus we were able to systematically map specific behaviors (including thoughts and feelings) targeted for change onto particular outcome measures. Where the intervention "worked", we had a pretty good understanding of *why* it was successful.

Interventions Should Have Multiple Components and Multiple Informants

We focused on social skills and academic motivation as two important pathways to reducing aggression and improving school engagement. The intervention would have been less novel, and probably less effective, if we had concentrated on only one of these components. It also is important for evaluation purposes that there are multiple sources of data from multiple informants. Relying solely on participant self-report is vulnerable to memory distortions, social desirability, and self-presentation concerns. Relying solely on teacher reports is susceptible to the subtle biases or unconscious stereotypes that teachers may have about some of their students (particularly problem behavior students). And relying solely on archival data like school grades or cumulative folders is constrained by the accuracy and completeness of school records, as well as the fact that achievement is determined by many factors outside of the range of most interventions (e.g., economic advantage, parental values).

Interventions Should Build In A Longitudinal Component So That
Cumulative Effects Across Critical Periods Of Transition Can Be Examined

Many of our intervention boys would be entering the major transition to middle school within 6 months or a year after the treatment. Because at-risk children are particularly vulnerable to delinquency and school disengagement during the middle school transition (Eccles, Lord, & Buchanan, 1996), it would be important to know whether the intervention served any protective or buffering function. Other successful interventions focusing on teen mothers and children of divorce have been guided by this transition or milestone approach (Durlack & Wells, 1997). The underlying assumption is that transitions can result in negative outcomes if they are not successfully negotiated or mastered by those about to experience them. An intervention like *Best Foot Forward* aimed at aggression reduction and motivation enhancement for 4th and 5th grade at-risk youth is ideal for testing this transition approach.

"Boosters" are Needed

Many successful interventions adhere to a public health model where problem behaviors are conceptualized much like diseases that must be both controlled and prevented. Part of prevention involves immunization, as in the prevention of small pox or polio, and booster shots at critical periods. As part of a longitudinal design, brief "doses" of *Best Foot Forward* (key lessons with new activities) should be implemented at regular intervals, especially during developmental transitions.

Interventions Need To Be Culturally And Developmentally Sensitive

Ethnic minority youth are at risk not only for poor academic outcomes but for early delinquency as well. As our world becomes increasingly diverse, minorities continue to be over represented among those experiencing negative academic and social outcomes. Acknowledging this reality, many school based interventions that address problem behaviors in urban areas are targeted for ethnic minority children (Gottfredson, 2001). Yet one rarely sees any discussion of the cultural relevance of curriculum materials to which participants are exposed.

In creating *Best Foot Forward*, we made special efforts to develop stories and role-play activities that reflected the life experience and cultural heritage of ethnic minority boys. For example, there is evidence that African American youth have learning styles that are more compatible with physical activity, communalism, and expressiveness (e.g., Boykin, 2000). Hence we made sure that our role-play activities allowed for freedom of movement, group work, and an opportunity to express feelings. We also know that the world of sports is a topic that generates a great deal of enthusiasm among inner city boys. We therefore focused our activities on sports as well as academics in the motivation training because the athletic arena is also an achievement domain where intermediate risk-taking, realistic goal-setting, and persistence in the face of challenge also are key determinants of success. The success of any intervention designed specifically for minority youth depends in part on the degree to which it is culturally sensitive

In addition to targeting students with diverse ethnic backgrounds, school-based interventions have also been developed at every level of schooling, from pre-K through high school. Children undergo major cognitive, emotional, social, and biological changes across these grade levels and interventions targeted for particular age groups must be sensitive to those developmental shifts. Again, we took great care and drew on our expertise as former teachers to create materials that were matched to the cognitive and social maturity of middle elementary age children.

Interventions Can Backfire

In a review of interventions for adolescent problem behavior, Lipsey (1992) reported that 29% of the studies examined were judged as harmful in that intervention participants displayed escalated problem behavior in comparison to their control group counterparts. Harmful outcomes of interventions are called *iatrogenic* effects. One factor known to produce those effects is aggregating high risk boys together in treatment groups. The social reinforcement that group members receive from one another for acting out and "talking trash" in discussions of risky behavior sometimes functions as a kind of deviancy training that results in increased problem behavior (Dishion, McCord, & Poulin, 1999). At times we ourselves were struck with how quickly our intervention boys' behavior could deteriorate when such deviancy training escalated. One solution is to have mixed intervention groups that include a balance of high and low risk boys. The presence of more adults and smaller adult-child ratios is also a good strategy.

A FINAL NOTE: COSTS VERSUS BENEFITS

Intervention development and implementation is expensive, if the amount of federal dollars devoted to this activity is an accurate gauge. It is sometimes difficult to reconcile the costs of intervention research in relation to perceived benefits. In the case of *Best Foot Forward*, if we think about reducing the risk that intervention boys will become delinquent as adolescents, then projected savings in terms of the costs of incarcerating even one juvenile (about $35,000 a year) are substantial. Add to this the savings in terms of *human capital*—increased opportunity among at-risk youth for education, personal growth, and responsible citizenship—then the potential benefits to society of effective school-based interventions are enormous.

REFERENCES

Atkinson, J. (1964). *An introduction to motivation.* Princeton, NJ: Van Nostrand.

Bandura, A. (1997). *Self-efficacy: The exercise of control.* New York: W. H. Freeman & Company.

Boykin, W. (2000). The talent development model of schooling: Placing student at promise for academic success. *Journal of Education for Students Placed At Risk, 5,* 3–25.

Coie, J., & Dodge, K. (1998). Aggression and antisocial behavior. In N. Eisenberg (Ed.), *Handbook of child psychology. Volume 3: Social, emotional, and personality development* (pp. 779–862). New York: John Wiley.

Dishion, T. J., McCord, J., & Poulin, F. (1999). When interventions harm: Peer groups and problem behavior. *American Psychologist, 54,* 755–764.

Durlak, J. A., & Wells, A. M. (1997). Primary prevention mental health programs for children and adolescents: A meta-analytic review. *Journal of Community Psychology, 25,* 115–151.

Eccles, J., Lord, S., & Buchanan, C. M. (1996). School transitions in early adolescence: What are we doing to our young people? In J. A. Graber, J. Brooks-Gunn, & A. C. Peterson (Eds.), *Transitions through adolescence: Interpersonal domains and contexts* (pp. 251–284). Mahwah, NJ: Lawrence Erlbaum.

Flannery, D., Williams, L., & Vazonyi, A. (1999). Who are they with and what are they doing? Delinquent behavior, substance use, and early adolescents' after-school time. *American Journal of Orthopsychiarty, 69,* 2, 247–253.

Gottfredson, D. (2001). *Schools and delinquency.* New York: Cambridge University Press.

Graham, S. (1994). Motivation in African Americans. *Review of Educational Research, 64,* 55–118.

Graham, S. (1997). Using attribution theory to understand social and academic motivation in African American youth. *Educational Psychologist, 32,* 21–34.

Graham, S., & Hudley, C. (1994). Attributions of aggressive and nonaggressive African American male early adolescents: A study of construct accessibility. *Developmental Psychology, 30,* 365–373.

Graham, S., & Taylor, A. (2002). Ethnicity, gender, and the development of achievement values. In A. Wigfield & J. Eccles (Eds.), *The development of achievement motivation* (pp. 121–146). San Diego, CA: Academic Press.

Graham, S., Taylor, A., & Hudley, C. (1998). Exploring achievement values in ethnic minority early adolescents. *Journal of Educational Psychology, 90,* 606–620.

Graham, S., & Weiner, B. (1996). Theories and principles of motivation. In D. Berliner & R. Calfee (Eds.), *Handbook of educational psychology* (pp. 63–84). New York: MacMillan.

Graham, S., Weiner, B., & Benesh-Weiner, M. (1995). An attributional analysis of the development of excuse-giving in aggressive and nonaggressive African American boys. *Developmental Psychology, 31,* 274–284.

Gresham, F. & Elliot, S. (1990). *Social skills rating system* [teacher form]. Circle Pines, MN: American Guidance.

Hudley, C., & Graham, S. (1993). An atrributional intervention to reduce peer-directed aggression among African American boys. *Child Development, 64,* 124–138.

Jencks, C., & Phillips, M. (1998). *The black-white test score gap.* Washington, DC: The Brookings Institution.

Lipsey, M. W. (1992). The effect of treatment on juvenile delinquents: Results from meta-analysis. In: F. Loesel & D. Bender (Eds.), *Psychology and law: International perspectives* (pp. 131–143). Berlin, Germany: Walter De Gruyter.

Scott, M., & Lyman, S. (1968). Accounts. *American Sociological Review, 23,* 46–62.

Suarez-Orozco, C., & Suarez-Orozco, M. (1995). *Transformations: Migration, family life, and achievement motivation among Latino adolescents.* Stanford, CA: Stanford University Press.

Weiner, B. (1986). *An attributional theory of motivation and emotion.* New York: Springer-Verlag.

Weiner, B. (1995). *Judgments of responsibility: A foundation for a theory of social conduct.* New York: Guilford Press.

CHAPTER 6

CROSS-CULTURAL VALIDATION OF SELF-CONCEPT MEASURES AND THEORETICAL MODELS IN THE CHINESE CONTEXT

Chit-Kwong Kong, Kit-Tai Hau, and Herbert W. Marsh

High self-concept has been considered both as a desirable outcome as well as an important mediator in enhancing other positive psychological variables and academic achievement (e.g., see reviews by Marsh, 1990a, 1993). In the past two decades, there has been much advancement in its measurement and theoretical model building, which unfortunately has been based primarily on studies in Western countries. Teachers and researchers in other societies are interested to know whether their students' self-concept is affected by the social milieu in the same way as those in the western culture. It is important, therefore, to understand whether such theoretical self-concept models and measures are universally valid and applicable.

In this chapter, we will first briefly review the major theoretical models and development related to self-concept. Then, we will report on a series of large-scale longitudinal studies among Chinese students that examines the cross-cultural validity of these major theoretical models. Specifically, we will discuss: (a) the validation of the measurement instrument, (b) the

Teaching, Learning, and Motivation in a Multicultural Context, pages 117–145
Copyright © 2003 by Information Age Publishing

internal and external frame of reference (I/E) model, (c) the big-fish-little-pond effects (BFLPE), and (d) the causal relationship between achievement and self-concept.

CULTURAL IMPACTS ON SELF-CONCEPT FORMATION

As current self-concept models and measures have been primarily developed in Western cultural contexts, they are criticized for being culturally bound to the ideology of individualism and may not be applicable to people in the collectivistic cultures (e.g., Yang, 1991). Two lines of research are particularly relevant to this issue. One is the contrast between the independent and the interdependent views of the construal of self (Markus & Kitayama, 1991). The other is the contrast between the private and the collective self (Triandis, 1989).

Markus and Kitayama (1991) have contrasted the differences in the construal of self between people from individualistic (e.g., Western) and collectivist cultures (e.g., Asian). In an individualistic culture, a person is typically viewed as "an independent, self-contained, autonomous entity who comprises a unique configuration of internal attributes" (Markus & Kitayama, 1991, p. 226). Based on these values, the self-concept model in an individualistic culture is characterized by a description of personal attributes and traits. However, people in a collectivistic culture tend to emphasize the interdependence and harmonious relatedness between one another (e.g., family members, working partners). In these cultural contexts, it is important to fit with others, to fulfill and create obligations, and to become part of various interpersonal relationships (Markus & Kitayama, 1991). Because of such differential cultural emphases, it has been challenged that the Western self-concept models may not capture the salient interdependent and related components of self-concept in the collectivistic cultures (Kitayama & Markus, 1995; Markus & Kitayama, 1998).

In another line of research, some theorists have attempted to describe the differences in the conception of self in terms of cultural variation in cognitions. Baumeister (1986) has proposed that self-information is organized in a systematic structure and can be classified into three aspects of self (the private, the public, and the collective self). The private self refers to the cognitions about traits, states, or behaviors of the person (e.g., "I am kind"), the public self involves the generalized other's view of the self (e.g., "Most people think I am kind"), and the collective self is related to views of the self found in collective contexts (e.g., "My family thinks I am kind"). Triandis (1989) has suggested that these three kinds of self are sampled with different probabilities in different cultures. In an individualistic culture, people use mostly the private self, while in a collectivistic culture, the collective self predominates. Triandis (1989) has further proposed that when the collective self is used, people are more likely to behave according to norms, rules, and customs. On the other hand, when the private self is preferably chosen, people are more likely to behave according to their attitudes, feelings, and beliefs, or their personal philosophy. In a number of cross-cultural studies, people of different cultural backgrounds have been asked to complete twenty statements each beginning with "I am ...." (referred to as the Twenty Statements Test or TST), the subjects have differentiated themselves in their self-description primarily in line with the predictions based on cultural differences as proposed by Triandis and other researchers (e.g., Cousins, 1989; Dhawan, Roseman, Naidu, Thapa, & Rettek, 1995; Ma & Schoeneman, 1997; Watkins et al., 1998).

In addition to previous research showing that Chinese students differ from Western students in being lower on the cultural value of individualism, higher on collectivism, and stronger on collective self (e.g., Bond, 1996; Hofstede, 1980; 1991; also see Markus & Kitayama, 1991; Triandis, 1989), results with Chinese students in Hong Kong also suggest they attribute their examination performance more to effort than to ability and concentrate more on their own improvement over time than on comparisons with other students as determinants of perceived academic achievement (Hau & Salili, 1991, 1996). Given these cultural differences, it is reasonable to ask whether Western models of self-concepts and their relations with other constructs (such as academic achievement) are also different for these Chinese students. Whereas we do not specifically hypothesize that there are cultural differences in these relations, Marsh, Byrne, and Yeung (1999) emphasized the need to evaluate the limits of the generalizability of the theoretical models across students from different cultures. Watkins (2000) also advocated the need of careful interpretation of differences between data from two countries as well as the necessity to replicate cross-cultural studies in very diversified conditions (or countries). Our intent here is to evaluate cross-cultural support for predictions derived from the Western self-concept models. The following series of studies offer an opportunity to evaluate the generalizability of our Western theoretical models and empirical findings for Chinese students in Hong Kong.

MULTIDIMENSIONAL AND HIERARCHICAL STRUCTURE OF SELF-CONCEPT

The Western Models

There is an increasing recognition of the multidimensional nature of self-concept and a pressing interest on the development of psychometrically strong self-concept measures. In particular, Shavelson, Hubner, and Stanton (1976) developed an operational definition and proposed a possible structure of self-concept. According to Shavelson et al. (1976), self-concept is broadly defined as a person's perception of himself/herself. These perceptions are formulated through interactions with the environment, and are influenced especially by evaluations by significant others, environmental reinforcements, and personal interpretations of own experience. Shavelson et al. (1976) also proposed a multifaceted and hierarchical model. This self-concept model can be represented by an inverted tree structure, with the global, general self-concept being placed at the apex of the hierarchy which then branched into academic and non-academic components. The academic component can further be divided into self-concepts of specific subjects, such as English, history, mathematics and science, and so on, while the nonacademic component can be divided into social, emotional, and physical subcomponents. At the bottom of the hierarchy, there are evaluations of behavior in specific situations.

The multifaceted and hierarchical model proposed by Shavelson et al. (1976) was heuristic and innovative and has been overwhelmingly conceived to replace the global and unidimensional model that predominated at the time of their review. Initially, empirical support for the multifaceted and hierarchical model of self-concept was extremely rare. In Shavelson et al. (1976) evaluation of commonly used instruments, the support for the separation of the academic, social, emotional, and physical facets of self-concept was only moderate. Typically, the different facets of self-concept could not identify and differentiate clearly. Though there was some evidence showing the possible hierarchical relationship between general self-concept and more specific self-concepts, the results were far from conclusive and were subject to alternative interpretations. Thus, the model could not be fully tested until more psychometrically strong measures are developed.

More recently, researchers have developed psychometrically stronger self-concept instruments to measure specific self-concept facets derived from theoretical models and have used factor analysis to support these *a priori* facets. For example, Harter (1982) identified academic, social, and physical as three distinguishable components of self-concept in her "Perceived Competence Scale" (Harter, 1982). Fleming and Courtney (1984) found clear and identifiable factors of physical appearance, physical abilities, social confidence, and academic (school ability) components of self-concept in their analyses of the "Feelings of Inadequacy Scale" (Fleming & Courtney, 1984). In both the Harter (1982) and Fleming and Courtney (1984) studies, a global, general self-esteem was also identified as a separate factor from the specific components of self-concept. Shavelson and

Bolus (1982) also demonstrated that the general, academic, and subject-specific self-concepts were distinguishable from each other.

Particularly strong support for the multifaceted self-concept model has been provided by Marsh and his colleagues (e.g., see reviews in Marsh, 1990a, 1993; Marsh & Craven, 1997) using their series of Self-Description Questionnaire (SDQ) measures. Based on Shavelson's model, Marsh et al. developed the set of three SDQ (I, II, III) instruments to measure the self-concept for pre-adolescents, early adolescents, and late adolescents, respectively (Marsh & O'Neill, 1984, Marsh, Parker, & Barnes, 1985; Marsh, Parker, & Smith, 1983). The instruments were designed to provide reliable and valid measures of the multifaceted self-concept and to reflect that self-concept becomes increasingly differentiated with age. Empirical studies using these SDQ measures have clearly identified the targeted factors and supported their convergent and divergent validity (Marsh & O'Neill, 1984, Marsh, Parker, & Barnes, 1985; Marsh, Parker, & Smith, 1983).

Recent reviews and empirical studies have provided very strong support for the multidimensional structure of self-concept (Marsh, 1990a; Marsh, Byrne & Shavelson, 1992; Marsh & Hattie, 1996). Furthermore, with the use of multidimensional self-concept measures such as SDQs, researchers have obtained much more valuable information and refined relations among constructs. Based on this research, Marsh concluded that "self-concept cannot be reasonably understood adequately if its multidimensionality is ignored" (1990a, p. 162).

Validation in the Chinese Culture

Between construct validation

Construct validation research can be broadly classified into within-construct and between-construct studies. The former focuses on the cohesiveness (or differentiation) of various components within the self-concept construct whereas the latter investigates its theoretical relationships with other constructs (e.g., with achievement behaviour and other attitudes). In a number of between-construct studies with Chinese students, the multidimensional nature of self-concept has been examined. Using an adapted Chinese version of SDQ-I, Lau (1989) showed his multidimensional measure helped to capture the specific relations between Hong Kong Chinese adolescents' sex role orientations and different self-concept domains. In another series of studies on adolescent delinquency using a more refined measured adapted from SDQ-I, Lau and Leung (1992) demonstrated that parent-child relation tended to have a closer linkage to adolescents' social development, whereas school-child relation was related more to their academic achievement. They also showed that adolescents' delinquency was related to specific components rather than to the global measure of general self-concept (Leung & Lau, 1989). The results were consistent with Chan and Lee's (1993) finding that psychological symptoms could be accounted for by specific self-concepts as predictors.

In another study with Chinese junior high school children, Leung and Leung (1992) found that life satisfaction was more strongly related to self-concept in relation with parents than to self-concept in relation with teachers. Distinctive developmental patterns across grades in specific self-concepts were also identified with the adoption of multidimensional measures of self-concept. For example, Lau (1990) found that academic ability self-concept increased while that of physical appearance decreased with age. In addition, these two specific self-concepts were related differently with other psychological variables such as locus of control, test anxiety and extraversion. In sum, these studies showed that the inclusion of specific components of self-concept in research revealed more refined relations, and hence a better understanding of the constructs. The results have provided strong support for the between construct validity of the multi-dimensional self-concept.

Within Construct Validation

It is important to provide stronger support for the within-construct validity in the cross-cultural validation of self-concept measures and models. In a number of construct validation studies with Chinese students using exploratory factor analysis (EFA), Watkins and his colleagues identified six out of the seven factors of the SDQ-I. However, the general-self dimension often submerged and 'dissolved' into other factors (Chung & Watkins, 1992; Watkins & Dong, 1994; Watkins, Dong, & Xia, 1995). The use of EFA in model testing in previous studies had strong limitations in that it could not evaluate and compare the *a priori* model against other alternative models (Marsh & Shavelson, 1985). Such problems and weaknesses could be overcome by the use of confirmatory factor analyses (CFA). Furthermore, previous self-concept research with Chinese subjects relied primarily on the SDQ-I measure regardless subjects' age, even though at times for subjects of Grades 7 to 11, the SDQ-II measure should be more appropriate.

Using confirmatory factor analysis, Yeung and Lee (1999) tested the applicability of the SDQ-II measure in the Chinese context. They measured the academic achievement and self-concept of 511 Grades 7, 8, and 9 students from a high school in southern China in a 2-wave longitudinal survey (6 months). A Chinese-translated version of the Verbal (Chinese), Math, Academic, and General self-concept scales was used while school examination scores and teachers' schoolwork ratings were used as academic achievement indicators. Confirmatory factor analyses clearly demonstrated that: (a) the self-concept factors were clearly defined, (b) the test-retest reliability of the self-concept factors were consistently high, (c) subject-specific self-concepts correlated more strongly with academic achievement in matching areas and less so in non-matching areas, and (d) Chinese and Math self-concept were uncorrelated or slightly negatively correlated. All these findings support the convergent and divergent validity of the self-concept measure.

In recent research, Cheung and Lau (2001) have proposed an indigenous self-concept model and developed a new self-concept measure to test their model. Consistent with recent emphasis on multidimensionality, their model consists of the important key self-concept components such as academic, social, physical, and general domains. The unique feature of their model is the systematic inclusion of sources of self-concept knowledge. Specifically, they consider the reflected parental appraisals, reflected school appraisals, upward comparison, and downward comparison as important sources of self-concept knowledge (self-concept perspectives). Based on this model, a new Multi-Perspective Multi-Domain Self-Concept Inventory (MMSI) was developed (Cheung & Lau, 2001). Items were constructed with reference to four domains (academic, social, physical, general) and four perspectives (reflected parental appraisal, reflected school appraisal, upward comparison, downward comparison). Results (Cheung & Lau, 2001) provided empirical support for the construct validity and multidimensionality of their measure. Based on confirmatory factor analysis of the responses of 981 Grades 2, 4, and 6 students in Hong Kong, they showed that: (a) all the factors were clearly defined (b) the reliability of each subscale was reasonable high, and (c) the self-concept model gave a reasonably good fit to the data.

Arguing the importance of using culturally relevant self-concept models and instruments in cross-cultural research, Cheng (1996) used open-ended questionnaires and semi-structured interviews to investigate how Hong Kong secondary students thought about themselves. Content analyses of the students' responses provided very strong support for the multidimensionality of self-concept. Five major categories of self-description information were identified, including the intellectual (academic), social, family, moral, and physical domains. Among these, the family self and the moral self were identified as two cultural-relevant and important aspects of the Chinese's self-concept. Cheng (1996) proposed the inclusion of filial piety and virtue as two important subscales of self-concept for Chinese and developed an indigenous self-concept measure for Chinese adolescents (the Chinese Adolescent Self-Esteem Scale). Subsequent analyses (e.g., Cheng & Watkins, 2000) based on this model and its measure provided preliminary support for its construction validity. Despite the predictive and concurrent validities of the measure have yet to be determined, this line of research represents an important contribution to cross-cultural self-concept research.

In a large-scale longitudinal study of the self-concept (two waves) and academic achievement (four waves) of Chinese secondary students in Hong Kong, Hau, Kong, Marsh, and Cheng (2000) tested the cross-cultural validity of the SDQ-II measure and the underlying model of self-concept upon which it is based. Confirmatory factor analyses provided very strong support for the construct validity of their Chinese translation of the SDQ-II measure. The 12 factors, including an additional one on Chinese language, were clearly identifiable and distinguishable from one another. Confirmatory factor analysis showed that all the self-concept factors were clearly defined, the factor loadings on the target factors were very high and statistically significant (median values = .74, and .78 for Grades 8 and 9, respectively). In addition, the factor loadings on each target factor were consistent across grades, indicating that the factor structure was replicable across the two years. The various goodness-of-fit indices showed that the model fitted the data very well (RMSEA was small, 0.0246; NNFI and CFI were high, .942 and .946, respectively).

Other Psychometric Properties

The psychometric properties of the Chinese version of the SDQ-II were strong and comparable to those reported with the original instrument. Specifically, in a large scale 6-year longitudinal (starting at Grade 6) study ($N = \sim 8500$) with Hong Kong Chinese students (for details see, Hau et al., 2000; Marsh, Hau, & Kong, 2000, in press; Marsh, Kong, & Hau, 2000, 2001), the reliabilities as estimated by Cronbach's alpha were satisfactory, ranging from .73 (Honesty) to .92 (Mathematics) with a median of .84 for Grade 8, and from .77 (Honesty) to .94 (Mathematics) with a median of .87 for Grade 9. These figures were comparable to the reliabilities from the Australian Normative Archive SDQ-II Sample ($N = 5494$, 2658 males and 2836 females) ranged from .84 (Honesty) to .91 (Physical Appearance) with a median of .87 (Marsh, 1990b).

The correlations among the latent self-concept factors based on these confirmatory factor analyses in the above large scale study were relatively low as hypothesized (median correlations = .26 and .25 for Grades 8 and 9 respectively). The results showed that the different subscales of self-concept were quite distinct and differentiable from each other, thus lending strong support for the multidimensional structure of self-concept. The convergent and divergent validity of the self-concept responses was further demonstrated by a multitrait-multitime analysis. As expected, while the correlations between the same self-concept factors at different occasions were consistently high (high convergent validities, or stability over time in this application), the correlations between different self-concept factors at the same test occasion were much lower and became even lower across differ-ent test occasions (high divergent validity).

The construct validity of the Chinese instrument and applicability of the Western self-concept structure have been further demonstrated in the fac-torial invariance analysis. In the Marsh et al. (2000, 2001) large scale stud-ies, this was tested by placing equality constraints across grade levels, on all factor loadings, and subsequently on factor covariances , factor variances, and item uniquenesses. The fit of each model with additional constraints was compared with that with no constraints. Furthermore, the correspond-ing modification indexes and expected changes for these constrained parameters were inspected to reveal the impacts of the invariance con-straints on the whole model. In brief, the results showed that the structure and size of parameters (factor loadings, variances, and covariances) were identical across the different educational level groups.

In summary, the psychometric properties of the Chinese instrument were very strong or even stronger than that of the original Australian (English) version. The converging evidences showed the stability of the fac-torial self-concept structure across various grade levels as well as the appli-cability of the western developed self-concept structure to be used with the Chinese students.

FRAME OF REFERENCE EFFECTS: THE INTERNAL/EXTERNAL MODEL

The Western Models

Internal and External Frame of Reference Model (I/E model)

In the multidimensional self-concept model, it was surprising to find that the verbal and mathematics self-concepts were nearly uncorrelated though their respective achievements (e.g., verbal and mathematics exami-nation scores) were substantially and positively correlated. This pattern of results also contradicted the original belief that the academic self-concepts of different specific school subjects should be substantially correlated so that they could be combined and incorporated as a single general aca-demic component. These seemingly contradictory results have led Marsh and his colleagues to revise the original self-concept model by positing two distinguishable academic components: the academic/numeric and the academic/verbal components (Marsh & Shavelson, 1985). Furthermore, Marsh (1986) has proposed the "Internal and External Frame of Reference Model" (I/E model) to account for this intricate correlation between mathematics and English self-concepts.

The I/E model (for further discussion, see Marsh, 1986, 1993; Skaalvik & Rankin, 1995) was initially developed to explain why math and verbal self-concepts were almost uncorrelated even though corresponding areas of academic achievement are substantially correlated (typically .5 to .8, depending on how math and verbal achievement are measured). According to the I/E model, academic self-concept in a specific school subject is formulated through two comparison processes: the comparison with other students in the same conext (the external process) and the comparison within self of competence in one school subject relative to competence in other school subjects (the internal process). Specifically, the external process refers to the comparison of the perceived own ability (e.g., mathematics ability) with the perceived same ability of other members (e.g., classmates, friends) in the reference group (social comparison). On the one hand, this relativistic impression serves as one basis for the gauging of own self-concept. On the other hand, Marsh also posits that people tend to compare their ability in one area (e.g., mathematics ability) with their own ability in other areas (e.g., verbal ability). This internal comparison serves as the second basis self-concept formation. So it is possible that students with high math ability may have average or even below-average math self-concept just because their verbal ability and hence their verbal self-concept are much higher.

Since verbal and mathematics abilities are substantially correlated, people with high verbal ability are likely to have high mathematics ability as well. They would tend to have higher self-concept in both verbal and mathematics domains when compared externally with others (e.g., classmates) in their reference group. Thus, the external comparison process would lead to a positive correlation between verbal and mathematics self-concepts. However, in the internal comparison, as own verbal ability and is compared to own mathematics ability (an ipsative comparison), people with mathematics ability higher than their verbal ability would tend to have a higher mathematics self-concept but a relatively lower verbal self-concept. The internal comparison process would, therefore, lead to a negative correlation between verbal and mathematics self-concepts. Subsequently, the joint operation of the external and internal processes, depending on the relative strength of each, would lead to a correlation either close to zero, which is substantially less than the typically large correlation between verbal and mathematics achievements.

Stronger tests of the I/E model are possible in the examinations of the relations among math and verbal achievements and their respective self-concepts (see Figure 6.1a). The external comparison process predicts that good math skills lead to higher math self-concepts and that good verbal skills lead to higher verbal self-concepts. According to the internal comparison process, however, good math skills should lead to lower verbal self-concepts (once the positive effect of good verbal skills on verbal self-concept is controlled). The better one is at mathematics, the poorer he/she is at verbal subjects (relative to his/her good math skills). Similarly, better verbal skills should lead to lower math self-concept (once the positive effect of good math skills on math self-concept is controlled). In models used to test this prediction (Figure 6.1a), the paths from math achievement to math self-concept and from verbal achievement to verbal self-concept (the grey horizontal lines in the figure) are predicted to be substantially positive (indicated by "++" in the figure). However, the paths from math achievement to verbal self-concept and from verbal achievement to math self-concept (the dark lines in Figure 6.1a) are predicted to be negative (indicated by "–"). These predictions have been supported from a large body of research based on a variety of self-concept measures and from different countries (Marsh & Craven, 1997; Marsh & Yeung, 2001; Skaalvik & Rankin, 1995).

Using longitudinal research data of 511 Grades 7, 8 and 9 students in southern China, Yeung and Lee (1999) tested the generalizability of the

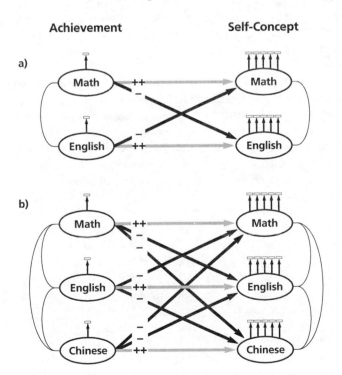

Figure 6.1.   Predictions based on the traditional I/E model (a) and the new extended I/E model (b) that incorporates native and nonnative languages ("+" and "–" refer to the predicted direction of the path coefficients).

western I/E model in the Chinese culture. As there were two waves (6 months in time span) of measures of subject-specific achievement and self-concept in Chinese and mathematics, the study was particularly suitable for the evaluation of the I/E model. Consistent with the a priori predications based on the I/E model, prior Chinese achievement had a strong positive effect on Chinese self-concept and a slightly negative effect on mathematics self-concept, whereas prior mathematics achievement had a strong positive effect on mathematics self-concept and a slightly negative effect on Chinese self-concept. Thus, the results lent strong support for the I/E model.

A number of researchers have proposed various extensions of the I/E model (e.g., Bong, 1998; Marsh & Köller, in review; Skaalvik & Rankin, 1995; Yeung & Lee, 1999). In particular, a number of studies in different countries have examined the relation of verbal self-concept to a native language other than English (e.g., Norwegian in Skaalvik & Rankin, 1995; German in Marsh & Köller, in review; Chinese in Yeung & Lee, 1999). For example, Bong (1998) tested the I/E model using a broader range of academic domains, including measures of self-concept and achievement in six school subjects. In her original analysis, the verbal constructs of self-concept and achievement were based on English, Spanish, and American history, whereas the mathematics constructs of self-concept and achievement were based on algebra, geometry, and chemistry. Bong found only partial support for the I/E model.

In a reanalysis of this data, Marsh and Yeung (2001) reported that Spanish self-concept was nearly uncorrelated with other verbal self-concept factors, and that the corresponding Spanish achievement was only moderately related to either verbal or mathematics achievements. Noting that a majority of the students in the study were native Spanish speakers living in Metropolitan Los Angeles, the authors suggested that the students might see English and Spanish self-concepts as very distinct. Following from this reasoning, they proposed a post hoc model with Spanish, English, and mathematics self-concepts and achievements instead of the typical I/E model based on only English and Math constructs. Extending the logic of the I/E model, they demonstrated that: (a) Spanish achievement had a positive effect on Spanish self-concept, but negative effects on mathematics and English self-concepts, (b) mathematics had a positive effect on mathematics self-concept, but negative effects on English and Spanish self-concepts, and (c) English achievement had a positive effect on English self-concept, but negative effects on Math and Spanish self-concepts.

Marsh and Yeung (2001) concluded that the results provided strong support for the original I/E model based on math and verbal constructs, and a potentially important extension of the model when native and non-native languages were both included in the model. An important implication of the Marsh and Yeung (2001) study is the juxtaposition of the self-concepts of native and nonnative languages. Their results suggested that self-concepts in native and nonnative languages are likely to be very distinct from each other and from math self-concept, and to have distinct patterns of relations with corresponding measures of achievement.

Evaluation and Extension of the I/E Model in the Chinese Culture

In a large-scale longitudinal study, Marsh et al. (2001) tested the extension of the I/E model proposed by Marsh and Yeung (2001) by studying the juxtaposition of self-concept in the native (Chinese) and nonnative language (English) among the Chinese secondary students in Hong Kong. As the Chinese and English languages were both very important in the high school curriculum in the Hong Kong context, Marsh et al. argued that Hong Kong students might use English as an additional frame of reference in formulating their subject-specific self-concepts. Standardized achievement test scores were collected at Time 0 (pre-test, Grade 6, the year prior to the start of high school), Time 1 (Grade 7, the first year of high school), Time 2 (Grade 8), and Time 3 (Grade .9), while the self-concept questionnaire (SDQ-II) was administered at Time 2, Time 3, and Time 4 (Grade 10). Marsh et al. first evaluated tests of predictions based on the extended I/E model (Figure 6.1b) separately for each wave of data (Grades 8, 9, 10 at Time 2, 3 and 4). Consistent with a priori predictions, critical parameter estimates provided strong support for the I/E model in separate analyses of each of the three waves of data, with the following major findings:

1. Correlations among the Chinese, English, and Math self-concept scales were very small (correlations of –.07 to .13) and substantially less than correlations among corresponding Chinese, English, and Math achievement scores (correlations of .67 to .79);

2. Mathematics achievement had a substantial positive effect on Math self-concept (path coefficients of .63 to .79), but smaller negative effects on English self-concept and Chinese self-concept (path coefficients of –.35 to –.14);

3. English achievement had a substantial positive effect on English self-concept (path coefficients of .48 to .62), but smaller negative effects on Math self-concept and Chinese self-concept self-concepts (path coefficients of –.26 to –.10); and

4. Chinese achievement had a substantial positive effect on Chinese self-concept (path coefficients of .50 to .61), but smaller negative effects on Math self-concept and English self-concept (path coefficients of –.40 to –.06).

For these path coefficients that were critical for evaluating predictions of the I/E model (see Figure 6.1b), every path coefficient was statistically significant and in the predicted direction in each of the separate analyses of self-concept responses at Time 2, Time 3, and Time 4. These results provided very strong support for the extended I/E model and the stability of the effects over time.

Even stronger tests were the evaluation of the longitudinal effects of the I/E model across three waves (Time 2, Time 3, Time 4) of self-concept data. With this set of multi-wave self-concept data, it was possible to evaluate the direct and indirect effects of Time 0 achievement on subsequent self-concept (Time 2, Time 3, and Time 4). Results showed:

1. The effects of Time 0 achievement on Time 2 self-concept were the same as those involving only the Time 2 data as if there had been no intervening variables.

2. Even with the control of the effects of prior self-concept on subsequent self-concept (e.g., Time 2 self-concept on Time 3 self-concept), the direct effects of Time 0 achievement on subsequent self-concept in the longitudinal model were still significant and consistent with the predictions based on the I/E model that the effects of achievements on matching self-concepts (e.g., Time 0 mathematics achievement on Time 3 Math self-concept, +.25) were significantly positive whereas those on non-matching self-concepts (e.g., Time 0 mathematics achievement on Time 3 Chinese self-concept, −.14) were either significantly negative or nonsignificant. Hence, the effects of prior achievement in the three academic subjects on subsequent (e.g., Time 3) academic self-concepts—even after controlling the effects of prior (e.g., Time 2) self-concepts—still supported predictions based on the I/E model.

In summary, these findings provided very strong support for (1) the generalizability of the I/E model in the Chinese culture, (2) an important extension of previous I/E model by demonstrating the juxtaposition of native language (Chinese) and nonnative language (English) self-concepts, and (3) the long-term effects of the I/E model on subsequent subject-specific self-concepts.

THE JUXTAPOSITION OF CONTRAST AND ASSIMILATION (REFLECTED GLORY) EFFECTS IN SOCIAL COMPARISON

The Western Models

Big-Fish-Little-Pond-Effects

One of the perhaps quite unexpected findings in recent self-concept research is the negative effect (disadvantage) in attending high average-ability competitive schools. It has been shown that students attending high average-ability school have lower academic self-concept than those attending low average-ability ones after adjusting for individual differences in prior ability (e.g., Marsh, 1991; Marsh & Parker, 1984). Initially, this finding might seem illogical and unexpected, as one would generally expect benefits in attending high-ability schools. However, the results are explicable in terms of the social comparison theory or the "Frame of Reference Model" (Marsh & Parker, 1984).

Social comparison theory posits that individuals tend to evaluate themselves by comparing their ability or attributes with those of their classmates. They would choose other people in their immediate context as their group of reference, and in particular those who are close to them in that particular ability or attributes under consideration (Festinger, 1954). In general, comparison with others who have performed better than or are better-off than the self (upward comparisons) results in more negative affect and lower self-perception than comparison with others who have performed worse than or are worse-off than the self (downward comparison).

Based on the principles of social comparison, Marsh proposed the "Frame of Reference Model" to explain why students in high average-ability school have lower self-concept than their counterparts (with similar ability) in low average-ability school, after adjusting differences for individuals' ability (Marsh & Parker, 1984). It is posited that academic self-concept is derived from one's comparison of own ability with that of other members in one's group of reference. In the school settings, students generally use their classmates or schoolmates as their immediate group of reference. Thus, students' self-concept is determined by their perception of their own ability relative to that of their classmates or schoolmates. Marsh further predicted that for two equally able students attending schools of contrasting school-average ability, the one attending a high average-ability school would have less favorable self-evaluation than the one attending a low average-ability one (Marsh & Parker, 1984). Because students attending high average-ability schools are constantly comparing unfavorably their ability with other equally smart or even smarter classmates, they are thus more likely to have an average or even below average judgment on their own ability. On the contrary, students attending a low average-ability school have higher chances to perform better than their classmates and are more likely to have superior or more positive feelings on themselves. These predictions have been examined and supported in empirical studies (e.g., Marsh & Parker, 1984). This phenomenon that equally able students would have higher self-concept in low average-ability schools than those in high average-ability schools has been called the "Big-Fish-Little-Pond-Effect" (BFLPE, Marsh & Parker, 1984). Because the BFLPE is typically negative, it should, perhaps, be called the "little fish in a big pond" effect, but we retain the traditional BFLPE label.

Evidence for BFLPE has been accumulated from studies at different education levels using a wide variety of research methodologies in different countries (e.g., Marsh & Parker, 1984). The BFLPE is typically demonstrated as a negative effect of school-average ability on student's self-concept after controlling for students' ability. For example, Marsh and Parker (1984) specifically sampled two groups of Grade 6 students from schools with contrasting social economic background and academic ability within the same city. In a series of regression analyses, academic self-concept was regressed on individual ability, family SES and school-average SES/ability. Results showed that individuals' academic ability and family SES had positive effects on academic self-concept, whereas the school-average measures of SES/ability showed a negative effect on academic self-concept, indicating a net detrimental effect on self-concept in high-ability schools after controlling for the effects of individual differences in ability and family background.

It has been shown that the negative school-average effect can also be extended to other valuable outcome variables such as grade-point-average (GPA), and educational and occupational aspirations (Marsh, 1991). A number of studies demonstrated that the negative effects of school-average ability on educational aspiration, were mediated through students' GPA or academic self-concept. For example, in a very large, nationally representative sample of U.S. students, Marsh (1991) greatly expanded the range of outcome variables to include: academic and general self-concept, coursework selection, academic effort, educational and occupational aspirations, school grades, standardized test scores collected in the sophomore year and again in the senior years of high school; and college attendance and aspirations measured two years after high school graduation. The effects of attending higher-ability high schools were negative for almost all 23 outcomes and were not significantly positive for any outcome. Whereas some effects were small (e.g., standardized test scores), none were positive for this set of outcomes including many of the most frequently cited goals of education. Furthermore, there were additional negative effects during the last two years of high school beyond the already negative effects earlier in high school. In addition to academic self-concept, school average achievement had a substantial negative effect on educational and occupational aspirations—even two years after graduation from high school. Finally, substantial proportions of the negative effects of school-average ability on the entire set of academic outcomes were mediated by the negative BFLPE on academic self-concept.

Reflected Glory or Assimilation Effects

If students in high-ability schools compare their accomplishments with those of other high-ability classmates, their academic self-concept may decline—a typical contrast effect in social comparison. "There are a lot of pupils smarter than me in this school, and perhaps I am not so smart as I thought." However, there is also ample evidence showing that individuals may have a better self-perception through reflected glory, identification or association effects in social comparison. Individuals in the highly valued social groups are generally evaluated more positively by others and have better self-evaluation than members in the lower status social group (e.g., Cialdini & Richardson, 1980). Based partly on this theoretical perspective, Marsh (1993; also see Felson & Reed, 1986) argued that pupils in high-ability school might have an additional gain in their self-concept because of their memberships in a high-ability school—an assimilation effect in social comparison. "This school is highly selective and I am selected, so I must be very smart as well."

Both the counter-balancing negative contrast effects and positive assimilation effects are likely to affect self-concept so that the typical observed BFLPE is actually a net effect (Marsh, 1993). This implies that an assimilation effect may be operating even though contrast effects overshadow it. Furthermore, controlling for the positive assimilation effects by including relevant variables in the model should result in purer, more negative contrast effects. Felson and Reed (1986) made a related distinction, emphasizing that these effects should be considered simultaneously because they are likely to suppress each other, but lamented that survey studies have not included such controls.

McFarland and Buehler (1995) described BFLPE as a paradox as individuals in a high-status group (e.g., high-ability school) reported even lower self-concept than did equally able individuals in a low-status group (e.g., low-ability school). While the reflected glory effects would predict members in the high-status group to have higher self-concept, the BFLPE suggests the contrary. McFarland and Buehler argued that self-perception might be affected by how one valued his/her social group. They posited that people who valued their social group more strongly would be less susceptible to BFLPE in their reactions to performance feedback. In a series of laboratory studies, McFarland and Buehler (1995) showed that people who valued their group membership in a social group evaluated themselves less unfavorably when performed poorly in a high-ability group and evaluated themselves less favorably when performed well in a low-ability group. It appeared that people who valued their social group would take into consideration of the performance of their social group in self-evaluation and they are benefited from their good performance of their social group when they do poorly and take advantage of their individual performance when their group does badly.

McFarland and Buehler (1995) also posited that people from different cultures value their group membership differently. They argued that people from collectivistic culture would value their group membership in social group than do people from individualistic culture. Based on the classification method from Hofstede (1991), they classified university students from first and second generation Canadian with an Asian or Latin American heritage as collectivistic, and university students from North American and Europe as individualistic. McFarland and Buehler (1995) successfully demonstrated that students with a collectivistic cultural heritage feel more strongly about their group membership in social group and are less susceptible to BFLPE. Their study is important because it provides strong support for the juxtaposition of the contrast and assimilation effects in social comparison as well as the empirical evidence on the cultural differences in BFLPE.

Evaluation and Extension of the BFLPE Model in the Chinese Culture

In a large scale longitudinal study with over 10000 students following for 6 years, Marsh, Kong, and Hau (2000) tested the BFLPE in the Hong Kong Chinese context. First, the typical negative contrast effect in attending high-ability school was replicated in the Chinese cultural context. Then, the juxtaposition of the contrast and assimilation effects in attending high-ability school was examined. The study extended previous studies by operationalizing the potentially positive component in social comparison as "school status" and attempted to delineate this positive component from the negative contrast effects. The authors also speculated that the positive reflected glory effect may be particularly strong among Chinese who are quite concerned about their face (Ho, 1976). It is because people who are so concerned with face should be benefited more by being members of the high status group. Thus, it is possible and would be interesting to compare the positive and negative contextual effects on Chinese students' academic self-concept.

The negative contrast effect was demonstrated by studying the effects of school average pretest (Time 0, Grade 6) achievement on subsequent academic self-concept (Time 2 and Time 3 academic self-concept, Grades 8 and 9 respectively) after controlling for individuals' pretest achievement (Time 0 Ach). Consistent with the findings from Western studies, academic self-concept was significantly positively related to achievement and the effect of school-average achievement on Time 2 academic self-concept was negative after controlling the effects of prior achievement. Specifically, the negative effect of school-average achievement on T2 academic self-concept varied from −.22 (when only T0Ach was controlled) to −.24 (when T0Ach, T1Ach, and T2Ach were controlled). The pattern of results was similar for Time 3 academic self-concept.

As there were two waves of academic self-concept data, it was possible to evaluate the additional negative effects of school-average achievement at Time 3 beyond the negative effects at Time 2. Of critical importance, the negative effect of school-average achievement on Time 3 academic self-concept was still significantly negative (−.09 to −.07) even after controlling the negative effect of school-average achievement mediated by Time 2 self-concept. Hence, there were new, additional negative effects of school-average achievement on Time 3 self-concept beyond the negative effects at Time 2.

In summary, results provided clear support for the negative BFLPE in Hong Kong high schools. Not only were there negative BFLPEs for Time 2 and Time 3 academic self-concept considered separately, but the negative BFLPEs for Time 3 academic self-concept were larger than those that could be explained by the negative BFLPE already experienced at Time 2.

In order to demonstrate the juxtaposition of the contrast and the assimilation effects, Marsh et al. (2000) included a new measure, students' perceived school status to tap the potentially positive impacts on self-concept in attending high-ability schools. The construct validity of the measure was demonstrated by confirmatory factor analysis and its predictive validity was further explicated by its distinctive relationships with academic achievement and self-concept (see Marsh et al., 2000; for a more comprehensive description). With the inclusion of this construct, Marsh et al. (2000) were able to demonstrate the juxtaposition of the contrast and assimilation effects in the Chinese secondary school setting in Hong Kong. The supporting evidence was:

1. Perceived school status was highly correlated with school-average achievement (.56 to .60) and had a consistently positive correlation with academic self-concept.

2. The effect of perceived school status on Time 3 academic self-concept was positive (.17) and continued to be positive even after controlling for Time 2 self-concept (.09). In marked contrast, the effects of school-average achievement on Time 3 academic self-concept were substantially negative (−.33 to −.31). Most importantly, these

negative effects of school-average achievement were substantially more negative (–.33 to –.31) than in corresponding models that did not include school status (–.23 to –.21).

3. School status did not seem to have much effect—positive or negative—on Time 3 achievement beyond what could be explained by school-average achievement and prior achievement.

In summary, the large-scale study successfully replicated the Western BFLPE with the Chinese students in showing a negative net effect on self-concept of being studying in high average-ability schools. However, the large-scale study extended Western findings in disentangling the simultaneous positive (assimilation) and negative (contrast) effects in attending a high-ability school. The juxtaposition of the positive reflected glory assimilation effects of school status and the negative contrast effects of school-average achievement supported a priori predictions. Furthermore, also consistent with the a priori predictions, the inclusion of school status into models of academic self-concept resulted in the negative effects of school-average achievement becoming more negative. These suppression effects are consistent with theoretical predictions that the BFLPE is a net effect of the positive assimilation and negative contrast effects. Hence, when the positive assimilation effects are controlled by the inclusion of school status, the negative effect of school-average achievement becomes a more accurate measure of the negative contrast effects and subsequently school-average achievement effects become more negative.

CAUSAL RELATIONSHIP BETWEEN ACADEMIC SELF-CONCEPT AND ACHIEVEMENT

The Western Models

The causal relationship between academic achievement and self-concept is a theoretically and pragmatically important issue in self-concept research. In spite of its importance, this issue has not received sufficient evaluation. It has been posited that self-concept is formulated, at least in part, through self-attribution and evaluative feedback from significant others (Rosenberg, Schooler, & Schoenbach, 1989; Shavelson et al., 1976). Success in academic striving would probably result in positive feedback from significant others (e.g., teachers, classmates, & parents) and favorable self-attribution to competency. In contrast, failure in academic striving would probably lead to unfavorable judgment from others and negative self-attribution to competency. Thus, it is likely that academic self-concept is at least partially influenced by prior academic achievement. This position is in line with the skill development model, which posited that academic self-concept is primarily the consequence of academic achievement, and the best way to enhance self-concept is through skill development (Calsyn & Kenny, 1977).

On the other hand, students' self-evaluations of their own competence are a significant predictor of success expectation, persistence of effort, and motivation for academic striving and learning. For example, based on the self-worth theory, Covington (1992) has argued that many students fail to learn because of a lack of self-confidence and a fear of failure in academic striving. This is consistent with the argument of the self-enhancement model that self-concept is primarily the cause of academic achievement and an enhancement in self-concept would result in improvement in academic achievement (Calsyn & Kenny, 1977).

Reviews of the empirical studies prior to 1980 showed that the support for the skill development model and the self-enhancement model was equivocal. In Byrne's (1984) review of 23 studies claimed to tackle the causal predominance issue of self-concept and academic achievement, she found that almost half of the studies supported the skill development model while the other half of the studies stood for the self-enhancement model. However, she also noted that the cross-sectional design used in most of the existing studies failed to meet the temporal precedence in the determination of cause and, hence, were methodologically inadequate to test the causal ordering of achievement and self-concept.

In a review and critique of this review, Marsh (1990a, 1990c, 1993) also argued that much of this research was methodologically unsound and inconsistent with academic self-concept theory. He pointed out that researchers had perhaps misplaced the central focus on arguing for the "either-or" conclusion. He emphasized that it was widely accepted that prior academic achievement was a determinant of academic self-concept. Therefore, the critical question is whether there also exists a causal link from prior academic self-concept to subsequent achievement. The statistical significance and size of this path is of critical importance, rather than the relative strengths between self-concept and achievement. Marsh further argued that a more realistic compromise between the self-enhancement and skill-development models was a "reciprocal effects model" in which prior self-concept affects subsequent achievement and prior achievement affects subsequent self-concept. Marsh's reciprocal effects model has major implications for the importance placed on academic self-concept as a means of facilitating other desirable outcomes, as well as being an important outcome variable.

Byrne (1984) and Marsh (1990c) have specifically recommended essential requirements in research design for testing the causal ordering of self-concept and academic achievement. In brief, these included the use of: (a) a multiwave longitudinal design to establish the logical time precedence, (b) multiple indicators to infer latent constructs, and (c) structural equation modeling (SEM) to compare various competing models. In a systematic review of these methodologically more appropriate studies, Marsh and his colleagues found general support for reciprocal effects model (e.g., Helmke & van Aken, 1995; Hoge, Smit, & Crist, 1995; Marsh, 1990c; Marsh, Köeller, & Baumert, in press). In their review of this research, Marsh, Byrne, and Yeung (1999) called for the need of further research to pursue cultural differences in the reciprocal effects models and the application of multilevel modeling to evaluate the extent to which this support generalizes across different schools within a particular study.

In a two-wave longitudinal study, Yeung and Lee (1999) studied the academic self-concept and achievement of 511 Chinese high school students in southern China. As there was a clear temporal precedence of self-concept and achievement measures across the two waves (with a time span of six months), their study provided a reaonsable basis for the evaluation of the causal relationships between academic self-concept and academic achievement. Structural equation modelling showed that prior academic self-concept had positive effects on subsequent academic achievement and that prior academic achievement had positive effects on academic self-concept, controlling the effects of prior achievement and self-concept respectively. The results clearly supported the reciprocal effects model of academic self-concept and achievement.

Evaluation and Extension of the Reciprocal Effects Model in the Chinese Culture

Marsh et al. (2001) evaluated the causal ordering academic self-concept and academic achievement in a large-scale ($N = 10000$ students) longitudinal (4-year) study. Prior academic achievement (Time 0 Ach, Grade 6) had significant effects on subsequent academic self-concept at Time 2 and Time 3 (Grades 8 and 9). Importantly, the effects of prior achievement on Time 3 academic self-concept was also significant even controlling the effects of Time 2 academic self-concept. On the other hand, the effects of self-concept (Time 2 academic self-concept) on subsequent achievement (Time 3 achievement, Grade 9) were also positive even after controlling measures of prior achievement (Time 2 achievement, Grade 8). These results contributed to the growing body of research based on longitudinal path models, showing that academic self-concept and achievement were mutual causes of each other.

Using additional waves (6-year from Grade 6 to Grade 11) of self-concept and achievement data, Marsh, Hau and Kong (in press) re-examined the causal ordering of academic self-concept and achievement, and investigated the influence of language of instruction for Hong Kong Chinese students. The results clearly demonstrated the following characteristics:

1. Prior academic achievement had positive effects on subsequent academic self-concept after controlling for the effect of prior academic self-concept, and

2. Prior academic self-concept affected subsequent achievement beyond the effects of prior academic achievement.

The results provided strong support for a reciprocal effects model. Specifically, there were significant effects of prior achievement on subsequent measures of self-concept after controlling prior self-concept and of prior academic self-concept on subsequent achievement after controlling the effects of prior achievement. These results demonstrate that academic self-concept and achievement are mutually reinforcing constructs, providing strong support for the cross-cultural generalizability of the reciprocal effects model that heretofore has been based primarily on research in Western countries.

CONCLUSIONS

We began by asking the theoretical question of whether the Western self-concept models and measures are applicable to the Chinese context. This is an important research question in the multicultural context. For example, Chinese teachers and parents would like to know whether the self-concept of students studying in high average abilty schools is negatively affected in the same way as those in the western culture. So, we are interested in whether the cultural contexts have any effect on the universality of western self-concept models.

In this systematic review, we found that the psychometric properties of a Chinese version of SDQ-II are as strong as or even stronger than that of the original Australian (English) version. The results lent very strong support for the generalizability of the self-concept models and the SDQ-II measure in tapping the multidimensional self-concept of Chinese adolescents.

Empirical studies on the I/E model in the Chinese context provided supportive results consistent with the predictions based on the original I/E model. When the model was extended to include native and nonnative language self-concepts and achievement, the results were also consistent with the predictions based on the extended I/E model. More importantly, the juxtaposition of the native and nonnative language self-concepts was also nicely demonstrated. Furthermore, when the longitudinal I/E model was examined, it was found that the I/E model had surprisingly long-term and consistent influence on the formulation of subject-specific self-concepts. The results, of course, were also supportive to the I/E model. All these findings converged to support the cross cultural validity of the I/E model and represented an important theoretical extension to the original I/E model.

The support for the BFLPE in the Chinese Hong Kong context was also very strong. Not only the typical negative contrast effect was clearly demonstrated, but also the two counteracting components in BFLPE—the positive assimilation effect and the negative contrast effect—were successfully delineated and empirically demonstrated (Marsh et al., 2000). Because the results were nicely consistent with the predications based on the BFLPE, or in the broader perspective, the social comparison effect, the cross-cultural generalizability of the BFLPE were strongly supported.

Review on the causal relationships between academic self-concept and academic achievement in the Chinese context also provided supportive results to the growing body of evidence of the reciprocal effects model. Consistent with the previous studies in Western studies, academic self-concept and academic achievement were found to be mutually affecting each other.

In sum, the major findings in self-concept research with the Chinese students were consistent with those in Western studies and provided very strong support for the cross-cultural generalizability of self-concept research. Furthermore, when the original self-concept model was extended and evaluated in the Chinese context, the results were also consistent with the predictions based on the extended model. Taken together, the series of analyses demonstrate the robustness of the SDQ instruments and the universality of the self-concept models and theories in Chinese culture.

NOTE

Parts of the manuscript have been based on the first author's Ph.D. dissertation submitted to the Chinese Univeristy of Hong Kong and have been partially presented at the Self-Concept Theory, Research and Practice: Advances for the New Millennium—Inaugural Self-Concept Enhancement and Learning Faciliation (SELF) Research Centre International Conference, Sydney, Australia, October 5–6, 2000.

REFERENCES

Baumeister, R. F. (1986). *Public self and private self.* New York: Springer.
Bond, M. H. (1996). Chinese values. In M. H. Bond (Ed.), *The handbook of Chinese psychology* (pp.208–226). Hong Kong: Oxford.

Bong, M. (1998). Tests of the internal/external frames of reference model with subject-specific academic self-efficacy and frame-specific academic self-concepts. *Journal of Educational Psychology, 90*, 102–110.

Byrne, B. M. (1984). The general/academic self-concept network: A review of construct validation research. *Review of Educational Research, 54*, 427–456.

Calsyn, R., & Kenny, D. (1977). Self-concept of ability and perceived evaluations by others: Cause or effect of academic achievement? *Journal of Educational Psychology, 69*, 136–145.

Chan, D. W., & Lee, H. C. B. (1993). Dimensions of self-esteem and psychological symptoms among Chinese adolescents in Hong Kong. *Journal of Youth and Adolescence, 22*, 425–440.

Cheng, C. H.-K. (1996). Towards a cultural relevant model of self-concept for the Hong Kong Chinese. In J. Pandey, D. Sinha, & D. P. S. Bhawuk (Eds.), *Asian contributions to cross-cultural psychology* (pp. 235–254). New Delhi: Sage Publications.

Cheng, C. H.-K., & Watkins, D. (2000). Age and gender invariance of self-concept factor structure: An investigation of a newly developed Chinese self-concept instrument. *International Journal of Psychology, 35*, 186–193.

Cheung P. C., & Lau, S. (2001). A multi-perspective multi-domain model of self-concept: Structure and sources of self-concept knowledge. *Asian Journal of Social Psychology, 4*, 1–21.

Chung, C. H., & Watkins, D. (1992). Some evidence of the reliability and validity of a Chinese version of the Self Description Questionnaire. *Bulletin of the Hong Kong Psychological Society, 28–29*, 39–48.

Cialdini, R. B., & Richardson, K. D. (1980). Two indirect tactics of image management: Basking and blasting. *Journal of Personality and Social Psychology, 39*, 406–415.

Cousins, S. D. (1989). Cultural and self-presentation in Japan and the United States. *Journal of Personality and Social Psychology, 56*, 124–131.

Covington, M. V. (1992). *Making the grade: A self-worth perspective on motivation and school reform.* Cambridge, UK: Cambridge University.

Dhawan, N., Roseman, I. J., Naidu, R. K., Thapa, K., & Rettek, S. I. (1995). Self-concepts across two cultures: India and the United States. *Journal of Cross-Cultural Psychology, 26*, 606–621.

Felson, R. B., & Reed, M. D. (1986). Reference groups and self-appraisals of academic ability and performance. *Social Psychology Quarterly, 49*, 103–109.

Festinger, L. (1954). A theory of social comparison processes. *Human Relations, 7*, 117–140.

Fleming, J. S., & Courtney, B. E. (1984). The dimensionality of self-esteem: II. Hierarchical facet model for revised measurement scales. *Journal of Personality and Social Psychology, 46*, 404–421.

Harter, S. (1982). The perceived competence scale for children. *Child Development, 53*, 87–97.

Hau, K. T., & Salili, F. (1991). Structure and semantic differential placement of specific causes: academic causal attributions by Chinese Students in Hong Kong. *International Journal of Psychology, 26*, 175–193.

Hau, K. T., & Salili, F. (1996) Prediction of academic performance among Chinese students: Effort can compensate for lack of ability. *Organizational Behavior and Human Decision Processes, 65,* 83–94.

Hau, K. T., Kong, C. K., Marsh, H. W., & Cheng, Z. J. (2000). Chinese students' self-concept: Multidimensionality, big-fish-little-pond effects and casual ordering. Paper presented at American Educational Research Association Annual Meeting, New Orleans, April 24–28.

Helmke, A., & van Aken, M. A. G. (1995). The causal ordering of academic achievement and self-concept of ability during elementary school: A longitudinal study. *Journal of Educational Psychology, 87,* 624–637.

Ho, D. Y.-F. (1976). On the concept of face. *American Journal of Sociology, 81,* 867–884.

Hofstede, G. (1980). *Culture's consequences: International differences in work-related values.* Beverly Hills, CA: Sage.

Hofstede, G. (1991). *Culture and organizations.* London: McGraw-Hill.

Hoge, D. R., Smit, E. K., & Crist, J. T. (1995). Reciprocal effects of self-concept and academic achievement in sixth and seventh grade. *Journal of Youth and Adolescence, 24,* 295–314.

Kitayama, S., & Markus, H. R. (1995). Culture and self: Implications for internationalization psychology. In N. R. Goldberger, & J. B. Veroff (Eds.), *The culture and psychology reader* (pp.366–383). New York: New York University.

Lau, S. (1989). Sex role orientation and domains of self-esteem. *Sex Roles, 21,* 415–422.

Lau, S. (1990). Crisis and vulnerability in adolescent development. *Journal of Youth and Adolescence, 19,* 111–131.

Lau, S., & Leung, K. (1992). Relations with parents and school and Chinese adolescents' self-concept, delinquency, and academic performance. *British Journal of Education Psychology, 62,* 21–30.

Leung, K., & Lau, S. (1989). Effects of self-concept and perceived disapproval of delinquent behavior in school children. *Journal of Youth and Adolescence, 18,* 345–359.

Leung, J. P., & Leung, K. (1992). Life satisfaction, self-concept, and relationship with parents in adolescence. *Journal of Youth and Adolescence, 21,* 653–665.

Ma, V., & Schoeneman, T. J. (1997). Individual versus collectivism: A comparison of Kenyan and American self-concepts. *Basic and Applied Social Psychology, 19,* 261–273.

Markus, H. R., & Kitayama, S. (1991). Culture and the self: Implications for cognition, emotion, and motivation. *Psychological Review, 98,* 224–253.

Markus, H. R., & Kitayama, S. (1998). The cultural psychology of personality. *Journal of Cross-Cultural Psychology, 29,* 63–87.

Marsh, H. W. (1986). Verbal and math self-concepts: An internal/external frame of reference model. *American Educational Research Journal, 23,* 129–149.

Marsh, H. W. (1990a). A multidimensional, hierarchical self-concept: Theoretical and empirical justification. *Educational Psychology Review, 2,* 77–172.

Marsh, H. W. (1990b). *Self description questionnaire (SDQ) II: A theoretical and empirical basis for the measurement of multiple dimensions of adolescent self-concept: An interim test manual and a research monograph.* San Antonio, TX: The Psychological Corporation.

Marsh, H. M. (1990c). The causal ordering of academic self-concept and academic achievement: A multiwave, longitudinal path analysis. *Journal of Educational Psychology, 82,* 646–656.

Marsh, H. W. (1991). Failure of high-ability high schools to deliver academic benefits commensurate with their students' ability levels. *American Educational Research Journal, 28,* 445–480.

Marsh, H. W. (1993). Academic self-concept: Theory, measurement, and research. In J. Suls (Ed.), *Psychological perspective on the self* (Vol. 4). Hillsdale, NJ: Erlbaum.

Marsh, H. W., Byrne, B. M., & Shavelson, R. J. (1992). A multidimensional, hierarchical self-concept. In T. M. Brinthaupt & R. P. Lipka (Eds.), *The self: definitional and methodological issues* (pp. 44–95). New York: State University of New York.

Marsh, H. W., Byrne, B.M., & Yeung, A.S. (1999). Causal ordering of academic self-concept and achievement: Reanalysis of a pioneering study and revised recommendations. *Educational Psychologist, 34,* 154–157.

Marsh, H. W., & Craven, R. (1997). Academic self-concept: Beyond the dustbowl. In G. Phye (Ed.), *Handbook of classroom assessment: Learning, achievement, and adjustment* (pp. 131–198). Orlando, FL: Academic Press.

Marsh, H. W., & Hattie, J. (1996). Theoretical perspectives on the structure of self-concept. In B. A. Bracken (Ed.), *Handbook of self-concept: Developmental, social and clinical considerations* (pp.38–90). New York: Wiley.

Marsh, H. W., Hau, K. T., & Kong, C. K. (2000). Late immersion and language of instruction (English vs. Chinese) in Hong Kong high schools: Achievement growth in language and nonlanguage subjects. *Harvard Educational Review, 70,* 302–346.

Marsh, H. W., Hau, K.T., & Kong, C. K. (in press). Multilevel causal ordering of academic self-concept and achievement: influence of language of instruction (English vs. Chinese) for Hong Kong students. *American Educational Research Journal.*

Marsh, H. W. & Köeller, O. (in review). Unification of two theoretical models of relations between academic self-concept and achievement: A cross-cultural comparison between East and West German students.

Marsh, H. W., Koeller, O., & Baumert, J. (in press). Reunification of East and West German school systems: Longitudinal multilevel modeling study of the big fish little pond effect on academic self-concept. *American Educational Research Journal.*

Marsh, H. W., Kong, C. K., & Hau, K. T. (2000). Longitudinal multilevel modeling of Big-Fish-Little-Pond-Effect on academic self-concept: Counterbalancing social comparison and reflected glory effects in Hong Kong high schools. *Journal of Personality and Social Psychology, 78,* 337–349.

Marsh, H. W., Kong, C. K., & Hau, K. T. (2001). Extension of the internal/external frame of reference model of self-concept formation: Importance of native and nonnative languages for Chinese students. *Journal of Educational Psychology, 93,* 543–553.

Marsh, H. W., & O'Neill, R. (1984). Self-Description Questionnaire III: The construct validity of multidimensional self-concept ratings by late adolescents. *Journal of Educational Measurement, 21*, 153–174.

Marsh, H. W., & Parker, J. (1984). Determinants of student self-concept: Is it better to be a relatively large fish in a small pond even if you don't learn swim as well? *Journal of Personality and Social Psychology, 47*, 213–231.

Marsh, H. W., Parker, J., & Barnes, J. (1985). Multidimensional adolescent self-concepts: Their relationship to age, sex, and academic measures. *American Educational Research Journal, 22*, 422–444.

Marsh, H. M., Parker, J., & Smith, I. D. (1983). Preadolescent self-concept: Its relation to self-concept as inferred by teachers and to academic ability. *British Journal of Educational Psychology, 53*, 60–78.

Marsh, H. W., & Shavelson, R. J. (1985). Self-concept: Its multifaceted, hierarchical structure. *Educational Psychologist, 20*, 107–123.

Marsh, H. W., & Yeung, A. S. (2001). An extension of the internal/external frame of reference model: A response to Bong (1998). *Multivariate Behavioral Research, 36*, 389–420.

McFarland, C., & Buehler, R. (1995). Collective self-esteem as a moderator of the frog-pond effect in reactions to performance feedback. *Journal of Personality and Social Psychology, 68*, 1055–1070.

Rosenberg, M., Schooler, C., & Schoenbach, C. (1989). Self-esteem and adolescent problems: Modeling reciprocal effects. *American Sociological Review, 54*, 1004–1018.

Shavelson, R. J., & Bolus, R. (1982). Self-concept: The interplay of theory and methods. *Journal of Educational Psychology, 74*, 3–17.

Shavelson, R. J., Hubner, J. J., & Stanton, G. C. (1976). Validation of construct interpretations. *Review of Educational Research, 46*, 407–441.

Skaalvik, E. M., & Rankin, R. J. (1995). A test of the internal/external frame of reference model at different levels of math and verbal self-perception. *American Educational Research Journal, 35*, 161–184.

Triandis, H. C. (1989). The self and social behavior in different cultural contexts. *Psychological Review, 96*, 506–520.

Watkins, D. (2000). *The nature of self-conception: Findings of a crsoss-cultural research program* (pp.108–117). In R. G. Craven & H. W. Marsh (Eds.), Collected papers of the inaugural self-concept enhancement and learning faciliation (SELF) research centre international conference, Sydeny, Australia, October 5–6.

Watkins, D., Alande, A., Fleming, J., Ismail, M., Lefner, K., Regmi, M., Watson, S., Yu, J., Adair, J., Cheng, C., Gerong, A., McInerney, D., Mpofu, E., Singh-Sengupta, S., &Wondimu, H. (1998). Cultural dimensions, gender, and the nature of self-concept: A fourteen-country study. *International Journal of Psychology, 33*, 17–31.

Watkins, D., & Dong, Q. (1994). Assessing the self-esteem of Chinese school children. *Educational Psychology, 14*, 129–137.

Watkins, D., Dong, Q., & Xia, Y. (1995). Towards the validation of a Chinese version of the self-descriptive questionnaire–1. *Psychologia, 38*, 22–30.

Yang, C. F. (1991). A review of studies on self in Hong Kong and Taiwan: Reflections and future prospects (in Chinese). In C. F. Yang & H. S. R. Kao (Eds.), *Chinese and Chinese heart* (pp. 15–92) (in Chinese). Taipei, Taiwan: Yuan Liu.

Yeung, A. S., & Lee F. L. (1999). Self-concept of high school students in China: Confirmatory factor analysis of longitudinal data. *Educational and Psychological Measurement, 59,* 431–450.

CHAPTER 7

DOES KNOWLEDGE EXIST IF NOBODY KNOWS ABOUT IT?

Exploring Eastern and Western Ontologies of Knowledge

Márta Fülöp and Ference Marton

INTRODUCTION

There seems to be a growing awareness of the fact that teaching is a cultural activity (see, for instance, Stigler & Hiebert, 1999). This means that educational systems, and even more the teaching practices within them, vary with the culture in which they are embedded. During the last two decades empirical research revealed differences *within* cultures as regards assumptions about learning and knowledge, ontological and epistemological commitments, underlying observed difference in educational achievements. Frequently, the different conceptions and beliefs have been interpreted in terms of hierarchical structures: some conceptions and some beliefs are seen as more powerful than others in relation to certain criteria of learning (see, for instance, Perry, 1970; Marton, Dall'Alba, & Beaty, 1993). But what if comparisons are made across different cultures:

Teaching, Learning, and Motivation in a Multicultural Context, pages 147–169
Copyright © 2003 by Information Age Publishing

147

can they all be projected into the same hierarchical structure of categories or do we find different, culturally unique categories in different places, which cannot be ordered preferentially in relation to each other. Certain findings indicate this to be the case in some instances at least (see, for instance, Paine, 1990, Marton, Dall'Alba, & Tse, 1996).

These days we witness increasingly the emergence of the multicultural classrooms inhabited by children with varying cultural backgrounds, with at least in part non-overlapping epistemological beliefs and assumptions about learning. This has certainly important pedagogical implications and if we want to find out what we can expect in multicultural classrooms we have to explore the cultural variation in relevant aspects. This is exactly what we are trying to do in this chapter.

EPISTEMOLOGICAL AND ONTOLOGICAL BELIEFS

During the past decade there has been a growing attention to those critical forces that exert significant influence on learning and teaching, but which are not readily identifiable, because they exist as implicit beliefs or concepts. Students' beliefs about knowledge are part of this powerful framework (Alexander et al., 1998). Epistemological and ontological beliefs are deeply rooted, but tacitly held views of the world (Alexander, 1998). They are beliefs about the nature and existence of knowledge, and about the process of acquiring it (Elliott & Chan, 1998). They are "socially shared intuitions" (Jehng, Johnson, & Anderson, 1993, p. 24) or implicit assumptions held by learners about the source and certainty of knowledge and about the ways to obtain knowledge (Youn, 1999) or they are simply personal theories of knowledge (Kvale, 1998).

Educational philosophers and researchers emphasize the force that epistemological beliefs have on individual thoughts and actions (Alexander, 1998). More specifically, students' beliefs about the nature of knowledge and learning or their personal epistemologies have become a study of interest primarily because of the assumption that they affect students' learning outcomes (Schommer, Crouse, & Rhodes, 1992).

One of the pioneers in the field was Perry (1968) who used in depth interviews to explore students' epistemological beliefs, and identified changes during college years from dualist to relativistic views and further on to personal commitment within relativism. Schommer (1990) who renewed the research on beliefs about the nature of knowledge had the hypothesis that they are far too complex to be captured in a single dimension. She constructed a questionnaire that was intended to capture the more complex and multidimensional nature of beliefs. Studies carried out with the 63-item Epistemological Belief Questionnaire indicated that epistemological beliefs are indeed related to certain aspects of students' learning, like their persistence, active inquiry, integration of information and coping with complex domains (see review by Schommer, 1994). Students seem to have beliefs about learning that may facilitate or hinder conceptual change (Hofer & Pintrich, 1997). The interaction of epistemological beliefs with achievement is also reported by many others using Schommer's questionnaire. For instance Windschitl and Andre (1998) found that students with more sophisticated epistemological beliefs performed better in a learning environment that allowed free intellectual discovery.

The bulk of the work on epistemological beliefs has been undertaken in the United States with white, middle-class university students. It is therefore important to determine if there are differences in research findings from one context to another and whether the assumptions behind much of the research in one context holds true in another. Findings from other research in other fields suggest that culture plays an important role in forming individuals' perception about knowledge (Alexander & Dochy, 1995).

The interest turned towards Asian students' epistemological beliefs not only because they represent a potentially different culture, but also because of the rapidly growing interest to explain the outstanding academic achievement of Asian students, mostly Japanese and Chinese (Stevenson et al., 1985, 1992, 1993, 1997, 1998). However, most of the studies concentrated on the role of academic and cognitive abilities (Stevenson, 1985), mathematics achievement (Stevenson, 1987), personality factors like motivation (Stevenson, 1993) or the teaching methods (Stigler et al., 1991, 2000).

Alexander et al. (1998) calls attention to the lack of insights about how the epistemological views of individuals from Asian cultures might differ from the Americans, and what kind of explanatory function they might have in Asian students' outstanding academic achievement. There is now a growing interest in studying epistemological beliefs in non-Western countries.

Those researchers who first turned towards this topic used Schommer's (1990) existing Epistemological Beliefs Questionnaire and found that her findings and factor structure gained from white middle-class respondents were not replicable in Hong Kong Chinese (Elliott & Chan, 1998) context. Youn (1999) compared students from the United States and Korea using his own questionnaire. While in the U.S. sample the factor structure he obtained was conceptually consistent with the one identified earlier by Jehng et al. (1993) the Korean sample did not display the same conceptual consistency and the collectivistic values of Korean students were reflected in their views on knowledge and learning, indicating that culture might significantly influence epistemological beliefs. It seemed that one cannot use the same questionnaire in different cultures, because different aspects might be in the foreground. This called attention to the need for explorative, qualitative research in the field.

Alexander et al. (1998) compared how students and teachers in Singapore and the United States conceptualize knowledge and beliefs. Their purpose was to provide an opportunity to the respondents to present the various ways in which they conceptualize and experience knowledge and beliefs in more versatile ways. They therefore made use of a mixed method consisting of graphic depiction of the students' potential beliefs followed by an open-ended questionnaire. Their suggestions were that tapping into conceptions of knowledge, without concomitant consideration of meta-beliefs, offers an incomplete picture about conceptual change or learning.

This line of work is related to the research on conceptions of learning, that are similar to epistemological beliefs, but the research originates, however, from a very different qualitative research tradition, phenomenography (Marton et al., 1993). Conceptions of learning are also considered to be related to learning outcomes (Marton et al., 1992, 1997; Watkins et al., 1991; Watkins & Biggs, 1996). Purdie et al. (1996) based her research on phenomenography when she examined differences between Australian and Japanese secondary school students' conceptions of learning, with a questionnaire with open-ended questions. She found that contrary to the stereotypical expectations Japanese students view learning from a much broader perspective. For them learning is not only related to what happens at school, it is also seen as a lifelong, experiential process leading to personal fulfilment.

The relatively new qualitative research on epistemological beliefs and conceptions of learning is related to the trend in social psychology to look at different phenomena from the cultural point of view. Researchers pursuing a cultural perspective seek to understand the various relations that may exist between the sociocultural and the individual, and to analyze the person as a cultural participant who is simultaneously a social construction and a social constructor of experience (Markus, Kitayama, & Heiman, 1998). In the past 50 years European and American psychology and education have been based on a set of largely unexamined ontological assumptions about the meaning of a person, the meaning of the self or even the meaning of knowledge. Differences in ontological assumptions are likely to be the source of many of the cultural differences being observed and require direct examination (Markus, Kitayama, & Heiman, 1998).

Cultural psychology so far differentiates between two different concepts of man. The concept of person as a seemingly separate and private store of thoughts, rooted in the ontological tradition of Cartesian split between mind and body, self and others, cognitive and affective is characteristic of the Western way of thinking. The "obvious" and "objective" reality of the individual, which is a conceptual consequence of an individualist notion of the person, implies the view that the social world is separate and "out there" and it exists independently from the perceiver, just as does knowledge. Western concepts of knowledge and learning assume the idea of a stable, objective world that once acquired, functions independently from their social context. The powerful ideological context of individualism affords and reinforces the separation between mind and knowledge (inside) on the one hand and the social world (outside) on the other hand. This is in accordance with the Western independent self concept based on individualism, stating that once somebody has a stable identity it is autonomous and decontextualized. In contrast to this, a number of studies in non-Western cultures for example, India and East-Asia (Markus, Kitayama, & Heiman, 1998) revealed that many Asian cultural groups emphasize interdependence of the individual with the collective. They have a non-Cartesian epistemology and they consider all of the basic cognitive processes interpersonal, societal and collective phenomena as well (Markus & Kitayama, 1994). Youn (1999) found, for instance, that Koeran students' beliefs about learning do involve the self and their educational level was positively related with their interdependent self-construal, but negatively with their independent self-construal.

Dahlin and Regmi's (2000) investigation was the first cross-cultural study about the question of the *mode of existence of knowledge* using a qualitative research approach comparing Swedish and Nepalese students' ontologies of knowledge. "Ontology of knowledge" refers to basic assumptions or beliefs about the mode of existence of knowledge. Dahlin and Regmi (2000) found when comparing the notions of students from the two different cultures, knowledge is often seen in Nepal as having a social mode of existence, namely that it exists only if it is communicated and used in society, while in Sweden it is seen as mainly personal, that is, it is enough if the individual is aware of possessing it.

These results alerted us to the possibility making a comparison with ontologies of knowledge. It is well known that learning and knowledge have a special, high value in Japanese culture and society. However, there has been only scattered research, like for instance Purdie's (1995, 1996), on how Japanese students think about learning and knowledge.

The exploratory research presented below, focuses mainly on Japanese students' concepts on the nature of knowledge and their different ways of thinking about its mode of existence. It is embedded in three research specializations: First, the rather recent qualitative research on epistemological beliefs about the nature of knowledge and about the ways in which it is acquired. Second, the perspective of cultural psychology suggesting that beliefs about knowledge and its acquisition are cultural. Third, the growing interest in studying learning and teaching processes in Asia, especially among Chinese and Japanese. The direct forerunner of this research is

Dahlin and Regmi's study and the goal was to explore how Japanese students think about the nature of knowledge and its mode of existence in comparison with the Swedish and Nepalese. In terms of economic development Japan, with its second largest economy in the world, is rather similar to Sweden, and is a large contrast to Nepal being one of the poorest countries in the world. Japanese are very successful in their studies in international comparisons, Nepalese students are not. However, in contrast to Sweden, Japan is considered to be a group oriented society (Nakane, 1970), the Japanese self concept is more interdependent, emphasizing the basic relatedness of the self to others, than independent (Markus & Kitayama, 1991, 1994). Both Japanese and Nepalese are considered to be more collectivistic than individualistic (Hofstede, 1980; Triandis et al., 1994). In this respect Japanese students can thus be expected to have beliefs about knowledge which are more similar to Nepalese than to Swedish beliefs.

A STUDY OF JAPANESE ONTOLOGIES OS KNOWLEDGE

The study that we are reporting and comparing with Dahlin and Regmi's (2000) study in this chapter is an exploratory study in the strongest sense of the word. What we could hope for at best was to come up with conjecture sufficiently interesting.

As the aim of Dahlin and Regmi was to reveal implicit beliefs and concepts they had to find an alternative and creative method to stimulate individual's reflection about those not easily available systems of beliefs. It had to be a tool that engages students in a discussion that unveils their ideas on the nature of knowledge. Therefore they decided to engage in an in-depth interview with the participants about a riddle, because it seemed to be a good way to explore different beliefs that otherwise could have been approached only in a very abstract way. Through the concrete story, an otherwise very abstract problem became approachable. The riddle served as a possible trigger and was followed up by the interviewer.

The interview itself was a phenomenographic one (Marton & Booth, 1997), that is, a type of clinical interview, which goes deeply into how each subject perceives the phenomena of interest. It is a method embedded into the phenomenographic approach that has a so called second order perspective, where the emphasis is on trying to reveal the qualitatively different ways in which people experience or conceptualise various phenomena in the world around them (Marton, 1981).

In our exploratory study conducted in Japan with seven university students majoring in different subjects (economics, physics, English, Psychology) we adopted the riddle from Dahlin and Regmi (2000) in their comparison of Swedish and Nepalese ontologies of knowledge. The title of the story is: "The story of the buried book" and it is a metaphor about the nature of knowledge and knowing. The story was introduced by the following instruction: "Now I would like to read a riddle to you. Afterwards you can read it yourself. There are no right answers to the questions the story poses. I am just interested in finding out about your way of thinking and reasoning about it."

After reading the story there was an individual in-depth interview with respondents about their thoughts in connection with the story. The interviews were carried out in English. It is commonly acknowledged that interviews, particularly of the character used here, are best conducted in the respondent's mother tongue. This was, however, not possible and therefore we chose students who had a good command of English. Using English maybe reduced the sensitivity of the discourse, but the interviewer lived in Japan at the time of the data collection and this gave her a deeper understanding of the culture and ways of thinking.

The interviews were transcribed verbatim and analyzed according to penomenograhy. Our guiding idea was that the system of thoughts concerning "existence" and "knowledge" are not just metaphysical by-products, but instead, they constitute a framework of lived experience and might be productively analyzed In the analysis we registered what kind of answer the subjects gave to the final question and what kind of explanation they gave to support it. We were looking for similarities and differences in terms of structure and content between the answers given by the students in order to arrive at a description of variations in the concepts expressed. Every statement that was of direct relevance to the concept being investigated was collected and compared with each other. From this analysis the qualitatively different views of the nature of knowledge gradually became visible.

The categories in terms of which we made sense of the participants' differing ideas were fully compatible with Dahlin and Regmi's (2000) system of categories. In this chapter we make comparisons between the participants in our study and the two groups of participants in their study. We make distinctions in these comparisons between the presence and absence of the conceptions captured by the categories, and occasionally between the most frequent conception and others for a certain group.

The Riddle: The Story of the Buried Book

Once upon a time there was a scholar who had wrestled with one big question the whole of her life. Eventually she found the answer. She sat a day and night in her chamber and wrote and wrote. She wrote an entire book in the end with everything in it what, she knew. She laid down the book in a box, which was not only water- but also air-tight. Then she walked out into the forest and buried the box with the book in it. She dragged herself home, lay down on her bed and died—happy and at peace. Her life was completed.

Can we say that her knowledge—that which the scholar so energetically wrote down in her book—survived her?

The dialogues following this question in the individual in-depth interviews were transcribed and analyzed in accordance with what was said above. We found important differences in the ways of reasoning among the participating students in three respects: (1) The existence of knowledge in the book; (2) What makes knowledge exist in general; and (3) The moral aspects of knowledge. We tried to capture the variation within each one of these dimension in terms of qualitatively different categories corresponding to qualitatively different meanings.

The Existence of Knowledge

Although according to all the Japanese students the knowledge itself that is in the book buried under the ground is non-existent, there were two qualitatively different ways to express this.

1. the knowledge is lost
2. the knowledge exists in material sense, but not in a human sense.

The Knowledge is Lost

Most of the Japanese students (all but one), conceive of the knowledge in the buried book as not existent in *any form*.

> Respondent: *"Her knowledge is lost ... I don't think that her knowledge has existed from the point she buried the book"* (Int.2.)[2]

Knowledge Exists in Material, but not in a Human Sense

One student differentiates between material or objective existence on the one hand and human or social existence, on the other and claims that knowledge does exist in the material sense.

> R: *"Yes, I think so. If the box is opened by someone and the book is exposed to someone and people can know the content of the book*

then that book exists. But in this case the book is just buried in the ground and no one can see it or even touch it. It is true that the book exists but no one can recognize the existence of the book. So..so... in material meaning it exists, but among people it doesn't exist. How can I say?"

Interviewer (I): *"According to your answer something exists in the human sense if it can be recognized by the human mind...."*

R: *"Yes......I think there are two sorts of existence..."*

I: *"How would you define them?"*

R: *(laughing) "I did not name them, but perhaps material existence and human existence or mind existence? Or mental existence?" (Int. 3.)*

If we compare the results of our separate analysis with Dahlin and Regmi's (2000) we find certain similarities and differences. The most striking difference is that most of the Swedes answered "yes" to the main question and said that knowledge exists in the book, and in this sense survives her. This means that knowledge can exist outside the learner's mind, the book contains the knowledge and the text has an autonomous existence.

Just the contrary, all but one of the Japanese and ninety percent of the Nepalese considered the knowledge in the hidden book as being completely lost.

The Swedes had two different concepts about the existence of the knowledge. A smaller group of respondents stated that the "Knowledge exists in the book in the same form as it existed in the author's mind." This view existed neither among the Japanese nor among

Table 7.1. The Existence of the Knowledge

Category	Japanese	Napalese	Swedish
Knowledge exists in the book.	O	O	X
Knowledge exists in material, but not human sense/ exits in a radically different form.	X	X	X The majority of Swedes gave this answer.
Knowledge does not exist. No form of knowledge is in the book.	X The majority of Japanese gave this answer.	X The majority of Nepalese gave this answer.	X
The roots of knowledge still exist in the surrounding world.	O	X	X

Note: O means that there was no such answer. X means that there was such answer.

the Nepalese. The majority of the Swedish students had the idea that "Knowledge exists in the book, but in a radically different form" (Dahlin & Regmi, 2000). Those Asians who did not consider the knowledge completely lost shared this latter concept.

Within this view the students made a distinction between objective, however "useless" existence and existence that is "relevant" in the human mind or brain, stating that "Knowledge exists in the book in the material sense, but does not exist in the human sense." Dahlin and Regmi (2000) meant that these students differentiate between the "personal" and the "social" mode of existence of knowledge.

There were Swedes and Nepalese, but no Japanese students saying that the roots of the knowledge still exist in the surrounding world. This means that the knowledge that has gone lost can be re-created by other people now or in the future.

NECESSARY CONDITIONS FOR KNOWLEDGE TO EXIST

Most Japanese and Nepalese students believe that knowledge does not exist in an objective, material sense: it is essentially social and socially constructed. In order to become knowledge it must be the result of an interaction between the person who produced it and other persons, the group and the society. Knowledge is understood as something that is socially defined as knowledge and that has significance for the society. Only in this way does knowledge exist and it has meaning that is fundamentally relational and is a result of joint efforts between people, rather than a result of an individual's journey through an impersonal and objective world. According to these students the purpose and also the result of learning is always something social. Therefore the knowledge in the book is non-existent in the human sense, but they had qualitatively different requirements about what it takes to make knowledge existent. This was also true for the Swedish participants in Dahlin and Regmi's (2000) study who did not think that knowledge exists in the book itself. We found three different concepts:

Knowledge Exists if it is Shared

According to this concept, if somebody shares his/her knowledge with others, the knowledge comes into being and materialises itself in the human world.

> R: "I think if she didn't show it to anybody it was just a waste of time..."
> I: "You mean that the knowledge disappeared?"
> R: "Yes." (Int. 6.)

Knowledge Exists if it is not only Shared, but also Reflected Upon and Understood

According to this view it is not enough to share a kind of knowledge it must be understood by others, otherwise it doesn't exist as knowledge just as "noise."

> R: "It exists to those people who are interested in it. Who are interested in this topic. I mean there can be something very important in that book, in case nobody is really interested in it, then it doesn't exist even if it exists. Even if it is not buried. The information in it is worthless and becomes nothing. Like rubbish." (Int. 7)

Or

> R: "As a scholar she found some answer....If I were a scholar I would probably show it to other people....I mean that knowledge. I would like to get some good reflection from others. But she hid and put the answer into a box. ....Normally people die, but their knowledge does not die with them, that can be still developed after their death. But in this case her knowledge cannot develop...That knowledge existed just for her." (Int.5)

One of the subjects speaks about existence in a broader sense and emphasizes that personal existence, just like the existence of knowledge can't be possible without others reflecting on us.

> R: "Hm...This is philosophical.....It is very difficult, but when I was 15 or 16 or 17, I thought about the same question. A very basic question. What does "exist" mean for me? What is the meaning of it? I wondered, what I am being for. Am I for my parents or am I for my lover or my future children? I couldn't find any answer and still I managed to live until now.....Existence.....but if I am the only person in the world I can't define me, I can't find my existence in this world. But there are people around so I can communicate with them, then I can tell who I am: I am such a kind of person and I should do this and that..."
>
> I: "It is very interesting what you say, because the question you put yourself is similar to the one we are talking about...... You asked: 'Do I exist for my parents, do I exist for my future lover, or for my children?' It is always a question that places you into a relationship with somebody."
>
> R: "Yes, it is."
>
> I: "Your life is 'for' somebody. It seems that your existence is justified by others. Do you exist for yourself?"

> S: *"I think it is also important, but if I think that way, I think it is difficult to define myself. So it is easier to think that I live for others, I live for this company or I live for this spouse or for my children. It is easier. But I know I have to live for myself not for others. But if I sometimes think that way I lose my way…(Int. 3.)"*

Knowledge Exists if it Contributes to Society and Improves It

This concept puts the existence of knowledge into an even wider social perspective. Sharing, and understanding in a rather narrow interpersonal framework are all important, but in themselves are not enough. Knowledge has to contribute to the development of the wider community, the society.

> R: *"Not just share it, but share a knowledge that can be used for…improvement….*
> *The academic thing or knowledge must be a thing that has to be used for the society. If the knowledge is not useful for the society, is not for the sake of the society, it is totally meaningless……Knowledge must be something that can improve our society….make people happier…..The reason we exist is that we must be useful for the society. It was unnecessary for this scientist to live in the world. Her life and death is meaningless."*
> (Int.1.)

Or

> S: *"I think it was buried not only in the material meaning, but buried anyway. It did not appear to anyone…I think she should have given that knowledge at least to someone who can contribute with at least some parts of it to society."* (Int. 4.)

The Swedes used one explanation: "if it is understood," the Nepalese two: "if it is understood" and "if it contributes to society," and the Japanese three that seemed to represent different levels of the social nature of knowledge from simple sharing via understanding to contribution to the society.

Table 7.2.   Concepts on what makes knowledge existent

Concept	Japanese	Nepalese	Swedes
Sharing	X	O	O
Understanding	X	X	X
Contribution to the society	X	X	O

Note: O means that there was no such concept. X means that there was such concept.

KNOWLEDGE IS A MORAL RESPONSIBILITY

Just like the Nepalese students in Dahlin and Regmi's study (2000), the Japanese students in this research also have some moral concerns in connection with the riddle. Sharing and distribution of the knowledge is not only a self-evident "cognitive" imperative for them, but also a kind of moral responsibility and an act that causes positive emotions.

> R: *"Do I understand well that her behavior makes her happy?"*— asks one of the students concerning the scholar who buried her book. She is puzzled, does not want to believe that something like that can happen.
> R: *"If I were her, I wouldn't do that...I cannot understand why she is satisfied with her behavior."* (Int.5.)

Or

> R: *"If I were her I wouldn't do that. Because if I had a big knowledge and I knew a lot of things I wouldn't write a book and take it into the forest and bury it...I would talk about it or teach it to someone. If I had children I would give them."* (Int.2.)

Not sharing someone's knowledge is not an acceptable individual choice, it means avoiding the moral commitment towards others and society. This idea is also present when these students speak about the significance of studying.

> R: *"Studying for me right now means the opportunity to bring back something to society. Maybe if I study right now and gain more knowledge and I learn new material and new things then I can bring back some new things to society. That is why I study now....Because my definition of studying is that I have to contribute with something to society..."* (Int.4.)

Neither Japanese, nor Nepalese students understand how somebody can be happy with finding out something, if it is not shared with other people and the society. According to both Asian groups knowledge is moral responsibility, it exists in order to be shared among people and used in society, in other words the mode of existence of knowledge is essentially social.

The concept of knowledge as something that is essentially beneficial for the society is in close connection with the central importance of personal obligation to the society in the Japanese way of thinking (Rosenberger, 1992). It seems that Asian students (e.g., Malaysian) in general focus more on the moral aspects of learning and knowledge (Wan Ali, 1996) than do Western students. Purdie et al. (1996) showed that Japanese students consider learning as a moral duty more often than for example, Australians. The Nepalese consider it to be a religious obligation to disseminate knowledge and teach others if one knows something (Dahlin & Regmi, 2000). This aspect did not appear in the interviews with the Swedish respondents.

HIDDEN CULTURAL ASSUMPTIONS UNDERLYING THE RESEARCH METHODOLOGY

By analyzing the students' answers, it became obvious that the riddle itself was a culturally biased story. We realized that the "story of the buried book" is a metaphor of the Western way of conceptualizing knowledge and caused a kind of cultural clash in both Asian groups. In an implicit way, the story is based on an individualistic concept of man and knowledge. It gives an epistemological priority to the separate, independent, autonomous, essentially non social, self-contained individual (Bellah et al., 1985; Sampson, 1989) who works on something individually, accomplishes something individually, is happy about this individuality and dies with this happiness individually without getting into the slightest contact with people around her or with her society. In this sense the individual is an entity separated from the external situation or social world, whose behavior is determined by some configuration of internal motives. The story gives the notion that you can live a happy and satisfied life without being related to others or having the need to relate to others. From this perspective the individual is the first fact, the purpose of thinking is the knowledge itself and the more knowledge the thinker can gain is the better, and sociality and relatedness to the group is secondary.

The Japanese students do not understand how somebody can be happy with finding out something, without getting into contact with other human beings and sharing it with other people and the society. This is in harmony with the cultural influence of shinto that makes the interest of the community and public paramount and that leaves no place for egoism (Ono, 1962). The individual cannot be separated from the society and it is an imperative to make contributions to the world through his own work in life.

Learning connects people to each other by giving them opportunities to discuss, helping them to make friends, and improves society. Learning and knowledge are not for individual improvement or pleasure:

> R: *"In learning I learn what people and society want to know. This has meaning, because it is not just I who is important"* (Int.1)

The notion of intrinsic motivation and intrinsic reward are therefore not very strong enough concepts for the Japanese students to explain what happened, while these until recently have been highly evaluated notions in the Western motivation theories (Deci, 1975, 1999) Task-oriented motivation and mastery motivation are considered to be the most mature reasons in the West, but the accomplishment of a task for only the sake of mastery is rather immature according to the Japanese way of thinking. When the Japanese student persists and does not give up the effort, it is for the benefit of the group. For the Westerner, an effort is made for personal gain. These meaning systems are different but equally viable and each one appears as right, obvious, or natural to its adherents, as it was the case when we constructed the riddle. Also, the story is counter to the notion of infinite improvement, meaning that somebody cannot be fully satisfied and die as if she accomplished a task perfectly. The success of the performance is properly judged by society's standards rather by standards the individual might create. Thus there is always room for improvement in this pursuit of excellence. It is a person's obligation continually to strive for greater improvement. Therefore the heroine of the story cannot die happily—this is counter to the cultural expectation (Thomas & Niikura, 1990).

The drive for meaning—making, be culturally resonant or appropriate (Baltes & Staudinger, 1995) is so strong that students become quite creative when they try to interpret the story in order to make sense of it for themselves. If somebody does not share the knowledge with others and is still happy, the only explanation that is in harmony with his or her cultural construct, that the discovered knowledge is unwelcome or dangerous.

> R: "I am a little bit curious, why she buried the knowledge under the ground. Probably she found some kind of forbidden knowledge or some extremely dangerous thing like the Atomic Bomb (laughing)...yes... " (Int.5.)

Another interviewee tries to accept the different way of thinking about happiness and tries to emphatically understand it, however for her the story is still sad.

> R: "She might be very-very happy, because she wrote what she felt....what she thought so she must be very-very happy. But it's very-very happy only for her. The knowledge can't be understood by anybody because she buried it. For other people it is nothing........ I think it is really a pity, it's really a pity."
> I: "Let us take that somebody finds that book."
> R: In that case the situation gets happier. (Int.6.)

Among the Swedish students there was no reaction of this kind, for them it was understandable that being able to solve a problem in itself is rewarding and can make somebody happy.

Another cultural message can be the fact that the scientist in the story "puts" her knowledge into a book. This is very much in accordance with the Western notion that knowledge exists in books (Dahlin & Regmi, 2000). However, in the Confucian cultures of East Asia the common view of knowledge is that it is something to be conserved and reproduced and given to one person from another by relationship and interaction (Kirby, Woodhouse, & Ma, 1996). In this respect the teacher's or master's role is essential, not the book itself. The person who has got the knowledge (sensei, the teacher) is entitled to give it away. The transference of personal "wisdom" from the teacher to the student is an important cultural value in Japan.

CULTURAL SIMILARITIES, ECONOMIC DIFFERENCES

Schommer (1990) identified four different dimensions of beliefs concerning knowledge: knowledge is simple or complex, knowledge is certain/tentative, ability to learn is innate/acquired, learning is quick/or not at all. We can certainly join Dahlin and Regmi (2000) and add another dimension: knowledge is personal/social/both by nature.

We find it strikingly interesting that the similarity of economic, technical and social institutional development between Japan and Sweden does not mean that the two groups' ontologies of knowledge are also similar to each other. At the same time it equally intriguing that Nepalese and Japanese students' beliefs are so similar. Although both countries are in Asia, they are not close geographically. Their history is also very different. Japan is a highly developed, high tech country with all the requisites of the most developed Western societies, while Nepal has dramatically lower GDP. In terms of religion, while Buddhism is present in both societies, Nepal is the world's only Hindu state and in Japan shinto and Confucianism have also some cultural influence. According to Purdie (1996) many Japanese educational practices are based on the Confucian conception of teaching and learning. The Confucian perspective conceives thinking in a social context and has a very important relational function (Azuma, 1994). Confucianism stresses the development of people as social beings, as elements of the family and the broader society (Lin, 1990). For the Japanese learning is a lifelong process that is not restricted to the school years. As long as somebody lives in a society his/her learning and gaining knowledge is not a private, cognitive matter but an action that has meaning and responsibility towards others. The shinto theory of human development also has an essential notion that the human world consists of the individual living harmoniously with others, working for the good of the group. Hinduism, the main religion in Nepal, does not have any specific teachings about social responsibility and the same is true for Buddhism, the common religion in Japan and Nepal. The latter rather stresses the development of intellectual autonomy (Marek, 1990).

In Japan, the number of students participating in higher education is almost 50% of a cohort and Japanese students are high achievers both at national and international levels, while in Nepal only a small fragment of the youth has the opportunity to go on to higher education.

In spite of the huge difference between the general educational level in Nepal and Japan the students' ontologies of knowledge show no major differences. But there can be still different causes leading to the same result. One explanation can be the significance of studying and learning in the two studied groups. For Japanese in general (not only for university students) learning is a way to contribute to the society's development, and the development of Japan. In Nepal, however, those who manage (like the respondents in Dahlin and Regmi's study) to get into higher education might feel responsibility towards the rest of the society, as they are those who are going to be the highly educated few in the country, thus they owe their knowledge to the country.

One cultural explanation can be that in cross-cultural research Asian societies are considered to be more collectivistic than Western ones. Yamaguchi (1994) characterizes Japan as a society with "collectivistic tendencies." There has been no specific study about Nepal, still it is also considered to be collectivistic with an emphasis on the group or community, where the individual is not separate from others, but inextricably linked with them or embedded in group (Dahlin & Regmi, 2000; Jansz, 1991). In collectivistic societies social norms and duty are rather defined by the group than by own pleasure seeking (Triandis, 1990).

If we interpret the results in the individualistic-collectivistic framework, then it is not surprising that Swedes prove to be rather individualists. They tend to assign a greater weight to personal goals than the goals of the collective.

DIFFERENT CULTURES, DIFFERENT PSYCHOLOGIES

We can interpret our results in the cognitive/situated cognitive framework too. The shift within cognitive science to situated cognition theory among some Western psychologists, anthropologists and educationalists is at least as profound as was the shift to cognitivism from behaviorism (Kirshner & Whitson, 1996). They represent two different epistemologies. The first one claims that knowledge exists objectively, outside the learner's mind and we individually acquire it, while the second one states the social aspects of learning and knowledge, claiming that these are essentially embedded into everyday social practices and we gain knowledge by participating in these social practices. The cognitive view follows the tradition of individualism when it wants to find the invariant laws of operation, the real processes of the mind underpinning subjectivity (Shweder, 1991), and aims at setting up a culturally decontextualized description. A person is a seemingly separate, private store of thoughts. Knowledge, when once acquired, functions independently from the social context and the purpose of learning is gaining this independent knowledge in itself.

In contrast to this, in the past decade the concept of socially shared cognition, the study of the social and cultural in cognition is systematically considered (Lave & Wenger, 1991) and the traditional dualism of the individual/social; self/society distinction is questioned. It is embedded into Vygotsky's (1965) idea that learning is always social, the student is not somebody who is alone with the book that contains the knowledge, but surrounded by the social world and this has its own significance. The situative cognition trend claims that knowledge is always relational, essentially social and is embedded in everyday social practices that are collaborative and socioculturally determined.

Our studies of ontologies of knowledge seem to suggest that the Western, Swedish students are rather cognitivists, and from the results it is evident that their idea of an external reality that is mostly free of the perceiver's grasp, works as a barrier against seeing the interdependence of the individual and the social world. Contrarily, the Japanese and Nepalese students are "in-born" situated cognitivists, having a deeply rooted belief that knowledge and learning are fundamentally social. They are certainly not engaged in the Western debate between the cognitive trend and the situated cognition movement, for them the idea that cognition is socially situated has got a self-evident nature.

Another possible interpretative framework is the independent-interdependent self-concept. The most recent studies on the self (Markus, Kitayama, & Heiman, 1998; Kitayama, Markus et al., 1997) show that Japanese have an interdependent self-concept, meaning that even the mature self cannot be separated from its social context, it is contextual and relational.

The energy and direction for individual behavior seem to reside in the expectations of others (Markus, Kitayama, & Heiman, 1998).

While cognitivism is in accordance with the Western independent self-concept based on individualism, stating that once somebody has a stable identity it is autonomous and decontextualized, the cultural perspective of cognition and the theory of situated cognition is in a great harmony with the Asian way of conceptualizing the existence, according to which the social world and the mind are mutually constitutive, that is, the interdependent self-concept.

We found that all the participants in this study at a certain point refer to the importance of the "other," and of relationally, connectedness, interdependence and the participatory, responsive, interpersonal nature of all behavior and they emphasise that social relatedness is an essential requirement of knowledge. According to Lebra (1992) what it means "to be" differs quite dramatically between East and West. In the Western way of thinking the goal of all existence from the ontological perspective is self-objectification—a highlighting of the division between the experiencer and what is experienced. However according to the Shinto-Buddhist submerged model, the nature of being is not self-objectification, but rather a kind of downplaying of the division between experiencer and the object of experience.

Qualitative studies like the ones discussed in this chapter indicate that what appears as personal epistemological belief or personal ontology of knowledge turns out to be fundamentally cultural. (And personal as well, of course.) This means that some of the categories are non-existent or very rare in one culture while they are frequent in another culture. The most straightforward pedagogical implication of this is that teachers should examine their own epistemological and ontological assumptions instead of taking them for granted. The second implication is that a teacher in the multicultural classroom should try to find out about his/her students' culturally diverse views. And the third implication is that a teacher should draw what he/she has found into the fore and by doing so enrich the students' understanding of what learning and knowledge is about.

ACKNOWLEDGMENT

The research was carried out in Japan while the first author was a fellow of Japan Foundation in 1997–1998 and it was supported by the Magnus Bergwall Foundation, Sweden. The first author was also supported by the Hungarian National Research Fund (No. T 029876) and the Johann Jacobs Foundation.

REFERENCES

Alexander, P. A., & Dochy, F. J. R. C. (1995). Conceptions of knowledge and beliefs: a comparison across varying cultural and educational communities. *American Educational Research Journal, 32*, 413–442.

Alexander, P. A., Murphy, P. K., Guan, J., & Murphy, P. A. (1998). How students and teachers in Singapore and the United States conceptualize knowledge and beliefs: positioning learning within epistemological beliefs. *Learning and Instruction, 8*(2), 97–116.

Anderson, John R. et al. (1996). Situated learning and education. *Educational Researcher, 25* (4), 5–11.

Azuma, H. (1994). *Japanese discipline and education.* Tokyo: Tokyo University Press.

Baltes, P., & Staudinger, U. (Eds.). (1995). Prologue. *Life-span perspectives on interactive minds.* New York: Cambridge University Press.

Bellah, R. N., Madsen, R., Sullivan, W. M., Swindler, A., &Tipton, S. M. (1985). *Habits of the heart. Individualism and commitment to the American life.* New York: Harper & Row.

Brown, S. J., Collins, A., & Duguid, P. (1989). Situated cognition and the culture of learning. *Educational Researcher, 1–2,* 32–42.

Bruner, J., (1993). Do we "acquire" culture or vice versa: Reply to Tomasello, M., Kruger, A. C., & Ratner, H. H. *Cultural learning Behavioral and Brain Sciences. 163*(3), 515–516.

Dahlin, B., & Regmi, M. P. (2000). "Ontologies of knowledge East and West—a comparison of the views of Swedish and Nepalese students." *International Journal of Qualitative Studies in Education, 13*(1); 43–61.

Deci, E. L. (1975). *Intrinsic motivation.* New York: Plenum.

Deci, E. L., Koestner, R., & Ryan, R. M. (1999). A meta-analytic review of experiments examining the effects of extrinsic rewards on intrinsic motivation. *Psychological Bulletin, 125,* 627–668.

Elliott, B., & Chan, K. W. (1998). *Epistemological beliefs in learning to teach: Resolving conceptual and empirical issues.* Paper presented at the European Conference on Educational Research, Ljubljana, Slovenia, September 17–20.

Hofer, B. K., & Pintrich, P. R. (1997). The development of epistemological theories: beliefs about knowledge and knowing and their relation to learning. *Review of Educational Research, 67*(1), 88–140.

Jehng, J. J., Johnson, S. D., & Anderson, R. C. (1993). Schooling and students' epistemological beliefs about learning. *Contemporary Educational Psychology, 18,* 23–35.

Kirby, J. R., Woodhouse, R. A., & Ma, Y. (1996). Studying in a secondary language: The experiences of Chinese students in Canada. In D. Watkins, & J. Biggs (Eds.), *The Chinese learner. Cultural psychological and contextual influences* (pp. 141–158). Hong Kong: Comparative Education Research Centre & Australian Council for Educational Research.

Kirshner, D., & Whitson, J. A. (1996). Preface. In D. Kirshner, & J. A. Whitson (Eds.), *Situated cognition. Social, semiotic, and psychological perspectives.* New Jersey: Lawrence Erlbaum Associates, Publishers.

Kitayama, S., Markus, H. R., Matsumoto, H., & Norasakkunkit, V. (1997). Individual and Collective Processes in the Construction of the self: Self-enhancement in the United States and self-criticism in Japan. *Journal of Personality and Social Psychology, 72* (6), 1245–1267.

Lave, J. (1988). *Cognition in practice.* Cambridge: Cambridge University Press.

Lave, J., & Wenger, E. (1991). *Situated learning: Legitimate peripheral participation.* Cambridge: Cambridge University Press.

Lebra, T. S. (1993). Culture, Self, and Communication in Japan and the United States. In. W. B. Gudykunst (Ed.), *Communication in Japan and the United States* (pp. 51–87). Albany, NY: State University of New York Press.

Limon, M. (2001). On the cognitive conflict as an instructional strategy for conceptual change: a critical appraisal. *Learning and Instruction, 11* (4–5), 357–380.

Lin Huey-ya. (1990). Confucian Theory of human development. In R.M. Thomas (Ed.), *The encyclopedia of human development* (pp. 149–152). Oxford: Pergamon Press.

Marek, J. C. (1990). Buddhist theory of human development. In: R. M. Thomas (Ed.), *The encyclopedia of human development* (pp. 144–149). Oxford: Pergamon Press.

Markus, H. R., & Kitayama, S. (1991). Culture and the self: Implications for cognition, emotion, and motivation. *Psychological Review, 98*, 224–253.

Markus, H. R., & Kitayama, S. (1994). A collective fear of the collective: Implications for selves and the theories of selves. *Personality and Social Psychology Bulletin, 20* (5), 368–379.

Markus, H. R., Kitayama, S., & Heiman, R.J. (1998). Culture and "basic" psychological principles. In: E. T. Higgins & A. W. Kruglanski (Eds.), *Social psychology, handbook of basic principles* (pp. 857–11). The Guilford Press.

Marton, F. (1981). Phenomenography: Describing conceptions of the world around us. *Instructional Science, 10*, 177–200.

Marton, F., Beaty, E., & Dall'Alba, G. (1993). Conceptions of learning. *International Journal of Educational Research, 19*, 277–300.

Marton, F., & Booth, S. (1997). *Learning and awareness.* Mahwah, NJ: Lawrence Erlbaum Associates, Publishers.

Marton, F., Dall'Alba, G., & Tse, L. K. (1996). Memorizing and understanding: The keys to the paradox. In D. Watkins & J. Biggs (Eds.), *The Chinese learner: cultural, psychological and contextual influences* (pp. 69–84). Hong Kong: Comparative Education Research Centre (CERC).

Marton, F., Watkins, D., & Tang, C. (1997). Discontinuities and continuities in the experience of learning: an interview study of high-school students of Hong Kong. *Journal of Learning and Instruction, 1*, 21–48.

Nakane, C. (1970). *The Japanese society.* Berkeley: PUBLISHER.

Ono, S. (1962). *Shinto, the kami way.* Tokyo: Tuttle.

Paine, W. L. (1990). The teacher as a virtuoso: A Chinese model for teaching. *Teachers College Record, 92* (1), 49–81.

Perry, W. G. Jr. (1968). *Patterns of development in thought and values of students in a liberal art college: A validation of a scheme.* Cambridge, MA: Bureau of Study Council, Harvard University.

Perry, W. (1970). *Forms of intellectual and moral development in the college years.* New York: Holt, Rinehart & Winston.

Purdie, N. (1996). Student conceptions of learning and their use of self-regulated learning strategies: A cross-cultural comparison. *Journal of Educational Psychology, 88* (1), 87–100

Purdie, N., & Hattie, J. (1996). Cultural differences in the use of strategies for self-regulated learning. *American Educational Research Journal, 33* (4), 845–871.

Rosenberger, N. R. (1992). *Japanese sense of self.* New York: Cambridge University Press.

Sachs, L. (1983). Evil eye or bacteria: Turkish migrant women in Swedish health care. Stockholm: *Stockholm Studies in Social Anthropology.*

Sampson, E. E. (1989). The challenge of social change for psychology, globalization and psychology's theory of a person. *American Psychologist, 6,* 914–921.

Schommer, M. (1990). Effects of beliefs about the nature of knowledge on comprehension. *Journal of Educational Psychology, 82*(3), 498–504.

Schommer, M. (1993). Synthesizing epistemological belief of research: tentative understandings and provocative confusions. *Educational Psychology Review, 6* (4), 293–319.

Schommer, M. (1993). Epistemological development and academic performance among secondary students. *Journal of Educational Psychology, 85* (3), 406–411.

Schommer, M., Crouse, A., & Rhodes, N. (1992). Epistemological beliefs and mathematical text comprehension: Believing it's simple doesn't make it so. *Journal of Educational Psychology, 84,* 435–443.

Shweder, R. A. (1991). *Thinking through cultures: Expeditions in cultural Psychology.* Cambridge, MA: Harvard University Press.

Stevenson, H. W. et al. (1985). Cognitive performance and academic achievement of Japanese, Chinese, and American Children. *Child Development, 56* (3), 718–734.

Stevenson, H. W. (1987). The Asian advantage: The case of mathematics. *American Educator: The Professional Journal of the American Federation of Teachers, 11*(2), 26–31.

Stevenson, H. W., & Stigler, J.W. (1992). *The learning gap.* New York: Summit Books.

Stevenson, H. W. et al. (1993). Motivation and achievement of gifted children in East Asia and the United States. *Journal for the Education of the Gifted, 16* (3), 223–250.

Stevenson, H. W. (1998). A study of three cultures: Germany, Japan and the United States—An Overview of the TIMSS Case Study Project. *Phi Delta Kappan, 179,* (7), 524–529.

Stigler, J. W., & Stevenson, H. W. (1991). How Asian teachers polish each lesson to perfection. *American Educator: The Professional Journal of the American Federation of Teachers, 15* (1), 12–20.

Stigler, J. W., & Hiebert, J. (1999). *The teaching gap.* New York: The Free Press.

Thomas, R. M., & R. Niikura (1990). Shinto theory of human development. In R. M. Thomas (Ed.), *The encyclopedia of human development* (pp. 152–155). Oxford: Pergamon Press.

Youn, I. (2000). The culture specificity of epistemological beliefs about learning. *Asian Journal of Social Psychology, 3,* 87–105.

Vygotsky, L. (1965). *Thought and language.* Cambridge, MA: M.I.T. Press.

Wan Ali, W. Z. (1997). Conceptions of learning: A Malaysian perspective. *Department of Education and Educational Research, Goteborg University* (14).

Watkins, D., & Biggs, J. J. (1996). *The Chinese learner: Cultural, psychological and contextual influences.* Hong Kong: CERC & ACER.

Watkins, D., Regmi, M., & Astilla, E. (1991). The Asian-learner-as-a-rote-learner stereotype: Myth or reality? *Educational Psychology, 11*, 21–34.

Wen Q., & Marton, F. (1993). *Chinese views on the relation between memorization and understanding*. Paper presented at the 5th European Association for Research on Learning and Instruction, Conference in Aix en Provence.

part III

MULTICULTURAL PERSPECTIVES ON TEACHING AND TEACHER EDUCATION

CHAPTER 8

PROGRAM DIFFERENCES IN VALUES TEACHING IN TEACHER EDUCATION PROGRAMS

Canada, Mexico, and the United States

Ratna Ghosh and Norma Tarrow

The phenomenon of globalization has intensified worldwide social relations and inextricably linked distant geographical areas that shape local events. Economic integration, such as through the North American Free Trade Agreement (NAFTA, 1994) is one "symptom" of a much larger change in modes of communication made possible by technological advances (Farrell, 1996). It is interesting to conjecture what impact the North American economic integration of such significant dimensions will have on the education of the respective societies. As trade barriers disappear, the movement of people for economic reasons will have important educational and cultural consequences.

Economic convergence within the countries of the United States, Canada, and Mexico will involve a supranational level of economic, political, and social organization that cuts across nation-states through social and communication networks made possible by new technology. The com-

Teaching, Learning, and Motivation in a Multicultural Context, pages 173–192
Copyright © 2003 by Information Age Publishing
All rights of reproduction in any form reserved.

bined onslaught of technological change, globalization of the economy, instant communication and information transfer, and mobility of people pose unprecedented challenges. The issues are not merely technological preparation for global competition and an information based economy. Living and working in an increasingly interdependent world involves societies becoming increasingly multicultural, the need for international knowledge and intercultural communication skills, as well as moral and ethical dimensions, which place a tremendous responsibility on educational institutions. The current political and economic convergence poses immense challenges for the education and development of future generations. Civil societies depend on harmonious relations and the values that underpin these relations. Internalizing values of justice, equality and equal opportunity for example, involves knowledge (cognitive domain) but also moral and ethical values (affective domain). Educational institutions and teachers cannot simply teach these values through instruction, since values are acquired, not given. Teachers must create the conditions that encourage the development of these moral values through the school curriculum and program of studies, the organizational culture, the processes of decision making, critical thinking, and communication in the classroom as well as in the larger school environment. Teachers are crucial in this process because they are the medium in delivering the messages that students ingest. Thus, attention or lack of attention to values in pre-service programs which produce teachers are of great significance, especially in the multicultural and multilingual societies of the twenty-first century.

Due to the growing tendency toward political, social and economic integration between Mexico and the North American countries, the three authors of this chapter, each from one of the three NAFTA countries, decided to examine teacher education programs in their institutions for their values content. One of the aims of this tri-national study (1996–1999) was to identify educational policies and practices in the development of values that are implemented in the participating institutions. This work is a preliminary study looking at commonalities and differences in what teachers consider most important values and how much attention is actually given to preparing teachers to deal with cultural conflict, especially when teachers are from one culture/language and children from another.

This chapter will provide an overview of the program of studies in three universities with large teacher education programs in the province of Quebec, Canada, in Mexico City and in Long Beach, California. Quebec was seen as highly interesting with respect to its multicultural and linguistic characteristics given its linguistic laws and emphasis on values education. While this study was conducted in an Anglophone institution, all universities in the province are subject to the Ministry of Education's prescribed teacher education program. The participating universities in Mexico and

California, on the other hand, have two innovative programs, and they collaborate in preparing bilingual, bicultural teachers on both sides of the border. However, Mexico and California are also subject to prescribed teacher education programs: Mexico has to conform to requirements of the federal government and California to the State's California Teacher Credentialing Commission.

This chapter has four parts. It begins with a brief description of the social and educational context in relation to values in each country. This is followed by an analysis of university mission statements and teacher education programs. The third section presents data from questionnaires and interviews of students and professors regarding their observations on values teaching. Finally, the authors compare the three institutions and draw conclusions from the data.

PART I: SOCIAL AND EDUCATIONAL CONTEXT

Values are defined in this chapter as conscious and unconscious preferences of the majority of people in a society. Garcia and Vanella (1992) define values as conscious and unconscious preferences with which the majority of people in any society comply. Values are socially determined. Values are construed as such in a particular moment in the history of humanity. They remain with us, not in an immutable form, but as ideas of value, not defined in themselves, but maintained by consensus even when not put in practice. From this perspective, the universal character of some values does not contradict their historical nature, given their origins and their limited use. While values are historically and culturally related and therefore socially constructed, they also have a universal quality.

Mexico

It was only in the 1990s that Mexicans began to recognize that they are a multicultural country with a strong indigenous heritage, where tradition and modernity coexist. This was the result of the North American Free Trade Agreement which brought about some changes to Mexico's role in the continent. There are 56 officially reported indigenous groups which, together, are made up of 10 million people in one state alone.

In Mexico the discussion of values was for a long time considered unimportant and avoided because of the secularization of education after the Mexican Revolution, and the perception of a schism between morality—considered part of the religious realm—and politics. On the one hand, values and ethics were considered to be outside the realm of public education, which, on the other hand, was given the job of citizenship education. The social function of the school was unrelated to political and ethical values because civic education was a combination of rituals and ceremonies that ignored what it means to be a good citizen and its relationship to political duty. The citizen was more a "patriot" dedicated to national symbols than one who was politically active.

The 1995–2000 Education Development Plan (Poder Ejecutive Federal, 1996), however, emphasized reinforcing values and attitudes that lead to optimal child development, as well as scientific and technological knowledge. The plan outlined a need to develop values, attitudes and behaviors which allow for more harmonious coexistence leading to authentic democratic behavior and contributing to a respect and vigilance for human rights in all aspects of society—from the family and the school to all spaces of coexistence. Specifically, it proposed to give priority and preferential treatment to the most vulnerable social groups, recognizing the cultural diversity of Mexico and its need for bilingual education. Attention was focused on values that help expand women's roles as well as create a consciousness of values related to environmental preservation. The plan also mentioned the need for Mexicans to have knowledge of their rights and the duties of citizenship as well as respect for laws. Personal maturity, curiosity and international understanding were identified as necessary for responsible civic participation. These statements of policy came up against serious difficulties due to the economic crisis, political problems and the inability of the government to implement appropriate programs.

Canada

Although Canada is officially a multicultural country, with a Multicultural Policy (1971) and Multicultural Act (1988) at the federal level, education in Canada is imbued with the values of its "founding nations," France and England. At the turn of the twenty-first century about 46% of the Canadian population belongs to various ethno-cultural groups, about 25% are of French origin and reside primarily in Quebec while 29% are of British origin.

Canada was founded by English and French settlers but Anglo-Saxon values and points of view have historically predominated in the country. More recently in Quebec, the Silent Revolution has focused on French values for the Francophone province of Quebec. The 1991 Census indicated that 81% of Quebec's population was of French origin, while 9% were of English origin and 9% described themselves as being of a different or mixed origin (Ghosh et al., 1995). The current education policies in the province reflect in many ways the predominance of the culture and values of the French Quebecois tradition.

Values were established for Quebec's educational system in the Policies and Plan of Action for the Quebec Schools of 1979 (Government of Quebec, 1979). Curricular programs in each subject had to specify the values they would promote.

Education is based on a number of values and more precisely on general instructional objectives. These values should be reflected everywhere, at the primary and junior high levels, and especially in the course objectives. These are often the object of study and discussion in the schools. However, they indicate goals whose attainment motivates young people to develop their potential. These values are not presented in any determined order since it is the responsibility of each school to identify the necessary values for their education project and to attain results that reflect the aspirations of the community (Government of Quebec, 1979).

The document organizes six categories of values: intellectual, emotional, aesthetic, social and cultural, moral, and spiritual and religious. In comparison to other provinces in Canada, Quebec has taken the lead in what constitutes moral education. Its position on moral and religious education in the school system was legalized with Law 107 which establishes a choice within three options, namely, Catholic, Protestant or moral education. Students must not only choose one option, but schools are required to provide 76 hours of instruction per week in each of these areas.

Various initiatives of the Quebec government involve school programs that aim to help in the integration process of immigrants. In 1960 special programs called welcoming classes or *classes d'accueil* were established for migrants who had recently arrived in order to accelerate the process of learning French. During the same period, programs were also established for learning the native tongue (McAndrew, 1994).

Quebec's multicultural population is concentrated in the Montreal metropolitan region. Traditionally, immigrants went to Protestant schools which were predominantly English, and French-speaking Catholic students went to French schools established by the Catholic School Commission of Montreal. In 1977, Bill 101 obliged all immigrant students to go to French schools. The aim of the Bill was to strengthen the French language, protect French culture, and accelerate the integration of immigrants into Quebec society (Ghosh, 1995).

Bill 101 suddenly and dramatically changed the demography of the Montreal schools. While the British North America Act (1867) had organized education along religious lines according to Catholic and Protestant denominations, the French Catholic system was homogenous and the heterogenous English Protestant system started giving attention to the development of multicultural education policies only since 1984 when a comprehensive multicultural education approach was attempted.

In 1998, the government introduced a policy on Intercultural Education recognizing the need for more than language teaching for immigrant students so as to develop values in all students to deal with increasing diversity in the province. With falling birthrates and the need to step up immigration, it was felt that future citizens of Quebec need to develop intercultural skills, values and attitudes. While the Ministry has mandated one course in the teacher education program, intercultural education is far from permeating the teacher education curriculum.

In summary, interest in the question of values can be observed in the education policy documents of Quebec as well as in those of the school committees. However, even when there is an interest in attending to multicultural questions, a contradiction can be observed between the needs of a highly diverse population and the ideological position with respect to culture that is held by the government of Quebec and the French sector.

The United States

Founded on the ideals of justice and democracy, the United States, like Canada, is an immigrant society with many diverse cultures. Historically, education in the United States aimed to teach universal values so as to encourage immigrants to develop an American identity.

By mid-nineteenth century, the "universality" of values was questioned by different racial and ethnic groups because the values were thought to represent the white majority culture in power. By mid-twentieth century, schools avoided values issues and even civic education was given a lower priority. Several external conditions, among them the weakening of social commitments, the development of pluralism, secularization and the belief that values education should be the province of home and religious institutions, caused the school to lose the privileged position it once had as vehicle for transmitting social values (Likona, 1993). The "Clarification of Values" and "Just Community" strategies enjoyed a brief period of success, until they fell victim to political, religious and ideological forces that demanded that the teaching of values be taken out of the school. The doctrine of the separation of church and state indicated that public schools should clearly refrain from any type of education that included the teaching of values with religious connotations. Kolberg (1981), who became very influential in developing a theory on values learning, says:

Even though the Bill of Rights prohibits the teaching of religious beliefs or specific value systems, there is no law against teaching awareness of rights and the fundamental principles of justice expressed in the Constitution (p. 169).

With a dramatic increase in youth violence and crime, and an increase in awareness of cultural diversity there has been increasing recognition that values education is significant. An educational system that explicitly focuses on values implies the need for qualified teachers in order to provide quality instruction. Since the majority of teachers identify with the white majority hegemonic culture, the education of future teachers should open new possibilities with respect to the conflicts between culture and values. As Likona (1993) points out, revived interest in values education in America's multicultural schools imposes a responsibility for teacher education institutions to deal with the training of teachers in this area.

To sum up, all three countries have gone through phases where "value-free" education was attempted. All three now see education as a moral endeavor where values and moral behavior are increasingly significant for upholding the ideals and responsibilities of democracy as well as for peace in their societies where ethnic, religious, class and other differences have inherent tensions. The next section will review policies and practices in the three institutions in Mexico, Canada and the United States.

PART II: UNIVERSITY MISSIONS AND TEACHER EDUCATION PROGRAMS

In any organization, its stated mission sets the tone for what is important for that culture. What follows is a brief description of the nature and mission statement of each of the universities in this study. Furthermore, in order to determine the degree to which attention is paid to the question of values in a multicultural context within teacher education programs, courses and study plans were reviewed. Analysis of this material revealed the following:

Mexico

The Universidad Pedagógica Nacional (UPN) is a federal higher education system that is comprised of 75 campuses and 272 branch campuses. The university's mission is the result of different tensions that have characterized the education of teachers in the country, such as the relationship between theory and practice, the debate about the role of the university in respect to teaching practice (previously regarded as the sole province of teacher training colleges) and the tension between state or federal control and the university's autonomy.

Recognition of the importance of values education and its relationship to Mexico's multicultural society is evident in the following statements by its National Pedagogical University:

The university should take heed of the following principles:

- Democracy... in order to contribute to social change and the creation of a more participatory, free and just society.
- Criticism... to strengthen critical thinking to resist any dogma and to respect different opinions with respect to, for example, the transformation of social practices and lifestyles in order to meet the challenges of modern life
- Science... to base actions on knowledge and quality research, which must be diverse, plural and relative to the process of permanent transformation.
- Nation... in order to respect the linguistic and cultural pluralism that predominates in the country and which defines our identity...at the same time that we must conserve, develop and promote the national culture (version translated and adapted from UPN: Proyecto Académico, 1993).

The mission emphasizes the sociopolitical dimension articulated at a time when the production of knowledge was being examined from a critical standpoint. Without forgetting the national university's tradition, the need to recognize the sociocultural pluralism of the country is incorporated into the statement.

Professors and students who participated in this study were involved in two different programs—one directed at Mexican teacher education students preparing to teach in Mexico and the other involving Mexican-American graduates of Mexican teacher training colleges preparing to teach in California. The two programs were:

1. Bachelor of Arts in Education, Plan 94 (offered at the national level although the studied population was from the eastern campus of Mexico City).
2. Credential in Bilingual-Bicultural Education offered at the California State University Long Beach for Mexican teachers who are residents of Los Angeles.

The Bachelor of Arts in Education program (Plan 94) preparing Mexican teachers to work in Mexican schools focuses on the propagation of values that create a stronger, more moral community and that provides skills that aid in developing independence. These values are taught in seven specific courses ranging from social relationships to values and the environment.[1] At the same time, the program attempts to promote the development of a professional attitude in teachers and to strengthen the idea of honesty as a way of life.[2] As a central point of articulation of the program's teaching strategy is the proposal to develop an inquisitive, free and capable attitude which recognizes the imperfection of existing knowledge and attempts to strengthen moral autonomy, taking the work of Piaget and Kolhberg as basic points of reference. Further, the concepts of human rights, respect for the environment, personal dignity, respect, tolerance, liberty and justice are thought to be important.

The course "Civic and Values Education" looks at the debate on national versus universal values, with emphasis on the contributions of minorities and the conditions which make value conflicts possible. At the same time, it especially focuses on visualizing the school as a vehicle for social action. This vision is especially emphasized in a context characterized by the challenges faced by humanity in a complex, interdependent and multicultural society.

In the case of the Credential in Bilingual-Bicultural Education for Mexican teachers living and preparing to work in Mexican-American communities in the United States' special emphasis is placed on intercultural education processes for integration of these teachers and their students into U.S. society. Although there are no specific courses dealing with values, the objective of the program is to educate teachers so that they are capable of promoting values such as the awareness of society's commitment to equality, justice and democracy. It proposes to produce teachers who are able to transform their teaching practice depending on the sociocultural characteristics, and primary language, as well as needs and interests of their students. The program strives to develop the capacity for self-criticism, an inquisitive attitude and a constantly searching intellect, and is delivered by faculty from both the Mexican and California universities. The program proposes, as one of its central objectives, to strengthen cooperative work, especially in diverse socio-cultural and linguistic contexts. It also seeks to produce teachers with a conscious commitment to the values of justice, democracy and respect for cultural diversity. Additionally, it looks to promote cultural sensibility and good habits of communication and self-esteem.

As can be observed, the orientation with respect to values of UPN's programs is closely linked to conditions of a socio-political order. In a more specific analysis, significant differences can be observed between the two programs. The Bachelor of Arts in Education program seeks to promote the development of a moral culture with the notion of respect as its basis. It establishes the need to open up the new fields of human rights and environmental education. The Credential in Bilingual-Bicultural Education program focuses the greater part of its effort on multicultural education.

Both programs have the objective of practicing reflection and developing research habits in order to identify problem areas and develop intervention strategies. They put a strong emphasis on the reexamination of the teaching practice in order to strengthen self-esteem. In both programs the teacher is considered a social activist capable of transforming his or her teaching and producing critically conscious students.

Canada

McGill University is a public university, like all the universities in Canada. It is one of the oldest (founded in 1829) and is considered to be among the ten largest research universities in the country. It is an English-speaking institution located in Quebec, a French-speaking province, which creates an ideal situation for uniting two worlds. The students of the university come from local areas, different parts of Canada and foreign countries.

The university's mission is based on the idea of excellence in its services, teaching and research (Fontanus, 1994). The Institution emphasizes its social responsibility in the area where it works best—the development of academic skills. Its mission is specifically described as the following:

> The mission of the university is to develop learning through teaching, the production of knowledge and service to society, offering the students who most stand out the best education possible; the university should offer scholastic activities judged to be excellent by international standards of quality, and give society services in those areas in which, by virtue of the academic strength of the institution, high quality can be offered (Fontanus, 1994, p. 33).

In an article, which appeared in the editorial page of *The Gazette*, the most important English newspaper in Montreal, the then-Chancellor of McGill University, Gretta Chambers stated the following:

> I humbly maintain that the mission of the universities is the production and transmission of knowledge in a process of permanent discovery; they can't be in and of themselves the arbiters of social change. They offer to society the objective results of research in a large variety the social, economic, cultural and political fields with the objective of choosing or designing the social changes society considers appropriate. The universities are an infinitely renewable resource, not a classification of a values systems or intellectual products.

> What is at stake in superior education are minds, not things, transactions or marketable tools. They cannot be produced at will, with a formula or in order to satisfy the needs of consumers. The best academic program on paper is only valuable for those who are involved in this exercise. To the degree which minds have will, which is what makes them valuable, they tend

to congregate where they will be most productive (*The Gazette*, Sunday, May 10, 1998, p. A8).

These paragraphs are significant because they allow for the recognition of the attitudes and values of the university—a faculty worried about the development of thinking, a way of seeing, with a flexible attitude, with a will to consider all aspects of a problem, which allows one to see the complexity of daily situations.

The Faculty of Education offers nine Bachelor of Education programs. Students as well as professors participating in this study were enrolled in the following two programs.

- Bachelor of Education in Elementary School Education (B. Ed)
- Bachelor of Education in Teaching a Second Language (B. Ed)

The non-specialist B.Ed. is a four year, 120 credit program. The Ministry of Education, Quebec (MEQ), which certifies the teachers and approves their programs, indicates that future teachers should have an education which includes work on professional ethics and skills for handling the values question, in both curricular and extracurricular activities. It is expected that elementary school teachers value cultural diversity and ethics and that they promote values considered to be most important in Quebec (Government of Quebec, 1987, p. 18).

Until June 1998, the schools in Quebec were organized along confessional lines (Catholic or Protestant). This meant that elementary school teachers had to be prepared to teach moral education as well as the Protestant or Catholic religions. Despite the recent change from a confessional organization to a linguistic one, the demand for the confessional or religious education has not been affected. This implies teachers taking a methodological course as well as various other courses in this area.

After a study carried out by a Committee on Intercultural and Interracial Education in the faculty, a course focusing on ethnicity was made obligatory for the Bachelor of Education degree (Milligan, 1990), which represented an important step in the reform process of the teacher education program. Similarly, two other courses were made obligatory in the area of philosophy of education on philosophical perspectives and professional ethics. The objective of the courses was to expose students to questions of pluralism, equality, social transformation and moral and spiritual values (Faculty of Education, McGill University, 1994).

The Department of Culture and Values[3] is responsible for offering courses on values. The department's function, as well as that of the faculty, is closely tied to the special characteristics of the Quebec school system. The duality of languages and the historic importance of religion in the province of Quebec are determining factors with respect to the nature of the programs that are offered. The underlying logic of the courses offered by the Department of Culture and Values is described in the following manner:

> We recognize that different values underlie education ideologies and that, in various ways, the ethos of the school and the classrooms is dynamically related with the values and the culture that they represent. The new configuration (for example, the creation of the Department) requires analysis of the philosophical basis of concepts such as intercultural education, educational development, education for peace, religious instruction, moral education and instruction in the arts (McGill University, 1997, p. 62).

The Department of Culture and Values offers education students studies in Catholicism, Judaism, Protestantism and moral education and sexuality education all of which are linked with the needs established by different elements of the Quebec school system. The Superior Council of Education of Quebec has two committees, one Catholic and one Protestant, which protect the schools' interests and those of their corresponding jurisdictions. Teachers of moral and religious education, in Catholic schools as well as Protestant ones, need the government of Quebec's certification as well as that of the Department of Culture and Values of McGill University. There is no indication that the committees in the new linguistic framework (replacing religious boards) are putting less emphasis on these programs. The department emphasizes the integration of different religious and moral perspectives that takes place in these programs:

> Students of moral education are motivated to take classes in Judaism (for example, a course on the Holocaust), ethics courses and classes on Catholicism (such as "Ethics in Practice" or "Moral Values and Human Action") or courses on Protestantism (for example, "Living With Questions"). Students who do course work in Catholic and Protestant studies are motivated to take classes in moral education (such as "Values and Human Sexuality"). Professors of Judaic Studies also contribute to classes in Catholicism (and vice-versa) (McGill University, 1997, p. 22).

While mandatory courses relating specifically to values range from intercultural education to philosophical foundations of education, several optional courses are specifically dedicated to values.[4] Even when these courses are not obligatory, the majority of the students can cover the Education Ministry's requirements by taking at least three courses directly related to values.

The United States

The California State University at Long Beach (CSULB) is part of a system which has 23 campuses in different regions of the state. The mission of the Long Beach campus is stated as the following:

> A fundamental goal of the university is to prepare students to function effectively in a culturally diverse society, strengthening the understanding of the diversity of our cultural heritage, including the achievements of women and ethnic minorities. Instruction places special emphasis on the ethical and social dimensions of all the disciplines, which relate to their application in contemporary affairs. These fundamental premises and the international character of the university's faculty strengthens the international nature of its curriculum. (Bulletin, California State University, LB, 1996, p. 11).

The College of Education of the university prepares students for the various professions in the field of public and private education. Its mission is defined in the following way:

> The college seeks to include and benefit the students whose academic and professional antecedents are ample and varied. It proposes to provide them with information and the cultural experiences of a world that is plural, interdependent and in the process of changing. Recognizing the importance of linguistic and cultural diversity, the College of Education welcomes the challenges and opportunities made possible by this situation. The college's programs assume the responsibility of offering an education that is equitable and sensible to differences of gender, age, race, sexual orientation, ethnicity, disablement and academic strengths (Bulletin, California State University, Long Beach, 1996, p. 11).

Both the institution's mission, as well as that of the college particularly emphasizes values related to the life of a culturally diverse society. Through use of resources from the Departments of Teacher Education, and Educational Psychological and Social Foundations and Administration the college offers the following programs as options to obtain a basic elementary school teaching credential:

- Cross-Cultural Language and Academic Development (CLAD)
- Bilingual Cross-Cultural Language and Academic Development (BCLAD)
- CSU system-wide BCLAD in Mexico City.

It must be realized that in California all students in a credential program are in a fifth year program following a B.A. degree. All students are required to have completed a prerequisite class (outside of the college) on societies and cultures in an international context and a course on culture and education. All three of the programs emphasize the development of intercultural competencies, while the two BCLAD programs also focus on bilingual education. Students are required to take the bilingual Spanish English concentration in their undergraduate Liberal Studies major and to pass the State Spanish language and culture examinations (Exams 5 and 6). Methods courses, field work and student teaching take place in bilingual situations, providing enrichment opportunities for bilingual candidates to practice primary language pedagogy.

Through the reading of course syllabi, one can identify a preoccupation with respect to values that is not explicitly delineated in official course outlines, but that are made evident in organizational forms, readings and teaching practices. It can also be said that in various suggested readings there is an emphasis on democratic values.

The introductory course for all education students (EDEL 380) requires that students understand "the implications that diversity has on learning material and communities, including questions of equity, the disabled and the gifted, multiculturalism, empowerment and global interdependence." For the three types of credentials, students take basic methods courses, which, for the CLAD and the BCLAD, have been revised to include studies of cultural and linguistic diversity in the classroom. The four methods courses (for language, reading, mathematics and social sciences) put special emphasis on multicultural factors, require field experiences in schools that have a significant minority population (at least 27%) and propose that children be given bilingual-bicultural support The methods course for social studies is the only one that specifically mentions the theme of values, dedicating at least one section to the topic of "The Citizen and Values."

All students take at least one of three courses in multicultural education (two at the 400 level and one at the 500 or graduate level). In the course rationale for EDEL 432, "Cultural Diversity in Education Settings," for example, it is indicated that the main interest is in "causing students to confront their own values, their ethnocentrisms and their prejudices," so that "students can find paths that help confront these issues in their current and future education." Special attention is paid to the treatment of the topics of racism, discrimination and violence, as well as diverse cultural manifestations (family socialization, learning styles, roles and status). This is also true of both of the other multicultural education courses.

In summary, it can be said that as long as there is no course exclusively dedicated to values, all the courses, to some degree, look at themes related to values in multicultural contexts.

PART III: OBSERVATIONS ON VALUES TEACHING

This section analyzes data from interviews and questionnaires adminis-tered to students and teacher educators in the different programs. Thirty participants, professors and future teachers were interviewed in each of the participating countries.

At the National University of Pedagogy participants came from the Bachelor of Arts in Elementary Education, Plan 94, offered in Mexico City locations, and the Credential in Bilingual-Bicultural Education, offered cooperatively by the Mexicali campus of the UPN and California State Uni-versity Long Beach.

In Canada the participants came from two programs within the Faculty of Education at McGill University.

The group interviewed in the United States came from three different programs: Cross-Cultural Language and Academic Development (CLAD), Bilingual Cross-Cultural Language and Academic Development (BCLAD), a credential program offered by the California State University system, and the BCLAD of Mexico, which is offered by the California State University, Long Beach and the National University of Pedagogy in Mexico City.

Mexico

The teachers and future teachers in the education programs in Mexico consider one of their most important functions to be the imparting of val-ues education. In accord with this, they place highest importance on values of a socio-cultural and political order, giving lower priority to those that refer to academic habits, even when the curriculum puts a strong emphasis on the latter. Even if the presence of programs dedicated to the teaching of values is recognized, there is still a special emphasis on classroom interac-tion and the hidden curriculum. Rather than specific curriculum, identi-fied teaching strategies for the imparting of values included viewing the teacher as a model, along with the use of "group dynamics," "strengthen-ing of the discussion" and "critical analysis." It is apparent that there is a need to recognize different perspectives for the same situation and to be able to locate the "Other" in its place.

An important difference between the two programs that were analyzed was that the focus on "individuality" as a value is found exclusively in the student population of Mexican immigrants residing in the United States and in the hybrid program. Also, the Mexican teachers in the joint UPN/CSULB program delivered in California claimed there was lack of congru-ence between what the (California) teacher educators said and did as well as what they labeled the abuse of authority with respect to assigning work and grading. This was, perhaps, an example of cultural difference. In reality, even when the participants in the program for immigrants explicitly recognized the topic of diversity, they did not recognize having experienced a conflict of values, always seeing the situation instead as a conflict of power.

Canada

The teachers and future teachers see themselves as agents in the imparting of values. It is worth mentioning that 50% of those interviewed qualified their answers, mentioning the specific context in which they taught, adding that certain scholastic content offers the opportunity to teach values. They offered a long list of values that are promoted in the classroom and recognized courses in which values are an obligatory part of the curricula (Muliculural/Intercultural Education and the Philosophical Basis of Education). Courses that include religious and educational studies were mentioned less frequently. It is of particular interest that they mentioned two courses related to the teaching of a second language as important to the teaching of values. A significant number of people in the sample recognized difficulties faced by people who had differences based on gender, race, ethnicity, religion, and so on. However, there was only a small percentage that recognized power issues that underlie the construction of differences. The conflicts they experienced were grouped in three categories: gender, culture and abuse of authority. As specific strategies in the teaching of values, those which most stood out were case studies, autobiographies, the use of examples, the acting out of roles, critical thinking exercises and visual media.

The United States

The teachers and future teachers did not see values education as a central part of their responsibilities. Instead, for this group, the teaching of values is done indirectly. A significant percentage of students said that course content determines to some extent whether or not values will be explicitly discussed. For example, social science teachers recognize this role more than those who teach natural sciences. In the United States, like the population in Mexico City, difference is not usually recognized and when it is, the difference is measured against standards established by the majority group so that all are expected to reach those standards.

Teachers who belong to minority groups point to differences in ethnicity, language, gender and color which need different treatment and understanding. Some teaching strategies identified were the discussion method, cooperative learning, the use of videotapes and the participation of invited guests. With respect to the recognition of conflicts experienced in their work, the majority thought that these problems were related to questions of power.

CONCLUSIONS

This chapter discusses the mission statements and teacher education programs of three educational institutions in relation to values and values education in three geographical locations in multicultural North America. It also explores the observation of students and professors on values teaching.

The analysis indicated policy differences in the three universities. These policy differences were related to historical and social contexts. Despite the differences, there were shared values. The objectives identified in the institutional missions demonstrate significant differences. While the National University of Pedagogy (UPN) puts special emphasis on its social commitment and the production of knowledge in order to achieve a more democratic society, McGill University emphasizes its achievement of excellence, by which it makes good on its social commitment. On the other hand, California State University (CSU) puts total emphasis on promoting multicultural education in all its dimensions.

In all three universities, the programs that were identified were explicitly or implicitly related to values education. However, there were differences in terms of their orientation. In Mexico's UPN, the development of an autonomous morality, commitment to justice, equality and democracy were important, with concern as well for human rights and the environment. It is necessary to mention that the topic of cultural diversity is closely examined in the joint UPN/CSULB Bachelor of Arts program directed to the immigrant population, although this is not the case in the programs directed to the urban population where these questions are completely absent. It is obvious that in the joint program specifically targeting former Mexican teachers currently living in the United States and preparing to teach in California's multicultural schools, issues of cultural diversity are of great importance for the teachers.

At McGill University there is a clear orientation toward religious and cultural plurality, which is also accompanied by a specific interest in the field of human sexuality. Of the three universities in this study, McGill indicated the strongest commitment to values education as evidenced by all the courses. Finally, it is interesting that while CSU does not have courses which explicitly teach values, or courses that deal with the philosophy of education, the program has a number of courses that analyze the question of diversity. Furthermore, it can be said that the component of cultural immersion in the third BCLAD program offered by CSU in Mexico is a highly innovative program and could have significant results.

In all three institutions, specific values were identified. The values mentioned include equality, cooperation, democracy, interdependence, community, having an open mind, respect for difference, tolerance and justice. While the programs in Mexico focus more on the sociopolitical dimension of values, the programs at McGill University place more emphasis on their moral and spiritual questions. In both Mexico and Canada, there are specific programs that look at values from a philosophical standpoint. The fact that McGill University has created a program on Culture and Values speaks for the importance of values in teacher education.

Information from the interviews and questionnaires indicated the way in which values related curricular policies are put into practice. There is seemingly a direct relationship between the official curricular policies on the teaching of values and the role played by the teacher. California was the only location that did not have an explicit policy in this area and was the only place where at least some of the teacher educators did not recognize themselves as agents of values education.

Independently from the values proposed in teaching programs, the existing social dynamic could be identified as a determining factor in which values were important. For example, in Mexico the majority of the answers given by students fell into a socio-political category. In Canada and the United States there was more of a tendency to cite values in the multicultural field, something which is just starting to happen in Mexico.

Universities in general and teacher education programs in particular must deal with the fundamental questions on the purpose and content of education. This means that attention must be paid not only to subject content in the curriculum but also to the values being transmitted both explicitly and implicitly. The unprecedented social, political and economic changes in contemporary society have posed tremendous challenges to all social institutions, and very specifically to educational institutions. Policies that only emphasize the utilitarian aspects of education will be useless if children go through school without developing values that will guide them in using the knowledge and skills to the benefit of the local and global communities.

Interactions between different cultures are increasing and integration will signal the importance of diversity in the process of globalization and the need to profit from diversity. Teacher education programs can play a significant role in shaping this new way of looking and utilising diversity by creating conditions in schools where values of justice and equity will define good citizenship in a multicultural world.

ACKNOWLEDGMENT

This research was made possible by a grant obtained from the Collegio de Mexico.

NOTES

1. "School Groups," "Schools, Communities and Local Culture," "Children and their Social Relationships," "Pre-School Children and Their Values," "Values Education in Elementary School," "Socio-cultural Environment and School Organization" and "Social Implications of Educational Integration."
2. These values are promoted in the following courses: "The School Institution," "Public Schools and the Professionalization of Teaching," "Values Education in Schools and Society," "Reference Frameworks in Education," "Management and Collective Relationships in Schools" and "Quality in Education and School Administration."
3. Since 2001, Culture and Values is a program in the Department of Integrated Studies in Education.
4. These values are promoted in the following courses: "The School Institution," "Public Schools and the Professionalization of Teaching," "Values Education in Schools and Society," "Reference Frameworks in Education," "Management and Collective Relationships in Schools" and "Quality in Education and School Administration."

REFERENCES

California State University, Long Beach. (1996.) *Catalog: Undergraduate and graduate studies,* 1996–1997.

Faculty of Education, McGill University (1994.) *Draft Report: Required Courses in Philosophy in Education.*

Farrell, J. (1996). *Changing conceptions of educational quality and educational planning under conditions of globalization.* Paper presented at the Conference on Education Reform in Canada, Mexico and the United States: An agenda for co-operation and research, Brown University, Oct.1996.

Fontanus. (1994). *Collections of McGill University.* Montreal: McGill University Libraries, VII.

García, S., & L. Vanella. (1992.) *Normas y valores en el salón de clases.* México, Siglo XXI.

Ghosh, R. et al. (1995.) Policies relating to the education of cultural communities in Quebec. *Canadian Ethnic Studies.*

Gouvernement du Québec, Ministère de l' Éducation. (1979.) *The schools of Québec: Policy statement and plan of action.*

Government of Quebec. (1987). *La valorization du pluralisme culturel dans les manuels scolaires.* Montreal: Conseil des Communautes Culturelles et de l' immigration du Quebec.

Kohlberg, L. (1981.) *Essays on moral development, volume I: The philosophy of moral development.* San Francisco: Harper & Row.

Lickona, T. (1993). The return of character education. *Educational Leadership,* 51 (3), 16.

McAndrew, M. (1994). Ethnicity, multiculturalism and multicultural education in Canada. In R. Ghosh & D. Ray (Eds.), *Social change and education,* 3rd edition. Toronto: Harcourt Brace.

McGill University. (1997). *Undergraduate programs: Undergraduate calendar,* 1997/98.

Milligan, C. (1990). *Education and interculturalism in the future: A report of the academic policy sub-committee on inter-cultural and inter-racial education.* Montreal: McGill University.

Poder Ejecutivo Federal. (1996) *Plan de desarrollo educativo, 1995–2000.* México: Secretaría de Educación Pública.

CHAPTER 9

MULTICULTURALISM IN NEW SOUTH WALES AUSTRALIA

A Retrospective and Prospective View

Valentina McInerney and Dennis M. McInerney

Since its European settlement just over two hundred years ago, Australia has become one of the most culturally diverse countries in the world. The most recent figures available from the Australian Bureau of Statistics (ABS, 2000) indicate that almost a quarter of the Australian population was born overseas, with over half of these from countries where English is not the first language.

Throughout the twentieth century, Australia has received waves of immigrants from a wide variety of regions, although the pattern of countries of origin of migrants has changed as global situations have altered. Successive Australian governments have maintained a moderately high level of migrant intake stimulated at different times by economic, cultural and humanitarian motives. From the end of World War Two until the early 1970s, the Australian government's position on immigration was called the "White Australia Policy" Under this policy, immigrants who were British or northern European were given preference because it was thought that they could more easily integrate into a homogenous culture (Hill & Allan, 2001), and to that end, assimilation of immigrants was expected.

Teaching, Learning, and Motivation in a Multicultural Context, pages 193–222

In the immediate post-World War II period in Australia migrants and their children were expected to assimilate as soon as possible. This process included assimilation to Anglo-Australian customs, to adopt English as their language and to give up any "ethnic" identity (Smolicz, 1971). Schools at this time were rather mono-cultural institutions in terms of outlook, if not in terms of their population. During the 1960s immigrant groups began to lobby for support for their children's maintenance of "ethnic" languages and cultures in the schools serving their needs. Multicultural programs—some as simple as food fairs and costume days, others with more depth—began to find favor too in the broader community around these schools. By the end of the 1960s it was, however, becoming clear that migrants were among the poorest and most disadvantaged groups in the country, and that children of migrants were significantly underachieving at school. In response to such concerns that were becoming increasingly voiced by migrant groups, a series of social welfare reforms were initiated that paved the way for a major shift in ideology from that of assimilation to one of integration. In 1971, for example, the Child Migrant Education Program (CMEP) was established to provide the teaching of English as a Second Language (ESL) for migrant children in schools (Cope, Kalantzis, & Poynting, 1997).

By the late 1970s, the discussion had moved a considerable distance, with governments and state education departments increasingly looking to schools to develop multicultural curricula in which cultural differences were not only respected but cultivated (Davis, 1982; Harris, 1980; New South Wales Higher Education Board, 1984). Community languages and cultures gradually became a normal part of many school programs and multiculturalism, supported by school systems, became more respectable and encouraged. Key multicultural policies were written in the late 1970s and early 1980s to address important issues related to the education of children of migrants, however, while written to address the necessity of introducing appropriate curriculum to schools with high cultural diversity, many aspects were, however, intended for *all* schools.

Influential in the development of multicultural policies within Australia was the *Participation* report written for the New South Wales State Government by the then Ethnic Affairs Commission (NSWGP, 1978). While other inquiries suggested that multiculturalism was a function of important but peripheral specifically "ethnic" concerns, the Ethnic Affairs Commission saw it as a determinant in the framing of central government policy. The Commission's interpretation of multiculturalism was given in the opening words of the *Participation* report: "The Commission in this Report has attempted to look beyond the concept of multiculturalism seen only as a need to preserve the cultural heritage of Australians with a non-English speaking background. It sees as the fundamental issue the right of minority groups to achieve total participation in the Australian and New South Wales' political and social systems."

The *Participation* report was adopted as the blueprint for multicultural policy development and implementation in NSW in 1978. Since that time, there has been a sustained stream of government funding dedicated to the cultivation of Australian minority groups' cultural heritage and to the achievement of Australian children of ethnic background in schools. The most recent statement of aims for multicultural Australia are to be found in the Commonwealth of Australia Document "A New Agenda for Multicultural Australia" (AusInfo, 1999). The general aims of multiculturalism presented in this document are threefold:

- Make Australia's administrative, social and economic infrastructure more responsive to the rights, obligations and needs of our culturally diverse population;
- Promote social harmony among the different cultural groups in Australian society; and
- Optimize the benefits of our cultural diversity for all Australians.

Within this context each State Department of Education has operationalized principles of multiculturalism in Multicultural Policy Documents which are continually being updated. In New South Wales, where the study reported below was conducted, the following aims are specified in the Multicultural Education Policy Statement (N.S.W. Department of Education, 1983; New South Wales DET, 1999). Multicultural education aims to provide students with the opportunity to develop: an understanding and appreciation that Australia has been multicultural in nature throughout its history both before and after European settlement; an awareness of the contribution which people of many different cultural backgrounds have made and are making to Australia; intercultural understanding through the consideration of attitudes, beliefs and values related to multiculturalism; behavior that fosters inter ethnic harmony; and an enhanced sense of personal worth through an acceptance and appreciation not only of their Australian national identity, but also of their specific Australian ethnic identity in the context of a multicultural society (N.S.W. Department of Education, 1983). Among important strategies of multicultural education that have been implemented in New South Wales Schools are the following:

- English as a Second Language (ESL) programs
- Community Language programs
- Anti-racism education programs
- Multicultural curriculum and resources

- Communication and consultation with parents and communities from diverse cultural and linguistic backgrounds, including interpreters and translations
- Vocational education and training (VET) programs that are accessible to students from diverse cultural and language backgrounds. (New South Wales DET, 2001)

Each of these strategies has specific goals, which we briefly report below as a number of these are dealt with in our research report.

English as a Second Language Program

ESL education is provided in both primary and high schools. It supports the English language development of students whose first language is not English. In 2001, approximately 85,000 ESL students were supported by 876 ESL specialist teachers in more than 750 government schools. Fifteen Intensive English Centres (IECs) are located in Sydney and Wollongong to cater for newly arrived high school-aged students who need intensive English language support before transferring to high school. As part of the new HSC English course, a Stage 6 English (ESL) course has been implemented in 110 schools across the state.

Community Language Programs

In an effort to increase multiculturalism primary school students in New South Wales can learn a community language as part of their primary school education. A wide range of community languages is currently taught in NSW government primary schools.

Anti-racism Education Programs

Another key element of multiculturalism is anti-racism education. Programs and resources are provided to schools to assist in ensuring that all students and staff can learn and work in an environment free of racism. Important in this is the training that is provided to key school, district and community personnel to assist with the implementation of anti-racism projects in school communities and to key district personnel. Some schools with special needs are targeted to receive funding for anti-racism projects.

Multicultural Curriculum and Resources

A variety of multicultural and curriculum resources are provided to schools throughout New South Wales to enhance their multicultural programs and, in particular, these resources provide teaching ideas to develop students' knowledge of Australia's diverse communities. Teaching units incorporating multicultural perspectives to the curriculum have been developed in a number of key learning areas.

Communication and Consultation

Currently there are 20 Community Information Officers—Non English Speaking Background (NESB) located across NSW. Their role is to assist in providing information and strengthening links between schools and their parents/caregivers and community members from language backgrounds other than English. These Community Information Officers can assist schools in:

- addressing meetings of NESB parents and community members on educational issues affecting their children
- speaking at school staff meetings and school development days on issues related to NESB communities
- advising schools and assisting in professional development programs related to cross-cultural issues.

Furthermore, to ensure effective communication takes place between schools and their parents/caregivers and communities from diverse cultural and linguistic backgrounds, the Department provides funds to pay for interpreting and translation services. Schools can use either the Telephone Interpreter Service or engage on-site interpreters. The Department also provides schools with a range of translated documents for communicating information to parents and community members, as well as vocational education and training programs. Currently the Department is developing programs to support VET students from diverse cultural and linguistic backgrounds.

It is apparent that a number of these significant initiatives have been taken in schools where there are a high proportion of students from migrant backgrounds such as the introduction of community language teaching and support in schools, ESL programs, ethnic aides, bilingual programs, and improved communication with communities through translators. The extent to which multicultural education policies have ever impacted on mainstream schools, however, especially those that have remained predominantly Anglo, has not been studied. This is despite the fact that a number of the elements of the multicultural policy are aimed at introducing all students to the broader multicultural society in which they live and eventually will work.

In this context we investigated a sample of teachers' understandings of, and commitment to, multicultural education policies in schools today and compared these with the attitudes of teachers twenty years ago when the recommendations of the *Participation* report were first translated into government policy for NSW schools.

Schools and Multicultural Education

As we have suggested above, schools have traditionally been seen as central agencies for implementing government social policy. Over the last twenty years, schools have been expected to play a major role in the acceptance and development of Australian Government multicultural policy under programs developed by State Education Departments (Kalantzis, Cope, Noble, & Poynting, 1990). Despite differences in interpretation, Australian schools have been required by law to provide equal educational opportunities for all students, irrespective of their backgrounds (Alcorso & Cope, 1986; Office of Multicultural Affairs, 1989). However, many Australian teachers and schools appear to have given lukewarm reception to multicultural curriculum initiatives, which have been perceived by some as unnecessary political social engineering (McInerney & McInerney, 2001).

In schools with large numbers of non English speaking background (NESB) students, school-based multicultural policies and practices were in place well before multiculturalism was an official policy, and have continued to flourish in such schools. In these schools, need was the mother of invention. However, anecdotal information suggests that the impact of multicultural education policies has been less than anticipated on schools where there does not appear to be any significant immigrant presence. This is despite the fact that many of the policies (particularly those related to Ethnic Studies, Intercultural Education, and Multicultural Perspectives to the Curriculum) are mandated for all schools. Many of the notions underpinning multicultural education (culture, ethnicity, equity, participation) appear somewhat vaguely defined in the policy documents (Hill & Allan, 2001; Phillip Institute of Technology, 1984; Poole, 1987; Sachs, 1989). Perhaps, as a result of this, the attitudes of many teachers (and the community at large) has been, and still is, somewhat ambivalent to multiculturalism. This may explain the lack of impact of the policies.

McInerney (1979, 1987a,b,c) conducted a study examining teacher attitudes towards multicultural curricula developments in a sample of New South Wales state primary schools prior to the publication and dissemination of the first state Multicultural Education Policy document in 1979. Specifically, he examined teacher attitudes towards language maintenance and the schools' role in this, as well as teacher attitudes towards cultural diversity and the schools' role in fostering cultural maintenance and diversity. McInerney found that teachers and administrators were divided over issues related to these central elements of multicultural education. While there was general support for children of immigrants retaining their community language and for including multicultural studies as part of the school curricula, there were quite ambivalent attitudes towards the retention of cultural traits by immigrants and their children for the social benefit of Australia. The school was not seen by many of the respondents as responsible for teaching or maintaining community languages, and there was only equivocal support for community languages being used as a medium of instruction for part of the day in schools having large numbers of non-English-speaking children. The role of the school was seen primarily as one of teaching the non-English-speaking child English as quickly and painlessly as possible. A sizeable number of respondents (22%) considered that non-English-speaking children should not be encouraged to retain their community language and that the maintenance of community languages and customs was unimportant to the child (15% of respondents). Responses varied by school type (i.e., level of diversity) and teacher position (e.g., ESL teacher). In general, less positive attitudes were expressed in schools with low ethnic diversity than high ethnic diversity, and by classroom teachers than by ESL teachers. The level of commitment to multiculturalism across schools having little diversity was low.

As we have indicated above, considerable resources have been applied to developing and disseminating multicultural programs across all schools over the last twenty years. The research literature and reports are quite inconclusive on whether multiculturalism has ever impacted on mainstream schools, and in particular those which were and continued to be culturally homogenous. As teachers and school administrators are responsible for implementing multicultural policies, it is important that they have knowledge of, and are positive towards, these policies. The purpose of this research was, therefore, to examine current teacher attitudes towards, and knowledge of, some key aspects of multicultural education, and to compare and contrast this with the knowledge and attitudes revealed prior to the implementation of the policies.

METHOD

Participants

Our intention was to broadly sample three types of schools, viz, schools that had been multicultural prior to the advent of the official policy documents in the late 1970's and continued to be so over the twenty year period, schools that were mono-cultural (Anglo) and remained so over the twenty year period, and schools that were transitional during that period, that is, becoming multicultural from a mono-cultural (Anglo) origin. We also wished to survey primary and secondary schools as we imagined that the impact of the policy would vary not only according to the level of multiculturalism at the school but also school type. The targeted population was all school administrators and teachers at each school. This was important as we wished to compare attitudes across levels of teacher experience, as well as perceived power within the schools.

Our plans were more difficult to implement than expected which sheds light on problems associated with studying the implementation of multicultural curriculum at all schools. While multicultural schools (those, for purposes of our classification that were either ethnically diverse or ethnically mono-cultural, such as schools with predominant Arabic or Asian students) were very keen to participate, Anglo mono-cultural schools were less enthusiastic. In one particular large Anglo mono-cultural school, which was to provide an important part of our data, there was decided resistance to completing the survey, with almost the entire staff not complying, despite school administrative support and two visits by the research team to the school site. The reason given for the poor response was that such a survey was irrelevant to the school! We deal with this issue more in the description of the results. However, we were able to elicit the support of enough schools at this stage of the study to make meaningful comparisons with the earlier data. We are continuing to supplement the data with extra schools as the study proceeds. The participants in the study reported below are school administrators and teachers at:

- Two secondary and one primary school that were multicultural prior to 1978 and continued to be multicultural over the following twenty year period.
- Two primary and one secondary school that were culturally homogeneous (Anglo) prior to 1978 but which progressively became ethnically diverse over the period 1978–1998, what we have termed transitional.

- One primary and three secondary schools that were culturally homogeneous (Anglo) prior to 1978 and remained homogeneous over the period 1978–1998.

A total of 345 teachers and administrators at these schools completed the survey (administrators = 58, teachers = 287, primary = 123, secondary = 222) with the response rate at most schools very good. Eighty-six teachers (25%) listed that they had a non-English speaking background. Approximately 35% of the teachers had taught 10 or less years, 32% from 11 to 20 years, and the remaining 33% had taught more than 20 years. The sample size was approximately half the sample size of the 1979 study.

Instruments

A quantitative survey consisting of fourteen questions was designed to replicate those used by McInerney (1979, 1987a,b,c) and to assess teacher attitudes to multicultural education in 2000 in comparison with attitudes expressed in 1979. Items were written to reflect three key themes: fostering community language maintenance (sample item: "Non-English speaking background students should be encouraged by the school to retain their family language"); fostering the maintenance of cultural identity and prestige (sample item: "Schools should encourage the preservation of cultural differences between students of ethnic groups in Australia"); and fostering the benefits of multiculturalism in the broader community (sample item: "The maintenance of community languages is good for Australia"). Table 9.1 presents the full text of these questions. These 14 questions were answered on a four-point scale anchored with "strongly agree" and "strongly disagree." This format was a forced choice format with no middle point "unsure." While this format has some disadvantages with respondents, at times, indicating that they are unhappy to make an 'agree' or 'disagree' response (attitudes are not always this simple) it has the decided advantage of limiting the number of neutral responses. Furthermore, the response format replicated the forced choice format of the original questionnaire, although in this case the response was anchored with 'yes,' and 'no.' In order to alleviate respondents' concerns about the forced choice format, and in order to provide further depth to the answers, each question was followed by several empty lines and respondents were invited to elaborate on their answers. We also sought information on respondents' knowledge, beliefs, and attitudes towards multicultural curricula and programs. The answers to these questions have been qualitatively coded and categorized, as well as quantified in order to make a comparison with the earlier data. This chapter specifically reports on the first fourteen questions and their elaborations as well as on the respondents' knowledge about multicultural programs, although space prevents us dealing with the qualitative responses in detail.

In addition to the survey questions a limited number of demographic questions were included in order to do appropriate analyses. These questions asked for details on staff position, current grade level taught, number of years teaching, schools previously taught at and language background. Because of the nature of the questions asked we needed to be very sensitive not to obtain demographic information that may have been used to identify particular respondents.

Table 9.1. Participation in Education Survey Questions

Question

1. The maintenance of the family language is important for the student.

2. Non-English speaking background students should be encouraged by the school to retain their family language.

3. It is the school's responsibility to help the students retain their family language

4. When there are large numbers of non-English speaking background students in a school, the school should play a significant role in teaching appropriate Community Languages.

5. It is desirable for Community Languages to be used as a medium of instruction for part of the day in schools having large numbers of speakers of languages other than English.

6. Schools should encourage the preservation of cultural differences between students of ethnic groups in Australia.

7. A study of the cultures from which Australian migrants have come should be incorporated into the curriculum for all Australian students.

8. Students from English-speaking backgrounds should attend Community Language/culture classes at school to learn about the culture of ethnic groups.

9. Teachers should be familiar with the customs and languages of the students in their classroom.

10. Schools should encourage students to wear the clothes, eat the foods, or play games of their ethnic groups at school.

11. The maintenance of the languages of migrant groups is good for the social fabric of Australia.

12. The maintenance of the religions of migrant groups is good for the social fabric of Australia.

13. It is beneficial for migrant groups to live together in ethnic communities long-term.

14. The existence of informal ethnic groupings within schools hinders students' integration into the school community.

Administration

The first author administered the survey to all staff at each school at a dedicated staff meeting. This was done to ensure that all respondents understood the purpose of the survey, and to provide the opportunity for teachers to clarify questions. Prior to commencing the survey at each school the researcher gave a brief standardized introduction. The survey was also conducted at staff meetings to maximize return rates. This approach had a number of advantages and disadvantages. At all schools, bar one described below, cooperation was excellent and return rates maximized. Furthermore, many teachers seized on the opportunity to discuss issues with the researcher and each other. Many schools suggested that the data be used to run in-service courses. So no doubt the survey was perceived as useful and timely by the majority of schools. However, there were some logistic difficulties with this approach. First, it was extremely difficult to schedule a dedicated staff meeting at most schools with already committed meeting schedules, and second, even when the meeting was "dedicated" much time was lost at some schools through administrative announcements, and the desire of teachers not to remain behind to complete the survey.

Analyses

As the 1979 questions were in a forced choice "yes"/"no" format, the four point response format in this study was recoded "strongly agree" and "agree" to "yes," and "strongly disagree" and "disagree" to "no" to compute new variables. The table below presents percentages answering with either response to each question. However, in order to examine differences between schools and teacher type, the original four point response scale was used in parametric analyses. As indicated above the items on the survey were designed to reflect three key components of multicultural education, viz., language preservation, cultural maintenance, and multiculturalism and the broader community. MANOVA was conducted to examine group differences within these bands of questions to account for any capitalization of chance owing to potential correlation between questions within any one band. Comparisons were made between school type, level of multiculturalism, language background, staff position and length of teaching service.

In addition, each participant was provided the opportunity to elaborate on their answers to the fourteen questions listed above. These qualitative elaborations are presented below, as well as a presentation of school and curriculum initiatives that participants indicated occurred within their school settings (in section 2 analyses). You will note that respondents qualify their response in both positive and negative ways within each question.

RESULTS AND DISCUSSION

Table 9.2 presents findings across the schools surveyed and presents some interesting features in comparison to the 1979 data. Figure 9.1 represents graphically the responses of the full sample across all 14 questions. In the original questionnaire questions 11 and 12 were represented by one question "Is the maintenance of cultural traits by migrants good for the social community of Australia." We decided to use two questions in this survey to make the notion of cultural traits more explicit.

Table 9.2.   Responses to Multicultural Questions
(full text of questions in Table 9.1)

Question	Yes	No	nesb	type	mult
Language Maintenance					
1. The maintenance of the family language is important for the student	97% (85%)a	3% (15%)i			
2. NESB students should be encouraged by the school to retain their language	91% (78%)	9% (22%)i			
3. It is the school's responsibility to help students retain their language	33% (24%)	67% (76%)i			
4. Schools should play significant role in teaching community languages	68% (36%)	32% (64%)i	*		*
5. It is desirable for community languages to be used for instruction	49% (44%)	51% (56%)i		*	
Cultural Maintenance					
6. Schools should encourage the preservation of cultural differences	74% (50%)	26% (50%)i	*	(*)	
7. A study of other cultures should be part of the curriculum for all students	84% (91%)	16% (9%)d	*		
8. English speaking background students should attend culture and language classes to learn about ethnic groups	41% (52%)	59% (48%)d			
9. Teachers should be familiar with customs and languages of students	84% (89%)	16% (11%)d			
10. Schools should encourage students to wear the clothes, eat foods...	35% (28%)	65% (72%)i		(*)	
Broader Community					
11. The maintenance of community languages is good for Australia	74% (73%)	26% (27%)s	*		
12. The maintenance of religions of immigrant groups is good for Australia	73% (–)	27% (–)			*

**Table 9.2. Responses to Multicultural Questions
(full text of questions in Table 9.1) (Cont.)**

Question	Yes	No	nesb	type	mult
13. It is beneficial for immigrant groups to live together in ethnic communities	22% (11%)	78% (89%)i			*
14. The existence of ethnic groupings within school hinders integration	57% (76%)	43% (24%)i		*	*

Note: (a) number in bracket represents percentages answering question in 1979 study.
nesb = Non-English speaking background, type = school type (primary or high school), mult = level of multiculturalism (monocultural (Anglo), multicultural, transitional)
i = increase in positive response, *d* = decrease in positive response, *s* = equivalent response
• Significant differences MANOVA. (*) Differences approaching significance

The four point scale used for each of the 14 items in the survey was 1 = strongly disagree, 2 = disagree, 3 = agree and 4 = strongly agree. A mean above 2.5 therefore records a positive response to the question, while a mean less than 2.5 records a negative response. Figure 9.1 reveals strong positive responses for questions 1, 2, and positive responses for questions 4, 6, 7, 9, and 11. There were negative responses to questions 3, 5, 8, 10 and 13 with the latter being the most negative. Question 14 is expressed negatively so responses to this question really indicate a negative attitude. In the next section we consider each of the questions in detail.

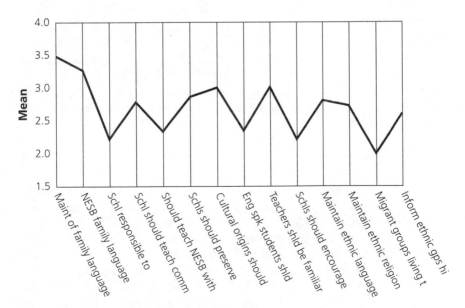

Figure 9.1.   Comparison of means across 14 multicultural questions.

Language Maintenance

In general, there has been an improvement in attitudes towards language maintenance since 1979. Across the five questions, there has been an improvement from 5% to 32% in positive responses. Very positive attitudes are expressed towards the importance of students' maintaining their family language (97%) and the role of the school in encouraging this (91%). Nevertheless, more negative attitudes are expressed towards the schools responsibility in this (only 33% indicating yes), the use of community languages for instruction (44% indicating yes), and the school playing a significant role in teaching community languages (68% indicating yes). The strongest improvement was with regard to this latter question with a 32% increase in positive responses since 1979. The weakest improvement was with regard to using community languages for instruction where there was an increase of only 5% in positive responses from the 1979 data.

There was a significant main effect on question 4, that is, "When there are large numbers of non-English speaking background students the school should play a significant role in teaching appropriate community languages" for language background ($F(5,414) = 3.49$, $p = .004$). Follow-up univariate F-tests indicated that non-English speaking background teachers ($M = 2.99$) are significantly more in agreement that schools should play a significant role in teaching community languages than English speaking background teachers ($M = 2.72$) ($F(1,318) = 6.98$, $p = .009$). There was a significant main effect for level of school multiculturalism on question 4 ($F(10,640) = 1.97$, $p = .035$). Follow-up one-way analyses indicated that transitional schools ($M = 2.60$) are significantly less in agreement than mono-cultural ($M = 2.83$) or multicultural ($M = 2.87$) schools ($F(2,335) = 3.55$, $p = .029$). There was a significant main effect for school type on question 5 ($F(5,320) = 5.77$, $p = .000$). Follow-up univariate F-tests indicate that primary schools are significantly more positive to community languages being used for instruction ($M = 2.59$) than high schools ($M = 2.21$) ($F(1,324) = 18.00$, $p = .000$).

Across almost all questions NESB respondents were more positive, however the only significant difference was on question 4. There was also a significant difference by level of multiculturalism with transitional schools being significantly less in agreement than either mono-cultural or multicultural schools. This could reflect the fact that multicultural schools already have programs in place, mono-cultural Anglo schools don't need to have such programs, while transitional schools are grappling, perhaps with limited resources, with the issue of introducing community languages. Across all language maintenance questions (except one, question 4) primary schools were more positive to each proposition than secondary schools. However, this difference was only significant on the one question: "It is desirable for Community Languages to be used as a medium of instruction for part of the day in schools having large numbers of speakers of languages other than English." The fact that primary schools were significantly more positive than high schools probably reflects the fact that it is, perhaps, less difficult to introduce community language programs within primary schools where students are housed within one home room, rather than in high schools with their more complex subject arrangements. It may also reflect primary teachers' greater awareness as a result of more intensive training in multiculturalism within their degree courses.

Perhaps the most striking feature of the findings on this bank of questions is that, although there has been improvement, there is still considerable ambivalence. Indeed, on two questions there is considerable negativity towards the role the school should play in language maintenance. Only 33% of respondents agreed that it is the school's responsibility to help students retain their language and only 49% agreed that it is desirable for community languages to be used for instruction in schools where there are large numbers of non-English speaking background students. In general, there were no differences by language background, type of school, or level of multiculturalism. Considering that community language programs have official backing and should be mandated at appropriate schools some distance needs to be gone to obtain fuller teacher commitment to this aspect of multiculturalism.

Cultural Maintenance

Across the five questions, reflecting attitudes to the schools' role in cultural maintenance there was marginal change from 1979 data. The strongest positive change was on question 6 with a 24% increase in positive attitudes towards schools encouraging the preservation of cultural differences. There was marginal improvement on question 10 with a 7% increase in positive responses to schools encouraging students to retain ethnic identity at school. Conversely, on three questions, 7, 8, and 9 there was a decrease in positive responses from the 1979 data. The emphasis in these questions was on what schools "should do" rather than what they "should encourage". On two questions (7 and 9) the response is still quite positive (84% from 91% and 89% respectively in 1979). However, on question 8, relating to English language background students attending culture and language classes to learn about ethnic groups, the response was quite negative with only 41% (down from 52% in 1979 data) agreeing with the proposition.

There was a significant main effect on this group of questions by language background ($F(5,306) = 2.80$, $p = .017$). Follow-up univariate F-tests revealed a significant difference for question 6 ($F(1,310) = 6.53$, $p = .011$)

with NESB respondents (M = 3.05) significantly more in agreement that schools should encourage the preservation of cultural differences than English language background respondents (M = 2.79). Follow-up univariate F-tests also revealed a significant difference for question 7 ($F(1,310)$ = 5.44, p = .020) with NESB respondents (M = 3.15) significantly more in agreement that a study of other cultures should be a part of the curriculum for all students than English language background respondents (M = 2.95).

The main effect for school type approached significance ($F(5,312)$ = 1.99, p = .08). Follow-up univariate F-tests indicated that primary schools (M = 3.02) are significantly more in agreement that schools should encourage the preservation of cultural differences than high schools (M = 2.78) ($F(1,316)$ = 6.89). Follow-up univariate tests also indicated that primary schools (M = 2.34) are significantly more in agreement that schools should encourage students to retain ethnic identity at school than high schools (M = 2.16) ($F(1,316)$ = 4.71, p = .031).

There are two striking features of these results. First, there has been a decrement in positive attitudes on key questions. This is concerning and perplexing given the fact that multiculturalism has been a mandated part of both pre and in-service teacher training courses over the last twenty years. Second, there are quite negative attitudes towards students from English-speaking backgrounds attending community language and culture classes at school to learn about the culture of ethnic groups (which seems innocuous enough), and towards schools encouraging students to wear the clothes, eat the foods, or play games of their ethnic groups at school. Both of these propositions are in line with the spirit of multiculturalism and the Participation Report. Even 26% of respondents are in disagreement with the proposition that schools should encourage the preservation of cultural differences. Across all questions NESB respondents are more positive to each proposition, although this was only significant for questions 6 and 7. Across all cultural maintenance questions primary schools were more positive than high schools, although there was only a significant difference on question 6 and 10. Again, as with the first bank of questions, this result might reflect the less complex nature of programming within primary schools, or perhaps their greater commitment as a result of more intensive training in multiculturalism within their degree courses. As with community language maintenance, the commitment of teachers to cultural maintenance across the full sample, and indeed within sub-samples, is less than envisioned within the multicultural policy document and the Participation Report.

Multiculturalism and the Broader Community

There was no change in attitude towards the maintenance of community languages being good for Australia since the 1979 data (74% of respondents in agreement with the proposition). Similar percentages apply to attitudes towards the maintenance of religions of immigrant groups being good for Australia (in the 1979 data these two aspects comprised one question). There was a slight increase in positive responses towards the proposition that it is beneficial for immigrant groups to live together in ethnic communities from the 1979 data (an increase from 11% to 22%), and a stronger increase in positive responses towards the proposition that the existence of ethnic groupings within school hinders integration (up from 24% to 43%). Note this question is negative so disagreement signals a positive attitude towards the existence of ethnic groupings.

There was a significant main effect for language background on this bank of questions ($F(4,283)$ = 2.36, p = .053). Follow-up univariate F-tests revealed a significant difference on question 11. Non-English background respondents (M = 2.96) were significantly more positive to the proposition that the maintenance of the languages of migrant groups is good for the social fabric of Australia than English background respondents (M = 2.75) ($F(1,286)$ = 8.59, p = .004).

There was a significant main effect for school type ($F(4,289)$ = 3.94, p = .004). Follow-up univariate F-tests revealed a significant difference on question 14 ($F(1,292)$ = 14.87, p = .000). High school respondents (M = 2.73) were significantly more in agreement that the existence of informal ethnic groupings within schools hinders students' integration into the school community than primary respondents (M = 2.38).

There was a significant main effect for level of multiculturalism ($F(8,578)$ = 2.66, p = .007). Follow-up univariate F-tests revealed a significant difference for question 12 ($F(2,291)$ = 4.11, p = .017) with mono-cultural Anglo schools (M = 2.5) significantly less positive to the proposition that the maintenance of the religions of migrant groups is good for the social fabric of Australia than either multicultural schools (M = 2.76) and transitional schools (M = 2.88). Follow-up univariate F-tests revealed a significant difference for question 13 ($F(2,291)$ = 3.04), p = .050) with transitional schools (M = 2.18) significantly more positive to the proposition that it is beneficial for migrant groups to live together in ethnic communities long-term than either multicultural schools (M = 1.95) or mono-cultural Anglo schools (M = 1.90). Finally, follow-up univariate F-tests revealed a significant difference for question 14 ($F(2,291)$ = 4.42, p = .013) with both mono-cultural Anglo (M = 2.67) and multicultural (M = 2.679) agreeing more strongly with the proposition that the existence of informal ethnic groupings within schools hinders students' integration into the school community than transitional schools ($M = 2.39$).

The most striking feature of these analyses is the relatively negative attitude of the respondents to each of the questions. Twenty-six percent of the respondents do not agree that the maintenance of community languages and religions is good for Australia. This negative attitude rises to 78% for the proposition that it is beneficial for immigrant groups to live together in ethnic communities for long periods of time. Fifty seven percent of the respondents believe that the existence of ethnic groupings within school hinders integration. Again, NESB respondents were more positive on each of the questions, although the differences were only statistically significant on question 11. Primary schools were also more positive on each proposition although the differences were only statistically significant on question 14. Type of school influenced attitudes on three of the four questions as elaborated above. Again the commitment to multiculturalism as reflected in these questions is less, perhaps, than envisioned in the multicultural policy documents and in the Participation Report.

We also conducted analyses by length of teaching service and position on staff (administrative or teaching). Length of teaching service was grouped in three streams—up to ten years, eleven to twenty years, and more than twenty years. Position on staff was broadly grouped into administrative and class teacher. There were no significant main effects for either grouping variable on any of the sets of questions. This was interesting as we had anticipated that teachers who had been in the service for more than twenty years would hold more negative attitudes than either of the other two groups who had been increasingly exposed to multicultural curricula within their teacher training courses. This result can be viewed positively, that is that older teachers have kept up to date with developments over the intervening years. Conversely, and probably more accurately, it can be viewed negatively, that is that even recently trained teachers hold no more positive attitudes towards multiculturalism in school contexts than teachers trained prior to the implementation of the policies. We had also anticipated that administrative staff, who are charged with implementing multicultural policies would be more positive than classroom teachers. Again, a result showing no difference in attitude is worrying and throws into relief that if the administrative staff are, at the best, ambivalent, and at the worst, negative towards multicultural initiatives, then what chance does the classroom teacher have.

The following presents the results of the qualitative elaborations of the quantitative study. For each question we present the percentages answering "yes" and "no" to each question across the full sample, and a range of elaborations for the "yes" and "no" responses made. You will note that even when respondents are positive they may qualify their response negatively, and vice versa.

Key Questions	Responses	Reasons Given
Language Maintenance		
1. Maintenance of the family language is important for the student	97% yes	YES: Important and valuable for developing literacy skills in English, for inter-generation communication, self-esteem, identity and pride in their culture. It is important to preserve cultural heritage and family traditions. Their home language should be encouraged and shared, however, learning English should be a priority too. It adds depth to the cultural pool.
	3% no	NO: Difficulties arise when students use the home language in school and the teacher is unable to understand what is being said to them.
2. NESB students should be encouraged by the school to retain their language:	91% yes	YES: Encouraged, yes, however this is a family/parental responsibility, and unless the language is official, it would be impossible to teach in an already overloaded curriculum.
	9% no	NO. Teachers don't have the time, funding or resources to do this and continue to teach all the other subjects. This is the parents' responsibility and there are various time constraints to implement this. Schools should be able to guide and direct students towards language opportunities in school or community.
3. It is the school's responsibility to help students retain their family language:	33% yes	YES: Enriches the school culture and promotes a feeling of being valued, leading to family co-operation and inclusion. We already have an over-crowded curriculum and lack of time to do this. It would depend on student numbers. English skills should take the priority. The local and ethnic communities could fund this, but we need trained staff and student willingness to choose a common language.
	67% no	NO: This is a family responsibility, not the schools. Overloaded curriculum. If resources were provided. Although very important, useful language classes are beyond the scope of our brief.

Key Questions	Responses	Reasons Given
4. Schools should play significant role in teaching community languages:	68% yes	YES: It depends on the resources the Department or the Community is prepared to give the school to teach these languages. There should be a greater emphasis on the language used in the community. Community languages of a particular school should be the only languages available to learn. Where there is community cooperation, endorsement and staff equipped for the job.
	32% no	NO: School staffing issues preclude this; timetable constraints, other situations can provide this, eg., family, Saturday school and distance education. It is difficult to accommodate all languages.
5. It is desirable for community languages to be used for instruction:	44% yes	YES: Gives students opportunity to strengthen their skills in their own language. Language acceptance increases students' feelings of acceptance. This can interfere with English instruction, which is equally as vital; this should not be done in mainstream classes, only in L.O.T.E classes. If they can understand English as well as their own language. In the ideal world this is an excellent idea, however lack of resources is a major problem. Important for Primary school children so that peers can communicate in language one and language two. It needs to be flexible, as school language groups change over time. In the Kindergarten and Year One levels, this would ensure understanding of key concepts.
	56% no	NO: Commonly those who disagreed cited lack of funding, resources and time as barriers to this as well as English being the schools priority. Family/community should play a role in this. These students need to assimilate into Australian culture and this would not assist them to learn English.

Cultural Maintenance

6. Schools should encourage the preservation of cultural differences	74% yes	YES: Teaches tolerance, understanding, cultural awareness and diversity. Where difference can be a basis of division, we have to be careful to make sure differences are valued.
	26% no	NO: Celebrate cultural diversity but aim to the integration of all ethnic groups in Australian laws, practices, culture etc. We should appreciate their differences, but not present and promote them. Schools should encourage unity and highlight similarities rather than differences.

Key Questions	Responses	Reasons Given
7. A study of other cultures should be part of the curriculum for all students	84% yes	YES: Promotes understanding and acceptance. Programming for this already, H.S.I.E Syllabus.
	16% no	NO: It is important for children to be aware and educated to avoid uninformed judgements. If possible in the given time and curriculum. Children need to be aware of the many cultures that make up the modern Australian identity. Time constraints. Curriculum overcrowded. Them and us mentality.
8. English speaking background students should attend culture and language classes to learn about ethnic groups	41% yes	YES: The majority who commented (yes and no responses) suggested it should be a personal/family choice. Cross cultural understanding.
	59% no	NO: Personal, family choice. Not compulsory.
9. Teachers should be familiar with customs and language of students	84% yes	YES: Majority agreed with Customs but not Languages. Promotes awareness, understanding and acceptance. Only within the practical limits and requirements of the job. This would be ideal. Awareness of minority groups.
	16% no	NO: Only to the extent where they are aware of cultural constraints affecting the student's ability to perform set tasks.
10. Schools should encourage students to wear the clothes, eat foods, wear the traditional dress	35% yes	YES: Multicultural days, food and games.
	65% no	NO: Not clothing; Important not to highlight *differences*, as this causes division. Best to develop a focus on *similarity* at school. Majority did not agree with Uniform—School uniform encourages unity. This limits integration, how do you achieve a sense of identity, creates a division which occurs naturally. Special days (cultural fairs) only.

Broader Community

11. The maintenance of community languages is good for Australia	74% yes	YES: Good for cultural diversity
	26% no	NO: English essential to their functioning in this country.

Key Questions	Responses	Reasons Given
12. The maintenance of religions of immigrant groups is good for Australia	73% yes	YES: Freedom of religion is important in Australia for everyone. As long as tolerance is included. Religious intolerance on any level is unacceptable—but so is religious conflict—perhaps this area needs lots of objectivity—no religious fervour.
	27% no	NO: Religion is the basis of many peoples whole outlook. This is difficult; some religions have highly political motivations and teachings that are misused as a focus of control. Religious belief that encourages bigotry and hatred is bad in any context—migrant or non-migrant alike.
13. It is beneficial for immigrant groups to live together in ethnic communities	22% yes	YES: Short term yes, long term, no. First or second generation Australian only.
	78% no	NO: Becomes exclusive. Integration and mixing is preferable to isolation. Eventually we must break out of the ghetto mentality and make a commitment to Australia.
14. The existence of ethnic groupings within school hinders integration	57% yes	YES: When students exclude others on any basis, it hinders integration into the community. Strong ethnic groups can reinforce some inappropriate behaviour at times and make it more difficult for individuals to understand the Australian culture and the school expectations.
	43% no	NO: It's natural to want to be with like-minded people. If the child is happy all will happen. Children generally accept people as they are. They need each other for support and understanding. Students can identify strongly with an ethnic group and still work very positively in the community.

Qualitative Analyses

An analysis of the qualitative data reveals the difficulty in forcing the choice for teachers, particularly on more contentious issues—many wanted a bit both ways, with qualifications. The quantitative data should be considered in this light as some of the negativity may be explained in terms of practical concerns teachers have regarding the effective implementation of many multicultural programs. These practical issues relate to resources, time allocation, the responsibility of the school vis a vis family responsibility, the availability of other agencies (for example, ethnic schools) to maintain language and culture. However, a considerable amount of negativity reflects the view that our society should be homogeneous, and multiculturalism works against the best interests of the society at large.

The qualitative data also reveal some of the reasons teachers give for positive responses to key elements of the multiculturalism. These include a reflection of the economic, personal and social benefits assumed to be obtained by the implementation of such programs. However, many of the positive responses, for example to schools playing a significant role in teaching community languages, are qualified by teachers. Many teachers indicate that unless appropriate resources and training are available these programs will not work. They also mention the potential of conflict between introducing multicultural programs (such as community language programs) and major curricula emphases (such as teaching effective English to all students). So the issue is very complex, and this complexity is best revealed through a cross-referencing of the qualitative material with the quantitative results. Unfortunately, this chapter does not allow the scope to go into this in great detail.

Section 2 Analyses

We also sought information on respondents' knowledge, beliefs and attitudes towards multicultural curricula and programs. The answers to these questions have been qualitatively coded and categorized, as well as quantified in order to make a comparison with the earlier data. In the following Table we present a brief overview of these. Again, these responses help illuminate the knowledge and practices teachers and schools have of multiculturalism.

Key Questions	*Summary of Responses*
Incorporating Cultures	
1. If your school's long-term plans are to incorporate the migrant cultures of students into the life of the school (e.g., through the curriculum and social activities), how is this carried out?	Multicultural and family days, language classes, bilingual and anti-racism programs, interpreters, religious festival days, guest speakers from many cultures and multilingual newsletters. One high school that had been Anglo dominant had set up a curriculum committee to design the school curriculum in order to incorporate the languages of the increasing number of new students from NESB.
Students' Difficulties	
2. What do you consider the most significant difficulties to be overcome by students of minority cultural groups in our society?	English language acquisition and first language are barriers to learning. Some groups (mainly Lebanese and Vietnamese) suffer from lack of acceptance and tolerance, social stereotypes, racist comments and attitudes, and bullying. Many have difficulties maintaining their own cultural background while learning a new culture.

Key Questions	Summary of Responses

Aims of Education

3. What do you see as the most important aims of the education of students of minority cultural groups?

Some Anglo dominant schools considered that the most important aim was fostering the integration and assimilation of minority group students. Schools with large numbers of minority groups considered important: ensuring equality of all cultures, valuing diversity, maintaining cultural identity and customs. All schools agreed that it was vital to teach students to communicate in English, improve their literacy and numeracy skills, and to learn tolerance and acceptance.

Parental Involvement

4. To what extent does your school foster the involvement of parents of children with language backgrounds other than English?

Only schools where there were large NESB student populations found it relevant to foster parental involvement through community liaison officers and interpreters, parent and teacher meetings, letters sent home in community languages, playgroups, community activities, parental information evenings and fundraisers.

Assisting New Arrivals

5. How do you think schools can help the newly-arrived child of migrant or refugee parents become accustomed to the Australian culture?

In terms of school assistance for the newly arrived child of migrant parents, schools used a variety of strategies such as; peer tutoring and buddy systems, E.S.L programs and classes, community liaison officers, and inviting parents to school activities, functions and meetings.

Resources for Languages

6. What resources does the school have for teaching Community Languages (CL)?

CL resources at schools with large numbers of NESB students included the provision of ESL teachers, language classes and programs designed to accommodate their community with some hosting community language classes on Saturdays. Other resources provided were library books/ videos, and NESB teacher expertise. In the same schools and also in the Anglo dominant schools, many staff were unaware of the resources in their school or perceived that there were none.

Resources for Cultures

7. What resources does the school have for teaching about the cultures of the groups that have settled in Australia?

The resources used for teaching about cultural groups were similar to the resources used for teaching community languages. This included; H.S.I.E syllabus content (multicultural kits and units of work), teachers and parents of non English speaking backgrounds and their expertise, family festivals, library resources, books, textbooks, posters, videos, guest

Key Questions	*Summary of Responses*
	speakers and computer software programs. There were still a lot of responses indicating that they were unaware of any resources or the school provided no resources at all.

Aboriginal Needs

8. If there are Aboriginal students at your school, comment on their learning needs and the school's role in addressing these.	The majority of schools considered the learning needs of Aboriginal students to be the same as any other students. Highlighted in the responses were; an Aboriginal perspective was integrated into the Key Learning Areas in the area of literacy and numeracy, individual programs, addressing cultural backgrounds, traditional home, dialects and celebrations, time and overcrowded curriculum restraints. There were a large number of responses indicating that they "didn't know" or simply didn't want to comment.

ESL Teaching

9. What does your school do to foster the English language acquisition of non-English speaking background students?	The common theme across all schools for language acquisition was teacher in-servicing, ESL teachers, classes, programs and individual or group withdrawal from class, support staff, buddies interpreting, whole school approach to literacy and numeracy, intensive reading in English and literacy programs, D.E.A.R program, resources and games. There were a large number of responses, which indicated there was little or no effort to assist ESL students, and a large number of staff chose not to comment at all.

Enrolment Procedures

10. How do the enrolment procedures at your school facilitate an understanding of the students' cultural and educational needs?	A large number of staff indicated that they were unaware of the enrolment procedures that facilitated an understanding of a student's cultural and educational needs. Community liaison officers were involved in enrolment interviews and assist in translating conversations, notes and forms for migrant parents and the child if needed. School reports from previous school, transfer forms and enrolment procedures.

Key Questions	*Summary of Responses*

Authentic Assessment

11. What does your school do to support the authentic assessment of non-English speaking background students' achievements? | The most common response for the assessment of ESL students was progress folders or portfolios, pupil records and reports sent home to the families in community languages. Other comments consisted of; the involvement of ESL teachers, community liaison officers and interpreters at verbal interviews with parents. There were a lot of staff responses indicating they did not know and a lot who did not comment at all.

Effective Reporting

12. How does your school facilitate effective reporting to parents of the achievements of non-English speaking background students? | The effective facilitation of reporting to parents was considered by the majority to be the role of the community liaison officers and/or ESL teachers at the school during parent and teacher interviews and letters translated into their home or community language. Portfolios and progress reports sent home to all students' parents. Alarmingly, there were a lot of staff who were unaware of the reporting procedures to parents of ESL children and a lot did not comment at all.

SUMMARY AND CONCLUSION

There is some evidence that there has been an improvement in attitude towards language maintenance through community language programs over the twenty years since the publication of the Participation Report, with the most positive attitudes being expressed by teachers in primary schools, and teachers from NESB backgrounds. However, there still appears to be considerable reluctance by many of the respondents to accept that language maintenance is a key responsibility of schools, and in particular, those schools with students from NES backgrounds. Considering that community language programs have Government backing and therefore should be mandated at appropriate schools further work appears necessary to get community language programs fully supported and implemented.

As indicated above, there are two striking features of the analysis of teacher attitudes towards cultural maintenance. There is a more negative attitude towards the school's active role in cultural maintenance than revealed in the original study (although, overall, responses are still very positive). There are also negative attitudes towards students from various backgrounds learning the languages and traditions of other groups, and members of ethnic groups appearing "ethnic" at school. This is of course, problematic, as it becomes increasingly common for various cultural groups to insist that school uniforms (the norm in Australian schools) allow for cultural customs, such as veils, turbans and so on. Again, these differences were moderated by school type and language background of teachers.

Finally, with regard to multiculturalism and the broader community there is still considerable ambivalence with regard to encouraging the maintenance of community languages and religions, as well as community groupings, as essential elements of a multicultural society. Again, these results were moderated by type of school, and language background of respondents.

An analysis of the qualitative data reveals the difficulty in forcing the choice for teachers, particularly on contentious issues—many wanted a bit both ways, with qualifications. The quantitative data should be considered in this light as some of the negativity may be explained in terms of practical concerns teachers have regarding the effective implementation of many multicultural practices. Even when positive attitudes are generally expressed some teachers have reservations related to resources and the training needed to implement the practices properly and effectively.

From our study it appears that primary schools are more positively disposed to implementing key elements of multicultural education than secondary schools. This may reflect the fact that, by and large, primary teachers receive compulsory teacher education courses that specifically emphasize the implementation of key multicultural programs, even in schools not characterized by ethnic diversity. Secondary teachers, on the other hand, may receive little, if any, direct training in multiculturalism as part of their core training. The results could also reflect the fact that primary schools are less complex places in which to introduce key multicultural programs, and perhaps, because they are less centered on external examinations, which drive much of the curriculum at secondary level, allow the space in the curriculum for such initiatives. There is also some evidence that transitional schools are less well disposed to multicultural initiatives than mono-cultural schools. We speculated, above, that this might be because transitional schools are grappling with the issues at a more intense level than schools that are mono-cultural anglo or ethnic. Certainly this points to the need for transitional schools to be given extra support in the implementation of specific programs that are needed within their evolving school contexts. This would include extra resourcing and the continuing education of the teachers at these schools to effectively implement multicultural strategies.

One problematic finding was that school administrators, charged with the implementation of multicultural programs were no more positive than the teachers. It would appear, therefore, that considerable effort still needs to be expended in communicating the nature and purpose of mandated policy to administrators and teachers. If administrators are not convinced of the usefulness of multicultural strategies and aware of effective methods for implementing them, it is not likely that the teachers under their supervision will be. This is particularly the case in mono-cultural anglo schools. Considerable effort therefore needs to be expended in providing the training and resources necessary for the proper commitment of teachers and administrators to the programs developed to implement these policies. It is obvious from the qualitative results that teachers do not think, as yet, that resources and training are sufficient.

Limitations in the Study

A study such as this has inherent weaknesses. First among these is a sampling problem. We cannot constrain schools or individuals to cooperate and hence we cannot guarantee that the responses from our sample schools are not biased and truly reflect teacher attitudes across the three broad categories of schools across the State of New South Wales, let alone Australia. Indeed, had we obtained usable data from one large anglo school that did not participate effectively the results may have been quite different, and perhaps a greater contrast drawn between mono-cultural, multicultural and transitional schools. The questions themselves were not necessarily the most appropriate but were written to reflect questions that were asked in the 1979 survey. We had to update the language of some of the questions as the way in which one talks about multiculturalism now is different from twenty years ago when "political correctness" was less powerful. Within the sampled schools there were not enough English as a Second Language teachers to make a comparison group. In 1979, we were able to include such a group. The forced choice response format no doubt annoyed some respondents who said that a 'black' or "white" answer was not possible. However, we alleviated this concern by allowing respondents to make open-ended responses to clarify their answers and these are detailed in another paper. Finally, our study reflects the attitudes of teachers at both primary and secondary schools. The 1979 study only sampled primary teachers. As we have seen in this survey primary teachers are generally more positive than secondary teachers across most questions and so the results comparing the two studies may be skewed and not as revealing of differences if the study had only used primary schools. This can be addressed by comparing the primary teachers in this sample with those of the earlier study, although the sample size for comparison is then reduced. We will conduct this analysis later.

ACKNOWLEDGMENTS

The support of the following colleagues contributed greatly to the original design and data collection for this study, and is gratefully acknowledged: Dr. Paolo Totaro, Dr. Madeleine Cincotta, Ms. Deborah Williams. We also thank Lana Jackson and Jane Breen for their assistance with the qualitative data.

REFERENCES

Alcorso, C., & Cope, B. (1986). *A review of multicultural education policy 1979–1986. NACCME Commissioned research paper No.6.* Woden, Australia: National Advisory and Coordinating Committee on Multicultural Education.

AusInfo. (1999). A new agenda for multicultural Australia. Canberra, ACT: Aus-Info.

Australian Bureau of Statistics. (2000). A statistical profile of Australia [Web Page]. URL. http://www.abs.gov.au/[2000]

Cope, B., Kalatnzis, M., & Poynting, S. (1997). Building unity out of diversity in Australian schools: Making 'one nation' the sum of its parts. [Web Page] URL http://www.edoz.com.au/educationaustralia/edoz/issues/intercultural.html.

Davis, D. A. (1982). *Galbally recommendation 14: Evaluation study.* Canberra: AGPS.

Hill, B., & Allan, R. (2001). Immigration policy, multicultural and anti-racist education in Australia: Charting the changes. In F. Salili & R. Hoosain (Eds.), *Multicultural education: Issues, policies and practices* (pp. 151–165). Greenwich, CT: Information Age Press.

Harris, J. (1980). *Identity: A study of the concept in education for a multicultural Australia* (ERDC Report No. 22). Canberra: AGPS.

Kalantzis, M., Cope, B., Noble, G., & Poynting, S. (1990). *Cultures of schooling: Pedagogies for cultural difference and social access.* London: Falmer Press.

McInerney, D. M. (1979). *Education for a multicultural society report.* Sydney: Milperra College of Advanced Education

McInerney, D. M. (1987a). Teacher attitudes to multicultural curriculum development. *Australian Journal of Education, 31* (2), 129–144.

McInerney, D. M. (1987b). The need for the continuing education of teachers: a multicultural perspective. *Journal of Intercultural Studies, 8,* 45–54.

McInerney, D. M. (1987c). The need for the continuing education of teachers in non-racist education—an Australian perspective. *Multicultural Teaching. Special Issue: Continuing Education, 6,* 31–35.

McInerney, D. M., & McInerney, V. (2001). *Educational psychology: Constructing learning. 3rd Edition.* Sydney: Prentice Hall.

New South Wales DET. (2001). *Multicultural education* [Web Page] URL http://www.schools.nsw.edu.au/learning/integrated/multiculturaled.php.

New South Wales DET (1999) *DRAFT Multicultural Policy.* Sydney: Government Printer.

New South Wales. Department of Education. (1983). *Multicultural education policy 1983*. Sydney: Multicultural Education Centre Directorate of Special Programs.

New South Wales. Ethnic Affairs Commission. (1978). *Participation*. Sydney: NSWGP.

New South Wales. Higher Education Board (1984). *Higher education in a multicultural society*. Sydney: The Board.

Office of Multicultural Affairs. (1989). *National agenda for a multicultural Australia...Sharing our future*. Canberra: AGPS.

Phillip Institute of Technology. (1984). *Review of the Commonwealth Multicultural Education Program: Volume 1* (Report to the Commonwealth Schools Commission). Canberra: The Commission.

Poole, M. E. (1987). Multiculturalism, participation and equity: Discussion on educational processes, policies and outcomes. *Australian Educational Researcher, 15*, 21–36.

Sachs, J. (1989). Match or mismatch: Teachers' conceptions of culture and multicultural education policy. *Australian Journal of Education, 33*, 19–33.

Smolicz, J. J. (1971). Is the Australian school an assimilationist agency? *Education News, 13*, 4–8.

CHAPTER 10

TEACHING IN HIGHER EDUCATION

International Initiatives Promoting Quality and Value

Alenoush Saroyan and Marian Jazvac

The illiterate of the 21st century will not be those who cannot read and write, but those who cannot learn, unlearn, and relearn.

—Alvin Toffler

In the past few decades we have witnessed fundamental change patterns in postsecondary systems worldwide. Changes include the shift from elite to mass education, the explosion of knowledge fields and specialties, reduced public funding, and the restructuring of universities (Blackburn & Lawrence, 1995; Clark, 1996; Ducharme, 1996; Everett & Entrekin, 1994; Fisher, 1994; Karpiak, 1997; Ramsden, 1998a; Thorsen, 1996). Of these factors, perhaps none have had as big an impact on the quality of teaching and learning as the phenomenal rate of increase in enrollments in postsecondary systems.

High enrollments have meant wider access and a greater diversity in student populations, hence a greater variation in intellectual abilities, motiva-

Teaching, Learning, and Motivation in a Multicultural Context, pages 223–241
Copyright © 2003 by Information Age Publishing
All rights of reproduction in any form reserved.

tion, learning styles and other factors known to be predictors of academic achievement (see e.g., Weiner, 1986). The preparation and goals that enabled students to succeed even in the worst teaching situations in the past are not sufficient for successful functioning in universities today. Moreover, expectations of employers from their educated employees have changed. Reasoning, problem-solving, and in general, the ability to learn new skills and content on demand have become more essential requirements than specialized knowledge for employment worldwide, particularly in knowledge-driven economies (Salmi, 2001).

Clearly, the successes of university students these days is largely dependent on the extent to which faculty make student learning their priority and adjust their teaching to motivate and actively engage students of diverse abilities and backgrounds in the learning process.

Teaching, however, is not the only academic duty that is placing greater demand on faculty time. Being productive in research and being able to integrate technology into academic work are examples of some of the other demands that require considerable amounts of time. With these competing demands, how can universities develop their academic staff such that they are able and motivated to provide quality teaching? What are the implications of greater focus on teaching and on the way teaching is valued and rewarded in the university? What are the implications on workload? In several countries, including Canada, the United States and the United Kingdom, significant steps have been taken to improve the quality of education in general and the value of teaching in particular. In this chapter, we discuss several international initiatives that have addressed university teaching and explore their implications on related policy and practice.

FACTORS AFFECTING THE QUALITY
OF TEACHING AND LEARNING

Increased Enrollment

The quality of teaching and learning has been a matter of serious concern for some time now in many of the OECD countries (members of the Organization for Economic Co-operation and Development), and more recently, this has become an issue of equal concern in developing countries (Task Force on Higher Education & Society [TFHES], 2000). The phenomenal growth in postsecondary enrollments since WWII has made this concern even more salient. Among OECD countries, Canada, which has been ranked first for tertiary participation from 1990 and has since maintained the highest level of tertiary school expectancy, shows an 18% rate of growth in full-time enrollment from 1987 to 1997 (Councils of Ministers of Education of Canada, 1999). The statistics are even more remarkable in developing countries where half of the world's postsecondary students live (TFHES, 2000). The Autonomous University of Santa Domingo in the Dominican Republic was established in 1538 to accommodate 6,000 students. Today it has an enrollment of 80,000 (Salmi, 2001). Enrollment numbers are even more staggering elsewhere. For instance, Cairo University shows enrollment of over 155,000 and The National Autonomous University of Mexico, over 200,000.

Student Diversity

One significant consequence of increased enrollments has been greater diversity in the abilities and motivation of student populations. The preparation and goals that enabled the elite students of the past to succeed even in the worst teaching situations cannot be expected to yield the same results today (Astin, 1998; Boyer, Altbach, & Whitelaw, 1994). The diversity of the student population demands that an instructor spend more time informing him/herself about the background, experiences and prior knowledge of students if they wish to avoid creating a situation that disadvantages certain students. An international survey suggests professors find today's students inadequately prepared in basic cognitive skills including written and oral communication and mathematics and quantitative reasoning (Boyer et al., 1994). Taken together, this means students are bound to put greater demands on faculty time and energy and their success is increasingly dependent on the extent to which faculty make learning possible for them (Laurillard, 1993; Ramsden, 1992).

Large enrollments have also had another consequence. They have given the student body the necessary voice and power to demand quality education. The student strikes in North America in the late sixties and early seventies, for instance, were born out of student discontent. At that time, the issue was the irrelevance of courses and uninspired teaching (Gaff, 1978). These concerns are still as relevant as they were four decades ago but now there is a stronger voice that demands quality education.

Expectation of Stakeholders

While the concern for quality teaching and learning has increased rather than diminished, the value attached to teaching has not increased. One reason is that institutional reward systems, particularly in doctoral granting research universities, still strongly favor research and research productivity vis à vis teaching. Another reason is the methods used to allocate funds in publicly funded postsecondary institutions. Some funding formulae give positive weighting only to research productivity defined in terms of number of publications and amount of acquired research grants (Ramsden, 1998a; see also funding system in the U.K.). This practice has gone a long way in altering academic priorities and affecting the nature of academic work (Knight & Trowler, 2001; Laurillard, 1993; McNay, 1995; Ramsden, 1998b; Scott, 1995). If research productivity is the primary outcome expected and favored by those who hold the purse strings, then a question that begs answering is why should faculty be motivated to take teaching seriously and actively engage in its improvement (Karpiak, 1996; Rice & Austin, 1990)?

IMPROVING TEACHING: WHY THE TROUBLE?

As higher education endeavors to accommodate a growing student body with diverse needs, intellectual skills and demands, professors are often left questioning their professional responsibilities and what priority they ought to give to teaching. Clearly, the extent to which teaching is valued and rewarded as an academic responsibility vis à vis research in their respective institutions will have a consequence in the course of action they take.

Cultural diversity is another aspect to be considered. In their ever increasing role as educators of society, teachers in higher education are called upon to create atmospheres of mutual respect, justice and equality within and outside of formal learning environments (Van Note Chism, 2002). Using multiple perspectives to view intellectual endeavors demonstrates the potential for growth through challenge and contrast, thus, promoting a greater societal tolerance of variation.

The significance of motivation in doing whatever it takes to improve teaching cannot be over emphasized in this respect. Centra (1993), has outlined motivation as one of four conditions in his model of improving teaching.[1] The first condition requires that the process of improvement result in some newly gained knowledge. The second stipulates that the individual investing time in the process perceives the improvement as having some value. The third is the availability of mechanisms and support systems to assist the individual in the process of improvement and change. And finally, the fourth condition is the presence of intrinsic or extrinsic motivation for improvement and in the case of the latter this implies rewards, promotions, salary increments and the like. These four distinct conditions make clear that implementing reward structures alone is inadequate to achieve a change in the perceived value of teaching. The establishment of mechanisms and support systems which aid individuals in the process of acquiring new and useful knowledge related to teaching are also necessary to foster change.

IMPROVEMENT INITIATIVES

In the following section of this chapter, we describe four initiatives which have attempted to address the concern about the quality of teaching as well as raise the value accorded to teaching and its scholarship. Three of these initiatives involve undertakings in the higher education systems of the United States, Canada and the United Kingdom whereas the forth is a forum on higher education convened by the World Bank and UNESCO. The selected countries have postsecondary systems that vary in terms of funding, types of institutions, autonomy and accreditation. The specifics of each are elaborated in the following section.

Country Examples

The United States

In the United States, there are both private and public institutions. While the private institutions are mainly funded from non-governmental sources, the main source of funding for public institutions are grants and taxes. Institutions vary in size and in the type of degree they grant. Bachelor, masters and doctoral degrees are granted by colleges and universities. Professional degrees such as medicine, law, and pharmacology are granted by professional schools that are often affiliated with a university. At the national level, there is no central authority that controls the system. Similarly, at the state level, the degree of control varies and in most instances, institutions are fairly autonomous. The outcome of this is a wide range of programs that differ greatly in character and quality and in the types of students they attract. The most visible form of quality control for an institution or program is the accreditation process which verifies whether established standards and criteria have been satisfied. Accreditation is obtained through private educational associations of regional or national scope many of which are linked to professional organizations (e.g., American Medical Association). The reliability of each accrediting agency is determined at a national level by the Secretary of Education (U.S. Department of Education). National level reviews of the accreditation agencies are carried out by the National Advisory Committee on Institutional Quality and Integrity which makes recommendation to the Secretary regarding recognition (U.S. Department of Education, 2000).

Canada

While the higher education systems in Canada are most similar to those in the United States, they differ in a fundamental way. High tuition fees which are common in many U.S. private universities are not a common feature of Canadian universities. The single largest sources of funding for universities are provincial governments which are in turn funded through a bigger envelope by the Federal Government. Tuitions, research grants and endowments provide the balance of university budgets. In this sense, Canadian universities are considered "public" (Jones, 1997), with relatively equal funding per student across the Canadian university system, with no institution being particularly rich or poor. In the past 10 years, however, systematic budget cuts have resulted in the creation of some private programs within this "public" system. The majority of these programs are professional programs such as Medicine or the Master of Business Administration (MBA). There are about 90 university-level institutions in Canada. They range in size from small liberal arts colleges to large, comprehensive institutions with a wide range of undergraduate, graduate, and professional degree programs. About 70 of these grant degrees in all of their own programs. A small number grant degrees in only one or two fields—usually theology—and the others do not grant degrees at all, but are associated with universities that do.

Universities in Canada are highly autonomous; they set their own admission standards and degree requirements, and have considerable flexibility in the management of their financial affairs and program offerings. As is the case in the United States, there is no accrediting body in Canada to evaluate the quality of general undergraduate programs, although a number of agencies perform this function for professional programs at both the undergraduate and graduate levels. While universities across Canada do not constitute a system, per se, there is considerable cooperation between and among Canadian universities through a variety of administrative and academic networks, such as the Association of Universities and Colleges of Canada. Membership in this Association is generally taken as evidence that an institution is providing university-level programs of acceptable standards. In fact, it is widely recognized that university undergraduate programs are remarkably uniform in quality across the country (Councils of Ministers of Education of Canada, 2001).

The United Kingdom

Similar to Canada, the government is the central source of funding for higher education institutions in the United Kingdom. The funds are distributed through regional funding councils in the form of grants. The balance of funds are provided through student tuition fees, individual research grants, private charities and industry. Allocation of the governmental funds, as is the case in Canada, is through the use of a funding formula (British Council, 1999). Central to this formula are the number of students studying in a given institution and a grouping of students into one of four categories representing costs related to different programs (e.g., programs requiring laboratories or high-tech equipment are grouped in a more expensive category than those requiring largely library resources). The quality of research is another factor in the allocation of governmental funds. For instance, a university department that scores highly will be allocated a far higher percentage of research funds than a department with a lower score. Standards of achievement and the quality of education are directly linked to funding and are open to public scrutiny and review by The Quality Assurance Agency for Higher Education (QAA), an independent agency which is funded directly by individual universities and colleges to carry out both institutional and subject quality reviews. The institutional reviews focus on managerial and administrative systems while the subject reviews include an assessment of the quality of courses and the quality of teaching with respect to the stated aims of the institution. The QAA also promotes quality enhancement through the dissemination of good practice. It creates reports to inform the public about all universities and colleges in the United Kingdom, it presents enrollment criteria, and registration trends (British Council, 1999). There are 169 institutes of higher learning in the United Kingdom. This number includes technical and vocational orientation, teacher training and art colleges, and professional schools including those that offer programs in health sciences (British Council, 1999).

Initiatives to Promote the Scholarship of Teaching

As will be noted in the section below, despite the differences in the higher education systems of these three countries, the vision and recommendations forwarded by reports on education conducted in these countries are quite similar. What is more surprising than this similarity is convergence among these recommendations and the views of the Task Force on Higher Education in Developing Countries.

The Boyer Report, U.S.A

In 1990 in the United States, the Carnegie Foundation for the Advancement of Teaching[2] commissioned a study to explore significant issues in undergraduate education. The president of the Foundation at the time, Ernest Boyer, conducted a survey of undergraduate education and prepared a report entitled *Scholarship Reconsidered: Priorities of the professoriate* (Boyer, 1990). This and a following report entitled *Reinventing Undergraduate Education: A blueprint for America's research universities* (Boyer Commission on Education, 1998) generated heated debates about the imbalance between research and teaching in American universities. This report was particularly critical of the fallacy of casting every type of institution in the mold of the European research university and using the criteria that these institutions use to measure academic performance.

Boyer's message to the higher education world was that "scholarship" and "scholarly activities" ought to pertain to every aspect of academic work and not just basic research and related work such as publishing, disseminating, and perhaps conveying research findings to students. He argued that since new knowledge is generated both from basic theoretical research as well as practical experience, a more inclusive definition of scholarship is warranted, "... one in which the rigid categories of teaching, research, and service are broadened and more flexibly defined" (p. 16). Boyer proposed an alternative vision of scholarship, one which comprised four categories: discovery, integration, application and teaching. "Such a vision of scholarship, one that recognizes the great diversity of talent within the professoriate, also may prove especially useful to faculty as they reflect on the meaning and direction of their professional lives" (p. 25).

Boyer's challenge was mainly addressed to the big research universities which, in the course of a few decades, had adopted the European university tradition that emphasized graduate education and research over undergraduate education. He found it ironic that at a time when universities were shifting from class to mass, the focus of these universities was moving from the student to the professoriate and "...the culture of the professoriate was becoming more hierarchical and restrictive" (p. 13).

The Boyer Report generated a vigorous conversation about valuing and rewarding teaching across North American campuses as it challenged the universities to "help faculty build on their strengths and sustain their own creative energies" (p. 43). The Carnegie Foundation and subsequently, the newly founded Carnegie Academy for the Scholarship of Teaching and Learning (CASTL)[3], in collaboration with the Pew Charitable Trusts and the American Society for the Study of Higher Education (ASSHE), began to provide resources for actual campus wide projects concerning the improvement of teaching and learning. Policies that supported the "scholarship" of teaching began to be formulated and acted upon. These comprised major steps toward promoting the scholarship of teaching.

The Smith Report, Canada

The second initiative, undertaken in Canada about the same time as the Boyer Report, was a commission appointed by the Association of Universities and Colleges of Canada (AUCC)[4] to look into the quality of education in Canadian universities. The mandate of the Commission of Inquiry was to examine the ability of universities to "adapt rapidly to the needs of a

Canada that is and will continue to be increasingly dependent on the essential national resource of well-educated citizens" (p. 3). Its goal then, was not just limited to finding out how well the universities were carrying out their educational mandate, but to also make recommendations for the future. This concern over quality was timely as the postsecondary systems, which had been confronted by rapid expansion in a short time span, were beginning to face severe institutional budgetary cuts and rising costs across Canadian provinces.

The Commission developed a report (hereafter referred to as the Smith Report) (Smith, 1991) based on extensive public hearings, hundreds of written briefs, and several commissioned research projects (see e.g., Donald & Saroyan, 1991). In fulfilling the mandate, the Smith Report concluded with a list of sixty-four recommendations concerning funding, curricula, international dimension, continuing and distance education, research on higher education, accessibility, attrition, tenure, links with the secondary school system, co-operation within higher education, future supply of faculty, quality control and performance indicators, and teaching and learning. There were fourteen recommendations pertaining specifically to teaching and learning. Among these were recommendations that each institution define scholarship in a much broader manner and consider pedagogical and technological innovations as scholarly contributions and support them as necessary. A central recommendation was that competence in teaching and graduate supervision and the development of these competencies be considered at every phase of academic life, including the time of hiring, and that it be made a condition for obtaining research grants. Moreover, that each university dedicate fixed funding for the pedagogical training of doctoral students and faculty members, as well as training teaching assistants before they are called upon to teach university students. Finally, the report recommended that senior professors share in the teaching of early undergraduate courses, and that the teaching dossier or portfolio be widely adopted as the basis for evaluating the teaching record of faculty.

The Dearing Report: Higher Education in the Learning Society, United Kingdom

The third national project was undertaken in the United Kingdom as part of the cyclical planning process which reviews each institution and all subjects once in a six-year cycle. This academic review reports on the establishment, maintenance and enhancement of academic standards, the quality of learning opportunities and institutional management of standards and quality. The most recent committee was convened in 1996 and charged to make recommendations on the purposes, funding, size and structure of the higher education system. This included recommendations for ways in which higher education should develop in order to meet the needs of the United Kingdom in the next 20 years, while recognizing that higher education embraces teaching, learning, scholarship as well as research.

Various sections of the report underscored the importance of teaching and learning from different perspectives. The Dearing Report highlighted the significance of life long learning and foresaw a national need and demand for higher education to expand, opening its doors to all kinds of students: young and mature, full-time and part-time, those with diverse cultural backgrounds, those with the highest intellectual potential as well as those who have struggled to reach the threshold of higher education. It challenged the system to enable all students to achieve beyond their expectations and to be at the leading edge of world practice in effective learning and teaching. Finally, the Dearing Report foresaw increasingly active partnerships between higher education institutions and the worlds of industry commerce and public service.

The Task Force on Higher Education, the World Bank and UNESCO

A more recent forum concerned with education systems world wide was convened in 2000 by the World Bank and UNESCO. This Task Force on Higher Education brought together experts from 13 countries for the purpose of exploring the future of higher education in the developing world. The priorities voiced by the task force were similar to those articulated in the 3 national reports. Recommendations placed emphasis on an education that could be used as a springboard for future learning; an education that would provide not only broader and more specialized skills but one that would hone students' higher order thinking and problem-solving skills; and an education that would be flexible, innovative, and relevant to the demands of a fast-changing world.

Points of Convergence

The three reports and forum described above have charted a converging course that is being threaded steadily, albeit slowly, in Canada, the United States, the United Kingdom, as well as elsewhere (e.g., Australia and New Zealand). Three main converging points are particularly salient. The first is that there is an intentional move to highlight the teaching mission of universities; to value teaching as an academic activity that is as important as research. The second is the subtle yet very important shift from characterizing universities from teaching to learner centered institutions and this is evident in recommendations that specifically address students and the quality of student learning. The third is a message to higher education institutions to create opportunities for their culturally and intellectually diverse student populations: to help them become life-long learners so that they can adjust to the needs of an ever changing society.

The more tangible outcomes of the three reports discussed above are the policies and practices that have emerged in the past 10 years in Canada, the United States and the United Kingdom. We highlight some of these in the following section.

Emerging Key Policies and Practices

One Impact of the Boyer Report

Following the Boyer Report, The Carnegie Foundation for the Advancement of Teaching launched The Carnegie Academy for the Scholarship of Teaching and Learning (CASTL) and began to use it as the venue through which the scholarship of teaching would be promoted. Since then, the Academy has sought to realize Boyer's vision by recommending that the same criteria which are used to evaluate research be applied to teaching. Making teaching public, that is, taking it out of the classroom and making it open to criticism by professional peers is one criterion that is being promoted. Another is the creation of a knowledge base that can both inform and be informed by innovative practices of the members of the community. As Lee Shulman, the present Carnegie Foundation President, has asserted, innovative teaching practices are seldom shared with others; nor do they become the basis for developing new pedagogical knowledge (Shulman, 1993). The goal of the Academy is to make this possible. To this end, the Academy has introduced 3 programs: one at the individual level, one at the campus level and one at the level of professional societies.

At the individual level, the program is referred to as The Pew National Fellowship Program for Carnegie Scholars. This program aims to bring together outstanding faculty committed to investigating and documenting significant issues in teaching and learning of their respective fields. The disciplinary differences of the scholars only add to the richness of the experiences and expertise shared and discussed. More importantly, they provide a wealth of information as to how students' learning experiences can be enhanced through innovative teaching. To date, around 120 scholars have benefited from this program.

At the campus level, a program entitled The Teaching Academy Campus Program provides support to those institutions which want to pursue a particular initiative of their choice that supports teaching and learning. The proposed initiatives are as varied in scope and nature as are the types of institutions that undertake them. Through this program, campuses collaborate to cultivate an environment which fosters the scholarship of teaching. As of Fall 2000, 180 campuses have signaled that they are working actively on a project to foster the scholarship of teaching and learning.

Finally, the third program involves work with the Scholarly and Professional Societies that are committed to advancing and supporting the scholarship of teaching and learning. Much of the work related to promoting the scholarship of teaching hinges on the availability of knowledgeable individuals who can contribute to the peer review process. In addition to supporting the development of networks, this initiative provides small grants to professional organizations to help develop such expertise.

Two Consequences of the Smith Report

Similar to the Boyer Report, the Smith Report, among other things, underscored the importance of valuing teaching and learning. It conveyed a deep concern about a trend being imported from the United States which placed greater value on the quantity of research publication than excellence in teaching. Notwithstanding this concern, it also noted that many Canadian universities had reinforced the primacy of their educational role in revised mission statements and had gone even further to carefully examine actual practice on campus with a view to maintain or reinstate proper balance between research and teaching. The actual implementations of the recommendations of the Smith Report were left to the discretion of the universities though many of them were swift in adopting and acting upon them. Two of the recommendations that have been implemented widely in Canadian universities are: (a) the teaching portfolio[5] as the basis for evaluating the teaching record of faculty, and (b) pedagogical training for doctoral students and faculty.

The teaching portfolio or dossier has a long history in Canada. The idea of the portfolio or dossier was initially developed under the auspices of the Canadian Association of University Teachers (Shore, Foster, Knapper, Nadeau, Neill, & Sim, 1986). Subsequently, it was taken on by the staff of American Association for Higher Education (AAHE) as one of the projects inspired by the Carnegie Foundation to improve teaching at all levels (Edgerton, Hutchings, & Quinlan, 1991). In 1993, Seldin suggested that about 400 colleges and universities in the United States were experimenting or using teaching portfolios as a way to put together evidence on teaching effectiveness. In the United Kingdom, the use of teaching portfolios is also widely supported by the Institute for Learning and Teaching (Centre for Academic Practice, 2000).

With respect to pedagogical training for doctoral students and faculty, four Canadian universities have created entire programs of study that offer either M.Ed. or M.A. degrees specifically in higher education or post-secondary education (e.g., University of British Columbia, University of Toronto, University of Manitoba, and Memorial University). The University of

British Columbia has also created a certificate program in teaching and learning in higher education specifically for faculty members. Faculty must apply to participate in this one year program which engages them in specific course-work, on-site practicum experiences and teaching dossier development (Hubball, 2001). As well, almost all Canadian universities now offer graduate courses in university pedagogy (Saroyan, Amundsen, & Cao, 1997). Courses such as these affirm that teachers are not born; that teaching is not a gift and that it can be developed with practice, experimentation, and reflection.

Impact of the Dearing Report

One of the visions forwarded by the Dearing report was that the United Kingdom would be at the leading edge of world practice in effective learning and teaching. To address this recommendation, the U.K. higher education funding bodies established a new Learning and Teaching Support Network to promote high quality learning and teaching in all subject disciplines in higher education. The network supports the sharing of innovation and good practices, including the use, where possible, of communications and information technology. The network consists of 24 subject centers, a generic learning and teaching centre and a technology integration center.

The subject centers are the main points of contact within subject communities for information and advice on good practices and innovations in learning, teaching, assessment, and provide support for many networks which already exist.

The generic learning and teaching centre (ILT—Institute for Learning and Teaching) promotes and disseminates information concerning practices that are common to all subjects. In short, it provides strategic advice to the sector on generic learning and teaching issues, disseminates good practice in the development and deployment of new methods and new technologies and acts as a knowledge broker for innovation in learning and teaching.

Finally, the technology integration centre investigates, develops and produces the applicability of new technologies in support of the whole education process in higher and further education. This includes technologies relevant to learning and teaching and their integration into wider student support and administrative systems.

Across the three countries there are also many other programs that have emerged in response to the growing discourse on the need to improve the quality of postsecondary education. Among these are programs for first year students which facilitate their transfer to university from the high school, programs for new faculty, interdisciplinary teaching conferences and subject area publications that focus on pedagogical issues. Collectively, these indicate that a solid base is being developed across higher education systems, that knowledge is being harnessed for the improvement of teaching and learning, and that we are becoming better equipped to face the challenges ahead.

CHALLENGES AHEAD

The initiatives discussed above have had some effect in making teaching a valued and more visible act on some campuses but these changes are not widespread. Redressing the imbalance between teaching and research, making teaching count, and improving the quality of teaching and learning remain to be big challenges in our universities. Some of these challenges will require unconventional solutions, for instance, substantive changes in the context and the approach to the teaching task.

To manage the learning process for more diverse and greater numbers of students, professors will have to consider the trade-off between the quantity and quality of time spent with students. They will also have to consider what optimal teaching means to them. For instance, the model of the expert who disseminates knowledge might be less relevant in a context where the learning goals are broad and include higher order thinking skills. In attempts to optimize student learning though various teaching practices, the often ignored or forgotten factors are culturally different ways of learning, various modes of expression, and the social context of students. A relevant example would be the student that does not engage in frequent questions and vocalizations in a classroom that expects and allocates grades to active participation. In such a situation, the teaching role may have to change dramatically if the teacher decides to take on the responsibility of first teaching the students how to become active participants so that no individual is disadvantaged because of background or lack of prior experience. As acknowledgment of the contextual factors that affect student motivation expands, a "competent" professor might no longer be someone who is just an expert in the subject matter but one who can facilitate the learning process.

If the quality of students' educational experience is to be maintained or improved, innovative teaching strategies which promote student learning will have to become widespread. Herein lies the most difficult hurdle: faculty members' resistance to change. Though many professors are ready to adopt new methods of teaching as circumstances change, others find change hard to accept. They do not reflect much on their teaching nor do they consider what good teaching practice is. The lack of incentives to develop teaching knowledge and skills and the limited opportunities for staff development in institutions/departments reinforce inertia. Universities need to continue to emphasize the centrality of learning and teaching in all their work. By explicitly stating how they intend to support their faculty in this regard, they can take a huge step in motivating their staff to take interest in their teaching and to make changes as required.

If institutions expect that their professors invest the time to learn about teaching, they need to send a message in a very tangible way that these sorts of activities are valued by the university. Engaging in new ways of teaching requires considerable time investment in order to develop a general knowledge of pedagogy and a specific knowledge of the pedagogy that pertains to the subject matter. Planning for learning and designing new forms of instruction which support learning ought to be considered as important as preparing the content of programs. Universities have to be prepared to acknowledge these contributions as efforts worthy of merit and rewards.

RESOURCES

As in all situations where there are threats, there are also opportunities. Within the universities, teaching development centers, the heads of departments, and the senior administration are resources that can play a major role in both heightening awareness about the importance of teaching and creating conditions that are conducive to teaching and learning.

Universities which have had the foresight to establish and support teaching development centers have signaled a commitment to their students and faculty that they are in the business of offering quality of education. These centers, used to their maximum potential, can both inform and form practice. Their formative role is in designing and implementing interventions which meet the specific needs of the disciplines, new faculty, and graduate students. They are also in the best position to inform senior administration of internal trends such as the quality of programs and their success in training competent graduates as well as external trends concerning university pedagogy.

A second rarely tapped resource that exists in every university is the department head. These individuals have a very important role to play in creating environments that faculty perceive as more conducive to teaching and learning. There is already evidence that academics' research productivity is conditioned by the characteristics of the department in which they work (Blackburn & Lawrence, 1995). Moreover, there is some evidence that approaches to teaching are related to perceptions that faculty have of the teaching environment (Prosser & Trigwell, 1997). These assertions, however, should be of no surprise. After all, organizational environments shape faculty attitudes, perceptions, and performance. We know that developing an environment which encourages teaching requires painstaking administrative undertaking. At a time when external factors such as reduced budgets and new management styles are quickly eroding the morale of faculty, department heads have a very important leadership role to play in creating environments that faculty perceive as more conducive to teaching and learning.

A third resource which is external to the university is the potential role that industry, business and government can play in promoting teaching. An example of the involvement of business in Canada is the 3M Canada Inc.'s collaboration with the Society for Teaching and Learning in Higher Education (STLHE). In 1986 this company created the prestigious 3M Teaching Fellowship Award. The award is given annually to professors who not only excel in the teaching of their own courses but also demonstrate an exceptionally high degree of leadership and commitment to the improvement of university teaching across disciplines. Up to ten Fellowships are awarded each year. One hundred and fifty Canadian university educators, representing 36 different universities and a range of disciplines have been recognized by this award since its inception.

An example of the involvement of government can be observed in the Australian context. The Australian Universities Teaching Committee (AUTC) was established in 2000 as part of the government's commitment to promoting quality and excellence in university teaching and learning. The AUTC has a mandate to identify emerging issues in teaching and learning in Australian universities. It administers a grants program designed to identify and support effective methods of teaching and learning and seeks to promote the dissemination and adoption of such methods across the higher education sector. The Committee is also responsible for the selection process for the prestigious Australian Awards for University Teaching.

The examples cited above only underscore the range and variety of resources that can be called upon to promote teaching and learning. None, however, can have as profound an impact on those who care and are concerned about the quality of teaching and learning than the unequivocal and supportive stance of a university's senior administration of teaching and learning. By generating relevant policies and allocating resources, an administration can send a clear message to its academic staff that the university's mission is as much about teaching and learning as it is about research.

CONCLUSIONS

In this current climate of change, the question of how universities could develop their academic staff such that they are able and motivated to provide quality teaching still requires attention. The increasing intensity in the level of discourse concerning teaching and learning is not accidental. It coincides with global trends that have emerged as major threats to the quality of teaching and learning. Student numbers have increased along with demands for better education, more competent graduates and more accountability among teaching staff. The Carnegie Foundation's sponsored programs, policies related to the evaluation of teaching and courses and programs on university pedagogy and the Institute of Teaching and Learning are all measures taken to ensure that the balance between teaching and research is not further eroded and that new as well as persisting challenges are met. These initiatives demonstrate the need for teaching and learning to be clearly etched not only in university mission statements, but in their policies and every day practices. At the same time, these measures can invite other stakeholders, including business and government, to be active participants in the promotion of teaching and learning.

NOTES

1.   Though Centra's model is presented in the context of formative evaluation, it can easily apply to improvement in general.

2.   The Carnegie Foundation is a national and international center for research and policy studies about teaching which aims to generate discussion and initiate sustainable long-term change in educational research, policy and practice.

3.   CASTL seeks to a) foster significant, long-lasting learning for all students, b) enhance the practice and profession of teaching, and c) bring to faculty members' work as teachers the recognition and reward afforded to other forms of scholarly work.

4.   The AUCC is a national, non-governmental, not-for profit body, which represents Canada's universities and degree granting colleges. Since education falls under provincial rather than Federal jurisdiction, the AUCC plays a particularly important role in providing a forum for discussion and a framework for action at the federal level, facilitating the development of public policy on higher education. The organization also encourages cooperation among universities and among partners who share the same interests.

5.   A teaching portfolio typically consists of a reflective piece of writing on one's philosophy about teaching and learning, a discussion of teaching responsibilities, evidence of effectiveness, and a description of steps taken toward teaching development and improvement.

REFERENCES

Astin, A. W. (1998). The changing American college student. Thirty-year trends, 1966–1996. *The Review of Higher Education, 21*(2), 115–135.

Blackburn, R. T., & Lawrence, J. H. (1995). *Faculty at work: Motivation, expectation, satisfaction*. Baltimore, MD: John Hopkins University Press.

British Council. (1999). *Higher education: The higher education systems, structure and funding, assessment and quality*. Retrieved November 2001 from The British Council Web site: http://www.britishcouncil.org/education/hed/hedindex.htm

Boyer Commission on Education. (1998). *Reinventing undergraduate education: A blueprint for America's research universities*. Princeton, NJ: Carnegie Foundation for the Advancement of Teaching.

Boyer, E. L. (1990). *Scholarship reconsidered: Priorities of the professoriate*. Lawrenceville, NJ: Princeton University Press.

Boyer, E. L., Altbach, P. G., & Whitelaw, M. J. (1994). *The academic profession: An international perspective*. Ewing, NJ: California/Princeton Fulfillment Services.

Centra, J. (1993). *Reflective faculty evaluation*. San Francisco, CA: Jossey-Bass.

Centre for Academic Practice. (2000). *Teaching portfolio: A staff resource pack*. United Kingdom: The Nottingham Trent University.

Clark, B. R. (1996). Substantive growth and innovative organization: New categories for higher education research. *Higher Education, 32*, 417–430.

Council of Ministers of Education of Canada. (1999). *Report of the Pan-Canadian education indicators program*. Ottawa, Ontario, Canada : Statistics Canada.

Council of Ministers of Education of Canada. (2001). *Postsecondary education systems in Canada: An overview*. Retrieved November 2001 from the Canadian Information Centre for International Credentials Web site: http://www.cicic.ca/postsec/vol1.overview.en.stm

Donald, J., & Saroyan, A. (1991). *Assessing the quality of teaching in Canadian universities* (Research report #3). Ottawa, Ontario, Canada: Association of Universities and Colleges of Canada, Commission of Inquiry on Canadian University Education.

Ducharme, E. R. (1996). *The lives of teacher educators*. New York: Teachers' College.

Edgerton, R., Hutchings, P., & Quinlan, K. (1991). *The teaching portfolio: Capturing the scholarship of teaching*. Washington, D.C.: American Association for Higher Education.

Everett, J. E., & Entrekin, L. (1994). Changing attitudes of Australian academics. *Higher Education, 27*(2), 203–227.

Fisher, S. (1994). *Stress in academic life*. Buckingham, UK: Open University.

Gaff, J. G. (1978). *Institutional renewal through the improvement of teaching*. (Vol. 24). San Francisco: Jossey-Bass.

Hubball, H. (2001) *UBC faculty certificate program on teaching and learning in Higher Education*. Retrieved November 2001, from University of British Columbia Web site: http://www.cstudies.ubc.ca/facdev/cert/index.html

Jones, G. A. (1997). Research on higher education in a decentralized academic system. In J. Sadlak & P. G. Altbach (Eds.), *Higher education research at the turn of the century* (pp. 189–208). Paris: UNESCO.

Karpiak, I. E. (1996). Ghosts in the wilderness. *Canadian Journal of Higher Education, 26*(3), 49–78.

Karpiak, I. E. (1997). University professors and mid life. *To Improve the Academy, 16*, 21–40.

Knight, P., & Trowler, P. (2001). *Departments and leadership in higher education.* Buckingham, UK: Open University.

Laurillard, D. (1993). *Rethinking university teaching.* London: Routledge.

McNay, I. (1995). From the collegial academy to the corporate enterprise: The changing cultures of universities. In T. Schuller (Ed.), *The changing university?* Buckingham: SRHE and Open University Press.

Prosser, M., & Trigwell, K. (1997). Perceptions of the teaching environment and its relationship to approaches to teaching. *British Journal of Educational Psychology, 67,* 25–35.

Ramsden, P. (1992). *Learning to teach in higher education.* London: Routledge.

Ramsden, P. (1998a). *Learning to lead in higher education.* London: Routledge.

Ramsden, P. (1998b). Managing the effective university. *Higher Education Research and Development, 17*(3), 347–370.

Rice, R. E., & Austin, A. (1990). Organizational impacts on faculty morale and motivation to teach. In P. Seldin (Ed.), *How administrators can improve teaching* (pp. 23–42). San Francisco: Jossey-Bass.

Salmi, J. (2001). Tertiary education in the 21st century: Challenges and opportunities. *Higher Education Management, 13*(2), 105–130.

Saroyan, A., Amundsen, C., Cao, & Li (1997). Incorporating theories of teacher growth and adult education in a faculty development program. *To Improve the Academy, 16,* 93–115.

Scott, P. (1995). *The meanings of mass higher education.* Buckingham, UK: SRHE and Open University Press.

Seldin, P. (1993). *Successful use of teaching portfolios.* Bolton, MA: Anker.

Shulman, L. (1993). Teaching as community property. *Change, 25*(6), 273–274.

Shore, B., Foster, S., Knapper, C., Nadeau, G., Neill, N., & Sim, V. (1986). *The teaching dossier: A guide to its preparation and use.* Montréal, Québec, Canada: Canadian Association of UniversityAlenoush Saroyan Teachers.

Smith, S. L. (1991). *Commission of inquiry on Canadian university education.* Ottawa, Ontario, Canada: Association of Universities and Colleges of Canada.

The Task Force on Higher Education and Society. (2000). *Higher education in developing countries: Peril and promise.* Washington, DC: The International Bank for Reconstruction and Development/The World Bank.

Thorsen, E. J. (1996). Stress in academe: What bothers professors? *Higher Education, 31*(4), 471–489.

U.S. Department of Education, Office of Postsecondary Education. (2000, November). *Overview of Accreditation.* Retrieved November 2001, from the Office of Postsecondary Education Web site: http://www.ed.gov/offices/OPE/accreditation.

Van Note Chism, N. (2002). Valuing student differences. In W. J. McKeachie (Ed.) *Teaching Tips.* Boston: Houghton Mifflin Company.

Weiner, B. (1986). *An attributional theory of motivation and emotion.* New York: Springer-Verlag.

CHAPTER 11

TEACHER THINKING AND PRACTICE FROM A CHINESE CULTURAL PERSPECTIVE

Lessons for East and West

David Watkins

INTRODUCTION

In the 1960s and 1970s most attempts in teacher education colleges and university staff development units to improve teaching focused on developing the instructional skills needed to transmit structured knowledge to students. However, over the last 20 years this approach has typically been replaced by one focusing on the teachers' thinking. Indeed the term "the reflective practitioner" has become synonymous with the aims of teacher education from America, Australia, and Great Britain to Hong Kong, the Philippines, and Zimbabwe.

This latter approach is based on the seemingly logical proposition that the way a teacher thinks about the nature of teaching will affect how he or she will teach, thence how their students will learn, and ultimately the quality of the learning outcomes they are likely to achieve. Surprisingly, despite

Teaching, Learning, and Motivation in a Multicultural Context, pages 243–258
Copyright © 2003 by Information Age Publishing
All rights of reproduction in any form reserved.

the plethora of research on teaching and learning, there is little evidence in the literature to support this proposition. Even less common is the demonstration of its validity in a non-Western culture. The purpose of this paper is to present such evidence for the teaching of Chinese students in Hong Kong and the People's Republic of China.[1] Specific questions asked in this research by the writer and his students and colleagues include: What conceptions of teaching are held by school teachers in China? How do such views compare with those of Western teachers? How does teacher education in Hong Kong impact on teacher thinking and practice? How do Chinese teachers cope with large class sizes? Are Western teachers more student-centered? Do Western innovations work in Chinese classrooms? Why? Can staff development change teachers conceptions and influence their students' learning? Finally I consider the implications of this research on teacher thinking for teaching innovations in both Chinese and Western cultures.

Levels of Teacher Thinking

The 'instructional skills' approach, according to Biggs (1999), is an improvement on the 'blame the student' view of poor learning outcomes favored by many teachers and parents worldwide. Teachers holding this latter view of teaching, which Biggs refers to as a Level 1 view, see their job as transmitting knowledge and it is the students' job to learn that knowledge. From this perspective, failures in learning outcomes are due to student deficits such as laziness, lack of intelligence, or lack of motivation. The 'instructional skills' model is based on what Biggs calls a Level 2 view of teaching where the focus is on what teachers do. From this viewpoint, good teachers have mastered a range of teaching competencies, including these days the latest in Instructional Technology. Biggs argues that this view is also based on a deficit model, only this time the deficit lies with the teacher not the student.

Level 1 and 2 views are also consistent with the teacher-centered/content-oriented conception found in a review of research on conceptions of teaching by Kember (1997) to be commonly held by Western university teachers. The second fundamental conception commonly held Kember termed student-centered/learning-oriented. This latter conception is also consistent with what Biggs refers to as a Level 3 view of teaching where the focus is on how well the students learn and on which teaching practices work within a particular learning context. It is the ability to be able to understand one's students' learning within its context and to adapt one's teaching appropriately to maximize the quality of their learning outcomes, that is at the core of the widely held desire of teacher educators to develop teachers to be reflective practitioners.

TEACHING IN A CHINESE CULTURAL CONTEXT

This writer has previously argued that classroom processes are complex and operate at many different levels: from that of individual teachers and learners to the class, the school, the school system, the particular society, the wider culture, and the global level (Watkins, 2000; see also Biggs, 1996). The implication is that any attempts to reform educational practices must take into consideration the complex, systemic nature of the processes involved. Too often educational reforms around the world have failed because they involved change to just one factor be it class size or teacher education.

It is the cultural and global levels of this system which are currently least understood. Schmidt et al. (1996) in their preliminary report of the Third International Mathematics and Science Study (TIMSS) described a "pedagogical flow" that characterizes teaching in each country of that study. The nature of this flow springs from socialization practices, values about education, and so on in the culture concerned. Therefore as Stedman (1997, p. 9) argued, achievement differences found between countries in TIMSS cannot be attributed "solely to school factors or to a single organizational or instructional factor."

Stigler and Hiebert (1999) were able to describe the nature of the pedagogical flow of educational systems in Germany, Japan, and the United States. After analyzing video-tapes of classroom in these countries "they were amazed at how much teaching varied across cultures, and how little it varied within cultures" (p. 10). It seemed that each culture had developed its own script and Stigler and Hiebert concluded that superior learning outcomes in Japan were due to a better script rather than the actor who delivered it. They concluded that the Japanese teaching script was both more student centered and more focused on higher quality learning outcomes than the American or German. Moreover, the Japanese had built in a quality enhancement mechanism.

The Chinese Cultural Context

In our edited book on the Chinese Learner (Watkins & Biggs, 1996) John Biggs and I point out that students and teachers from Confucian-heritage cultures (CHC) such as China, Hong Kong, Japan, Korea, Singapore, and Taiwan share a similar set of internal dispositions and external values which influence educational practices and outcomes today. Lee (1996) characterized this set as including a high degree of commitment to and involvement in the education of their children; these children show a basic eagerness to learn and positive attitudes toward school; a high status afforded teachers and a strong commitment by the latter to be involved in the overall development of their students; a premise of equal access to the rewards of successful learning through effort; and the valuing of education as an appropriate preparation for work.

By Western standards students in most CHC classrooms are taught in conditions that are likely to lead to poor learning: large classes, frequent norm-referenced assessment, relentless drilling for these examinations, expository whole-class teaching methods, and a harsh classroom environment. Moreover, there are common beliefs (referred to by Chang, 2000, as "vernacular Confucianism") including those about teaching and learning held by many CHC teachers, parents, and teachers which Western educators view skeptically. Such beliefs include "children are spoiled if praised", "failure is the result of laziness", and "no pain no gain" (see Watkins & Biggs, 2001, for further details). As we argue there, many such current beliefs derive not from the rather constructivist Confucius but from the far grimmer Xun Zu. But it does not matter from which ancient philosopher such beliefs come from but rather that these beliefs are commonly held today within Chinese cultures at least, and that they influence how teachers teach in Chinese classrooms today.

While Hong Kong and mainland China share a common cultural background a basic characteristic of "vernacular Confucianism" is that it may be operationalized in different ways in different Chinese societies leading to different practices in these societies (Chang, 2000).[2] Hong Kong education has clearly been strongly influenced by the British system on which it is largely based. Indeed many of the teachers of Hong Kong students, particularly at university level, are expatriate Westerns (such as the writer). Yet Hong Kong students and teachers have probably held more closely to traditional beliefs about teaching and learning than their PRC peers. The cultural revolution led to a questioning (and at that time often the violent rejection) of traditional beliefs about praise and blames and the student-teacher relationship which still have their repercussions today (see Watkins & Biggs, 2001, for a further discussion). Students from Singapore, Taiwan, and Hong Kong regularly outperform Western students in international comparisons of educational achievement and not just in math and science (e.g., TIMSS) and as students at Western universities (see Watkins & Biggs, 1996, for details). Chinese teachers must be doing something right, just as the work of Stigler and Hiebert (1999) has demonstrated for their Japanese counterparts. In the research described below we probe the thinking and practice of teachers of Chinese students in Hong Kong and China to see if we can identify the reasons for their apparent success.

TEACHER THINKING

What consistently comes through the research in this area is that teachers in China and Hong Kong believe that they have the role of "cultivating" not only their students' cognitive development but also promoting positive attitudes to society and responsible moral behavior. Whereas Australian teachers saw their major responsibility as limited to teaching the curriculum inside the classroom, Hong Kong teachers typically espoused in addition a pastoral view which extended far beyond the classroom.

Based on the analysis of in-depth interviews and classroom observation of 18 secondary school teachers of Physics in Guangzhou, China, Gao, and Watkins (2001) developed a model of the teaching conceptions held by these teachers (see Figure 11.1). This model was supported in a quantitative study of over 700 such teachers. The model we developed involved two higher orientations of Molding (with sub-areas of Knowledge Delivery and Exam Preparation) and Cultivating (with sub-areas of Ability Development, Attitude Promotion, and Conduct Guidance). These two orientations have some elements in common with the teacher-centered/content-oriented and student-centered/learning-oriented identified in Kember's (1997) review of research on Western university teaching. Not surprisingly though there was more emphasis placed on examination preparation given the much greater focus on external exams at secondary school level in both China and Hong Kong.

The emphasis on cultivating attitudes and good citizenship is consistent with the Chinese cultural value of "Jiao Shu Yu Ren" (which means teaching involves developing a good person). As one of our respondents put it (Gao & Watkins, 2001, p. 31):

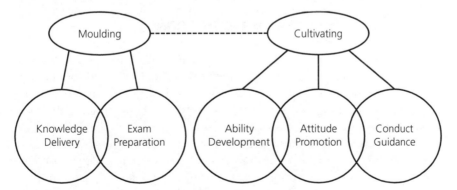

Figure 11.1.   The model of conceptions of teaching (after Gao & Watkins, 2001)
Key: A dotted line indicates a weak relationship whereas a solid line indicates a strong relationship

> However, teaching should involve far more than knowledge delivery. It should include educating and cultivating students. Help them to learn how to be a person. That's what we call 'Jiao Shu Yu Ren'. This should be more important than other things.

However, it is important to realize that the teaching of such values, supported by all 700 Chinese teachers in our research, is primarily conveyed implicitly in the teacher's performance and teacher-student interaction. The Chinese teacher is expected not only to have good instructional skills but also to be a good moral role model in all areas of life (this is known in China as "Wei Ren Shi Biao").

It might be argued that this view of teaching would also be commonly held by Western school teachers rather than the university teachers who were the focus of the research review by Kember (1997). However, Ho (2001) in a comparison of Australian and Hong Kong secondary school teachers, found that the former felt their responsibilities ended in teaching the curriculum inside the classroom. The Australians typically did not feel responsible for their student's personal or family problems or even unfinished homework. The Hong Kong teachers saw things very differently, and like their Guangzhou counterparts described above, voiced a pastoral as well as an instructional view of teaching.

The research of Cortazzi and Jin (2001) also depicts a similar picture of Chinese teachers. They refer to education as "books and society" and the teacher as friend and parents. They too argue that this reflects the Chinese holistic view of teaching, where teaching refers not only to the cognitive but also the affective and moral, including teaching children their place in society.

TEACHER EDUCATION

As described earlier a major aim of teacher education in Hong Kong and China, as elsewhere, is the development of reflective practitioners. Two investigations indicate that teacher education institutions in Hong Kong are indeed succeeding in this aim at least in terms of encouraging their students to reflect on the processes of teaching.

An in-depth follow-up study of 24 primary science teacher education students (So, 2001) shows how these students become increasingly more constructivist in their conceptions and planning of teaching and in their teaching practices as they progress through their course. For example they tended to make greater use of their pupils' existing knowledge in planning their teaching, to choose more activities designed to allow pupils to test their own ideas, and to provide a classroom environment more conducive for the discussion of such ideas.

Further evidence comes from a longitudinal study by Tang (2001). Responses to questionnaires on conceptions of and approaches to learning and conceptions of teaching administered before and after one year of study in teacher education or graduate education courses by 220 students were analyzed using structural equation modeling and other statistical methods. The results indicated that during their year of studying, students move towards a more meaning-focused conception of learning but there is little change in teaching approaches and orientations. However, using partial correlation analysis to control possible response sets, it was found those who increased use of a deep learning approach were also less likely to consider teaching as preparing students for examination or as transmitting knowledge. In addition in-depth interviews were conducted with 25 of these education students early in their course and after their final exams. Phenomenographyic analysis (see Marton & Booth, 1997) of the initial interviews yielded six conceptions both of learning and of teaching. Both sets of conceptions formed a hierarchy from the superficial 'transmission of knowledge' to the sophisticated 'development as a person.' The follow-up interview data supported the independently conducted quantitative analysis, by finding that many of these education students tended to change to more meaning-oriented conceptions of learning and of teaching. In addition, the qualitative analysis indicated that these education students' views on learning were closely related to and in fact seemed to limit their views on teaching.

CHINESE TEACHING PRACTICES

Teacher- versus Student-centered Teaching

Western educators, as reflected in the research of Kember (1997), often seem to think about teaching in terms of teacher- or student-centered polarities: with the latter being the desired pole. However, just as in our review of research on Chinese learners (Watkins & Biggs, 1996), it appears that once again an established Western dichotomy breaks down in the Chinese educational context.

This can be seen in the research of Gao and Watkins (2001) where, although the conceptual model developed (see Figure 11.1) had echoes of this dichotomy, it was found that many teachers in our sample espoused both student- and teacher-centered views. Moreover, when this was pointed out to them most both acknowledged the point and saw nothing strange about it.

Research of actual classroom practice sheds further light on this issue. Of course, one must always be careful generalizing about such a huge, diverse country on the basis of a few investigations. Yet studies of PRC school classrooms are consistent in reporting how actively involved in the desired learning tasks they found students even in classes of 60–70. Thus Gardner (1989) described how in several visits he made to China to study art and music teaching he first thought how highly directive and imitative was the teaching. However, he came to realize that once basic skills were mastered by repetition, Chinese students were actually encouraged to be far more creative and individualistic and typically achieved much higher standards than their U.S. peers.

In like vein, Stigler and Stevenson (1991) after observation of teaching in China, Taiwan, and Japan, reported that the teachers they observed saw their job as posing provocative questions, encouraging reflection, and individualizing their methods for particular students. Stigler and Stevenson commented that while Western educators espoused such constructivist methods they were seldom encountered in U.S. schools. O'Connor (1991) came to similar conclusions after studying PRC teachers.

Cortazzi and Jin (2001) explain how teachers in China are able to actively engage students even in large classes. While the Western approach is typically to encourage activity through small group teaching, PRC teachers prefer to utilize whole group teaching. Their students are expected not to be passive as they may appear to Western eyes, but rather to learn through 'listening-oriented learning'. As one eight year old quoted by Cortazzi and Jin (2001, p. 123) put it:

> I may be listening but I am not passive. I am learning in my head. I learn from my teacher. I also learn from what my friends do. If they make a mistake, I learn from that too.

The challenge for the Chinese teacher is to arouse and maintain their pupils' attention, concentration, listening, and interest and also to enable as many individual pupils as possible to speak however briefly. Cortazzi and Jin (2001) provide details of how and how well PRC teachers can achieve this using basically Socratic questioning techniques.

Further evidence of how Chinese teachers can use highly teacher-controlled methods to actively involve students in a student-centered way was provided in an investigation of Hong Kong classrooms by Mok, Chik, Ko, Kwan, Lo, Marton, Ng, Pang, Runesson, and Sze-To (2001). What Mok et al. argue is happening in many cases is that highly active and attentive students are learning within the framework of lessons skillfully orchestrated by the teacher. They describe in detail a language lesson where the teacher seemed to have:

an invisible script. He choreographed what the students were supposed to perform. In spite of the students acting spontaneously, the teacher constructed meanings upon their participation and managed to expose the variations of the critical dimensions related to the objects of learning (Mok et al., 2001, p. 174).

Adapting Western Methods

Hong Kong is currently undertaking major reforms of its highly ability-grouped, over-assessed, pressurized, academically-oriented educational system. Hong Kong in the past has imported (and ultimately rejected) many innovations from the West. The most spectacular failure, that of the Target Oriented Curriculum (TOC), should serve as an exemplar of how not to introduce an innovation (see Morris, Chan, & Lo, 1998, for an in-depth evaluation of its implementation). TOC seemed to be just what Hong Kong needed. As John Biggs and I put it:

> (TOC was) a carefully designed criterion-referenced scheme that replaced the rigors of norm-referencing with individually paced learning. But (Hong Kong) teachers with a theory-in-use deriving from vernacular Confucianism simply would not see what the problem was. Moreover, the innovation was prescribed top-down with little attempt to change teachers' or parents' thinking about the function of assessment (Watkins & Biggs, 2001, p. 17).

Two recent examples have shown how innovations based on Western ideas can be successfully implemented in Hong Kong Chinese classrooms and emphasized where TOC went wrong. Crucial elements seem to be first convincing teachers of the need for change and that the new approach makes sense and then involving them all in the implementation of the innovation.

Thus Stokes (2001) described how Problem Based Learning (PBL), which was first used as an alternative teaching and learning paradigm to the traditional lecture/tutorial/practical at a Canadian university was successfully applied at undergraduate level in Hong Kong. The typical elements of PBL are small-group work, a tutor, and resources and a study/work program designed to aid self-directed, independent learning. While the PBL approach generally worked well some lecturers found it difficult to adjust to the new role demanded of them: a facilitator of learning rather than a dispenser of knowledge.

Chan (2001) described how ordinary Hong Kong secondary school teachers could utilize Western constructivist learning principles for encouraging conceptual change such as cognitive conflict and confrontation, modeling, explanation, and scaffolding to improve the quality of learning of their students. Chan further reported the success of a graduate course she taught using computer-supported collaborative learning based on the methods advocated by Scardamalia and Bereiter (1994) which emphasize building on prior understanding, articulation of ideas, metacognition, and collaborative enquiry. She found that those students who showed more conceptual growth were more involved in deep collaborative learning on the computer network.

Chan (2001, p. 197) also emphasized that the teachers played a pivotal role in the success of these 'imported' innovations:

> If the approach was implemented without the teachers' understanding, it would not work whether it is based on Eastern or Western traditions … Similar to good teachers from any culture, they understood that the most important thing is not how they teach but how students learn.

Chan also described how these Hong Kong teachers developed ways of adapting and thinking about constructivist approaches which were consistent with Chinese educational beliefs and cultural values. As reported earlier, Chinese teachers tend to place more emphasis on their students' moral and personal development than do their typical Western peers. So it may seem that constructivist approaches which have been criticized for their 'cold' cognitive view of teaching which ignores affective aspects would be less appropriate for Chinese classrooms. However, one of Chan's Hong Kong teachers commented how the constructivist style of instruction he had utilized for the first time brought him closer to his students. As Chan comments, future research could test the proposition that such instruction can lead to better teacher-student relationships in both Western and Chinese classrooms.

CHANGING TEACHING PRACTICE

Conceptual Change

It is now well understood that teachers at all levels hold their own idiosyncratic views of teaching based largely on their own experiences as both a student and a teacher and, moreover, these views have a major influence on how they teach. Unfortunately too often these personal theories are inadequate for promoting high quality teaching and learning. Indeed Ramsden (1993) argued that the improvement of teaching and learning in higher education first required improving the personal educational theories of lecturers. Surprisingly, as discussed earlier, this presumed link between teacher thinking and practice has not been adequately researched (but see Prosser & Trigwell, 1998). However, a recent applied study by A. Ho (2001) provides not only evidence of such a causal link in a Hong Kong context but also how to bring about conceptual change which can ultimately improve student learning.

Based on her synthesis of four major Western theories of conceptual change, Ho identified four crucial elements of a conceptual change program: confrontation leading to dissatisfaction with the current situation; self-awareness of any mismatch between their own theory-in-use and the ideal; the awareness of alternative conceptions; and a commitment building and refreezing process. Ho designed and conducted a four-session staff development program which aimed to produce conceptual change about teaching. The success of this program was demonstrated in an evaluation involving longitudinal in-depth qualitative analysis. Further longitudinal research using quantitative methods and incorporating control teachers and students in the design, showed that the students of all those lecturers who showed real evidence of conceptual change reported an improvement in their teaching and many of these students also showed deeper level learning.

Action Research

During the 1990's action research (Carr & Kemmis, 1986; Zuber-Skerrit, 1992) was widely used in Western countries to try to enhance teaching practices. Action research has been hailed for making educational research relevant to the work of classroom teachers. It assumes that there is a body of such teachers who are sufficiently insightful to recognize weaknesses in their own teaching practices, sufficiently committed to their students' learning to want to improve, and sufficiently confident to collaborate with other teachers and researchers to plan, implement, and monitor new practices designed to improve their students' learning.

Hong Kong has been the scene of not only the major non-Western test of action research but also of undoubtedly the largest action research program in the world to date (see Kember, 2000, 2001 for details). Known as the Action Learning Project, it involved initial trials first in one university and then a second and finally to all tertiary institutions in Hong Kong. Two large research grants from the University Grants Committee of Hong Kong enabled the funding of over one hundred action research projects, which were all initiated by lecturers and later implemented in collaboration with project educational specialists. An independent evaluation of the projects in the first grant (Biggs & Lam, 1997) was strongly supportive of their value in enhancing teaching and learning.

Kember (2001) commented that skeptics who had argued that the reflection of one's own teaching, at the core of action research, was inconsistent with Chinese culture were proved wrong in this project. The collectivist nature of such a culture (see Watkins & Biggs, 1996) undoubtedly enhanced the close teamwork needed for successful action research.

CONCLUSION

This review of selected current research has indicated that while many views and practices are generalizable across cultures, there are a number of differences at least of degree between teaching in Hong Kong, China, and the West:

(a)   Chinese teachers tend to place more emphasis on the affective/ moral development of their students (Gao & Watkins, 2001; I. Ho, 2001).

(b)   At least some Chinese teachers are able to handle large class sizes through whole-class teaching (Cortazzi & Jin, 2001). While such teaching is often criticized in the West for leading to bored, passive students, Chinese teachers are often able to engage each student actively by this approach. Mok et al. (2001) reported similar use of such cognitively engaging whole-class teaching carefully orchestrated by the teacher in Hong Kong. Of course such instances of good practice do not mean that all Hong Kong or PRC teachers utilize such methods or do so as effectively.

(c)   The Western dichotomy of teacher-centered/student-centered seems to break down in Chinese classrooms (particularly the assumption that a student-centered, small group approach is needed for high quality learning outcomes). As explained above highly teacher-controlled, whole group teaching can be cognitively engaging in the hands of Chinese teachers. Also Gao and Watkins (2001) reported that teachers in China did not consider this an either/or dichotomy. They were quite happy to support both positions in different contexts.

The review also points to a number of Western innovations and theoretical principles which seem to be suitable for Hong Kong. Thus teacher education in Hong Kong seems to be able to encourage student teachers to adopt a more constructivist view of teaching and learning (So, 2001; Tang, 2001). Whether they will be as constructivist in practice is another matter, of course. Moreover, innovations consistent with a constructivist approach can work well in Hong Kong schools and universities (Chang, 2001). This suggests that Hong Kong teachers and students will be able to cope well if school assessment is reformed as planned to place more emphasis on conceptual understanding rather than reproduction of model answers. Also in Hong Kong, a conceptual change approach to staff development has also been shown to lead to improve teaching and better learning strategies (A. Ho, 2001) while a massive action research project has shown the benefits of such an approach for improving university teaching.

The applied research discussed above highlights that there are many instances of excellent practice of teaching and its enhancement in Hong Kong. The common element in all these studies is that if we wish to bring about improvement in learning we must start with teacher thinking. For virtually the first time we also have evidence of how thinking precedes action at least in the area of education.

When as in TOC well-intentioned innovation was implemented top-down it did not work. The reason for that is clear, the teachers who had to implement the innovation did not understand the need for it. TOC was doomed from the start. I would hope the massive educational reforms currently underway won't make the same mistake (but I would not bet on it!).

Too often approaches that have worked well in schools in one culture have been assumed to work well in another. As evidenced above such innovations can work if implemented bottom-up with teacher support and adapted to the learning and cultural context where it is to be adopted. However, this will not always by the case. In this paper I have described how teachers in Hong Kong and China are able to teach large classes through a cognitively engaging whole-class approach. Yet I would hope that Western education policy makers do not seize on such a finding to save money through increasing class sizes (a typical Level 1 response!) and discouraging small group teaching. The introduction of any teaching approach must consider the cultural values of the learning environment where it is to be adopted. As Cortazzi and Jin (2001) and Mok et al. (2001) emphasized the whole-class learning they observed worked well only because well because Chinese students come to class eager and trained to learn by "active learning" through the efforts of the teacher and other students (see also Watkins & Biggs, 1996). Until Western cultures can socialize their children to possess such attitudes and capabilities this Chinese whole-class approach would be doomed to failure in the typical Western classroom.

NOTES

1.   Much of the material in this chapter represents a synthesis of research presented in "Teaching the Chinese learner: psychological and pedagogical perspectives" co-edited by John Biggs and myself. I would like to thank Professor Biggs for his contribution to the views expressed in this chapter.

2.   The studies described were carried out either in Hong Kong or mainland China and because of the contextual nature of 'Vernacular Confucianism' it

is dangerous to assume findings in one context are generalizable to another without further research. In this chapter the context of each piece of research will be designated as either Hong Kong or China/PRC meaning mainland China. Where reference is made to more general aspects of Chinese culture the term 'Chinese' is used.

REFERENCES

Biggs, J. B. (1996). Western misperceptions of the Confucian-heritage learning culture. In D. A. Watkins & J. B. Biggs (Eds.), *The Chinese learner: Cultural, psychological, and contextual influences* (pp. 45–67). Hong Kong/Melbourne: Comparative Education Research Centre/Australian Council for Educational Research.

Biggs, J. B. (1999). *Teaching for quality learning at university.* Buckingham: Open University Press.

Carr, W., & Kemmis, S. (1986). *Becoming critical: Education, knowledge, and action research.* Brighton, Sussex: Falmer Press.

Chan, C. K. K. (2001). Promoting learning and understanding through constructivist approaches for Chinese learners. In D.A. Watkins & J.B. Biggs (Eds.), *Teaching the Chinese learner: psychological and instructional perspectives* (pp. 179–202). Hong Kong/Melbourne: Comparative Education Research Centre/Australian Council for Educational Research.

Chang, W. C. (2001). In search of the Chinese in all the wrong places! *Journal of Psychology in Chinese Societies, 1*(1), 125–142.

Cortazzi, M., & Jin, L. (2001). Large classes in China: 'good' teachers and interaction. In D. A. Watkins & J. B. Biggs (Eds.), *Teaching the Chinese learner: psychological and instructional perspectives* (pp. 113–132). Hong Kong/Melbourne: Comparative Education Research Centre/Australian Council for Educational Research.

Gao, L. B., & Watkins, D. (2001). Towards a model of teaching conceptions of Chinese secondary school teachers of physics. In D. A. Watkins & J. B. Biggs (Eds.), *Teaching the Chinese learner: psychological and instructional perspectives* (pp. 23–43). Hong Kong/Melbourne: Comparative Education Research Centre/Australian Council for Educational Research.

Gardner, H. (1989). *To open minds.* New York: Basic Books.

Ho, A. S. P. (2001). A conceptual change approach to university staff development. In D. A. Watkins & J. B. Biggs (Eds.), *Teaching the Chinese learner: psychological and instructional perspectives* (pp. 237–252). Hong Kong/Melbourne: Comparative Education Research Centre/Australian Council for Educational Research.

Ho, I. T. (2001). Are Chinese teachers authoritarian? In D. A. Watkins & J. B. Biggs (Eds.), *Teaching the Chinese learner: psychological and instructional perspectives* (pp. 97–112). Hong Kong/Melbourne: Comparative Education Research Centre/Australian Council for Educational Research.

Kember, D. (1997). A reconceptualisation of the research into university academics' conceptions of teaching. *Learning and Instruction, 7*, 255–275.

Kember, D. (2000). *Action learning and action research: improving the quality of teaching and learning*. London: Kogan Page.

Kember, D. (2001). Transforming teaching through action research. In D. A. Watkins & J. B. Biggs (Eds.), *Teaching the Chinese learner: Psychological and instructional perspectives* (pp. 253–271). Hong Kong/Melbourne: Comparative Education Research Centre/Australian Council for Educational Research.

Lee, W. O. (1996). The cultural context for Chinese learners: conceptions of learning in the Confucian tradition. In D. A. Watkins & J. B. Biggs (Eds.), *The Chinese learner: cultural, psychological, and contextual influences* (pp. 25–41). Hong Kong/Melbourne: Comparative Education Research Centre/Australian Council for Educational Research.

Marton, F., & Booth, S. (1997). *Learning and awareness*. Mahwah, NJ: Lawrence Erlbaum.

Mok, I. A. C., Chik, P. M., Ko, P. Y., Kwan, T., Lo, M. L., Marton, F., Ng, F. P., Pang, M. F., Runesson, U., & Sze-To, L. H. (2001). Solving the paradox of the Chinese teacher? In D. A. Watkins & J. B. Biggs (Eds.), *Teaching the Chinese learner: Psychological and instructional perspectives* (pp. 159–178). Hong Kong/Melbourne: Comparative Education Research Centre/Australian Council for Educational Research.

Morris, P., Chan, K. K., & Lo, M. L. (1998). Changing primary schools in Hong Kong: perspectives on policy and its impact. In P. Stimpson & P. Morris (Eds.), *Curriculum and assessment in Hong Kong: two components, one system* (pp. 201–222). Hong Kong: The Open University of Hong Kong Press.

O'Connor, J. E. (1991). A descriptive analysis of Chinese teachers' thought processes. Paper presented at conference on Chinese Education for the 21st Century, Honolulu, November 21.

Prosser, M., & Trigwell, K. (1998). *Understanding learning and teaching: the experience in higher education*. Milton Keynes: Open University Press.

Ramsden, P. (1993). Theories of learning and teaching and the practice of excellence in higher education. *Higher Education Research and Development, 12*(1), 87–97.

Scardamalia, M., & Bereiter, C. (1994). Computer support for knowledge building communities. Special Issue: Computer support for collaborative learning. *The Journal of the Learning Sciences, 3*(3), 265–283.

Schmidt, W., and 14 others (1996). *A summary of characterizing pedagogical flow: An investigation of mathematics and science teaching in six countries*. London: Kluwer.

So, W. (2001). Teacher thinking in science: a longitudinal investigation of Hong Kong primary school teachers. Ph.D. thesis submitted to the University of Hong Kong.

Stedman, L. C. (1997). International achievement differences: An assessment of a new perspective. *Educational Research, 26*(3), 4–15.

Stigler, J., & Hiebert, J. (1999). *The teaching gap*. New York: The Free Press.

Stigler, J., & Stevenson, H. W. (1991). How Asian teachers polish each other to perfection. *American Educator, 15*(1), 12–21 43–47.

Stokes, S. (2001). Problem-Based Learning in a Chinese context: faculty perceptions. In D. A. Watkins & J. B. Biggs (Eds.), *Teaching the Chinese learner: Psychological and instructional perspectives* (pp. 203–216). Hong Kong/Melbourne:

Comparative Education Research Centre/Australian Council for Educational Research.

Tang, T. K. W. (2001). The influence of teacher education on conceptions of teaching and learning. In D. A. Watkins & J. B. Biggs (Eds.), *Teaching the Chinese learner: Psychological and instructional perspectives* (pp. 219–236). Hong Kong/Melbourne: Comparative Education Research Centre/Australian Council for Educational Research.

Watkins, D. (2000). Learning and teaching: A cross-cultural perspective. *School Leadership and Management, 20*(2), 161–173.

Watkins, D. A., & Biggs, J. B. (Eds.) (1996). *The Chinese learner: Cultural, psychological, and contextual influences.* Hong Kong/Melbourne: Comparative Education Research Centre/Australian Council for Educational Research.

Watkins, D. A., & Biggs, J. B. (Eds.) (2001). *Teaching the Chinese learner: Psychological and pedagogical perspectives.* Hong Kong/Melbourne: Comparative Education Research Centre/Australian Council for Educational Research.

Zuber-Skerrit, O. (1992). *Action research in higher education: Examples and reflections.* London: Kogan Page.

part IV

SUCCESS AND FAILURES
IN MULTICULTURAL SETTINGS

CHAPTER 12

EDUCATIONAL ACHIEVEMENT IN A MULTICULTURAL CONTEXT

Diverse Demographics with Shared Family Values

Oliver C.S. Tzeng

The little world of childhood with its familiar surroundings is a model
of the greater world. The more intensively the family has stamped its character
upon the child, the more it will tend to feel and see its earlier miniature world again
in the bigger world of adult life.

—Carl Jung (1913)

INTRODUCTION

This study is to evaluate the needs and possibility for contemporary families with diverse objective cultural backgrounds to develop similar ideals and values for successful practices in children education. This evaluation is conducted to address the critical question faced by educators in contempo-

Teaching, Learning, and Motivation in a Multicultural Context, pages 261–288
Copyright © 2003 by Information Age Publishing
All rights of reproduction in any form reserved.

rary, multicultural and international societies: Whether and to what extent children with diverse—and frequently disadvantageous—objective family backgrounds may achieve designated national standards of educational achievement. Toward this evaluation goal, this paper will address the need for families to foster appropriate developmental goals and expectations for children to attain maximal benefits from the uniform educational ideals, objectives and practices.

Modernization and Education

In the past few decades, advanced nations have surpassed the last stages of industrialization and modernization. Traditional cultures at all levels, and in all places, have undergone radical transformations (Tzeng & Henderson, 1999). Institutional organizations, communities, and families have become increasingly diverse, resulting in uncertain and even conflicting values and functions, as predicted a century and more ago by the social theories of those such as Durkheim (1984), Freud (1961) and Weber (1946).

Modernization within each society has been assessed cross-culturally in terms of: (1) the temporal progression from traditionalism to modernism, (2) ecological (societal- environmental) changes in both objective (concrete) and subjective (conceptual) cultures, and (3) subjective cultural values reflecting individual needs and group norm expectations. In the process of societal modernization, educational investment has been found in a 20-nation comparative study, to be most important in predicting correlative advancements in technology and industrialization (Tzeng & Henderson, 1999). Globalization and convergence, or the internal impacts of external challenges by other nations through economic or social pressures have further accelerated the process of modernization for all nations. Thus, all member nations of the present one-world community need to fully cooperate in their endeavors for successful modernization and education.

Within this framework, each nation should adopt a multicultural and multidisciplinary approach for simultaneously considering all—objective and subjective—societal changes of the contextual and outcome domains of the modernization processes. When such objective—versus—subjective cultural changes are consistent, they would facilitate a harmonious national movement—in both reinforcing the positive changes (as modernization benefits) and defusing the negative changes (as new societal problems). On the other hand, when the changes are inconsistent, they will inevitably cause disharmonies or conflicts within and between people in all ecological environments (family, community, work places, nations and international relations). Apparently, educational process within each nation plays a major role to address such cultural changes and resolve associated issues for better developments of individuals, nations, and international relations.

Multicultural American Education

Modernization, along with its correlative revolutions in family composition, racial demographics, educational objectives, community cohesion and economic mobility, has forced societies to accommodate, if not entirely assimilate, previously excluded groups. Thus, two important issues across all modern nations are the uniform school education for children in a multicultural context, and the possibility and practicability of expecting universal achievement among children with diverse backgrounds. For this reason, it would be necessary to first gain an insight into the role of contemporary diverse families in their contributions to the realization of national policy and objectives of school education.

The goals and objectives of the national education system in the United States are set to accommodate multiculturalism in society. Educational research literature has thus focused on six broad contextual areas that define the common processes and goals of contemporary school education for all American children.

First, *American values* refer to a sense of "commonality" and "social solidarity" in attitudes, beliefs and behaviors that are beneficial to life development in general.

Second, *patriotism* refers to the optimism about the future of American, and the sense of responsibility to society, and the motivation to contribute to the common good via various activities (Morris, 1992).

Third, *individualism* refers to the circumstance under which students who have strong self-concepts are more likely to express and discuss their views.

Fourth, *distinction* refers to the fact that students who are independent thinkers, assertive, goal-directed and willing to do whatever it takes to achieve their goals are more likely to experience academic success.

Fifth, *diversity* refers to the idea that high achieving students see diversity in race, ethnicity, aspirations, family backgrounds, and individual differences as a crucial part of the American culture. These students value their own uniqueness and that of others and are open to a variety of new experiences (Reglin & Adams, 1990).

Sixth, *traditional beliefs* refer to the idea that high achieving school students have strong belief systems, a strong sense of morality, and adherence to family tradition (Austin & Martin, 1992).

With these six objectives, the primary functions of American school education are, on one hand, to foster the positive, rather than antisocial, unique characteristics of individual students, and on the other hand, to successfully cultivate the desirable national characteristics of its citizens (DeBaryshe, Patterson, & Capaldi, 1993).

Specifically, American primary and secondary schools have always been characterized as learning institutions in which the "fundamental" values of a democratic society are transmitted, for example, independence, freedom, tolerance, mutual respect, and community involvement (Calabrese, 1994; Peshkin, 1995; Sommers, 1993; Wragg, 1993). However, these values tend to accommodate diversity rather than enforce uniformity (La Belle, 1994). Although schools may thus be recognized as first and final "havens" of equality in terms of providing the same educational opportunity for all children, students still exhibit extremely distinct levels of academic achievement and occupational readiness (Jencks; 1988, Landsberg, 1993; Sayfie, 1994).

Contemporary Families and Impact

Contemporary societal problems in the United States, such as violence, intolerance and injustice, have long been grave concerns for public personalities and private citizens (Hamburg, 1994; Myers, 1992). These problems pose distinct challenges for schools and families in their preparations of upcoming generations to adopt and cope as productive future citizens (Fege, 1993; Ingram, 1995; Lickona, 1993; Martin, 1992; Ryan, 1987).

Many educators attribute student failures in educational achievements and behavioral problems to students' particular family backgrounds. Empirical studies further confirm the impact of diverse family structures on children's disparities in intellectual and personality developments (Amoroso, 1986; Fitzpatrick, 1992; Watt, 1990; Weston, 1989; Zill, 1993). These findings are especially significant for developing new educational theories and practices in today's pluralistic society that are unprecedently diverse in family compositions and social values.

More specifically, the contemporary concept of family denotes not only the traditional uni-racial, heterosexual couple with two children of direct descent, but also households consisting of step-parents, adoptive parents, inter-racial parents, common-law companions, homosexual partners, and foster families (Freedman, 1988; Hanson & Lynch, 1992; McCarthy, 1992). These households may further represent diverse and even antagonizing life styles and value systems. Thus, the contemporary family concept is no longer a uniform institution circumscribed and perpetuated by traditional societal norms, but is an almost exclusively self-defined private domain, where household heads have the ultimate prerogative of defining the atmosphere in which children develop their personalities and ethics.

Although the causal impact of families on child development is well documented in the literature, most empirical studies tend to focus on the negative effects of household environments, especially in the areas of child abuse and neglect (e.g., Eckenrode, 1993; Tzeng, Jackson, & Karlson, 1991). On the other hand, studies of positive family characteristics tend to treat causal characteristics as esoteric, ethnically based or socio-cultural anomalies. They frequently fail to delineate the implicit—cognitive as well as perceptual—meanings of family structures or other underlying determinants of family behavior (e.g., Cusinato, 1990; Lee, 1984; Schneider, 1994; Sue & Okazaki, 1990; Milne, 1989; Mulkey, 1992; Goldstein et al., 1994; Lamont et al., 1995). The challenge for educators, household heads and researchers alike is therefore to identify some desirable functional characteristics that are directly contributing to the success of child development and school performance across all forms of contemporary households.

Objectives of this Cameo Analysis

This study is designed to assess common characteristics among structurally diverse families that are known to be successful in child-rearing practices. Three specific empirical issues are examined in order. First, whether high school graduates selected for this study are "model students" as the representative products of "successful families." Second, whether their families recapture the structural diversity of contemporary households (in such important demographics as ethnicity, religion, income and household composition.) Third, whether these families possess similar attitudes regarding their children's education and also exhibit similar behavioral patterns in their child rearing practices. Finally, results from empirical findings on these issues will be used to discuss the appropriateness and attainability of developing an ideal "subjective family culture" that will help students overcome their disadvantages in ecological backgrounds for equal and better education.

METHOD AND PROCEDURE

Participants

This study involves the 141 graduating high school seniors recognized as Presidential Scholars in 1995. These participants fall into two general categories: academic and artistic. In the academic category, two scholars from each of the 50 states and two regions (Puerto Rico and Americans Abroad) were selected, along with 15 at-large scholars, on the basis of demonstrated intellectual ability, leadership quality and community service.

The selection of academic scholars involved a three-step procedure. First, 2,500 semifinalists were chosen from six million high school graduates in 1995 for having the highest SAT and ACT scores per state. Second, 500 finalists were identified by the College Board, based on comprehensive essays, academic transcripts, recommendations and other documents. Finally, 141 academic scholars were selected from the finalists by the presidentially appointed White House Commission, a group of some 30 eminent academic and professional leaders.

In the arts category, the selection involved a three-stage procedure: First, from some 5,000 high school seniors applying to a 1995 nationwide talent competition hosted by the National Foundation for Advancement in the Arts, 100 award-winners in the visual, creative writing and performing arts categories were chosen as semifinalists. Second, these winners were asked to provide those records required of the academic category. Based on these records, the White House Commission selected twenty students as Presidential Scholars of the Arts.

In the summer of 1995, the Department of Education conducted its annual one-week recognition program for the 141 scholars in Washington D.C. This study, conducted during that week, consisted of a questionnaire survey of all scholars, interviews and a follow-up survey of a small group of scholars.

The results presented in this study are based on 114 of the 141 scholars who completed the questionnaire. Geographically, these participants represented all 50 states and the two regions, with an average of two scholars per state. Ethnically, 73.7% were White, 10.5% Asian, 7.0% Black, 0.9% Hispanic, 1.8% mixed, and 4.5% others (unspecified). The participants ranged in age from 16 to 19, with the majority (92%) between 17 and 18. 44% were men and 56% were women. 86% were in the academic and 14% in the arts categories. Among the arts scholars, 73% represented the performing arts subcategory, 20% the creative arts, and 7% the visual arts.

Measurement

The survey questionnaire was constructed to gather four types of information from all subjects: (1) personal information, including demographics, educational goals and career plans, (2) perceptions of the family environments, (3) attitudes and beliefs on social and civic issues, and (4) opinions about themselves and the program. The questionnaire was administered individually during the recognition week in Washington D.C. by Sophia Tzeng (a 1991 scholar). Participation was voluntary, with the assurance of anonymity and confidentiality of responses. Completed questionnaires were excluded from analyses if they failed the reliability and validity tests built into the questionnaire.

Analysis

For the first objective of this study—to assess the appropriateness of treating these participants as "model high school graduates," the relevant archival materials on the Presidential Scholars program were compiled and evaluated. They include: (1) the mission statement of the program, (2) the criteria and process for selecting scholars, and (3) official remarks by the seven Presidents since 1967 at the annual White House ceremony to all previous and present scholars during the National Recognition Week. These results were further cross-validated by the participants' own attitudes and beliefs in social values and civic responsibilities, as well as by their opinions of themselves and the program.

Under the second objective—to assess whether the participants' family structures were representative of contemporary diversity, the demographics of the participants were compared, first between the two genders, then between the scholars and the national high school population.

Under the third objective—to assess whether these families possessed similar functional characteristics in child rearing practices, the participants' perceptions of their family environments were measured by semantic differential (SD) ratings. The ratings involved 28 bi-polar continua (scales) anchored by contrasting adjectives, for example, good/bad, active/passive, and structured/loose (Osgood, May, & Miron, 1975). A two-step statistical procedure was employed. First, the inter-correlations among all SD scales were computed and factored in order to identify *implicit attribute* (*components*) underlying the ratings. Second, the frequency distributions of subjects' responses to the 7 gradients of each rating continuum were computed and grouped into three "endorsement vs. rejection" levels ("agree," "neutral" or "disagree") of each implicit component.

RESULTS

Objective 1: Model High School Graduates

The central issue under the first objective (whether Presidential Scholars are recognized as "model students" and "successful products" of families and schools) seems to be confirmed by the four sources below:

A. Purpose of the Program

The original purpose of the program was to forge a sense of shared conception of educational excellence between the intellectual community and the government (Goldman, 1969). In 1964, President Johnson signed an executive order establishing the Presidential Scholars Program with a two-fold mission: to encourage high attainment by all students in secondary schools, and to enhance their future accomplishments and further potential by national recognition of model students.

Operationally, this mission led to the founding of National Recognition Week, in which 121 distinguished high school seniors were honored annually by President Johnson in a special White House ceremony. In 1979, President Carter expanded the program by Executive Order 12158 to include recognition of 20 additional scholars demonstrating exceptional talent in the visual, creative and performing arts.

B. Selection Criteria and Processes

Since 1964, the annual nationwide selection has been made from all graduating high school seniors. The winners are generally recognized as the "cream of the crop" of the American education system. As given in program statements, press releases and other official documentation (e.g., Goldstein et al., 1994; U.S. Commission, 1974), three specific selection criteria were established:

"Brain Power." Scholarship is the most dominant criterion, and is measured by College Board test scores, cumulative grade point averages, class rank, scholastic interests, and academic awards. As President Johnson (1966) put it: "(T)hese awards are to recognize the most precious resource of the United States—the brain power of its young people—to encourage the pursuit of intellectual attainments among all our youth."

Leadership. This criterion is measured by individual attainment in various scholastic and extra-curricular activities. Scholars are required to demonstrate extraordinary potential or recognized success as initiators, planners and executors of group activities. Both quantity and quality of involvement are emphasized in the selection process.

Community Service. Scholars are required to demonstrate sincere concern and earnest commitment to the advancement of the public interest (e.g., founding programs for the disabled, tutoring disadvantaged children, and volunteering at hospitals and nursing homes). Scholars are required to evidence the meaning, role, and impact of their community service through recommendations and essays.

The above three-step procedure resulted in the selection of 121 academic scholars (or .000024%) from the six million high school graduates who took the College Board tests in 1995, and of 20 arts scholars (.004%) from the 5,000 NFAA annual competitors.

C. Official Remarks of the Presidents (1964 - 1995)

All seven Presidents since 1964 have personally addressed the scholars in White House ceremonies. These addresses (21 in total) reiterated the program's general purposes, stringent criteria and rigorous selection process. All Presidents' appraisals of the scholars fall along three broad dimensions:

Recognition of Individual Achievement. All Presidents have contextually recognized the "outstanding achievement" of individuals with reference to specific selection criteria on scholarship, leadership, and service. This acknowledgment ranged from overt praise to generic congratulations. A typical laudatory remark was President Reagan's 1983 statement: "On behalf of a proud nation, I congratulate the scholars on their achievements. You are America's future and symbolize her greatest hopes. You're among our best young achievers."

Accreditation of Contributing Sources. The Presidents generally attributed the scholars' achievement to three primary sources: the scholars' individual motivations, family support, and school learning. For example, President Clinton summarized in 1995, "As I look out at this group today of proud parents and family members and friends and educators, I'm reminded once again of the curious mix of things that produces the sort of achievement that we see embodied in the young people on this stage today."

National Interest. All Presidents linked the national interest to the scholars' individual achievements. Although the seven Presidents diverged politically, they unequivocally urged the scholars to not only continue their achievements but also dedicate their efforts to national imperatives:

President Johnson (1966) stated, "I bring you the pride and the hope of a Nation that cherishes excellence and commitment, and that has never needed your kind of excellence and commitment more than it needs it right now."

President Nixon (1970) stated, "The fact that you have been selected as a Presidential Scholar means that the Nation has a stake in you as the leaders of the future."

President Ford (1975) stated, "I trust that you will contribute, through your scholarship and your practical experience, new theories and new insights into our national wisdom. In this way you will strengthen the American democracy which all of us cherish."

President Carter (1978) stated, "I not only congratulate you on your achievement so far, but I expect great things from you in the future."

President Reagan (1983) stated, "America needs your commitment, your knowledge, and your education. Your country has made an enormous investment in you, and we're relying on your energies and abilities to carry us into the next century—free and strong and prosperous."

President Bush (1989) stated, "Let this award be both a recognition of past accomplishment and a challenge to excel in the years ahead... We're counting on you to understand and shape a better world tomorrow."

President Clinton (1995) stated, "One thing only you owe your country—your devotion to making sure that every other young person in this country will always have the opportunity that brought you to this day."

Overall, these Presidents acknowledged the scholars' personal achievement, reminded them of the important contributions of families and school institutions, and encouraged them to continue to pursue excellence for the future of the nation. These students are explicitly regarded as "model graduates" whose accomplishments represent the success of American families and schools as well as the future promise of the nation.

D. Self Perceptions of Scholars

In the questionnaire survey, six items were specifically designed to measure whether the scholars perceived themselves as model high school graduates and ideal American citizens. As shown in Table 12.1, 73% of the scholars agreed that the program was designed to recognize each scholar as a "role model for all children" (Item 1). Over 59% of the scholars considered themselves as model citizens (Items 2 and 3). And 56% agreed that they possessed personal traits of "ideal American citizens" (Item 4). Further, the scholars strongly agreed that the program promoted ideal national values as reflected by the scholars themselves (84% and 63% respectively on Items 5 and 6). Overall, less than 19% of the scholars disagreed with any of the above measures. These positive self-perceptions seem to be consistent with the designated missions and goals of the Program and also with the evaluative remarks of the seven Presidents.

Table 12.1.   Perceived Characteristics of the Participants[a]

Perceptual areas [Rating item]	Endorsement (1–3)	Neutrality (4)	Rejection (5–7)	P[b] level
Model children				
1. One of the goals of the presidential scholars program is to recognize scholars as role models for all children.	73%	20%	7%	.01
Model citizens				
2. People in today's society should be more like the scholars you have met.	64%	21%	15%	.01
3. You consider yourself a model citizen in the community in which you live.	59%	25%	16%	.01

Table 12.1.   Perceived Characteristics of the Participants[a] (cont.)

Perceptual areas [Rating item]	Endorsement (1–3)	Neutrality (4)	Rejection (5–7)	P[b] level
Ideal traits of citizens				
4. In general, scholars possess the personal traits of ideal American citizens.	56%	27%	18%	.01
Program recognition and promotion of national values				
5. This program promotes values that all Americans should believe in.	63%	26%	12%	.01
6. Meeting other scholars broadened your idea of America as a national community.	84%	12%	4%	.01
Overall average	67%	22%	12%	.01

[a] Each item was rated on a 7-step continuum with steps 1–3 for "endorsement," 4 for "neutrality" and 5–7 for "rejection." The percentages of the three categories on each item were based on the 114 subjects involved in the study.
[b] P value indicates significance level of difference between the "endorsement" subcategory and the higher value of the other two subcategories.

Objective 2: Objective Family Characteristics

To assess the second and third objectives of whether the scholars have similar family environments, the scholars' household characteristics were examined in terms of two (objective and subjective) "cultures" (Osgood et al., 1975). Objective culture consists of the countable demographic facts of students, such as family composition, siblings, birth order, income, school size, and region of residence. Subjective culture regards personal impressions, feelings and attitudes about their childhood environments where the participants were raised. The students' objective (demographic) distributions and between-gender comparisons are shown in Table 12.2.

Table 12.2.   Proportions of Male and Female Scholars on Demographic Subcategories[a]

Demographic Variables	Female (N = 64)	Male (N = 50)	Total (N = 114)	P Level[b]
A. Relations with guardians				
1. Both natural parents	84%	70%	78%	.01
2. Single parent				
Mother only	6%	10%	8%	ns
Father only	2%	6%	4%	ns
(sub-total)	(8%)	(16%)	(11%)	
3. Step parent (scholar living in one household)				
Mother + stepfather	1%	6%	4%	ns
Father + stepmother	1%	2%	2%	ns
(sub-total)	(2%)	(8%)	(5%)	.05
4. Stepparents (scholar living between two households)				
<Mother + stepfather> and <father + stepmother>	2%	6%	1%	.05
<Mother + stepfather> and <father only>	2%	—	1%	ns
<father + stepmother>and (mother + other>	2%	—	1%	ns
(Sub-total)	(6%)	(6%)	(6%)	ns
B. Number of children per household				
1. Single child	8%	10%	9%	ns
2. Two children	56%	52%	54%	ns
3. Three children	21%	26%	20%	ns
4. Four children	8%	8%	8%	ns
5. Five children	7%	2%	4%	ns
6. Six children	—	2%	1%	—
7. Eight children	2%	—	1%	—
C. Birth order				
1. Single child	8%	10%	9%	ns
2. First child	56%	46%	52%	.01
3. Second child	30%	34%	32%	ns
4. Third child	5%	8%	6%	ns
5. Fourth child	2%	2%	2%	ns

[a] Percentages in this table were based on frequencies of each gender falling within each of the three demographic variables (A–C).
[b] P level indicates the significance level of difference between the two genders in each comparison subcategory.

Parentage. The relationships between the students and guardians of the households in which they resided during their senior years indicate that the overwhelming majority of scholars (84% for females and 70% for males) lived with both natural parents. But only 11% lived with single parents; 5% with one natural parent and one stepparent; and 6% lived in two households on a regular basis. No significant differences existed between genders on the natural parent, single parent, or stepparent subcategories.

Siblings. The distribution of the number of siblings is presented in Table 12.2B. The majority of scholars (54%) were principally raised in households with only two children; and significantly fewer came from families of three children (20%), four or more (14%), or even single children (9%). No significant gender differences were found in the number of siblings.

Birth Order and Gender Difference. The birth order statistics are presented in Table 12.2C. The majority of the scholars were first-born children (52%), followed distantly by second-born children (32%). The numbers of third and fourth-born children were much lower (8%), as was the number of single children (9%). Being first-born mattered less to males than to females. A male scholar was 46% likely to be a first-born compared to being second (34%), third (8%), fourth-born (2%), or even a single child (10%); while a female scholar was 56% likely to be first-born compared to being second (30%), third (5%), fourth-born (2%) or even a single child (9%).

Presented in Table 12.3 are results from comparisons between scholars and the comparable youth population. In general, the scholars of both sexes were distributed across all subcategories of each demographic variable, recapturing the demographic diversity of the general youth population. However, significant differences emerged, including:

Hometown Size. Scholars resided more in populated areas than the general population.

Ethnicity. Asian scholars were markedly over-represented, while Black and Hispanic scholars were significantly underrepresented.

Religion. Protestant faith was significantly underrepresented (26% of scholars compared to 56% of general population) while those of Jewish (14% to 2%) and no faith (32% to 9%) were highly over-represented.

Household Composition. Nearly 90% of scholars' households were comprised of two parents, whereas only about 75% of general households were comprised of two parents. Among these households, more scholars than general high school students resided with natural parents.

Number of Children. The majority of scholars' households were similar to general households in the number of children; i.e., single child (9% compared to 13%), two children (54% to 56%), three children (20% to 22%). Quite unlike the general population, however, a significantly high proportion of scholars came from families with four or more children (14% compared to 8%).

Family Income. Scholars were more likely to come from financially able families than typical American families with children aged 18 years or younger. No scholars reported family income less than $15,000, although 20% of the general family population earned less than that amount. The difference was also significant for the other income levels less than $29,999. Further, the scholars significantly over-represented the highest income brackets. Almost two-third of all scholars (73%) reported income above $50,000, although only one-third (33%) of the general family population earned that amount. Moreover, while the median income for scholars' households was about $65,000, the national median income for families with children was about $35,719 (U.S. Bureau of Statistics, 1995). Thus, scholars were typically reared in upper-middle-income households with both parents and two or three siblings.

Table 12.3.   Comparison of Demographics with National Youth Population

Demographic Categories	Subgroups	Scholar Distribution	General Youth Distribution	Difference (P-level)
Gender	Male	44%	49%	ns
	Female	56%	51%	ns
Hometown	Less than 100K	45%	65%	.001
	100K–500K	24%	18%	ns
	Over 500K	30%	17%	.001
Ethnicity	White	75%	68%	ns
	Asian	11%	4%	.001
	Black	7%	15%	.016
	Hispanic	1%	13%	.001
	Mixed/other	4%	0%	ns
Religion	Protestant	26%	56%	.001
	Catholic	19%	26%	ns
	Jewish	14%	2%	.001
	Mormon	4%		
	Other Christian	3%	7%	ns
	Islamic	1%		
	None	32%	9%	.001
Household composition	Two parents	89%	74%	.001
	Single parent	11%	26%	.001

Table 12.3.   Comparison of Demographics with National Youth Population (cont.)

Demographic Categories	Subgroups	Scholar Distribution	General Youth Distribution	Difference (P-level)
	Among two-parent families			
	Two natural parents	88%	81%	ns
	Natural + Step	12%	16%	ns
	Adoptive/unknown	0%	3%	.043
	Children in all families			
	Single child	9%	13%	ns
	Two children	54%	56%	ns
	Three children	20%	22%	ns
	Four or more	14%	8%	.019
Family income	Less than $5K	0%	5%	.019
	$5K–10K	0%	8%	.001
	$0K–15K	0%	7%	.001
	$5K–25K	4%	14%	.001
	$25K–30K	0%	7%	.004
	$30K–40K	9%	13%	ns
	$40K–50K	14%	12%	ns
	Above 50K	73%	33%	.001
High schools attended	Public	77%	91%	.001
	Private	23%	9%	.001

Note: The 1994 U.S. Census statistics of the national youth population were used for the demographic categories of Gender and Ethnicity (15 to 19 year olds), Religion, Household Composition, and Family Income (for Families with children). The 1993 statistics for hometown size by Hall and Slater (1993) were used for Hometown size. The National Center for Educational Statistics on 1993 secondary school enrollment was used for High School Attended. Blanks in the table indicate the data were unavailable in the cited references.

Objective 3: Subjective Family Characteristics

The ratings of home environments on the 28 semantic differential (SD) scales were statistically factored through principal component analysis. Six components were retained by the scree test of the eigen values accounting for 68.5% of the total variance.

Table 12.4 presents the SD "marker items" (after varimax rotation of the factor matrix) that define the resultant six components. Further, each participant's response on each marker item was further coded into one of three categories. They are "endorsement" (for choosing any of the three response alternatives toward the positive pole of the SD scale, "neutrality" (choosing the center—neither or both agree/disagree—alternative), and "rejection" (choosing any of the three response alternatives toward the negative pole of the SD scale). By summing the trichotomous codlings over all subjects across all marker items for each component, we derived three proportions that would reflect the entire subject group's relative "endorsement," "indifference" (neutrality) and "rejection" of each component. Psychologically, the proportions presented in Table 12.4 would thus denote the "attributions" of all scholars as a whole to each underlying component.

Table 12.4.   Endorsement Ratios on Semantic Differential Scales[a]

Component [SD scales]	Endorsements of			P Level b
	Left term	Neutrality	Right term	
1. Family bonding				
CARING/aloof	92%	1%	7%	.01
GOOD/bad	91%	4%	5%	.01
WARM/cold	85%	4%	11%	.01
UNITED/disparate	72%	11%	18%	.01
(Overall)	(85%)	(5%)	(10%)	(.01)
2. Achievement-orientation				
STRONG/weak	80%	13%	7%	.01
FUTURE/present	55%	32%	13%	.01
COMPETITIVE/submissive	51%	19%	29%	.01
(Overall)	(62%)	(21%)	(16%)	(.01)
3. Family activation				
STABLE/unstable	77%	12%	12%	.01
SOCIABLE/isolated	53%	12%	35%	.01
FAST/slow	43%	39%	18%	.01
(Overall)	(58%)	(21%)	(22%)	(.01)
4. Financial security				
RICH/poor	60%	28%	12%	.01
OPEN/tight	56%	23%	21%	.01
(Overall)	(58%)	(25%)	(17%)	(.01)
5. Discipline				
STRUCTURED/unstructured	64%	12%	24%	.01
STRICT/loose	58%	10%	32%	.01
HEAVY PARENT/freedom	58%	22%	20%	.01

Table 12.4.   Endorsement Ratios on Semantic Differential Scales[a]

	Endorsements of			
Component [SD scales]	Left term	Neutrality	Right term	P Level b
PRECISE/uncertain	50%	30%	19%	.01
(Overall)	(58%)	(19%)	(24%)	(.01)
6. Parental influence				
MOTHER/father dominant	44%	44%	12%	.01

[a] For each semantic differential (SD) scale, the sum of three response ratios equals 100%.
[b] P level indicates the proportion for the left term of a SD scale is significantly greater than that for the right term.

Family Bonding. This first, most dominant component is defined by four marker items with *caring, good, warm,* and *united* on one pole, and *aloof, bad, cold,* and *disparate* on the other. This component clearly reflects the scholars' perceptions of home environments as having a cohesive bounding relationship as opposed to a disintegrated indifference.

For the proportions on these four markers as a whole, the subjects had an average of 85% overall endorsement, with only 5% neutrality, and 10% rejection. On individual markers, the majority of subjects perceived their families as being *caring* (92%), *good* (91%), *warm* (85%), and *united* (72%). Such endorsements seem to indicate that the scholars experienced happy family lives with significant physical, emotional, financial and intellectual supports.

Achievement-Orientation. This second component is defined by three scales with apparent endorsements of *strong* rather than *weak* (80% compared to 7%), *future-oriented* rather than *present-oriented* (55% to 13%), and *competitive* rather than *submissive* (51% to 29%). Overall, the majority, 62%, of the scholars endorsed the positive pole of this component, 22% the neutral, and 16% the negative pole. This result clearly suggests that their families emphasized achievement, which is naturally conducive to producing highly motivated, confident and determined individuals.

Family Activity. This component is defined by three marker items, characterizing the family environments as more *stable* rather than *unstable* (77% compared to 12%), *sociable* than *isolated* (53% compared to 35%) and *fast* than *slow* (43% compared to 18%). Overall, the scholars perceived their family environments at a higher level of energetic activation (58%) than withdrawn passivity (21%).

Financial Security. The third component is dominated by two maker items with *rich* and *open* on one pole, and *poor* and *tight* on the other. In average, the majority (58%) of participants perceived their families as having sufficient financial means, while 25% as neutral and only 17% as insufficient. On individual markers, 60% perceived their families as *rich* and 56% as *open*, while only 12% as *poor* and 21% as *tight*. This result seems to suggest that the scholars perceived their families to have enough material resources for meeting daily living expenses, even though the families may not be "wealthy" in terms of actual monetary assets. Indeed, their self-reported annual family incomes were rather dispersed, ranging from $17,000 to $450,000, with the majority (73%) at the $50,000 level.

In comparison with the national median income of $35,719 for households with married couples and children (U.S. Bureau of the Census, 1995), the median income for the scholars' households was almost twice the national level, or about $65,000. Further, in considering that only 7% of all American families had incomes above $80,000, over 42% of scholars reported family incomes exceeding that level (with 12% exceeding $150,000). These differences seem to support the general belief that a traditional middle class family with two parents (especially with natural parents) more positively contributed to the educational attainment of children (Milne, 1989; Mulkey, 1992). However, despite income discrepancies among the scholar households, the majority believed themselves to be "rich" or at least financially sound, and "open" or having the feeling of freedom in utilizing family resources.

Discipline. This component is marked by four SD scales related to the discipline of children. Their family environments were perceived as very *structured* (by 64% of scholars), *strict* (58%), and *precise* (50%) and were also governed by heavy parental *involvement* (58%). Over all, 57% of the scholars reportedly grew up in well-disciplined environments with precise rules and limitations. On the contrary, only 20% reported living in loose, disorganized environments.

Parental Influence. This component is represented by a single marker measuring the relative dominance between two parents. Overall, 44% of the participants reportedly had more dominant mothers, 44% equally dominant parents, and only 12% more dominant fathers. More specifically, in the two-parent households of female scholars, 48% reported primary maternal dominance, and 40% reported equal dominance. However, in the two-parent households for male scholars, only 30% reported primary mother dominance, and 53% reported equal dominance. It seems clear that in two-parent households, mothers constituted principal roles in childcare and supervision, while fathers played equally or less apparent roles. Fathers themselves were only uniquely dominant for 18% of the male scholars and 12% for the females.

CONCLUSION AND DISCUSSION

The present study examines the common characteristics of families of a highly selective group of high school graduates. Three general conclusions confirm the initial research objectives. First, the participants are "model" young adults and their families are "successful" on the basis of four sources of evaluation—the founding purposes of the Presidential Scholar Program, stringent selection criteria, Presidential remarks, and the subjects' self-perceptions. Second, the demographics of these families are rather diverse, consisting of the various segments of the contemporary American society in the areas of ethnicity, family size, home residency, religious denomination, family income, and high school types. Third, these families, despite their objective diversity, share similar subjective characteristics in child rearing practices. These results seem to have significant implications for family contributions to modern education. Specific topical issues are discussed below.

Objective Cultural Diversity

Among the demographic results, two salient patterns emerged regarding the scholars' status within the family: number of children in the family, and birth order.

Number of Children. The majority of scholars tend to come from families with two children. This result may be explained in part by the contention that students with more than three siblings are less prone to outstanding achievement in high school than those with only two or three siblings (Blake, 1989; Heer, 1985). Parents with a larger number of children are reported to have difficulty in providing enough the quality time, energy, and financial resources that are necessary to accommodate the needs of each child to excel in scholastic achievement, extra-curricular activities, and community involvement. It is interesting to note, however, that the families with four or more children are relatively fewer when compared within the study sample, but are over-represented when compared to the general population. This finding seems to suggest the need to examine how the theoretical scarcity of attention in larger families is overcome by other environmental factors, especially subjective family characteristics.

On the opposite extreme, in single-child families, parental attention is likely to be overbearing, and standards of achievement for the child relatively lower. Whatever the single child does tends to be exaggerated as "remarkable" by proud parents, so the child is less likely to challenge external norms of achievement. In contrast, in the families with two or three children, parental attention and guidance are more objective and reasonably focused than in larger families, but not to the extent of positive over-reinforcement and lowered expectations as with the single child.

Birth Order. Scholars also tend to be the first-born children. This significant association between early birth and scholastic attainment is confirmed by other independent studies (Hauser, 1985; Polit, 1988). First-borns are reported to receive greater attention, expectations and educational effort from their parents than younger siblings. In this process, first-borns are more likely to be encouraged to take on personal responsibilities and leadership roles over younger siblings (Lackie, 1984). First-borns become more emotionally close to their parents, and thus tend to have greater regard for conventional social norms, and a stronger motivation to achieve in later life (Ishiyama, 1990; Neaves, 1990). Parental entrustment tends to motivate the first-borns to maintain competitive edges in rival sibling relationships, as well as to elevate personal expectations and self-esteem. Usually, first-borns are more confident and competitive than younger siblings throughout later education and socialization processes.

One noticeable quality about birth order, however, is its differential impact on each gender: significantly more female scholars are first-born than male scholars. This gender difference may be explained in part by the different expectations traditionally imposed on children by parents and society. Stereotypically, male children are often encouraged to be assertive, outgoing, motivated, and achieving, while female children are encouraged to be more sensitive, deferent, docile, and complying (Wittig, 1985; Buss, 1995; Kaminski, 1984; Wynn, 1987). Such expectations lead to the development of categorically different personalities for each gender, usually portrayed as beneficial for males, and repressive for females (Chellsen, 1984). In academic and career pursuits, male children are given a "leg up" in individual achievement regardless of birth order, while female children seem to need a counteracting influence for achievement—namely, the "mother role" of being the responsible, path-finding, and ground-breaking eldest child.

Overall, the demographic results of this study seem to trace the contour of a "model family" consisting of both natural parents and two or three children. This finding should not be construed as a challenge to the non-traditional family concept, nor as support for policies that condemn divorce or degrade single parents and other family forms. Indeed, the above structural implications of the family form, and especially the following examination of the subjective characteristics of the subjects' household environments, should reveal important and attainable lessons for all types of contemporary families.

Subjective Common Characteristics

The family environments of the participants were perceived to be strongly positive in all six psychological components. The findings clearly imply that diverse contemporary households can achieve equal success if they strive for the similar ideals and values in rearing children. Such ideals and values may be inferred from the six underlying components identified in this study.

Cohesive Family. Family members should "bond" by establishing a caring, warm, good, and united environment. This provides the empathic security and emotional stability necessary for the development of self-assurance and confidence in children. Family bonding as such makes the family an optimum springboard for children's societal achievement, while, at the other extreme, incohesive family environments may breed juvenile pathologies as current literature indicates (e.g., Bischof, 1995; Bush, 1995).

Achievement-Orientation. Parents and guardians should create achievement-oriented environments based on strength, future-orientation and healthy competition. This family will establish a decisive, determined, and forward-looking family mentality and engender in the child a capacity to cultivate ideas, be self-motivated and plan for the future. Specifically, strong household environments encourage assertion, control and decisiveness in individual and group activities; future-orientation cultivates an ethic of work and short-term sacrifice, and competition enhances leadership rather than followership tendencies. Together, strength, future-orientation and competition develop a sense of empowerment, self-purpose, and determination as a basis for motivated achievement in life.

Activity. The family should be psychologically "active," behaviorally energetic, yet emotionally stable. Where daily interactions and household chores are constructive, decisive and efficient, children naturally learn to be spontaneous in adapting to new challenges, as well as able and knowledgeable about life routines and responsibilities. Furthermore, an active and sociable home environment enables and encourages children to interact with one another and the external world, thus precluding emotional isolation or alienation. Healthy interaction teaches children the communicative and interpersonal skills necessary for school leadership and adulthood, while introducing them to the socialization process they will inevitably encounter in their future, fast-paced adult lives.

Financial Security. The family environment should emphasize "managing" instead of "having" or "missing," regardless of whether the family is objectively "wealthy" or "poor." The child needs to perceive family finance to be structurally stable in order to feel adequate, sufficient and safe. This perception induces confidence and security, empowering students to pursue excellence in school.

Constructive Discipline. Parents and guardians need to create a disciplined environment that is structured, precise, smooth, and governed by caring and loving parental involvement. However, discipline should not be independent of other components, especially evaluative bonding, achievement-orientation, and family-activation. Without felt warmth or unconditional support, sterile academy-like environments typically result in repressed emotion, bitter hostility and interpersonal indifference. Children raised in an unreasonably disciplined, stern and militaristic environment may suffer from stunted social skills and a great deal of insecurity.

The importance of this finding may be viewed from the impact of discipline, family structure and parental involvement on a child's psyche. If a child is conditioned in a relatively stable, structured and precise environment with constrained personal freedom, he/she should be expected to reinvent those qualities for themselves in their normal social and scholastic worlds.

On the other hand, if a child is raised in a caring, nurturing environment, yet with no sense of order, that child is less likely to develop the respect for authority, self-discipline and organizational skills necessary for leadership and scholastic achievement. Furthermore, parental involvement in the lives of children is crucial for creating and heightening the sense of personal responsibility and duty each child attaches to activities, attitudes and individual self-concepts. These effects have long been confirmed by relevant literature (e.g., Leung, 1987). Thus, the component of discipline, along with parental involvement, is crucial for the balanced development of academic and social skills.

Parental Influence. In heterosexual families, the paternalistic father figure should not be the only source of dominance. This result seems to confirm theoretical accounts of maternal influence in the literature. Mothers usually assume the pivotal role in establishing family bonding, promoting educational activities, and maintaining discipline in child development (Cone, 1985; Bartle, 1992). The cultivation of filial cohesion in children depends on the internal emotional bonds brought about through the nurturing process and disciplinary patterns of early childcare. However, although strong mothers become role models for young women, males seem to become more independent of maternal influence as they become older and more closely allied with the male role (Hess, 1984). This result does not, therefore, imply that the fathers should be absent for early child-rearing; indeed, father-presence has been shown to provide the sense of financial and emotional security necessary for preventing anxiety in young children (Shinn, 1979). The result indicates, rather, that the household environments should be overtly nurturing, and that parents should be intimately involved with their children's activities.

The established "role model" characteristics of the subjects, as well as their significantly shared endorsement of the above household factors, indicate that these factors may be regarded as meaningful, attainable and desirable standards for all child-rearing environments.

Although the evolving diversity of family structures in contemporary society might never be homogenized, these model characteristics may be recognized and striven for by all family forms, traditional or not. Unlike static demographic differences in birth order, income, place of residence, ethnicity, and so on, beneficial subjective characteristics are effectively "learnable" by all parents and guardians (Duman, 1989; Zeitlin, 1994; Weiss, 1988). Parenting courses, marriage counseling, and family dynamics training have all proven useful for this purpose (e.g., Mohan, 1983; Faria, 1994). Subjective family environments are thus attainable, depending on the willingness and adaptability of contemporary guardians. As far as child rearing in contemporary society is concerned, all motivated families may provide ideal learning environments for the cultivation of most productive future societal members.

Multicultural and International Implications

Contemporary educational institutions are generally "uniform" in both structure and process for providing students with "equal opportunities" in learning experiences. However, these students come into the educational system with diverse backgrounds both in objective and subjective cultures. The present research has clearly identified that some family characteristics are more desirable than others to make positive contribution to student achievement. While objective family environments (e.g., size of family, location of residency, and birth order) are not easily altered or controlled, subjective family values and interaction patterns can and should be improved to meet the genuine needs of child development and education. Undoubtedly, such improvement would involve the fundamental issue of whether certain unique characteristics of one family type (or a nation) should be required to adopt or harmonize with contemporary, and perhaps repugnant, values of another family type (or nation). This issue is prevalent in the modernization process of all nations. Perhaps, the natural law of family love of children would be the most effective means for parents to recognize and accept the needs of children in wholesome development. Under this premise, the development and implementation of multicultural education in schools would be the only means across all modern societies to cultivate students to appreciate or accept common values (such as those set forth in the U.S. national goal of school education.)

LIMITATIONS

One possible limitation of the present study is that the conceptualization of "model students" from the 114 subjects is too simple; that is, the sampling occurred in 1995 alone and did not evaluate past and latest scholars or otherwise equally qualified individuals. However, these subjects may safely be regarded as "successful products" of family and school environments because of the multi-tiered process involved in their selection (These subjects do, after all, represent the upper 0.1% of college-bound high school seniors in 1995.).

Another possible limitation regards the reliance on quantitative rather than qualitative methodology. In anticipation of this potential deficiency, personal interviews and follow-up questionnaire surveys for reliability and validity checks were administered to a small group of subjects over the entire National Recognition Week. The consistency and quality of their responses overwhelmingly confirmed the conclusions of this study. Finally, the semantic differential technique was chosen for the present study because of its multidimensional measurement efficiency, free-choice gradience, and bi-polar comparability. Overall, the consistency of these results seems to affirm this methodological strategy.

ACKNOWLEDGMENT

The completion of this study was assisted by Sophia Tzeng-Okamoto while she was at Harvard University and Columbia Law School.

REFERENCES

Amoroso, D. (1986). Adolescents' perception of aspects of the home environment and their attitudes toward parents, self and external authority. *Adolescence*, 21, 81, 191–204.

Austin, J., & Martin, N. (1992). College-bound students: Are we meeting their needs? *Adolescence*, 27(105), 115–121.

Bartle, S. (1992). Similarity between parents' and adolescents' levels of individuation. *Family Therapy*, 19, 173–184.

Bischof, G. (1995). Family environments of adolescent sex offenders and other juvenile delinquents. *Adolescence*, 30, 117, 157–170.

Blake, J. (1989). Number of siblings and educational attainment. *Science*, 245, 4913, 32–36.

Bush, E. (1995). A quantitative and qualitative analysis of suicidal preadolescent children and their families. *Child Psychiatry and Human Development*, 25(4), 241–252.

Buss, D. (1995). Evolution and human mating. *Harvard Journal of Law and Public Policy*, 18(2), 537–546.

Calabrese, R. (1994). The principal: A leader in a democratic society. *NASSP Bulletin*, 78, 3–11.

Chellsen, J. (1984). *The influence of sex-typing and attributional style on depression and attributions for success and failure*. DAI 44: 3925B.

Cone, J. (1985). Assessing parent participation: The parent/family involvement index. *Exceptional Children*, 51(5), 417–424.

Cusinato, M. (1990). Is there a psychology of the healthy family? *Japanese Journal of Family Psychology*, 4, 77–93.

DeBaryshe, B. D., Patterson, G. R., & Capaldi, D. M. (1993). A performance model for academic achievement in early adolescent boys. *Developmental Psychology*, 29, 795–804.

Duman, J. (1989). Treating antisocial behavior in children: Child and family approaches. *Clinical Psychology Review*, 9(2), 197–222.

Durkheim, E. (1984). *The Division of labor* (Translation by L. A. Coser). New York: The Free Press.

Eckenrode, J. (1993). School performance and disciplinary problems among abused and neglected children. *Developmental Psychology*, 29(1), 53–62.

Executive Order No. 11,155. (1964–1965). 3 C.F.R. 1968.

Executive Order No. 12,158. (1979). 15 Weekly Compilation of Presidential Documents. 1688.

Faria, G. (1994). Training for family preservation practice with lesbian families. *Families in Society*, 75(7), 416–422.

Fege, A. F. (1993). A tug-of-war over tolerance. *Educational Leadership*, 51(4), 22–24.

Fitzpatrick, K. (1992). Policy, school structure, and sociodemographic effects on statewide high school dropout rates. *Sociology of Education*, 65, 76–94.

Freedman, J. (1988). *The changing composition of the family and the workplace*. New Haven: Yale University Press.

Freud, S. (1961). *Civilization and its discontents* (Translated and Edited by James Strachey). New York: Norton.

Goldman, E. (1969). *The tragedy of Lyndon Johnson*. New York: Dell Publishing.

Goldstein, D., V. Stocking, L. Porter, & E. Berg. (1994). The presidential scholars: A portrait of talent and its development. *American Association for Gifted Children Working Paper No. 2*. Durham: AAGC.

Hall, G. E., & Slater, C. M. (1993). *Places, towns, and townships*. Lanham, MD: Bernan Press.

Hamburg, D. (1994). *Today's children: Creating a future for a generation in crisis*. New York: Time Books.

Hanson, M., & Lynch, E. (1992). Family diversity: Implications for policy and practice. *Topics in Early Childhood Special Education*, 12(3), 283–306.

Hauser, R. (1995). Birth order and educational attainment in full siblings. *American Educational Research Journal*, 22(1), 1–23.

Hess, R. (1983). Some cognitive consequences of maternal intervention techniques: A longitudinal study. *Child Development*, 55(6), 2017–2030.

Ingram, D. (1995). If preaching won't work, try practice. *Times Educational Supplement*, 9 June, 24–25.

Ishiyama, F. (1990). Birth order and fear of success among mid-adolescents. *Psychological Reports*, 66(1), 17–18.

Jencks, C. (1988). Whom must we treat equally for educational opportunity to be equal? *Ethics*, 98(3), 518–533.

Johnson, L. B. (1966). Remarks at the ceremony honoring the presidential scholars of 1966. *Public Papers of the Presidents*, No. 257, Washington: General Publication Office, 1967.

Kaiser, J. (1994). The role of family configuration, income, and gender in the academic achievement of young self-care children. *Early Child Development and Care*, 97, 91–105.

Kaminski, D. (1984). Children's perceptions of sex stereotyping: A five-year study. *International Journal of Women's Studies*, 7, 24–36.

Kaplinsky, R. (1984). *Third world industrialization in the 1980s: opening economies in a closing world.* UK: Frank Cass.

LaBelle, T. (1994). *Multiculturalism and education: Diversity and its impact on schools and society.* Albany: State University of New York Press.

Lackie, B. (1984). Learned responsibility and order of birth. *Smith College Studies in Social Work*, 54(2), 117–38.

Lamont, M., J. Kaufman, & M. Moody. (1995). The best and the brightest: Definitions of personal and cultural excellence among the 1991 presidential scholars. Paper presented at the meetings of the American Sociological Conference. Washington, August 1995.

Landsberg, B. K. (1993). Equal education opportunity: the Rehnquist Court revisits Green and Swann. *Emory Law Journal*, 43(2), 921–961.

Lee, C. (1984). An investigation of psychosocial variables related to academic success for rural Black adolescents. *Journal of Negro Education*, 53(4), 424–434.

Leung, J. (1987). Perceived parental influence and adolescent post-secondary career plans. *High School Journal*, 70(4), 173–179.

Lickona, T. (1993). The return of character education. *Educational Leadership*, 51(3), 6–12.

Martin, R. (1992). A model for studying the effects of social policy on education. *Equity & Excellence*, 25(2–4), 53–57.

McCarthy, A. (1992). The American family. In L. Kaplan (Ed.), *Education and the family* (pp. 3–26). Boston: Allyn and Bacon.

Miller, T. (1995). Clinical and preventive issues in child custody disputes. *Child Psychiatry and Human Development*, 25(4), 267–280.

Milne, A. (1989). Family structure and the achievement of children. In W. Weston (Ed.), *Education and the American family* (pp. 32–65). New York: New York University Press.

Mohan, V. (1983). Counseling of the socially disadvantaged child. *Asian Journal of Psychology and Education*, 11, 1–8.

Morris, G. G. (1992). Adolescent leaders: Rational thinking, future beliefs, temporal perspective and other correlates. *Adolescence*, 27(105), 173–181.

Mulkey, L. (1992). One-parent households and achievement. *Sociology of Education*, 65(1), 48–65.

Myers, S. (1992). Schools find that diversity can place values in conflict. *New York Times*, 6 Oct. 1992, natl. ed., p. A20.

Neaves, R. (1990). Deidentification in two-child families. *Journal of Adolescent Research*, 5(3), 370–386.

Osgood, C. E., May, W. H., & Miron, M. S. (1975). *Cross-cultural universals of affective meaning.* Urbana: University of Illinois Press.

Osgood, C. E., Suci, C. J., & Tannenbaum P. H. (1957). *The Measurement of meaning.* Urbana: University of Illinois Press.

Peshkin, A. (1995). Learning to be good: Quo Vadis. *American Journal of Education,* 103(2), 213–218.

Polit, D. (1988). The intellectual achievement of only children. *Journal of Biosocial Science,* 20(3), 275–285.

Reglin, G., & Adams, D. (1990). Why Asian-American high school students have higher grade point averages and SAT scores than other high school students. *High School Journal, 73*(13), 143–149.

Ryan, K. (1987). Character development: the challenge and the model. In K. Ryan & G. F. Maclean (Eds.), *Character Development in Schools and Beyond* (pp. 3–35). New York: Praeger.

Sayfie, J. J. (1994). Education emancipation for inner city students: a new legal paradigm for achieving equality of educational opportunity. *University of Miami Law Review,* 48(4), 913–947.

Schneider, B. (1994). East-Asian academic success in the United States: Family, school, and community explanations. In P. M. Greenfield & R. R. Cocking (Eds.), *Cross-cultural roots of minority child development* (pp.323–350). New Jersey: Lawrence Erlbaum Associates, Inc.

Shinn, M. (1979). Father absence and children's cognitive development. *Annual Progress in Child Psychiatry and Child Development,* 292–330.

Sommers, C. (1993). Teaching the virtues. *The Public Interest.* CITY: PUBLISHER.

Sue, S., & Okazaki, S. (1990). Asian-American educational achievements: A phenomenon in search of an explanation. *American Psychologist,* 45, 913–920.

Tzeng, O. C. S., & Henderson, M. M. (1999). Objective and subjective cultural relationships related to industrial modernization and social progress. *International Journal of Intercultural Relation,* 56(4), 1–35.

Tzeng, O. C. S., Jackson, J. W., & Karlson, H. C. (1991). Theories of child abuse and neglect: Differential perspectives, summaries and evaluations. New York: Praeger.

U.S. Bureau of the Census. (1995). *Statistical abstract of the United States,* 115th edition. Washington: GPO.

U.S. Commission on Presidential Scholars. (1974). *Presidential scholars.* Washington: GPO.

Watt, N. (1990). *Children's adjustment to parental divorce: Self-image, social relations and school performance.* New York: Cambridge University Press.

Weber, M. (1946). Religious rejections of the world and their directions. In H. H. Gerth & C. W. Mills (Eds.), *From Max Weber* (Translation). New York: Oxford University Press.

Weiss, H. (1988). *Evaluating family programs.* Hawthorne, New York: Aldine de Gruyter.

Weston, W. J. (1989). *Education and the American family: A research synthesis.* New York: New York University Press.

Wittig, M. (1985). Sex-role norms and gender-related attainment values: Their role in attributions of success and failure. *Sex Roles,* 12(1–2), 1–13.

Wragg, T. (1993). Don't put the moral lead on our necks. *Times Educational Supplement,* 2 April 1993, p. 72.

Wynn, R. (1987). Sex role development and early educational experiences. In D. B. Carter (Ed.), *Current conceptions of sex roles and sex typing: Theory and research* (pp. 79–88). New York: Praeger.

Zeitlin, S. (1994). *Coping in young children: Early intervention practices to enhance adaptive behavior and resilience.* Baltimore: Paul H. Brooks Publishing Co.

Zill, N. (1993). The changing realities of family life. *Aspen Institute Quarterly,* 5, 27–51.

CHAPTER 13

THE MAKING OF SCHOOL SUCCESS AND FAILURE

The Case of the New Immigrant Students from Mainland China

Benjamin K.P. Leung

INTRODUCTION

This paper examines the impact of change in the socio-cultural environment on the school performance of *new immigrant* secondary school students who came to Hong Kong from Mainland China for the purpose of family reunion. These immigrant students were born in the Mainland, but because one of their parents, usually the father, is a Hong Kong permanent resident, have been allowed under the Basic Law of the Hong Kong Special Administrative Region to join their parents as the territory's permanent residents. These new immigrants (usually referred to as *new arrivals* in the local literature) are ethnically the same as the overwhelming majority of the Hong Kong population, but having been in the territory for less than three or four years, have had to cope with problems and difficulties in adapting to a new environment. They have had to come to grips with a dis-

Teaching, Learning, and Motivation in a Multicultural Context, pages 289–314
Copyright © 2003 by Information Age Publishing
All rights of reproduction in any form reserved.

continuity in school experiences, a change in family life, a break with past friendships, as well as unfamiliarity with a social-cultural setting which is more modernized and westernized than their places of origin. In addition, new immigrants (and visitors) from the Mainland have been the subject of ridicule and discrimination in the local media and among the local population (Government Secretariat, 1997, pp. 17, 28–29). In short these new immigrant students have faced difficulties and obstacles which can be expected to detract from their performance at school. Yet as the data from the respondents in my study show, while some have fallen behind in their school performance, many others have surpassed their local counterparts in academic achievement. What factors and conditions, then, have contributed to the success and failure of these new immigrant students? To what extent can their success and failure be attributed to differences in the way they respond to changes and challenges in the new environment? What is the role of socio-cultural change in the making of academic success and failure? Indeed questions such as these have been the subject of numerous studies on minority education in multicultural and multiethnic societies such as the United States and Britain. I will now take a cursory look at those studies which bear a thematic affinity to our inquiry, in order to draw explanatory insights to guide our analysis.

The Differential Educational Achievement of Minority Groups: Does Culture Matter?

Research on the education of non-mainstream children in the United States has shown that certain minority groups not only perform academically better than other minority groups, but also surpass the educational achievement of the mainstream group. This phenomenon is intriguing, for the term 'minority' suggests a position of social, cultural and political disadvantage or even subordination. Margaret Gibson, for instance, in her concluding chapter in an edited volume on minority education (Gibson & Ogbu, 1991) conceives of minority as "a group occupying a subordinate position in a multiethnic society, suffering from the disabilities of prejudice and discrimination, and maintaining a separate identity" (Gibson, 1991, p. 358). The phenomenon is also bewildering from the perspective of Pierre Bourdieu's explanation of educational success and failure in terms of the amount of *cultural capital* in the students' possession (Bourdieu, 1977; Bourdieu & Passeron, 1977). The school, Bourdieu argues, is an institute of social and cultural reproduction. School knowledge and school experiences, or in short school culture, in Bourdieu's view mirrors the values, dispositions, and life-styles of the society's dominant groups. The higher socio-economic groups are thus advantaged in education for their culture prepares and equips them with the appropriate dispositions and abilities for learning at school. In contrast, the lower socio-economic groups, to the extent that their culture differs from that of the dominant groups, are disadvantaged in their educational performance. The differential educational achievement (and hence the differential occupational and social achievements), of the higher and lower socio-economic groups, according to Bourdieu, is to a significant degree attributable to the different amounts of *cultural capital* they possess. Bourdieu's theory bears on our discussion of minority education, especially immigrant minority education, for immigrant minorities can be expected to possess less cultural capital than the mainstream social groups. In view of the disprivileges and disadvantages faced by minority groups, the academic success of some of them begs the questions of how these successful minorities manage to surmount the odds against them and how they differ from those who fail.

One group of explanations (Caudill & De Vos, 1956; Kitano, 1969; Caplan, Choy, & Whitmore, 1991) attribute the school success of the pertinent minority groups, Asian Americans in particular, to the high value which their cultures place on education. According to this view, there is a compatibility between the Asian cultural emphasis on achievement through education and hard work and central tenets of the middle-class American culture. This cultural trait, from the perspective of Bourdieu's concept of cultural capital, facilitates the Asian Americans' adaptation to the American *mainstream* way of achieving success and thus promotes their performance in education. A related group of explanations (Hsu, 1971; Sung, 1987; Chen & Stevenson, 1995; Hao & Bonstead-Brun, 1998) view the family-centred nature of Asian cultures as the prime contributing factor to academic success. Asian children, according to these authors, work hard in school to please their parents who have high educational expectations for their children and who view school success as a matter of family pride and honor. The above *cultural* explanations, however, falter in the light of studies which reveal that the same ethnic group may have widely different levels of academic achievement in different countries or even within the same country. De Vos (1978, 1992) and Lee (1991), for instance, have discovered that Korean students in the United States perform academically much better than Koreans in Japan. Buriel (1994), Stanton-Salazar and Dornbusch (1995), and Rumberger and Larson (1998), on the other hand, have found higher academic achievement among bilingual (i.e., from Spanish-speaking backgrounds but proficient in English) than monolingual (i.e., either English-speaking only or from Spanish-speaking backgrounds but not proficient in English) Mexican American students. Obviously an ethnic group's cultural characteristics alone do not offer a sufficient or convincing explanation of its performance in education.

Another set of studies (Suzuki, 1980; Hirschman & Wong, 1986; Sue & Okazaki, 1990; Goyette & Xie, 1999) overcome the inadequacy of the cultural explanation through combining an ethnic group's cultural traits and its experiences in the host country in accounting for its school success. Thus according to this argument, in the face of discrimination in the recipient country, Asian Americans regard education—something which they already venerate in their native countries—as the most reliable means to overcome disadvantages and attain upward social mobility. Goyette and Xie (1999), in proposing an explanation for the high educational expectations of the Asian Americans in their study, dwell on their position as an ethnic minority. Asian Americans, they argue, maintain a marginal presence in the United States because of their small numbers. "Because of their marginal status in the United States, Asian Americans of all ethnic groups may view education as the best means to overcome discrimination and other barriers to achieving high social status" (Goyette & Xie 1999, p. 23). This set of explanations, however, do not address the question of why other ethnic minorities subject to discrimination, such as the African Americans and Mexican Americans, have disproportionately high levels of academic failure. The cultural ecological theory (Ogbu, 1978, 1987, 1991, 1997; Matute-Bianchi, 1986, 1991; Gibson & Ogbu, 1991; Suarez-Orozco, 1987, 1991; Rumberger & Larson, 1998), to which I now turn, offers perhaps the most comprehensive explanation of the differential educational achievement of minority groups through highlighting their different responses to the discrimination they face.

Ogbu, the foremost and the best known proponent of the cultural ecological theory, makes a distinction between what he calls *voluntary* minorities and *involuntary* minorities. The former "have generally moved to their present societies because they believed that the move would lead to more economic well-being, better overall opportunities or greater political freedom" (Ogbu, 1991, p. 8). Examples are the Asian Americans, Koreans in the United States, Sikhs in Britain and in the United States. The involuntary minorities, in contrast, are "people who were brought into their present society through slavery, conquest or colonization" (Ogbu, 1991, p. 9). Examples are the African Americans, the American Indians, and Koreans in Japan. This difference in the two categories' *historical* experience of becoming a minority, according to Ogbu, conditions their responses to discrimination in the present society. The voluntary minorities adopt an accommodating and acquiescent adaptive strategy for they see the host society as offering them a better life than the life "back home." This *positive dual frame of reference* and their perception that they are "foreigners" or "strangers" in the present society, Ogbu argues, enable them to put up with the discrimination and barriers against them as a price worth paying in order to attain the goals of their emigration. Further, from their belief that the present society affords them better opportunities, these voluntary minorities have developed a *folk theory of success* which holds that they will surmount the obstacles and attain socio-economic advancement through hard work and education. Finally, Ogbu maintains that the voluntary minorities often retain, and even take pride in, their former *social and cultural identity*, which has the effect of insulating them from a sense of inferiority to the mainstream majority. Ogbu cites what a Sikh informant said about the ways of the American majority: "If we become like them, we shall fail" (Ogbu 1991, p. 13).

But the involuntary minorities, Ogbu argues, interpret and respond to the social barriers against them differently. They perceive their minority status and the attendant discrimination as something imposed on them by the mainstream majority; their historical experiences of subordination and oppression at the hands of the dominant majority lead them to develop an oppositional "we against them" consciousness and identity. They do not think that the social institutions in the present society, including *education*, afford them fair opportunities for success. Their main strategy for betterment, according to Ogbu, is collective struggle in the form of protests and civil rights activities rather than school success. Indeed, trying hard and doing well at school could be viewed by fellow members of their group as acquiescing with the mainstream "oppressors" and hence as a threat to their solidarity and collective identity. In short, while the voluntary minorities have strong incentives for performing well at school, the involuntary minorities have disincentives for doing so.

The Differential Educational Achievement of Minority Groups: Conceptual Implications for The Present Study

To derive from the above review conceptual insights and guidelines for our study, we need to take note of some basic differences between the present inquiry and the studies surveyed in the last section. First, this study is not concerned with inter-group comparisons; it is an analytic account of the factors impacting on the school experiences and performance of one minority group—new immigrant students from Mainland China. Second, the students in my study are not an *ethnic* minority; they are Chinese like the mainstream majority in Hong Kong. The first qualification suggests that we have to tease out from the above studies conceptual insights for application in a within-group study. The second cautions against any injudicious application of a cultural mold of explanation. In respect of the first issue, Ogbu in fact alludes to the applicability of his model (which he refers to as a cultural model) in within-group studies: "…within a given minority group, too, there are subgroup and individual differences in school success attributable in part to *differences in the influence of the cultural model*" (Ogbu, 1991, p. 8; italics mine). Indeed, Lee (1996) takes Ogbu's cultural ecological model as a useful (though in her view inadequate) conceptual starting point in her study of academic achievement among Asian Americans. Trueba and Zou in their study of the educational experiences and achievement of the Miao university students in China describe Ogbu's theoretical contribution as "very positive" (Trueba & Zou, 1994, p. 20). More recently, Rumberger and Larson (1998) have applied Ogbu's theoretical insights in their analysis of differences in educational achievement among Mexican American students. With regard to the second issue, we may note that the new immigrant students came from a socio-cultural environment somewhat different from that of the Hong Kong majority. For this reason we can explore to what extent, and in what way, their socio-cultural background has impacted on their school experiences and performance in the present society.

Thus my inquiry will revolve around the central issue of how the change in the socio-cultural environment of the new immigrant students bears on their student career in Hong Kong. More specifically, I will pursue the inquiry in the light of Ogbu's concepts of *dual frame of reference* and *folk theory of success* as well as his arguments in respect of the *"foreigner perception"* and *social and cultural identity*. I will use these as the conceptual guidelines in my investigation, which will begin with the characteristics of the new immigrant students as a group and then continue with an explanatory account of within-group differences. In my attempt to explain within-group differences, I will explore to what extent, as Ogbu suggests, such differences are attributable to differences in the influence of the cultural ecological model. In this connection, I will also delve into explanatory factors and conditions which lie outside the theoretical compass of the cultural ecological model.

The Sample

This study is based on data which I collected through in-depth interviews with forty-two new immigrant secondary school students and some of their teachers over a six-month period beginning from August 2000. The majority of these students came to Hong Kong within the past four years, from provinces in the southern part of Mainland China. Many either spoke Cantonese (the daily language of the Hong Kong majority), or learned it through Hong Kong-made television programs, in their home country. Most of those who learned the language after arrival in Hong Kong became conversant with it in about three to four months. Indeed I was able to conduct interviews with them in Cantonese, though in many cases they spoke the language with an accent which would reveal their identity as recent immigrants from the Mainland. The main academic difficulty they faced was the English language, a subject which they did study in their Mainland schools, but at a standard which fell far short of that at a comparable level of education in Hong Kong. Though in Hong Kong all of them entered schools where the medium of instruction, except for the subject of English, was Chinese, the overwhelming majority had to repeat the grade which they had completed before arrival in order to catch up with English. All except two students came from working class family backgrounds. The two exceptions belonged to the middle class.

The New Immigrant Students as a Voluntary Minority

The students in my study have come to Hong Kong primarily for the purpose of family reunion. Though some reported in the interviews that they were reluctant to leave their friends in the Mainland, they were nevertheless longing to join their father, sometimes also their mother and siblings, in Hong Kong. All the students believed at the time of departure that Hong Kong would offer them better overall opportunities. Almost all of them mentioned better job prospects; many referred to better opportunities for education; some alluded to greater political freedom. And they all held the view that Hong Kong is a society where success goes to those who are able and hardworking. Thus while family reunion was uppermost in their mind at the time of departure, they also harbored the belief that opportunities for personal development and success in Hong Kong were better than those in the Mainland. The students in my study, in other words, are what Ogbu calls a *voluntary* minority. To what extent then do they share the characteristics which Ogbu associates with voluntary minorities?

Here I need to note first a feature which makes the new immigrant students in my study somewhat different from the voluntary minorities in Ogbu's discussion. The majority of these students did not think that they were discriminated against in the present society. Several reported unfriendly and pejorative treatment from fellow "local" classmates; a few others mentioned *unfriendly stares* from people in the street upon hearing these students conversing in Putonghua. But they all considered these to be isolated incidents involving a few individuals. They all thought that they had the same opportunity for education and success as the rest of the Hong Kong population. In other words, unlike the voluntary minorities in Ogbu's discussion, these students did not think that there are structural barriers against new immigrants as a group in the present society.

But like Ogbu's voluntary minorities, these students were aware that they were "*strangers*" or "newcomers" who had to accept certain disadvantages they faced in the host society. Thus they readily accepted having to repeat the grade they had already completed before arrival, because their English was not up to standard. Many were assigned (by the Education Department) to academically inferior schools, but none complained about it because they did not think that as "newcomers" they were entitled to a better choice, or indeed any choice. Many also spoke of the hard lives of their parents, usually their recent-immigrant mothers, who had to work long hours for very low wages, but they thought it natural that new arrivals had to endure hardships and disadvantages to make a living. They seemed to view these and other disadvantages as the inevitable predicament of "newcomers" rather than as discrimination or exploitation from the "host" society. In addition, they accepted these disadvantages because they considered their life in the present society better than the life "back home." They have, in Ogbu's terminology, a *positive dual frame of reference.*

But the *folk theory of success* which these new immigrant students and their parents held is not entirely resonant with that of Ogbu's voluntary minorities. These students and their parents did strongly believe that in Hong Kong a good education is the best way to achieve success, but they did not view education, as Ogbu's voluntary minorities do, as a means to *overcome structural discrimination and barriers.* Their strong belief in the importance of education seems to have emerged in the context of their *positive dual frame of reference* and their *class position.* Thus in the interviews many of the students expressed views such as the following:

> In the Mainland, having a good education, even a university education, is no guarantee that you will have a good job. There are few high-paying jobs in the Mainland, and connections with the right kind of people often count a lot in getting a good job; many university students there earn very low incomes. In Hong Kong, in contrast, people with a good education have much better job prospects and earn much higher incomes. In addition, with grants and loans provided by the Government, even poor people like myself stand a reasonable chance of entering university.

> Even before I came here, my parents filled my mind with the idea that Hong Kong is a land of abundant opportunities, and that to avail myself of these opportunities, I must have a good education.

> My parents kept telling me that because they had a poor education, they have very strenuous jobs and earn very low incomes. They told me not to follow their path. They told me that in Hong Kong, I must have high educational achievement in order to make use of the plentiful opportunities here and to be successful in life.

In other words, while these students and their parents subscribe to the Hong Kong Dream like the Hong Kong majority (see Wong, 1992), their *positive dual frame of reference* (that is, education has much better payoffs here than in the Mainland) adds a reinforcement that strengthens their belief in the value of education. That characterizes their folk theory of success.

I come now to the issue of these new immigrant students' *social and cultural identity*. In the interviews, I deliberately asked them the general question of what they considered their identity to be. All of them found the question vague and asked me for clarification. This suggests that their "new immigrant status" was not uppermost in their minds in terms of identity. I then followed up by asking them whether they considered themselves a Mainlander or a Hong Kong person. Their responses were mixed. Most said that they were both; some considered themselves Hong Kong people; while a handful thought they were Mainlanders and said they would continue to think so irrespective of their length of stay in Hong Kong. It seems their responses were determined largely by their perception of how well they were integrated into Hong Kong society, and partly by their views of its people and way of life. But it is obvious that identity was not an issue which bothered them, for they did not think it made a difference in their opportunities in the present society. In this respect, they are different from the voluntary minorities in Ogbu's discussion. Yet almost all the students in my study were aware that as *students* from the Mainland, they were different in thinking and behavior from their local counterparts. It turns out, as my discussion later will show, that it is this "student identity"—and in this connection their past Mainland school experiences that shaped this identity—rather than the wholesale Mainland—versus—Hong Kong identity, that has a significant bearing on their present school performance.

Ogbu suggests, as I noted earlier, that for a voluntary minority, within-group differences in school success can be attributed *in part* to differences in the influence of the variables in the cultural ecological perspective. I attempt in the following sections to explore to what *extent* the within-group differences in school success in my study can be explained as Ogbu maintains. I also search for explanatory variables that lie outside the compass of the cultural ecological perspective. I begin with the high achievers.

Student Identity and Perceptions in the Making of School Success

The high achievers are students who at the time of the interview were *either* studying in some of Hong Kong's academically above-average schools and reaching the top few positions in their class, *or* had excelled themselves in recent public School Certificate examinations. As my account below demonstrates, Ogbu's cultural ecological perspective does not seem to provide an adequate or satisfactory explanation of their school success.

Kwan who was at the time of interview a Form 3 student came to Hong Kong four years ago. His academic performance since arrival had been outstanding, and he attributed this partly to the "higher academic standards, except for the subject of English, back home than here" and partly to his strong motivation to learn and his hard work. At the time of coming he knew that Hong Kong offered better opportunities for his future development, but he had hardly any expectations about his future because he was feeling too miserable about having to leave his friends and teachers. His parents were concerned about his study, but he thought that his strong motivation to do well at school came from within himself, "an attitude which I developed while studying in the Mainland." In fact he thought it odd that some students worked hard because of pressure or expectations from their parents or because they wanted to please their parents, for "we study and learn for our own benefits." He was not expecting to enter university in his first two years in Hong Kong; he was now because his teachers had told him he stood a very good chance of getting into university if he kept up his good performance.

Wong came to Hong Kong about three years ago without expectations though he knew that educational and job opportunities were better here than in the Mainland. He came first in his class in Forms 3 to 5, and he came within the top five per cent in the School Certificate Examinations which he took a few months before the interview. He thought that his serious attitude towards his study and his effort rather than family pressure were the reasons behind his school success, for his father, who was not at all concerned about his schoolwork, died when he was studying in Form 4, and his mother did not even know what grade he was studying. He went on to explain: "Back in the Mainland, I studied in a very good school where the students were very serious about their studies. Before I came to Hong Kong, I thought school life would be very competitive here. I was very surprised to see the students here so lax about their study. I found myself very different from them as a student. They seem to regard schoolwork as a burden. I see studying as an interest and an opportunity to learn. I do well mainly because it is easier to attain good academic results here than in the Mainland. Besides, my teachers knew I was a new immigrant and gave me strong support and encouragement; this helped me to perform well."

Fung came to Hong Kong primarily for family reunion, but also because "here people are rewarded according to their ability and effort, while in the Mainland people can often get ahead through bribery and corrupt practices." She then continued: "I stand a good chance of entering university back home, but what's the use if after graduation I still have to live in a society I don't like? Besides, unlike in Hong Kong, university students there often have to take up low-status jobs with low incomes." Yet at the time of coming to Hong Kong, she was uncertain about her future, for she was not even sure whether she could get into a school here. Six months later, after taking an entrance examination, she was admitted into a good secondary school where she subsequently performed at the top of her class. She completed Form 4 there, and then skipped Form 5 and took the School Certificate Examinations. She did well enough in these Examinations to be admitted into Form 6. She did not think her parents put pressure on her to do well at school. "They gave me encouragement, but that was only a way of expressing care; they did not really mind how well I performed at school." She was not thinking about entering university here; she preferred to proceed step by step and not to look too far into the future. What then motivated her to strive so hard and to do so well? "I just enjoy studying. I work hard at school because of my sense of duty as a student. In addition, I receive a lot of encouragement at school from very supportive and helpful teachers."

It is obvious from the above three cases that the *positive dual frame of reference* (i.e., better opportunities here than in the Mainland) was not a significant factor in motivating them to work hard and perform well at school in the present society. Nor was the *folk theory of success* important in this respect. None of them considered family pressure or expectation pertinent to their school success, though in the interviews they did say their parents held the view that a good education was essential to success in Hong Kong society. What counted most in their school success, it seems, was their self-concept as student. They all saw themselves as serious students with a strong motivation to learn and a keen interest in doing well at school. This self-concept was shaped primarily by their experiences at school, especially while they were in the Mainland but also after their arrival in Hong Kong. In this regard, they were no different from the other high achievers in the study. Though some of the other high achievers did have high expectations about their school performance at the time of coming, they reported that these expectations were a continuation of those which they already held while studying in the Mainland. And while two of them admitted that family pressure and expectations did play a part in their school success, they viewed these as secondary; they thought that they were committed and hardworking students anyway and that family pressure only gave them a reinforcement. Indeed, in the course of my research I became increasingly aware that for most of these high achievers, their past "Mainland" school experiences were crucial in setting the path for their present school success. What then were such experiences which, as I pointed out above, shaped their self-concept or identity as student and which motivated them to perform well at school? Kwan and Fung's experiences are good illustrations.

Kwan described his classmates in his Mainland school as "very attentive in class, very interested in learning, and very respectful to teachers." Though in Hong Kong he attended a school noted for its academic strength and good student discipline, he thought it still lacked his Mainland school's atmosphere of learning. Recalling the first few days of his schooling in Hong Kong, he observed: "I was surprised to see some classmates so playful and inattentive during a lesson. I never saw such naughty students before." He then described with zest how his classmates and himself "back home" *were* prepared for the primary-to-secondary public promotion examinations: "In order to help, parents studied with their children. They woke their children up at four or five in the morning to prepare for the examinations. Some rented a room in a hotel at the time of the examinations so that their children could study in a good environment. My mother got me a private tutor." Kwan considered his classmates and students in his Mainland school to be far more industrious than those he saw in Hong Kong. He added: "Back in the Mainland, my main concern was to do well at school, and I was then even more hardworking than my classmates." He consistently reached the top few positions in class in his Mainland school.

Fung reported similar school experiences in the Mainland. She studied in a "key" secondary school which admitted the best students in her town, a school which she described as "really outstanding in producing very good students." She considered the pressure to work hard in her Mainland school to be much greater than in Hong Kong—despite the fact that here she skipped Form 5 and had only about three months to prepare for the School Certificate Examinations. She explained with examples: "My school back home published after every examination a list of the students' current as well as past examination results side by side so that everybody could easily tell whether you were doing better or worse than before; this put a lot of pressure on students. And if your performance dropped, your class teacher would have a meeting with you to talk about it. The school I attended was a boarding school. Classes started at 6.30 in the morning, and finished at 5 in the afternoon. Then in the evening we had to attend revision classes from 7.30 to 11, with teachers around to help with our schoolwork. After the lights were turned off shortly after 11, some students would continue to study with a torch. There was a strong atmosphere of learning; everybody was working hard and you just felt you had to work hard." She usually came within the top fifteen in a class of some sixty students in her Mainland school. In Hong Kong, she considered herself more hardworking and serious than her classmates, but still she thought she was less industrious than in the Mainland. The change in school atmosphere, she said, had somehow weakened her drive to work hard.

For high achievers such as Kwan and Fung, it seems their diligence and strong motivation at school in the present society were largely a continuation of their past "Mainland" school experiences and *student identities*, though many also reported encouraging help and support from teachers in Hong Kong. However, in the case of Lam, another high achiever I will look at next, there was a sharp change in her self-concept as a student after her arrival in Hong Kong. She considered herself a "hopelessly poor performer at school" back in the Mainland. She was now a confident and outstanding student with a strong aspiration to enter university. Was it the lure of better opportunities here together with a strong belief in the importance of education in the present society, as Ogbu suggests, that motivated her towards high academic achievement?

The Emergence of a New Student Identity and its Bearing on School Performance

Lam was at the time of interview a Form 3 student in a academically strong school which catered in particular to new immigrant students from the province where she came from. She heaped praises on this school and its teachers, describing it as her "second home." She went through a rebirth as a student, she said, largely through the help of teachers in this school but also through the care and support of her parents.

In the Mainland, Lam studied in a school "where the students were not at all serious about their studies and where the teachers did not care much for students." She considered it to be a very weak school in terms of the students' academic performance and conduct, and she "did not feel like a student at all studying in that school." She performed very poorly at school then, and at the time of coming to Hong Kong, had "lost all hope of doing well at school." In her first two years in Hong Kong, she had a very hard time catching up with her study, especially English. But her teachers were very patient with her and gave her a lot of help and encouragement. "The English language teacher, for instance, gave me an extra lesson everyday after school for a few months. He asked me to learn five new words a day, and told me that if I could manage that, I should be able to catch up. I gradually realized that the teachers here cared deeply for me; they also led me to believe that I could do well as a student. My confidence in my academic ability grew. I not only felt like a student; I also felt I could be a competent student. In my first year here, I was near the bottom of my class; but by the end of the second year I was level with my classmates. From Form 2 on, I reached the top five in my class. Those first two years were a very difficult time for me; I never worked so hard in my life as I did then. I can now see that my efforts have been richly rewarded. I now feel good about being a student and I have a strong sense of attachment to my school."

Lam then went on to talk about the support she received from her family. "Back in the Mainland, my mother was too busy with her work and paid hardly any attention to me; father was then away in Hong Kong. I had the feeling that my family did not care for me. But shortly after my arrival in Hong Kong, I began to feel the warmth and care of my parents. Mother changed drastically after my elder sister's serious illness some two years ago; the incident made mother feel that she had been neglecting her children. After that she spent much more time with us, although she was still very busy with her work in Hong Kong. I could see how hard my parents were working to support us and how deeply they cared about my education. They were making a huge sacrifice, and I thought I must do well at school to repay them." At the end of the interview, Lam told me she had not only become a much better student, she had also become a much more considerate and caring person. She explained the change with insight: "I got these qualities here because my teachers and parents have treated me with great care and consideration."

Lam, as we have just seen, developed a *positive* student identity with the support of her teachers and parents. The student I look at next did so in the context of a poor and conflictual relationship with her parents.

Yu was not a high achiever but an above-average performer in an academically mediocre school in Hong Kong. Her school experiences in the three years before she came to Hong Kong, she told me early in the interview, were miserable. She originally studied in a school in the countryside where she worked diligently and performed very well academically. After completing primary four there, she changed to a school in the city, and there her nightmare started. She had a dark complexion, and her classmates in the new school called her "the dark girl from the countryside." Some of them spread the view that "if you touch her, you will get bad luck for ten years." She was soon ostracized by her class, and her academic performance dropped drastically for she "did not even want to go to school." When she entered a different school for her secondary education, she thought her torment would be over. "But a couple of my old classmates entered the same school. They spread that old view and my suffering was even worse than before." She described her coming to Hong Kong as "an escape from hell."

In Hong Kong, she experienced a rebirth as a student. "None of the teachers or students here discriminated against me. Indeed the teachers were very supportive of me because I was a new immigrant student. I was very happy at school and I got along well with everyone in class. Because I enjoyed school life, I became once again a motivated and hardworking student." She was very fond of drawing, an interest which she developed during her childhood in the Mainland, and which became a main source of conflict between her and her parents. "They keep saying that I am wasting my time in drawing. They say that drawing would not enable me to make a living in Hong Kong and that it is distracting me from my schoolwork. They do not at all appreciate my hard work and good performance at school. They say that I am doing well only because my school has low academic standards. They keep referring to my poor school performance in the Mainland, and they seem to have given up on me. They don't trust me; they don't trust my friends; and they don't trust I have the ability to do well at school. I find their attitudes very discouraging. I have quarrels with them almost everyday. But I am determined to prove to them that I can keep on drawing and perform well academically." She was aiming to complete Form 7 and then look for a career in drawing.

I will now look at a case where the appeal of *better opportunities* and the *stranger* position were instrumental in the forming of a new student identity which, as in the last two cases, was crucial in orienting the student towards hard work and higher academic achievement. The *stranger* position in this case, however, as the following account shows, is somewhat different from that in Ogbu's theory.

> Lee described herself as "by no means a serious or hardworking student back in the Mainland." At the time of departure for Hong Kong, she was told by her friends back home that she had to work very hard to survive the keen competition in Hong Kong schools. "But I was ready to accept the challenge because I knew opportunities in Hong Kong are much better." After arrival, she was allocated by the Education Department to an academically weak school, and she soon discovered that doing well there was in fact easier than in her Mainland school. "I thought then that if I worked hard, it would not be difficult for me to attain success here." She added: "Besides, I was a stranger in this place. I had no friends here and I did not know the place well, so I spent most of my time studying. And I knew that as a stranger I faced more disadvantages than the locals; I knew I must work hard in order to do better than the locals. The teachers here told me the same. They also kept telling us that a good education is the key to success in Hong Kong. This had a great influence on me." She then told me that the stranger mentality motivates people to work hard to attain success in a host society *with better opportunities* and she gave examples: the new immigrant students in Hong Kong, and the Chinese immigrant students in the United States.
>
> In her first year in Hong Kong, Lee came first in her class. But in the following two years, she faced a much greater challenge which reinforced her achievement motivation at school. "In Form 2 and now, I have had to compete against several new immigrant students who are very hardworking and performing extremely well. They got ahead of me in Form 2, and I knew I had to work at least as hard as they in order to reach the top few positions in my class. This competition made me completely different from the student I was in the Mainland. Back in the Mainland, I did not feel bad even when I failed; now I would feel unhappy if I did not reach the top few positions in my class." Lee was hoping to enter university, but she knew she was studying in an academically weak school, and she was worried whether she could achieve her goal. "But here I have at least some chance of reaching university. Back home, I didn't even think about having a university education." Like some of the other students I looked at above, Lee did not think that her family played any significant part in motivating her towards high educational achievement.

The cases we have considered so far were either high achievers or above-average performers. What then about the underachievers? How do they differ from the cases we looked at above? What explanations can we find for their poor performance at school in the present society?

The Underachievers: Factors and Circumstances Inhibiting the Achievement Motivation

The underachievers in my study share the following characteristics: they were below-average performers at school in the Mainland; they considered their school experiences in Hong Kong boring and unpleasant; they did not think their family understood or cared about the difficulties they encountered in adjusting to school life in Hong Kong. Most of them said that they came to Hong Kong for the better opportunities and the better life here; and all said that they considered education important to achieving a good career in the present society - yet this did not seem to have motivated them towards high academic achievement. The case of Chan, which I now look at, illustrates how past school experiences interacted with present circumstances in the making of these students' failure at school.

Chan came from a Mainland school where "the students were not interested in studying at all," and where "many students expected to find a job after completing junior secondary education." His description of the behavior of some of the teachers and students there was shocking: "Some teachers were very violent and would throw punches at misbehaving students, and these students would fight back." He belonged to the lazy group of poor performers; they often went out to play all night and returned to school the next day to sleep. Indeed, at the time of departure, he had reservations about coming to Hong Kong, for his friends back home had told him about the harsh school life here. Yet he still chose to come for "it's easier to find jobs here, and one also earns more money here." In Hong Kong he had a very hard time adapting to the "very strict discipline and boring life at school." Nevertheless, he became a more hardworking student and felt much more like a student. "After all, my relatives and my parents told me I must work hard at school here for a good future. No one said such things to me back home."

But he could not get used to school life in Hong Kong. In particular he could not cope with the subject of English. "It is too competitive and I can't get along with my classmates. They are too serious and just not my type." So in his second year in Hong Kong, he found a part-time job in the Ocean Park, "not for money but for the company of people like myself." Many of these people were working in jobs which required no more than secondary education, and he would like to follow their example, for he did not think he could attain a higher level of education in Hong Kong. His parents told him that if he so wished, he could seek employment after completing Form 3. With this orientation, his academic performance, which was already poor, got even worse. He told me he missed the good times in the Mainland, for there "it was all play and no work" and he "did not have to worry about his future."

It seems that in Chan's case, his past student experiences—his poor academic performance in the Mainland and the "all play and no work" inertia—together with the lack of demands and pressures from his parents in the present society oriented him towards an easier alternative than hard work at school for his future career. Indeed most of the underachievers in my study fell into this pattern. But in the case of Ng, another underachiever I look at below, it appears that even demands and pressures from the family were ineffective for fostering the motivation to achieve.

Ng was an unmotivated poor academic performer in the Mainland. In her first year in Hong Kong, she did make an effort to work harder than before for she had to catch up with English. Besides, her parents especially her father pressed her to work hard because they believed that "I would not be able to find a good job in Hong Kong without a good education." Her father would switch off the television during examination times so that she could concentrate on her study. Her parents also did not allow her to go out to play because "they thought there were many bad people in Hong Kong and I might fall into the company of bad people." She went on: "If I wanted to go out, they would accuse me of trying to escape from schoolwork and housework. They simply do not trust me. They scold me almost everyday, often for very trivial reasons" She thought her parents were trying to exercise too much control over her and she was very resentful of such control. And she thought her parents were not at all sympathetic about the difficulties she faced in adapting to school life here. "They never asked me how I felt at school. They didn't at all understand or care about my school experiences. They just looked at my examination results and would scold me badly if I did not do well." She did try to work harder every time after getting poor academic results; but she just could not keep up her effort. She became lazier after her first year in Hong Kong and she dropped to the bottom of her class in the past two years. "I just cannot concentrate on my study, and I am not keen about schoolwork except copying from other students."

The "New Immigrant Student" Identity and its Implications for School Performance

I argued in the discussion above that the student identity or student self-concept of the respondents in my study was a major factor in determining their school performance in the present society. My focus was on their *individual* student identities. I was not looking at their *collective* identity as new immigrant students. What has been missing are the important questions of how they view themselves as new immigrant students, and whether and if so how such views bear on their school performance in the present society. But these questions, I must here point out, cannot be adequately answered without first considering these students' *individual* past school experiences and in this connection their *individual* student identities. The reason is simple. In talking about the "new immigrant student" identity, these students were *generalizing* from their *individual* Mainland student experiences and student identities, and on the basis of this *generalization,* commenting on their situation and experiences as new immigrant students in the present society. This constructed, or generalized, "new immigrant student" identity in turn exerts an influence on their student behavior in the host society. This collective identity is the subject of my discussion below.

It is the high achievers and the above-average performers who held the most distinct "new immigrant student" identity. They were well aware of their differences from the local students, and in the interviews often referred to the "we" and "they" distinction in describing their student experiences in the present society. Thus, many reported a feeling of surprise or even shock during their first few days of schooling in Hong Kong. The following is an example:

> I was shocked to see the local students so playful and inattentive during a lesson, and so disrespectful to their teachers. In the worst cases, I could hardly hear what the teachers were saying. Back home, we had very high respect for our teachers … We were so quiet and attentive during a lesson that you could hear a fly flying by.

Many also considered new immigrant students to be more serious and motivated, or better students. A high achiever expressed her views in this respect in rather strong language:

> The local students are conceited. They think they are much better than students from the Mainland. If they keep their eyes open, they will see that they are totally wrong … I perform well at school here because I am so different from the local students. They are too passive and too dependent on their teachers; I work independently and I think critically. Our schools back home trained us to be critical and analytical. I was only an average performer back home: I excel here simply because the locals are not good.

Her teachers indeed described her and another new immigrant student in her class—an above-average performer in my study—as "quiet and independent students who are friendly with other classmates but who keep very much to their own company."

Most of the high achievers and above-average performers also considered it natural that the new immigrant students were better performers than the locals. One high achiever offered the following explanation:

We came from a poorer country, and we knew we had to work hard to make a living. But here in Hong Kong, the students are spoiled by affluence. They take a good life for granted and so they do not work hard. Besides, they face too many material temptations and they are distracted from their study. It is just natural that we are better students.

The pattern of these high achievers' leisure activities indeed show that they seemed to be "unspoiled" and "unsusceptible" to Hong Kong's "material temptations." None had gone to a discotheque or karaoke bar since their arrival in Hong Kong, for they considered such leisure pursuits "unhealthy and decadent." Most of them viewed window-shopping—a favorite pass time of local students—as a waste of time. Many did not even watch television except the news and educational programs, for they found the other programs, especially the popular drama series, "not making much sense." Their favorite leisure pursuits were taking part in their school's extracurricular activities, doing voluntary service in youth centers, picnicking and barbecuing, and ball games.

They also said that their teachers were particularly fond of them because "they found us more disciplined and motivated students in comparison with the locals." Some told me that their teachers spent extra time to teach them more advanced materials because they were far more eager to learn than the local students. Most thought that they stood out as model students in the eyes of their local classmates and their teachers. Indeed their teachers told me they did enjoy teaching the new immigrant students more than the locals because "they were well-behaved and strongly motivated to learn." In short these high achievers and above-average performers had a positive, even high, self-regard as new immigrant students. Many did report having gone through a very hard time adjusting to the new environment here; the vast majority considered coping with the subject of English their toughest challenge in Hong Kong. But their positive self-image as new immigrant students, and their perception that "we are used to challenge and hard work and we are prepared to endure the hardships here" have enabled them to persevere and rise above the hurdles and succeed with stoical determination. All of them still retained this "new immigrant student" identity at the time of the interview, though most had been in Hong Kong for three or four years.

The underachievers, however, differed sharply from the high achievers and the above-average-performers in their "new immigrant student" identity. In the first place, they did not seem to harbor a "we" and "they" distinction in terms of academic performance; they thought that "the students here are more or less the same as the students back home; some are hardworking and some are lazy, and some do better than others." Nor did they think that the local students were spoiled by affluence or distracted by material temptations. In fact they considered affluence and material abundance to be Hong Kong's main attractions. When they talked about their differences from local students, they referred to their unfamiliarity with the new environment which "restricted their leisure pursuits and friendship circles", and the great difficulty they had in catching up with English; they seldom mentioned attitudes towards learning or student behavior in class. They viewed the successful new immigrant students as "special cases who were already very hardworking and outstanding students in the Mainland." In short they did not see new immigrant students as having any qualities or characteristics that would help them towards higher academic achievement. They saw only the handicaps and difficulties they face. In both their *individual* and *collective* student identity, these underachievers had neither the perception nor the confidence that they could be good performers in the present society. So they easily gave up in the face of challenges and difficulties.

CONCLUSION

Student Identity and the Cultural Ecological Perspective

I have argued in this paper that student identity—that is, how the students view themselves as students and as new immigrant students—appears to be the most important factor in determining the school performance of the participants in my study. I have in earlier parts of this paper backed up this argument with descriptive accounts of the school experiences of several new immigrant students. I would like to add here that reports from the students in my study on the whole lend support to my contention. Thus all except two of the *twenty-four* high achievers and above-average performers in my sample had exemplary academic performance in Mainland schools, which they held to be the basis of their high self-esteem as students. The two exceptions—Lam and Yu, whose experiences were reported earlier—were able to acquire a new *positive* student identity after their arrival in Hong Kong, mainly because of favorable school experiences in the host society. On the other hand, all the *eight* underachievers came to Hong Kong not only with a poor academic record, but also a negative attitude towards schooling. Here the question arises as to why these students remained poor performers while the "two exceptions" mentioned above were able to improve themselves substantially after arrival. The main explanation seems to lie in their pre-arrival attitude towards schoolwork. The underachievers, as I pointed out in my account of Chan, had developed an "all play and no work" orientation; indeed they loathed schoolwork. In contrast, the "two exceptions" despite their mediocre academic performance were not rejecting schoolwork. To a large extent, it was *circum-stances*—a school with uncaring teachers, poor academic standards and lax student discipline in the case of Lam, and discriminatory treatment from fellow classmates in the case of Yu—that accounted for their pre-arrival poor performance. With a favorable change in school circumstances in Hong Kong, they were thus able to develop new student self-concepts and improve their school performance. Finally there are the *ten* average performers. I have not dwelt on this category of students because they did not *stand out* for the purpose of analysis. Since arrival in Hong Kong, some had improved their academic performance marginally while others had dropped slightly. But all were by and large average students both in their Mainland and Hong Kong schools.

In other words, findings from my study suggest that in coming to grips with school life in Hong Kong, the new immigrant students were drawing on their pre-arrival school experiences as a basis for *positioning* and *orienting* themselves in the new socio-cultural environment. On this basis they made their judgments about how they should conduct themselves, and how they were likely to fare, as students in the present society. On this basis they also interpreted the socio-cultural environment of Hong Kong—for instance its attractions and temptations, its popular culture, and its popular leisure pursuits. This basis—their *individual* past student histories and identities— in interaction with their experiences in the present society shaped their self-concept or identity as new immigrant students. For the vast majority of the students in my study, it seems that it was not what they thought about opportunities in the present society which had the most significant bearing on their school performance. Rather it was their experiences and perceptions at school that seem to count most. As students, they acted first and foremost with reference to their experiences and identities at school. Thus, we have seen from our case reports that the two underachievers Chan and Ng remained unmotivated students in spite of expectations and pressures from their families; the three high achievers Kwan, Wong, and Fung on the other hand were able to sustain their commitment to schoolwork in the absence of family pressures. A broader look at the other students in the sample reveals that family pressure was indeed by no means a significant factor in motivating the students to strive for school success. The high performers often considered it an unnecessary interference and even a nuisance. The underachievers rebelled against it. Almost all the students, however, deemed *support and understanding* from their families valuable in coping with the challenges of schooling in a new socio-cultural environment. In other words, their school experiences and the problems they encountered at school were their immediate and main concern. Family pressure on them to work hard for a "better tomorrow", in the absence of accompanying care and support, often generated ill feeling and conflict between these students and their parents. This brings me back to the main thrust of my argument in this paper. It was these students' identities and experiences in the socio-cultural environment of *the school*, rather than better job opportunities in the larger society, that had the most direct and crucial bearing on their school performance.

My findings and argument thus suggest an explanation that appears to differ from the main tenets of Ogbu's cultural ecological perspective. This difference warrants a closer examination.

At the heart of Ogbu's theory is the argument that the perception of better opportunities together with their folk theory of success motivates the voluntary minorities to rely on educational achievement as the best means to attain success in the present society. The voluntary minorities, according to this perspective, came to the host society for a "better tomorrow"; many were indeed running away from severe, even brutal, conditions of deprivation in their home country (Suarez-Orozco, 1991, pp. 46–47). In contrast, the new immigrant students came to Hong Kong primarily for the purpose of family reunion, not to escape from severe conditions of deprivation back home, though they were *aware* the host society offers them better opportunities. In other words, "better opportunities" was not the prime factor in their consideration at the time of coming and so not their dominant frame of reference in their post-arrival student career. For this reason, we can expect their awareness of "better opportunities" to have been submerged under and superseded by their more immediate and urgent task of coping with the demands of schooling in the present society. It was in this context that their *resources and perceptions as students* emerged as the most relevant and important factor in shaping their orientation and performance at school. My findings thus suggest that for certain kinds of voluntary immigrants—for instance those who come to the host society for family reunion—Ogbu's arguments have to be qualified as an explanation for their school performance in the present society.

This brings me to the issue of the *dual frame of reference*, which is an integral part of Ogbu's argument about *better opportunities* in the present society. The students in my study did have a dual frame of reference, but what appears to have had the most bearing on their current school performance was the dual reference they made to their experiences and opportunities as *students*, rather than the dual reference to opportunities for success in the larger society. Thus the high achievers and above-average performers often referred to the better school facilities, more caring teachers, and greater opportunities for university education in the present society as factors motivating them towards high academic achievement. They also referred to the challenge—especially English—which they currently faced as nevertheless not as difficult as the school demands back home. And they attributed their serious attitude towards schoolwork in the present society to the school culture they were exposed to before arrival—in particular to the strong atmosphere of learning and the work ethic among students. This school-based dual frame of reference gave them the motivation, the confidence as well as the disposition to strive for school success in Hong Kong.

But this does not mean that the dual frame of reference in regard to *opportunities in the larger society* had no part to play at all in the new immigrant students' school performance. For a student like Lee (whose case I considered earlier in the discussion), who was not a serious or hardworking student in the Mainland, the appeal of better opportunities in the present society helped to motivate her towards hard work and academic success after arrival. For underachievers like Chan (case considered earlier), who already had a strong dislike for schoolwork back home, better opportunities in the present society meant plenty of opportunities and alternatives to build a career than through school achievement. This perception, as we have seen, had a deleterious effect on his already poor school performance. It is highly probable that better career opportunities played a subsidiary *instrumental* role in sustaining the motivation and hard work of most of the high achievers and above-average performers, although their student self concepts seem to have been of prime importance in orienting them towards high academic achievement. In this respect, Lee's comment on what she viewed as the "new immigrant student disposition" is worth noting.

> As new comers to this society, we know we have to work hard at school in order to compete successfully with the locals. But we are ready to work hard only because we find ourselves in a *better* society. I don't think we'll do so in a worse-off society.

Implicit in Lee's observation is also a *folk theory of success*—the belief that education offers the best means to attain success in the host society. All the students in my study—be they high achievers or poor performers—subscribed to this belief, and this suggests that differences in their academic performance could not be attributed to differences in how they viewed the significance of education in the present society. The case of Chan, an underachiever, offers a good illustration in this regard. He spoke of the paramount importance of education for future success in Hong Kong, but he was planning to leave school and seek employment as soon as possible for he found school life boring and he did not think he had the ability to do well at school.

My study of the new immigrant students' *within-group* differences in school success shows that the *part* explainable in terms of Ogbu's theory is indeed small. While differences between the new immigrant students and the voluntary minorities in Ogbu's theory undoubtedly detract from its applicability to my study, my findings do suggest that school experiences and student identities do not seem to have been accorded their due importance in the cultural ecologists' explanation of minority students' school performance. In this connection, Pollard and Filer's concluding remarks to their study of the relationship between identity and learning are highly pertinent to our discussion:

> This analysis leads us to re-emphasize a need for attention to the individual qualities of learners and their learning. It is important to recognize and 'hear' pupils' individual perspectives ... This process is particularly important where a child's identity is distinct from, or in tension with, those of the mainstream peer or school culture ... The interaction of socio-cultural contexts and learners is highly complex but extremely powerful ... Individual capabilities are related to perceptions and self-confidence in particular social contexts (Pollard & Filer, 1999, p. 166).

The findings of my study indeed suggest that "the individual qualities of learners" and" the interaction of socio-cultural contexts and learners" are crucial in shaping the new immigrant students' motivation and school performance. My study shows that these students' orientation and school performance in the present society are very much the product of the *complex interaction* between their present school experiences and their past student histories and identities. It seems that in emphasizing minority students' perceptions in the larger socio-cultural contexts—their dual frame of reference, their folk theory of success and their stranger position—the cultural ecological perspective has not given due attention to their perceptions and self-confidence *within the school contexts*.

NOTE

1.   Secondary school education begins from Form 1, which is equivalent to grade 7 in the U.S. school system. Students take the public School Certificate Examinations after completing Form 5 (equivalent of grade 11), and the public University Entrance Examinations after completing Form 7.

REFERENCES

Bourdieu, P. (1977). Cultural reproduction and social reproduction. In J. Karabel & A. H. Halsey (Eds.), *Power and ideology in education* (pp. 487–511). New York: Oxford University Press.

Bourdieu, P., & Passeron, J. C. (1977). *Reproduction in education, society and culture*. London: Sage.

Buriel, R. (1994). Immigration and education of Mexican Americans. In A. Hurtado & E. E. Garcia (Eds.), *The educational achievement of Latinos: Barriers and successes* (pp. 197–226). Santa Cruz: Regents of the University of California.

Caplan, N., Choy, M. H., & Whitmore, J. K. (1991). *Children of the boat people: A study of educational success.* Ann Arbor: University of Michigan Press.

Caudill, W., & De Vos, G. (1956). Achievement, culture and personality: The case of the Japanese Americans. *American Anthropologist, 58,* 1102–1127.

Chen, C., & Stevenson, H. (1995). Motivation and mathematics achievement: A comparative study of Asian-American, Caucasian-American, and East Asian high school students. *Child Development, 66,* 1215–1234.

De Vos, G. (1978). Selective permeability and reference groups sanctioning: Psychocultural continuities in role degradation. In M. Yinger (Ed.), *Major social issues: A multi-community view* (pp. 9–14). Glencoe, IL: Free Press.

De Vos, G. (1992). *Social cohesion and alienation: Minorities in the United States and Japan.* San Francisco, CA: Westview Press.

Gibson, M. A. (1991). Ethnicity, gender and social class: The school adaptation patterns of West Indian youths. In M.A. Gibson & J. U. Ogbu (Eds.), *Minority status and schooling: A comparative study of immigrant and involuntary minorities* (pp. 169–203). New York: Garland.

Gibson, M. A., & Ogbu, J. U. (1991). *Minority status and schooling: A comparative study of immigrant and involuntary minorities.* New York: Garland.

Government Secretariat. (1997). *Equal opportunities: A study of discrimination on the ground of race.* Hong Kong: Home Affairs Branch.

Goyette, K., & Xie, Y. (1999). Educational expectations of Asian American youths: Determinants and ethnic differences. *Sociology of Education, 72,* 22–36.

Hao, L., & Bonstead-Brun, M. (1998). Parent-child differences in educational expectations and the academic achievement of immigrant and native students. *Sociology of Education, 71,* 175–198.

Hirschman, C., & Wong, M.G. (1986). The extraordinary educational achievement of Asian Americans: A search for historical evidence and explanations. *Social Forces, 65*(1), 1–27.

Hsu, F. L. K. (1971). *The challenge of the American Dream: The Chinese in the United States.* Belmont, CA: Wadsworth.

Kitano, H. H. L. (1969). *Japanese Americans: The evolution of a subculture.* Englewood Cliffs, NJ: Prentice-Hall.

Lee, Y. (1991). Koreans in Japan and the United States. In M. A. Gibson and J.U. Ogbu (Eds.), *Minority status and schooling: A comparative study of immigrant and involuntary minorities* (pp. 131–167). New York: Garland.

Lee, S. J. (1996). *Unraveling the "Model Minority" stereotype.* New York: Garland.

Matute-Bianchi, M. E. (1986). Ethnic identities and patterns of school success and failure among Mexican-Descent and Japanese-American Students in a California high school: An ethnographic analysis. *American Journal of Education, 95,* 233–255.

Matute-Bianchi, M. E. (1991). Situational ethnicity and patterns of school success and failure among immigrant and nonimmigrant Mexican-descent students. In M. A. Gibson & J. U. Ogbu (Eds.), *Minority status and schooling: A comparative study of immigrant and involuntary minorities* (pp. 205–247). New York: Garland

Ogbu, J. U. (1978). *Minority education and caste: The American system in cross-cultural perspective*. New York: Academic.

Ogbu, J. U. (1987). Variability in minority school performance: A problem in search of an explanation. *Anthropology and Education Quarterly*, 18(4), 312–334.

Ogbu, J. U. (1991). Immigrant and involuntary minorities in comparative perspective. In M. A. Gibson & J. U. Ogbu (Eds.), *Minority status and schooling: A comparative study of immigrant and involuntary minorities* (pp. 3–33). New York: Garland.

Ogbu, J. U. (1997). Racial stratification and education in the United States: Why inequality persists. In A.H. Halsey, H. Lauder, P. Brown, & A. S. Wells (Eds.), *Education: Culture, economy, society* (pp. 765–778). New York: Oxford University Press.

Pollard, A. & Filer, A. (1999). Learning, policy and pupil career: Issues from a longitudinal ethnography. In M. Hammersley (Ed.), *Researching school experience: Ethnographic studies of teaching and learning* (pp. 153–168). London: Falmer Press.

Rumberger, R. W., & Larson, K. A. (1998). Toward explaining differences in educational achievement among Mexican American language-minority students. *Sociology of Education, 71, 68–92.*

Stanton-Salazar, R. D., & Dornbusch, S. M. (1995). Social capital and the social reproduction of inequality: Information networks among Mexican origin high school students. *Sociology of Education*, 68, 116–135.

Suarez-Orozco, M. M. (1987). Towards a psychosocial understanding of Hispanic adaptation to American schooling. In H. T. Trueba (Ed.), *Success or failure: Linguistic minority children at home and in school* (pp. 156–168). New York: Harper and Row.

Suarez-Orozco, M. M. (1991). Immigrant adaptation to schooling: A Hispanic case. In M. A. Gibson & J. U. Ogbu (Eds), *Minority status and schooling: A comparative study of immigrant and involuntary minorities* (pp. 37–61). New York: Garland.

Sue, S., & Okazaki, S (1990). Asian-American educational achievements: A phenomenon in search of an explanation. *American Psychologist*, 45(8), 913–920.

Sung, B. L. (1987). *The adjustment experience of Chinese immigrant children in New York City*. New York: Centre for Migration Studies.

Suzuki, R. H. (1980). Education and the socialization of Asian-Americans: A revisionist analysis of the "model minority" thesis. In R. Endo, S. Sue, & N. N. Wagner (Eds.), *Asian-Americans: Social and psychological perspectives* (Vol. 2, pp. 155–175). Ben Lomond, CA: Science and Behavior Books.

Trueba, H. T., & Zou, Y. (1994). *Power in education: The case of Miao university students and its significance for American culture*. London: Falmer Press.

Wong, T. W. P. (1992). Personal experience and social ideology: Thematization and theorization in social indicators studies. In S.K. Lau, S.L. Wong, M.K. Lee, & P.S. Wan (Eds.), *Indicators of social development: Hong Kong 1990* (pp. 205–238). Hong Kong: Institute of Asia-Pacific Studies, The Chinese University of Hong Kong.

CHAPTER 14

WHAT DOES LABELING DO
TO STEREOTYPING?

Beyond Prototypes and Cognitive Economy

Takashi Yamauchi and Kevin D. McGuire

INTRODUCTION

Overcoming stereotyping is one of the most substantial challenges for successful multicultural education. Stereotyping has many different forms. A Catholic university that bans interracial relations demonstrates one form of institutionalized stereotyping. A Hollywood movie that singles out a certain ethnic group for a denigrated role also perpetuates cultural stereotypes. In addition to institutionalized stereotyping, another crucial source of stereotyping is misattribution that people commit in everyday situations (Henning-Stout & Brown-Cheatham, 1999). In this chapter, we will examine a specific aspect of misattribution, namely labeling, and will investigate cognitive regularities governing stereotyping.

In what follows, we will first introduce a general phenomenon related to labeling and its implications to multicultural education. Then, we will propose a new account that explains a cognitive-basis of stereotyping. Finally,

Teaching, Learning, and Motivation in a Multicultural Context, pages 315–344
Copyright © 2003 by Information Age Publishing
All rights of reproduction in any form reserved.

we will describe four empirical studies, which intend to shed new light on this issue.

"Susan is a liberal." "Susan is liberal." These two sentences literally mean the same thing. For example, given these sentences, one can easily infer what political party Susan supports. The indefinite article "a" distinguishes the two sentences. The first sentence involves labeling Susan with a noun, "liberal," while the latter describes Susan with an adjective, "liberal." This subtle distinction, however, invites a wide variety of cognitive effects. Given a label, people implicitly assume that an attribute associated with the object is long-lasting, powerful, and central to its identity (Markman, 1989).

This phenomenon, which I call hereafter "the labeling effect," is prevalent even in young children (e.g., Gelman & Markman, 1986; Gelman & Heyman, 1999; Waxman & Markov, 1998) and is revealed in our social as well as cognitive judgments by fostering many forms of biases, such as stereotypes, false expectations, generalizations, and erroneous inductions (see for review Fiske & Neuberg, 1990; Hamilton & Sherman, 1994; Maass, 1999). For example, Crick and Dodge (1996) found that fifth and sixth graders who tended to respond with aggression when confronted with frustration and provocation were more likely to label neutral situations as hostile than non-aggressive children did.

A number of cognitive psychologists suggest that the labeling effect is linked to the principles of forming categories (Gelman & Heyman, 1999; Markman, 1989). Because the organism's chance for survival hinges on the environment in which it resides, forming categories with maximum accuracy is of primal importance. Accuracy, however, entails processing costs. To reduce the costs, some form of abstraction takes place (e.g., forming a prototype, see Rosch, 1978; Rosch & Mervis, 1975). Social stimuli that people encode in everyday situations are also far too complex for regular processing. This complexity requires an abridgement of actual data. Because natural kind categories cohere with prototypes arising from family resemblance (Rosch & Mervis, 1975), prototypical features of a category are enforced, and, as a result, stereotypes dominate. Stereotypes thus arise as a cognitive side effect of forming categories (Allport, 1954; Takfel, 1969, 1970). Reflecting this characterization of stereotyping, policy related to multicultural education has been centered around reducing or re-structuring social categories by introducing social contact among students from different groups (Hewstone, 1996; Stangor, 2000; Stephan, 1999).

A potential problem with this account is the prevailing notion that stereotypes stem from a rigid category structure that enforces abstract prototypes, dominant exemplars, or a mixture of the two (Cantor & Mitchell, 1977; Kruschke, 1992; Medin & Schaffer, 1978; Nosofsky, 1986; Reed, 1972). Recent studies in concept formation, however, reveal much more flexible aspects of category representation. For example, research found that the way people interact with categories influences the way people represent categories (Ross, 1996a, 1996b, 1997; Yamauchi, Love, & Markman, 2002; Yamauchi & Markman, 1995, 1998, 2000a, 2000b). Attributes of a category are also adaptable to the background knowledge, intentions, and goals of a category learner. Different types of background knowledge are known to render different kinds of categories (Medin, Lynch, & Coley, 1997; Murphy & Medin, 1985; Ross & Murphy, 1999; Wisniewski & Medin, 1994). Accordingly, the impact of labeling may be more flexible than once believed. Rather than enhancing the perception of stereotypical features, labeling may also upgrade the perception of unrelated features.

In this chapter, we will focus on the flexibility of category representation and will investigate the relationship between categorical representation and stereotyping. Specifically, we will propose that categories by default have a resilient structure, and that labeling enhances this structural adaptability of categorical representation. As a consequence, labeling bolsters the perception of insignificant attributes as much as that of stereotypical attributes. On this basis, we would like to suggest that the stereotypes that arise from labeling are amenable to a variety of corrections. In multicultural education, rather than eliminating social categories or inducing assimilation of different cultural groups, we would like to suggest that positive interactions between social groups help reduce stereotypes and cultural biases.

OVERVIEW OF THE EXPERIMENTS

Gelman and Heyman (1999) investigated the relationship between labeling and inductive inference of five to seven year olds. Their study demonstrated a robust labeling effect on young children's inductive judgments. For example, when a person is described with a label ("Rose is a carrot-eater"), five year old children tend to think that a characteristic of that person (e.g., "Rose eats a lot of carrots") was present in the past ("Rose ate a lot of carrots when she was four years old.") and stays in the future ("Rose will eat a lot of carrots when she grows up") (Gelman & Heyman, 1999). We employed a similar procedure as developed in the Gelman and Heyman study and investigated the influence of labeling on college students.

In four experiments described below, we will compare the impact of categorical statements (e.g., "Linda is a feminist") and non-categorical statements (e.g., "Linda believes in and supports feminism") on people's inductive judgments (e.g., "Did Linda major in philosophy in college?"). Specifically, participants were assigned randomly to one of two conditions—a Label condition and a Non-label condition—and were asked to make estimations of the likelihood of attributes associated with each item.

In the Label condition, each item was characterized categorically (e.g., "Linda is a feminist"), and in the Non-label condition, each item was characterized descriptively without any labels (e.g., "Linda believes and supports feminism"). We measured participants' estimation scores as a function of these two conditions. In this study, we defined the labeling effect as an overestimation of a feature due to a categorical statement. In the following studies, we will demonstrate that categorical statements bolster people's estimations of attributes (i.e., labeling effect), and that a labeling effect emerges from the structural flexibility associated with categorical representation.

The main logic of the experiments is as follows. If the labeling bias occurs solely due to associations with the prototype of the corresponding category, then the bias should be limited in cases when underlying categories portray a family resemblance structure. In contrast, if the labeling bias arises also from the flexibility associated with category representation, then the bias should be ubiquitous, not limited to taxonomic categories but also non-taxonomic categories (Barasolou, 1983, 1985; Ross & Murphy, 1999). More importantly, the labeling bias should be present in attributes that contradict prototypical notion of the category (e.g., endorsing the attribute "John supports tax cuts for the rich" given the label "liberal").

In Experiment 1, we will employ social and personal categories (i.e., categories related to personal characteristics, occupations, and habits), and will demonstrate that the labeling bias is present in adult subjects as observed in young children (Gelman & Heyman, 1999). We will further show that the labeling bias emerges not for dominant attributes but for attributes that are inconsistent with the prototypical notion of the category. In Experiments 2 and 3, we will use ad hoc categories and this would demonstrate that the labeling bias is ubiquitous and could appear in categories that do not have a clear family resemblance structure. Finally, in Experiment 4, we will pinpoint the source of labeling bias by modifying the nature of categorical representation.

EXPERIMENT 1

The stimulus materials of Experiment 1 were descriptions about people. Each description conveys personal information related to occupations, characteristics, status, and identities. Given each description, participants were asked to judge the likelihood of attributes associated with each person. In one condition (Label condition), each person was characterized categorically (e.g., "Linda is a feminist"), and in the other condition (Non-label condition) each person was characterized descriptively without any labels (e.g., "Linda believes in and supports feminism"). The main goal of

Experiment 1 was to examine the presence of labeling bias, that is, overestimation of these attributes in the Label condition relative to the Non-label condition (e.g., "Did Linda major in philosophy in college?" given the label "feminist").

METHOD

The stimulus materials of Experiment 1 were fifteen person statements shown in a booklet (see Table 14.1 for samples). These person statements were based on some form of personal categories, such as occupations (a truck driver, an aerobic instructor, an art collector), characteristics (an over-achiever, a competitor, a feminist, a liberal, a party-animal), status (a millionaire, a high-school drop-out, a drug addict), hobbies (a stamp collector, an amateur poet), and national or cultural origins (a Korean, a New Yorker).

The task of the participant was to estimate the likelihood of personal characteristics about hypothetical people. This experiment consisted of two between-subjects conditions—a Label condition and a Non-label condition. In the Label condition, the stimulus statements characterized each person with a categorical label (e.g., "Laura is an amateur poet"). In the Non-label condition, the stimulus statements characterized each person descriptively without any labels (e.g., "Lora writes poems for a hobby"). After reading a person description, the participant was asked to estimate the likelihood of four possible attributes (A-D) with a 0–100 scale (see Table 14.1).

Table 14.1.   Samples of the stimulus materials used in Experiment 1

Label condition

Linda is a feminist. She is concerned with issues of discrimination and social justice.
   A. Linda likes to watch presidential debates.
   B. Linda majored in philosophy in college.
   C. Linda likes to watch presidential debates, and she works as a bank teller.
   D. Linda works as a bank teller.

Jack is a truck driver. He frequently talks on his CB radio and goes to sporting events when he can.
   A. Jack's hobby is watching birds.
   B. Jack began his job immediately after completing high school.
   C. Jack likes to play softball on Sundays, and his hobby is watching birds.
   D. Jack likes to play softball on Sundays.

Ted is a fierce competitor. He does anything to win.
   A. Ted's hobby is writing poems.
   B. Ted works in a big law firm.
   C. Ted likes action movies, and his hobby is writing poems.
   D. Ted likes action movies.

Table 14.1.   Samples of the stimulus materials used in Experiment 1

Mike is a high-school drop-out. He has been working since and loves riding his motorcycle.
  A. Mike plays the flute for a hobby.
  B. Mike works as a mechanics.
  C. Mike bowls several times a week, and he plays the flute for a hobby.
  D. Mike bowls several times a week.

Non-Label condition

Linda believes in feminist philosophy at heart. She participates in feminist activities as often as she can, and thinks that men and women should be equal in every aspect of their social and private lives. She is also concerned with issues of discrimination and social justice.
  A. Linda likes to watch presidential debates.
  B. Linda majored in philosophy in college.
  C. Linda likes to watch presidential debates, and she works as a bank teller.
  D. Linda works as a bank teller.

Jack has driven a truck in a moving company for the last 10 years. Jack thinks that watching football games while drinking draft beer is the best way to spend Sunday evening. He frequently talks on his CB radio, and goes to sporting events when he can.
  A. Jack's hobby is watching birds.
  B. Jack began his job immediately after completing high school.
  C. Jack likes to play softball on Sundays, and his hobby is watching birds.
  D. Jack likes to play softball on Sundays.

Ted loves to compete for anything. He thinks that winning is everything, and whenever he competes, he must beat his opponents. He does anything to win.
  A. Ted's hobby is writing poems.
  B. Ted works in a big law firm.
  C. Ted likes action movies, and his hobby is writing poems.
  D. Ted likes action movies.

Mike dropped out of his high school when he was 16 years old. He hanged around with his high school buddies for a while, but after he got a job in downtown, he got along with different pals. He has been working since and loves riding his motorcycle.
  A. Mike plays the flute for a hobby.
  B. Mike works as a mechanics.
  C. Mike bowls several times a week, and he plays the flute for a hobby.
  D. Mike bowls several times a week.

Among the four attributes, two attributes were concerned with major characteristics of the category (A&B, "Laura writes short stories for a hobby"), one was about an attribute that was inconsistent with that category (D, "Laura trades stocks using the Internet"), and the remaining statement was a conjunction of a consistent attribute and an inconsistent attribute (C, "Laura writes short stories for a hobby and she likes to trade stocks using the Internet"). The order of presenting these four attribute questions was determined randomly for each person description.

A pilot study employing 186 college students indicated that the two types of person statements convey analogous information. Given the statements in the Non-label condition, participants indicated more than 95% of the time that the person described in each stimulus belongs to the categories that are specified in the Label condition. Thus, the two types of statements literally purport the same categorical information.

In total, 102 college students participated in this experiment for course credit. These participants were randomly assigned to either the Label condition or the Non-label condition. There were 52 participants in the Label condition and 48 participants in the Non-label condition.

RESULTS AND DISCUSSION

The dependent measure was the participants' estimation scores. Categorization is known to modify the way people extract features of an item. When an item is categorized to a particular group, features shared in that group become dominant (Gelman & Markman, 1986; Goldstone, 1995; Tversky, 1977; Wisniewski & Medin, 1994; Yamauchi & Markman, 2000b). Thus, if the labeling bias is present, participants in the Label condition would overestimate the likelihood of prototypical attributes more often than participants in the Non-label condition would. If labeling bias occurs due to the formation of prototypes, then the effect should be limited to prototypical attributes related to the category (e.g., "Laura writes short stories for a hobby" given a label "amateur poet"). In contrast, if the adaptability of category representation plays an important role in the labeling bias, then the bias should also extend to attributes that contradict prototype information (e.g., "Laura trade stocks using the Internet" given a label "amateur poet").

All participants in the two conditions estimated the same attributes. Because these attributes were highly subjective, and participants were allowed to assign any number between 0–100 for their estimation, the range of participants' responses varied widely. In order to increase statistical resolution, the data were analyzed with respect to individual items. Specifically, average estimates were calculated for each item from individual participants, and the impact of the two conditions was compared with a paired t-test, along with two other non-parametric measures such as the Wilcoxon signed rank test and the binomial distribution test.

The main results of Experiment 1 are summarized in Table 14.2. All in all, the results of Experiment 1 were consistent with the flexibility hypothesis. For the consistent features, items characterized with labels received higher estimation scores than items characterized without labels. A paired t-test showed that participants in the Label condition gave significantly higher estimation scores than participants in the Non-label condition did; Label condition, $m = 67.9$, Non-label condition, $m = 63.1$, $t(14) = 4.17$, $p < 0.001$.

Table 14.2.   Estimation Scores for the Label and Non-label Conditions in Experiment 1

Categories	Consistent features		Inconsistent features	
	Label	Non-label	Label	Non-label
Feminist	65.05	64.35	30.10	27.50
truck driver	65.04	50.11	19.13	15.58
avid art collector	51.30	49.93	9.35	8.98
fierce competitor	74.13	70.83	20.87	13.96
avid stamp collector	56.62	53.23	19.73	18.71
aerobics instructor	77.98	71.85	7.96	7.90
Amateur poet	69.88	59.43	32.37	27.60
Korean	68.84	65.36	27.17	22.94
New Yorker	60.84	55.05	18.73	14.81
Outspoken liberal	69.02	71.45	24.06	21.46
typical over-achiever	66.25	62.78	16.10	14.52
high-school drop-out	67.96	58.95	13.65	13.44
party animal	69.20	65.14	27.73	21.42
Millionaire	76.16	68.13	6.69	6.29
drug addict	79.95	79.88	16.08	12.94
Average	67.88	63.10	19.31	16.54

Note: These numbers represent average estimation scores.

A Wilcoxon signed rank test, which measured the ranked sum of signed differences between the two conditions by subtracting average estimates in the Non-label condition from average estimates in the Label condition, showed that the sum of positive ranks exceeded the sum of negative ranks. This result indicates that higher estimations were given in the Label condition than in the Non-label condition; positive rank sum = 116, negative rank sum = 4, $Z = 3.18$, $p < 0.01$.

In a binomial distribution test, we also examined the difference between the two conditions by counting the number of positive and negative differences for each item. In 14 out of 15 items, the average estimation scores were higher in the Label condition than in the Non-label condition, and in only 1 out of 15 items, the average estimation score was higher in the Non-label condition than in the Label condition; $p < 0.01$ (Table 14.2).

Clearly, for the prototypical attributes, the estimation scores given by participants in the Label condition were significantly higher than the estimation scores given by participants in the Non-label condition. This result agrees with the finding from the Gelman and Heyman study, and confirms that there is a significant labeling bias in adult participants.

For the attributes that contradict prototype information (e.g., "Laura trades stocks using the Internet" given a label "amateur poet"), the labeling bias was also substantial. A paired t-test indicates that participants in the Label condition were more likely to make overestimations than participants in the Non-label condition; Label condition m = 19.3, Non-label condition, m = 16.5, $t(14)$ = 4.80, $p < 0.001$. The difference between the two conditions was also apparent in non-parametric measures. A Wilcoxon signed rank test revealed that the distinction between the two conditions was highly significant; the sum of positive ranks, 120; the sum of negative ranks, 0; Z = 3.41, $p < 0.01$. In 15 out of 15 items, average estimation scores were higher when items were characterized categorically (Label condition) than when items were characterized descriptively (Non-label condition); binomial distribution test, $p < 0.001$.

There are two important points in interpreting the results in Experiment 1. First, the labeling bias was conspicuous even among college students. This result extends Gelman and Heyman's (1999) finding, and confirms that the notion that bias stemming from categorical statements is indeed widespread and it is not limited to young children. Second, labeling elevates the perception of prototypical features as well as the perception of atypical features. For example, given a categorical statement "Laura is an amateur poet," participants were likely to overestimate the presence of atypical features ("Laura trades stocks using the Internet"). This result is hard to interpret with the prototype-based account. The prototype-based account posits that the labeling bias occurs due to an association with of prototypical features of a category. It is unlikely that the feature "trading stocks using the Internet" is part of prototypical attributes of the category "amateur poet." Clearly, along with prototype information, some other factors should be involved in the labeling bias.

EXPERIMENT 2

In Experiment 2, we employed a different type of categories and scrutinized the distinction between the prototype-based account and the flexibility hypothesis further. *Ad hoc* categories and script categories, which were used as stimuli in Experiment 2, are organized with norms, goals, ideals or situations, and are quite different from social and personal categories that are arranged primarily with a prototype structure (Barsalou, 1983, 1985; Cantor & Michel, 1977; Cantor, Mischel, & Schwartz, 1982; Ross & Murphy, 1999). These categories are unlikely to have direct associations with natural categories because their structures are markedly different from the structure of taxonomic categories. Thus, if the prototype-based account is valid, then the labeling bias should disappear with these categories. In contrast, if the labeling bias arises from the structural flexibility of categorical representation, then the bias should remain even with *ad hoc* categories.

METHOD

Materials

The basic procedure of Experiment 2 was analogous to the one described in Experiment 1. Stimulus materials consisted of fifteen ad hoc categories, which include *diet food, health food, winter clothing, birthday gift, wedding gift, vacation site, summer food, holiday activity, winter sport, suburban car, honeymoon site, children's game, Asian food, tabloid journal, and ethnic restaurant.* All item names were specified with six letters of arbitrary three consonant-vowel pairs (e.g, "NUMATA"). Given each stimulus description, participants were asked to estimate the likelihood of two consistent attributes and two attributes that are irrelevant to the category label. For example, given a category label "health food" ("'NUMATA' is a health food"), participants estimated the likelihood of consistent attributes such as "'NUMATA' is rich in calcium," and irrelevant attributes such as "'NUMATA' is popular in Texas but not in Louisiana." These irrelevant attributes were introduced to minimize the influence of family resemblance information. Given the label "health food," for example, it is difficult to conceive that the attributes such as "sells more in Texas than in Louisiana" are part of the internal representation of the concept "health food." Table 14.3 illustrates eight samples of the stimulus materials.

Table 14.3. Samples of the stimulus materials used in Experiment 2

Label condition

"KOMITA" is a birthday gift. It is particularly popular among young couples.
   A. KOMITA costs about $40.
   B. KOMITA sells well during summer.
   C. People can buy KOMITA in a department store.
   D. Many lawyers own KOMITA.

"NUMATA" is a health food. It regulates blood pressure. Many doctors recommend NUMATA to stay healthy.
   A. NUMATA contains virtually no fat.
   B. NUMATA is popular in Texas but not in Louisiana.
   C. NUMATA can be found in a drug store.
   D. Many high school teachers like NUMATA.

Table 14.3.   Samples of the stimulus materials used in Experiment 2

"TASIRO" is winter clothing. Without it, people can barely survive in winter.
   A. TASIRO is thick and heavy.
   B. TASIRO is sold in Wal-Mart but not in K-Mart.
   C. Many people in Canada wear TASIRO in winter.
   D. People who like to wear TASIRO also like to play basketball.

"HITASI" is a popular holiday activity. In Easter or Labor's day, many people get together and enjoy HITASHI.
   A. HITASI involves eating.
   B. Liberal people are particularly fond of HITASI.
   C. HITASI makes people happy.
   D. People who like HITASI eat lots of chocolate.

Non-label condition

Many people give "KOMITA" to their friends and relatives for their birthdays. It is particularly popular among young couples.
   A. KOMITA costs about $40.
   B. KOMITA sells well during summer.
   C. People can buy KOMITA in a department store.
   D. Many lawyers own KOMITA.

Eating NUMATA regularly helps people stay healthy. It regulates blood pressure. Many doctors recommend NUMATA to stay healthy.
   A. NUMATA contains virtually no fat.
   B. NUMATA is popular in Texas but not in Louisiana.
   C. NUMATA can be found in a drug store.
   D. Many high school teachers like NUMATA.

Everybody wears "TASIRO" in winter. It makes people stay warm and cozy. Without it, people can barely survive in winter.
   A. TASIRO is thick and heavy.
   B. TASIRO is sold in Wal-Mart but not in K-Mart.
   C. Many people in Canada wear TASIRO in winter.
   D. People who like to wear TASIRO also like to play basketball.

During holidays, people love to do HITASHI. In Easter or Labor's day, many people get together and enjoy HITASHI.
   A. HITASI involves eating.
   B. Liberal people are particularly fond of HITASI.
   C. HITASI makes people happy.
   D. People who like HITASI eat lots of chocolate.

Procedure

The procedure of this experiment was identical to the one described in Experiment 1. Two hundred and thirty-four participants participated in this experiment. These participants were randomly assigned to either the Label condition or the Non-label condition. There were 133 participants in the Label condition, and there were 101 participants in the Non-label condition.

RESULTS

The 15 *ad hoc* categories were organized with particular norms or goals, rather than general similarity among category members. As in natural categories, *ad hoc* categories are said to have a graded structure centered around typical items. However the typicality of *ad hoc* categories derives from shared ideals and norms, rather than overall similarity (Barsalou, 1983, 1985). It is interesting to see if labeling bias occurs in these categories.

If prototype information is the only source of labeling bias, the bias is expected to disappear in this experiment. However, if the adaptability of category representation plays an important role in the labeling bias, then the bias should remain in this setting. In this case, labeling should increase estimations of related (A&B) as well as unrelated features (C&D).

Major results from this experiment were consistent with the flexibility hypothesis. Overall, the labeling bias was present in both the major attributes and the unrelated attributes. For the major attributes, an item-based paired t-test showed that participants' estimation scores were significantly higher in the Label condition than in the Non-label condition; Label condition, $m = 70.2$, Non-label condition, $m = 66.9$, $t(14) = 3.12$, $p < 0.01$ (Table 14.4).

Table 14.4.   Estimation Scores for the Label and Non-label Conditions in Experiment 2

Categories	Consistent features		Unrelated features	
	Label	Non-label	Label	Non-label
birthday gift	64.32	55.50	36.34	37.01
diet food	63.03	66.42	36.37	34.34
health food	66.39	63.57	33.05	32.03
winter clothing	84.04	81.06	23.14	20.71
summer food	71.64	66.56	31.76	27.24
holiday activity	70.38	64.92	36.44	32.35
winter sport	63.20	62.11	26.71	23.45
vacation site	76.17	71.00	25.59	23.15
Asian food	74.61	77.39	23.12	21.16
suburban car	70.10	70.01	40.31	38.97
tabloid journal	80.55	78.23	30.02	23.61
children's game	76.50	66.74	41.24	32.94
Healthy exercise	68.41	61.54	31.43	31.11
Honeymoon site	69.95	71.73	25.83	24.43
Ethinic restaurant	53.83	46.93	41.45	35.08
Average	70.21	66.91	32.19	29.17

Note: These numbers represent average estimation scores.

A Wilcoxon signed rank test also showed that the sum of positive ranks significantly exceeded the sum of negative ranks, indicating that higher estimations were given in the Label condition than in the Non-label condition; positive rank sum = 104, negative rank sum = 16, $Z = 2.50$, $p < 0.05$.

By counting the number of positive and negative differences for each item, in 12 out of 15 items, the average estimation scores were higher in the Label condition than in the Non-label condition, and in only 3 out of 15 items, the average estimation scores were higher in the Non-label condition than in the Label condition; $p < 0.05$.

For the unrelated attributes (C&D), the impact of labeling was in fact intensified. Consistent with the flexibility hypothesis, but inconsistent with the prototype-based account, the difference between the Label condition and the Non-Label condition was highly substantial. A paired t-test showed that participants in the Label condition made higher estimates ($m = 32.2$) than participants in the Non-label condition did ($m = 29.1$); $t(14) = 4.68$, $p < 0.001$. Results from a Wilcoxon signed rank test and a binomial test also agreed with this description. The sum of positive ranks (118) was significantly larger than the sum of negative ranks (2); $Z = 3.29$, $p < 0.01$, indicating that higher estimations were made by participants in the Label condition than by participants in the Non-label condition. In 14 out of 15 items, the average estimation scores were higher in the Label condition than in the Non-label condition, and only in 1 out of 15 items, the average estimation score was higher in the Non-label condition than in the Label condition; $p < 0.001$.

Unlike social and personal categories, *ad hoc* categories do not have a clear similarity structure (e.g., family resemblance). These categories are arranged mainly by the norms, ideals, goals and situations associated with a category learner (Barsalou, 1983, 1985). The organization of these categories varies considerably as people interact with these categories in different manners. Furthermore, these categories do not have rich cultural connotations that personal and social categories convey. It is hard to conceive that an association with a prototype of a category is the only force for the labeling bias. Furthermore, the labeling bias was observed not only in dominant attributes but also in attributes that are unrelated to the category norm. These attributes have no clear links with the prototype of each category. Once again, it is difficult to ascribe prototypes as a primal impetus for biases. Taken together, the results from Experiment 2 clearly contradict the prototype-based account, and favor the view that there is a structural basis for the labeling bias.

EXPERIMENT 3

Experiment 3 was designed to control three external factors that might have contaminated the labeling bias in Experiment 2. First, the number of sentences that were used to describe each item was different in the two conditions of Experiment 2. For example, in the two samples shown in Experiment 2, only two sentences characterized "NUMATA" in the Categorical condition, while three sentences characterized "NUMATA" in the Descriptive condition. This disparity might have caused the overestimation of attributes in the Label condition relative to the Non-label condition. Second, it is not clear to what extent a descriptive statement was semantically compatible with a categorical statement. Participants might have interpreted descriptive statements (e.g., "Lora writes poems for hobby") as semantically distinct from categorical statements (e.g., "Lora is an amateur poet"). Third, presenting unrelated attributes together with prototypical attributes might have influenced participants' behavior (e.g., an anchoring effect). Experiment 3 was designed to control these external variables by balancing the number of sentences used to describe each item and by gauging closely the semantic connotations of categorical and descriptive sentences.

METHOD

Procedure: The procedure, design, and materials of Experiment 3 were similar to those described in Experiment 2. In Experiment 3, however, the organization of the stimulus materials was modified. Table 14.5 shows two sample stimuli and the structure of the stimuli used in the two conditions.

Table 14.5.   (a) Samples and (b) the Structure of the Stimulus Materials used in Experiment 3

(a) Samples

Label condition

"KOMITA" is a birthday gift. It is particularly popular among young couples.
  A. KOMITA sells well during summer.
  B. Many lawyers own KOMITA.

"NUMATA" is a health food. It regulates blood pressure. Many doctors recommend NUMATA to stay healthy.
  A. NUMATA is popular in Texas but not in Louisiana.
  B. Many high school teachers like NUMATA.

Table 14.5. (a) Samples and (b) the Structure of the Stimulus Materials used in Experiment 3 (cont.)

"TASIRO" is winter clothes. It makes people stay warm and cozy. Without it, people can barely survive in winter.
   A. People who like to wear TASIRO also like to play basketball.
   B. TASIRO is sold in Wal-Mart but not in K-Mart.

"HITASI" is a popular holiday activity. In Easter or Labor's day, many people get together and enjoy HITASHI.
   A. Liberal people are particularly fond of HITASI.
   B. People who like HITASI eat lots of chocolate.

Non-label condition

Many people give "KOMITA" to their friends and relatives for their birthdays. It is particularly popular among young couples.

   A. KOMITA sells well during summer.
   B. Many lawyers own KOMITA.
   C. KOMITA is a birthday gift.

Eating NUMATA regularly helps people stay healthy. It regulates blood pressure. Many doctors recommend NUMATA to stay healthy.
   A. NUMATA is popular in Texas but not in Louisiana.
   B. Many high school teachers like NUMATA.
   C. NUMATA is a health food.

Everybody wears "TASIRO" in winter. It makes people stay warm and cozy. Without it, people can barely survive in winter.
   A. People who like to wear TASIRO also like to play basketball.
   B. TASIRO is sold in Wal-Mart but not in K-Mart.
   C. TASIRO is winter clothes.

During holidays, people love to do HITASHI. In Easter or Labor's day, many people get together and enjoy HITASHI.
   A. Liberal people are particularly fond of HITASI.
   B. People who like HITASI eat lots of chocolate.
   C. "HITASI" is a popular holiday activity.

(b) The structure of the stimuli used in the two conditions:

Label condition:
   Statement:
     C1, D2,
   Attribute Questions:
     A1, A2

Non-label condition:
   Statement:
     D1, D2
   Attribute Questions:
     A1, A2, A3 (= C1)

As Table 14.5 illustrates, the stimuli in the two conditions had analogous structures. In the Label condition, the stimulus statement started with a categorical sentence (C1: "'NUMATA' is a health food") followed by some description about the item (D2: "It regulates blood pressure. Many doctors recommend 'NUMATA' to stay healthy"). The participant in the Categorical condition was asked to estimate the likelihood of two irrelevant attributes (A1 & A2; e.g., A1: "'NUMATA' is popular in Texas but not in Louisiana," A2: "Many high school teachers like 'NUMATA'"). The statements employed in the Non-label condition were identical to those shown in the Label condition except that the categorical sentence C1 was replaced with a descriptive sentence (D1: "Eating 'NUMATA' regularly helps people stay healthy"). Thus, the same number of sentences characterized each item in the two conditions. In addition, in the Non-label condition, the categorical sentence (C1) is augmented at the end of a stimulus and is used as another attribute question (A3/C1). Thus, in the Non-label condition the stimulus statement started with a descriptive sentence (D1) followed by some description about the item (D2). The participant in the Non-label condition was asked to estimate the likelihood of two irrelevant attributes. In addition to these attribute questions, participants in the Non-label condition were given another attribute question (A3/C1), which was the first sentence of the stimuli in the Label condition (C1). This question A3/C1 was introduced to gauge the extent to which participants in the Descriptive condition would endorse categorical information. In this manner, the participant in the Non-label condition received item statements (D1 & D2) and three attribute questions (A1, A2, A3/C1).

The procedure of this experiment was identical to the one described in Experiment 2. In total, 285 participants participated in this experiment. These participants were randomly assigned to either the Label condition or the Non-label condition. There were 162 participants in the Label condition and there were 123 participants in the Non-label condition.

RESULTS

Experiment 3 was designed to control three external variables with the following measures. First, the number of sentences used in each stimulus was balanced so that the same number of sentences characterized each item in the two conditions. Second, the attribute questions in this experiment consisted solely of unrelated features. This measure was taken to prevent an anchoring effect. Third, the compatibility between categorical statements and descriptive statements was closely gauged. For this purpose, the categorical questions (A3=C1) were inserted at the end of each stimulus in the Non-label condition, and participants in the Non-label condition provided estimations of the category statements used in the Label condition. In these attribute questions (A3/C1), the average estimation scores of participants in the Non-label condition were 87.4. On average more than 50% of participants endorsed the categorical statement of each item with a score of 100%. Thus, the statements characterized in the two conditions (Label condition and Non-label condition) were semantically compatible.

As in Experiment 2, results from this experiment were consistent with the flexibility hypothesis. The labeling bias was present in all measures with a significant level well below $p < 0.001$. An item-based paired t-test revealed that participants in the Label condition ($m = 40.0$) were much more likely to provide higher estimation scores than participants in the Non-label condition did ($m = 28.7$); $t(14) > 100$, $p < 0.0001$. Results from a Wilcoxon signed rank test and a binomial test agreed with this description. The sum of positive ranks (120) far exceeded the sum of negative ranks (0); $Z = 3.41$, $p < 0.01$. This result indicates that higher estimations were given by participants in the Label condition more often than by participants in the Non-label condition. In all items (15 out 15 items) the average estimation scores were higher in the Label condition than in the Non-label condition; $p < 0.0001$ (Table 14.6).

Table 14.6. The Label and Non-label Conditions in Estimation Scores for Experiment 3

	Label	Non-label
Birthday gift	44.4	36.0
diet food	45.4	33.0
Winter clothes	30.9	22.1
Popular holiday activity	43.6	26.1
Popular vacation site	34.2	18.6
Suburban car	50.2	34.4
Children's play	43.5	33.9
Honeymoon site	34.8	26.4
Health food	46.3	28.8
Summer food	39.1	21.6
Popular winter sport	33.8	22.1
Asian food	25.8	14.9
Tabloid journal	39.1	23.6
Healthy exercise	41.3	29.0
Ethnic restaurant	48.9	34.9
Average	40.1	27.0

Note: These numbers represent average estimation scores.

In order to ensure the compatibility of the categorical statements and the descriptive statements further, additional analyses were carried out. Specifically, in the Non-label condition, the data were taken from participants who gave a score of 100% for each of the category question (A3=C1). On average, there were 62.7 cases in which participants gave 100% estimation scores to the category question (A3/C1). Even with these selected data, a robust labeling bias was apparent. A paired t-test showed that participants in the Label condition gave higher estimation scores ($m = 41.0$) than participants in the Non-label condition did ($m = 27.0$); $t(14) > 100$, $p < 0.0001$. Results from a Wilcoxon signed rank test and a binomial test were also consistent with this description. The sum of positive ranks (120) exceeded the sum of negative ranks (0); $Z = 3.41$, $p < 0.01$, indicating that higher estimations were made by participants in the Label condition more often than by participants in the Non-label condition. In all items (15 out 15 items), the average estimation scores were higher in the Label condition than in the Non-label condition; $p < 0.0001$.

In Experiment 3, we introduced a number of remedial measures to reduce external differences between the two conditions, such as balancing the number of sentences used to describe each item. Even with these measures, participants in the Label condition showed a strong tendency to overestimate the attributes of a category member (i.e., labeling bias). This tendency is noteworthy because it is observed not only in social categories but also in ad hoc categories (e.g., "holiday activities" or "wedding gift"). Clearly, the labeling bias seems to have some structural origin. The fact that the labeling bias is present even in unrelated attributes also suggests that the bias is relatively independent of the semantic content of the attributes themselves. This finding further supports the view that the labeling bias is tied with the structure of categorical representation.

As discussed earlier, we have hypothesized in this chapter that the labeling bias arises from the structure associated with categorical representation. This hypothesis assumes that categories have fundamentally adaptable representational structure. The main impetus for this hypothesis is that categories are formed to facilitate cognitive tasks that require symbolic manipulations. Because symbolic manipulation often entails highly malleable structure (Deacon, 1997; Fodor & Pylyshyn, 1988; Langacker, 1986; Marcus, 1998; Pinker, 1999), we reasoned that categories, which operate as symbols, must have flexible representational structure (e.g., Gentner, 1983). In the previous 3 experiments, we have provided two sets of evidence that support the flexibility-based account for the labeling bias. First, the labeling bias was observed even using ad hoc categories that do not have a family resemblance structure. Second the labeling bias was also present in attributes that are unrelated to the category. In Experiment 4, we will test the adaptability hypothesis directly by removing flexibility from categorical representation.

Consider the following two sentences: (a) I have a mango, (b) A mango is a tropical fruit. "Mango" in the sentence (a) refers to a specific item that "I" have, while "mango" in the sentence (b) refers to "mango" in general. Although "mango" in the two sentences is syntactically identical (i.e., count noun), they correspond to different conceptual structures. "Mango" in (a) functions as a token, while "mango" in (b) works like a type. Now consider the following sentence "'NUMATA' is a health food." In this case, "NUMATA" points genetically to a group of entities labeled as "health food" (i.e., type). By modifying this sentence with an adjective close, "'NUMATA' is the health food that Jane eats every morning," "NUMATA" can be linked to a specific entity (i.e., token). Jackendoff (1983) suggests that "type" and "token" are distinguished in conceptual structure. If the symbol "NUMATA" is used as a token, then it is no longer linked to a categorical structure. Accordingly, the labeling bias should disappear if the bias originates from the representational structure associated with a category. This prediction was tested in Experiment 4.

EXPERIMENT 4

Experiment 4 consisted of 3 between-subjects conditions—a Label condition, a Non-label condition, and a Specific condition. The first two conditions— the Label condition and the Non-label condition—were control conditions. They were similar to the Label and the Non-label conditions in Experiment 3 with some minor modifications (see the Method section below). The Specific condition was similar to the Label condition except that each categorical statement was modified with an adjective clause. For example, a categorical statement, "'NUMATA' is a health food," was modified with a clause, "'NUMATA' is the health food that Craig bought last week." In this manner, the arbitrary name, "NUMATA," signifies a concrete entity in the Specific condition while it points to a general "type" in the Label condition.

In other words, in the Specific condition, these arbitrary names no longer correspond to a categorical representation. As a consequence, if the flexibility associated with category structure is a source of the labeling bias, then the bias should be reduced substantially with this manipulation.

METHOD

Participants

Participants were 320 college students who participated in this experiment for course credit. These participants were randomly assigned to one of three conditions—the Label condition, the Non-label condition, and the Specific condition. There were 106 participants in the Label condition, 110 participants in the Non-label condition, and 104 participants in the Specific condition.

Materials

The materials of this experiment were similar to those described in Experiment 3 except for some important modifications. The structure of stimulus materials is shown in Table 14.7. As Table 14.7 shows, the stimuli used in the Non-label condition were identical to those used in the Non-label condition in Experiment 3. A stimulus statement consisted of descriptive statements D1 and D2, and participants were asked to provide estimates of three attributes, A1, A2 and A3 (=C1). The attributes A1 and A2 were unrelated to the category labels. The attribute A3 is the categorical statement used in the Label condition. In the Label condition, a stimulus statement consisted of a categorical statement (C1), followed by a descriptive statement (D2). The participant in the Label condition were asked to estimate the likelihood of three attributes—A1, A2 and A'3(=D1)—while the attribute A'3 was the first descriptive statement used in the Non-label condition. In the Specific condition, the participant received a statement (C'1) that was modified with an adjective clause (see Table 14.7) along with a descriptive statement D2. The participant was then asked to estimate the likelihood of three attributes (A1, A2, and A'3/ D1). In this manner, the Specific condition was identical to the Label condition except that the first categorical statement was modified with an adjective clause. All the other aspects of this experiment were identical to those described in Experiment 3.

Table 14.7. Samples of the Stimulus Materials Used in the Specific Condition of Experiment 3

Specific condition
"KOMITA" is the birthday gift that John bought for his wife this year. It is particularly popular among young couples.
A. KOMITA sells well during summer.
B. Many lawyers own KOMITA.
C. Many people give "KOMITA" to their friends and relatives for their birthdays.
"NUMATA" is the health food that Craig bought last week. It regulates blood pressure. Many doctors recommend NUMATA to stay healthy.
A. NUMATA is popular in Texas but not in Louisiana.
B. Many high school teachers like NUMATA.
C. Eating NUMATA regularly helps people stay healthy.

Table 14.7. Samples of the Stimulus Materials Used in the Specific Condition of Experiment 3 (cont.)

"TASIRO" is winter clothes that Jane loves to wear. It makes people stay warm and cozy. Without it, people can barely survive in winter.
    A. People who like to wear TASIRO also like to play basketball.
    B. TASIRO is sold in Wal-Mart but not in K-Mart.
    C. Many people wears "TASIRO" in winter.

"HITASI" is the popular holiday activity that the Smiths enjoy every year. In Easter or Labor's day, many people get together and enjoy HITASHI.
    A. Liberal people are particularly fond of HITASI.
    B. People who like HITASI eat lots of chocolate.
    C. During holidays, people love to do HITASHI.

RESULTS

The flexibility hypothesis predicts that the labeling effect disappears with this manipulation. That is, the estimates obtained from participants in the Specific condition and those from the Non-label condition should be statistically indistinguishable, while participants in the Specific condition should underestimate the likelihood of attributes relative to participants in the Label condition. Because there were three between-subjects conditions, the alpha level was set with 0.05/3 in all analyses employed in this experiment (Bonferroni adjustment).

Results from this experiment were consistent with the flexibility hypothesis. Comparisons between the Specific condition and the Descriptive condition revealed that there were no noticeable differences between the two conditions.

An item-based paired t-test showed that the average estimation scores obtained in the Label condition and the average estimation scores obtained in the Non-label condition were statistically equivalent; Non-label condition, $m = 28.0$, Specific condition, $m = 27.0$; $t(14)=2.67$, $p > 0.10$. Results from a Wilcoxon signed rank test and a binomial distribution test were consistent with this assessment. The sum of positive ranks was 20 while the sum of negative ranks were 100; $Z = -2.27$, $p > 0.10$. A binomial distribution test also showed that in 2 out of 15 items participants in the Specific condition made higher estimations than participants in the Non-label condition did (Table 14.8).

Additional analyses were carried out with the data taken from the participants who provided an estimation score of 100% for the descriptive question (A'3=D1—in the Specific-label condition) or the categorical questions (A3=C1—in the Descriptive condition). These additional analyses did not change the interpretation of the data. An item-based paired t-test showed that the difference between the two conditions was not significant; $t(14) =$

2.16, $p > 0.10$. The sum of positive ranks was 98 and the sum of negative ranks was 22; $Z = 2.16$, $p > 0.10$. In 11 out of 15 items, participants in the Non-label condition made higher estimates than participants in the Specific condition. However this difference did not reach the significance level; $p > 0.10$. Clearly, the adjective clauses introduced in the Specific condition eliminated the labeling effect.

Table 14.8.   Estimation Scores for the Label and Non-label Conditions in Experiment 4

	Label	Specific	Specific	Non-Label
birthday gift	**35.51**	32.50	32.50	**35.75**
diet food	**38.27**	27.71	27.71	**32.16**
winter clothes	**22.69**	21.02	21.02	21.01
popular holiday activity	**39.57**	32.47	32.47	**32.72**
popular vacation site	**25.52**	20.12	20.12	20.12
suburban car	**42.97**	35.59	35.59	**43.14**
children's play	**36.10**	31.50	31.50	**34.06**
honeymoon site	**27.72**	19.76	19.76	**23.00**
health food	**37.32**	26.61	26.61	**30.68**
summer food	**32.93**	25.11	25.11	24.56
popular winter sport	21.03	22.98	22.98	17.32
Asian food	**17.46**	16.98	16.98	**18.89**
tabloid journal	**23.45**	18.42	18.42	**21.85**
healthy exercise	**39.09**	25.47	25.47	**28.25**
ethnic restaurant	**41.61**	33.04	33.04	**33.48**
Average	**32.08**	25.95	25.95	**27.80**

These numbers represent average estimation scores.

Comparisons between the Label condition and the Specific condition further confirm that modifying the categorical statements with a specific adjective clause depressed participants' attribute estimations. An item-based paired t-test revealed that participants in the Label condition ($m = 31.3$) were much more likely to provide higher estimation scores than participants in the Specific condition did ($m = 27.0$); $t(14) > 6.93$, $p < 0.0001$. Results from a Wilcoxon signed rank test and a binomial test were consistent with this description. The sum of positive ranks (120) exceeded the sum of negative ranks (0); $Z = 3.41$, $p < 0.01$, indicating that higher estimations were made by participants in the Label condition more often than by participants in the Specific condition. In all items (15 out 15 items), the average estimation scores were higher in the Label condition than in the Specific condition; $p < 0.0001$.

To increase the compatibility of the two conditions further, additional analyses were carried out with the data taken from the participants who provided an estimation score of 100% for the descriptive question (A'3=D1). Results from these data did not change the overall difference between the Label condition and the Specific condition. As in the previous analysis, the difference between the Label condition and the Specific condition was highly substantial. An item-based paired t-test indicates that participants in the Label condition made significantly higher estimations than did participants in the Specific condition; Label condition, $m = 32.1$, Specific-label condition, $m = 26.0$; $t(14) = 5.71$, $p < 0.0001$. A Wilcoxon singed rank test and a binomial distribution test also revealed a significant disparity between the two conditions. The sum of positive ranks (117) exceeded the sum of negative ranks (3); $Z = 3.24$, $p < 0.01$, indicating that higher estimations were made by participants in the Label condition more often than by participants in the Specific condition. In 14 out 15 items, the average estimation scores were higher in the Label condition than in the Specific condition, and in 1 out 15 items, the average estimation score was higher in the Specific condition than in the Label condition; $p < 0.001$. Clearly, the specific adjective clause attached to the categorical statements reduced participants' estimation scores in the Specific condition.

Finally, comparisons between the Label condition and the Descriptive condition further enforce the notion that the labeling effect arises from the flexibility associated with categorical representation. As in Experiment 3, the difference between the Label condition and the Non-label condition was substantial in all measures. An item-based paired t-test showed that participants in the Label condition gave significantly higher estimation scores ($m = 31.3$) than participants in the Non-label condition ($m = 28.0$); $t(14) = 6.85$, $p < 0.0001$. A Wilcoxon signed rank test showed that the difference between the two conditions was substantial; $Z = 3.35$, $p < 0.01$. In 14 out of 15 items, participants in the Label condition made higher estimations than participants in the Non-label condition; and only 1 out of 15 items, participants in the Non-label condition gave a higher estimation score than participants in the Label condition did; $p < 0.001$.

The data taken from the participants who responded with an estimation score of 100% for the attribute question A3 or A'3 also agreed with the results described above; the paired t-test, $t(14) = 4.58$, $p < 0.01$; the Wilcoxon signed rank test, $Z = 3.07$, $p < 0.01$; and the binomial test, $0.05 < p < 0.10$.

In the Specific condition, each categorical statement was modified with an adjective close. The results of this experiment indicate that this modification reduced the labeling bias substantially. The estimation scores made by participants in the Specific condition were statistically indistinguishable from those made by participants in the Non-label condition. Comparisons between participants in the Specific condition and participants in the Label condition further revealed that participants in the Specific condition made estimations significantly lower than participants in the Label condition did. As discussed earlier, the adjective clauses in the Specific condition were introduced to generate a conceptual structure that works as a "token" rather than as a "type." Assuming that "type" and "token" are represented differently in conceptual structure (see Jackendoff, 1983), the results from Experiment 4 confirm the notion that the flexibility associated with a categorical statement is indeed a leading force for the labeling bias.

GENERAL DISCUSSION

Bias is not a simple and straightforward phenomenon. It is neither just a social problem nor just a cognitive problem. It arises from a mixture of many converging factors. In this chapter, we have examined the labeling bias from a perspective based on recent findings in cognitive science, and have attempted to provide some cognitive interpretation of the labeling bias.

Traditionally, labeling bias has been studied primarily in the context of "cognitive economy." According to this view, bias emanates from processing burdens pertinent to the way people form categories. Because the capacity of cognitive processors is limited, bias is expected to develop as a side effect of categorization.

The studies introduced in this chapter, however, reveal a drastically different account. In addition to "cognitive economy," the labeling bias can derive directly from the representational structure of categories. On the one hand, categories direct people's attention to a particular aspect of category members; on the other hand categories also engender flexibility that helps integrate new information. Because of its flexibility associated with categorical representation, people tend to overestimate the presence of a particular attribute when objects are characterized categorically. Thus, labeling not just bolsters the perception of stereotypical attributes, it also yields an opportunity to modify existing knowledge.

In the four experiments described in this chapter, we have shown that labeling bias can arise even after controlling a semantic disparity between categorical and descriptive statements (Experiment 3). The labeling bias was present even in adult participants as well (Experiment 1). It was also observable in attributes that were not related to the prototype of the corresponding category, and it was present even in *ad hoc* categories (Experiments 2). Only when the flexibility associated with categorical statements was removed, the labeling bias disappeared (Experiment 4). These results clearly favor the view that the labeling bias is associated with some representational components of categories.

STEREOTYPING AND MULTICULTURAL EDUCATION

Categorization is an integral part of stereotyping (Allport, 1954; Duckitt, 1992; Hamilton & Sherman, 1994; Takfel, 1969, 1970). The main assumption underlying this view is the notion of cognitive economy. To facilitate cognitive processing, stereotypes emerge from the formation of social categories. The basic means to cope with stereotyping in multicultural education has thus been to appease restrictive effects of social categories (Hewstone, 1996; Salili & Hoosain, 2001; Stangor, 2000). Reflecting this theorization, multicultural education in the United States has embraced integrative measures such as bilingual education, study-abroad programs, or the multi-racial classroom that enhances contact among students from different cultural backgrounds. Enhanced social contact, however, resulted in change in the perception of individual outgroup members but not the perception of the outgroup as a whole (Hewstone, 1996; Stangor, 2000). As a consequence, stereotypes toward specific social and ethnic groups remained robust during these years despite drastically increased intergroup contacts among students (Cooper & Slavin, 2001; McConahay & Hough, 1976).

The present findings provide several new implications for multicultural education. On the negative side, this study confirms the notion that labeling can cultivate a "myth" of a certain ethnic group. When a person in a particular social group is defined with a categorical label, people are more likely to associate that person with dominant features in the group. On the positive side, however, the impact of labeling seems more dynamic. Labeling not only strengthens a stereotypical notion of category members, but it could also help generate new knowledge because labeling can evoke a flexible structure that can blend new information easily (see Spears & Haslam, 1997; Yzerbyt, Rocher, & Schadron, 1997; for a similar view).

The present studies indicate that categorization, while bringing stereotypes, also helps dissolve stereotypes. The studies show that the categories people form are much more flexible than once envisioned (Allport, 1954; Hamilton & Sherman, 1994; Takfel, 1969, 1970). For example, "Islam" can be associated with "violence" and "fanaticism" in one context; yet, the same label can provide a new notion about the social group (e.g., "Islam" stands for "tolerance"). In other words, the key to successful multicultural education seems to lie not in "decategorization," but in clarifying the differences and similarities between social groups. Some educational practices that publicize specific information about a social group may break the "group myth." Educational practices that provide students with an opportunity to experience different cultures would also help transform existing stereotypes. In other words, bias can be resolved not by eliminating differences between groups but by adequately informing differences between groups.

In the following subsection, we will briefly describe a case study of how concrete data about students can redress stereotypes and school policies. Specifically, we will chronicle the events and strategies that took place in Valley Middle School, Pittsburgh, Pennsylvania, and show how concrete data can eliminate teachers' prevailing stereotypes on special education students.

A CASE STUDY

In October 2001, staff in a school improvement meeting brought up the concern of Special Education students, specifically about their behavioral problems. The staff members expressed vehemently that these students were getting in many behavioral troubles at school assemblies. The following were statements voiced by staff members. "What do you expect from this type of students?" "They all act like animals when they come to an assembly." "They are incapable of acting in the proper way and should not be permitted to attend school assemblies."

One of the authors (KM) then formed the school improvement team and asked the team members if they wanted to have well-behaved students in school assemblies and permit all students to attend school assemblies. They stated that having all students attend school functions has been part of the school mission.

One of the authors (KM) then asked the school improvement team to list those areas where they believed Special Education students were not doing well—such as "Special Education students cannot stay in their seat," "Special Education students cannot pay attention," or "Special Education students argue with everyone."

After recognizing the improvement team's beliefs and how the team members labeled Special Education students, KM conducted meetings with all Special Education teachers and created a plan of action to change and rebuild the rest of the staff perspective.

KM then collected data on behavior problems that occurred in assemblies and found that Special Education students exhibited a slightly higher incident rate when compared to other students. Their behavior problems were not as drastic as the group had perceived.

Along with the Special Education teachers, KM planned several school assemblies that highlighted Special Education students and the positive things that they were involved in inside and outside the school. The other students watched and listened as Special Education students presented hobbies, skills and projects they had completed.

At the end of the semester, KM again asked the school improvement team how they perceived Special Education students in general. And even though the rate of behavioral incidents involving Special Education students had not changed substantially, feedback from the team had moved to a much more positive position and they believed Special Education students should attend all school assemblies.

This brief chronicle exemplifies how stereotypes can be resolved and how new school policies can be implemented in a multicultural educational setting. As discussed earlier, to change prevailing misconceptions, it appears crucial to provide adequate data about a certain social group. Although stereotypes and biases are widespread in multicultural education, the biases that people form can be adaptable and malleable to corrections. Once again, not eliminating social categories but clarifying the differences and the similarities between social groups seems crucial for successful multicultural education.

ACKNOWLEDGMENT

This research was supported by Texas A&M University Faculty Mini-Grant FMG-R1-037 awarded to the first author. We thank Arthur B. Markman for his valuable comments and encouragement.

REFERENCES

Allport, G. W. (1954). *The nature of prejudice.* Cambridge, MA: Addison-Wesley.

Barsalou, L. W. (1983). Ad hoc categories. *Memory & Cognition, 11*(3), 211–227.

Barsalou, L. W. (1985). Ideals, central tendency, and frequency of instantiation as determinants of graded structure in categories. *Journal of Experimental Psychology: Learning, Memory, and Cognition, 11*, 629–654.

Cantor, N., & Mischel, W. (1977). Trait as prototypes: Effects on recognition memory. *Journal of Personality and Social Psychology, 35*, 38–48.

Cantor, N., Mischel, W., & Schwartz, J. C. (1982). A prototype analysis of psychological situations. *Cognitive Psychology, 14*, 45–77.

Cooper, R., & Slavin, R. (2001). Cooperative learning programs and multicultural education: Improving intergroup relations. In F. Salili, & R. Hoosain (Eds.), *Research in multicultural education: Issues, policies and practices, Vol 1* (pp. 15–33). Greenwich, CT: Information Age Publishing.

Crick, N. R., & Dodge, K. (1996). A Social information-processing mechanisms on reactive and proactive aggression. *Child Development, 67*(3), 993–1002.

Duckitt, J. (1992). Psychology and prejudice: A historical analysis and integrative framework. *American Psychologist, 47 (10),* 1182–1193.

Deacon, T. W. (1997). *The symbolic species.* New York: W. W. Norton & Company.

Fiske, S. T., & Neuberg, S. L. (1990). A continuum of impression formation, from category-based to individuating processes: Influences of information and motivation on attention and interpretation. *Advances in Experimental Social Psychology, 23,* 1–74.

Fodor, J. A., & Pylyshyn, Z. W. (1988). Connectionism and cognitive architecture: A critical analysis. *Cognition, 28.*

Gelman, S., & Heyman, G. D. (1999). Carrot-eaters and creature-believers: The effects of lexicalization on children's inferences about social categories. *Psychological Science, 10,* 489–493.

Gelman, S., & Markman, E. M. (1986). Categories and induction in young children. *Cognition, 23,* 183–209.

Gentner, D. (1983). Structure-mapping: A theoretical framework for analogy. *Cognitive Science, 7,* 155–170.

Goldstone, R. L. (1995). Effects of categorization on color perception. *Psychological Science, 6,* 298–304.

Hamilton, D. L., & Sherman, J. W. (1994). Stereotypes. In R. S. Wyer, & T. K. Srull (Eds.), *Handbook of social cognition* (Vol. 2, pp. 1–68). Hillsdale, NJ: Lawrence Erlbaum.

Hewstone, M. (1996). Contact and categorization: Social psychological interventions to change intergroup relations. In C. Racrae, C. Stangor, & M. Hewstone (Eds.), *Stereotypes and stereotyping* (pp. 323–368). New York: The Guilford Press.

Henning-Stout, M., & Brown-Cheatham, M. (1999). School psychology in a diverse world: Considerations for practice, research, and training. In C. R. Reynolds & T. B. Gutkin (Eds.), *The handbook of school psychology* (pp. 1041–1055). New York: John Willey & Sons.

Jackendoff, R. (1983). *Semantics and cognition.* Cambridge, MA: MIT Press.

Kruschke, J. K. (1992). ALCOVE: An exemplar-based connectionist model of category learning. *Psychological Review, 99*(1), 22–44.

Langacker, R. W. (1986). An Introduction to Cognitive Grammar. *Cognitive Science, 10,* 1–40.

Maass, A. (1999). Linguistic intergroup bias: stereotype perpetuation through language. *Advances in Experimental Social Psychology, 31,* 79–121.

Marcus, G. F. (1998). Rethinking eliminative connectionism. *Cognitive Psychology, 37,* 243–282.

Markman, E. M. (1989). *Categorization and naming in children: Problems of induction.* Cambridge, MA: MIT Press.

McConahay, J. B., & Hough, J. C. (1976). Symbolic racism. *Journal of Social Issues, 32,* 23–45.

Medin, D. L., & Schaffer, M. M. (1978). Context theory of classification. *Psychological Review, 85,* 207–238.

Medin, D. L., Lynch, E. B., & Coley, J. D. (1997). Categorization and reasoning among tree experts: Do all roads lead to Rome? *Cognitive Psychology, 32,* 49–96.

Murphy, G. L., & Medin, D. L. (1985). The roles of theories in conceptual coherence. *Psychological Review, 92,* 289–316.

Nosofsky, R. M. (1986). Attention, similarity, and the identification-categorization relationship. *Journal of Experimental Psychology: General, 115*, 39–57.

Pinker, S. (1999). *How the mind works.* New York: W. W. Norton & Company.

Reed, S. K. (1972). Pattern recognition and categorization. *Cognitive psychology, 3*, 382–407.

Rosch, E., & Mervis, C. B. (1975). Family resemblances: Studies in the internal structure of categories. *Cognitive Psychology, 7*, 573–605.

Rosch, E. (1978). Principles of categorization. In E. Rosch & B. B. Lloyd (Eds.), *Cognition and categorization* (pp. 27–48). Hillsdale, NJ: Lawrence Erlbaum Associates.

Ross, B. H. (1996). Category learning as problem solving. *The Psychology of Learning and Motivation, 35*, 165–192.

Ross, B. H. (1996). Category representations and the effects of interacting with instances. *Journal of Experimental Psychology: Learning, Memory, and Cognition, 22*(5), 1249–1265.

Ross, B. H. (1997). The use of categories affects classification. *Journal of Memory and Language, 37*(2), 240–267.

Ross, B. H., & Murphy, G. L. (1999). Food for thought: cross-classification and category organization in a complex real-world domain. *Cognitive Psychology, 38*, 495–553.

Salili, F., & Hoosain, R. (2001). Multicultural education: History, issues, and practices. In F. Salili, & R. Hoosain (Eds.), *Multicultural education: Issues, policies and practices* (pp. 1–13). Greenwich, CT: Information Age Publishing.

Spears, R., & Haslam, S. A. (1997). Stereotyping and the burden of cognitive load. In S. Russell, P. J. Oalkes, N. Ellmers, & S. A. Haslam (Eds.), *The social psychology of stereotyping and group life* (pp. 171–207). Oxford, UK: Blackwell Publishers.

Stangor, C. (2000). Volume Overview. In C. Stangor (Ed.), *Stereotypes and prejudice: Essential readings* (pp. 1–16). Philadelphia: Psychology Press Francis.

Stephan, W. (1999). *Reducing prejudice and stereotyping in schools.* New York: Teachers College Press.

Tjfel, H. (1969). Cognitive aspect of prejudice. *Journal of Social Issues, 25*, 79–97.

Tajfel, H. (1970). Experiments in intergroup discrimination. *Scientific American, 223* (2), 96–102.

Tversky, A. (1977). Features of similarity. *Psychological Review, 84*, 327–352.

Waxman, S. R., & Markow, D. B. (1998). Object properties and object kind: Twenty-one-month-old infants' extension of novel adjectives. *Child Development, 69*(5), 1313–1329.

Wisniewski, E. J., & Medin, D. L. (1994). On the interaction of theory and data in concept learning. *Cognitive Science, 18*, 221–281.

Yamauchi, T., Love, B. C., & Markman, A. B. (2002). Learning non-linearly separable categories by inference and classification. *Journal of Experimental Psychology: Learning, Memory & Cognition.*

Yamauchi, T., & Markman, A. B. (1995). Effects of category learning on categorization—An analysis of inference-based and classification-based learning. In J. D. Moore & J. F. Lehman (Eds.), *The proceedings of the seventeenth annual meeting of the cognitive science society* (pp. 786–790). Pittsburgh, PA: Lawrence Erlbaum.

Yamauchi, T., & Markman, A. B. (1998). Category-learning by inference and classification. *Journal of Memory and Language, 39,* 124–148.

Yamauchi, T., & Markman, A. B. (2000a). Inference using categories. *Journal of Experimental Psychology: Learning, Memory and Cognition, 26*(3), 776–795.

Yamauchi, T., & Markman, A. B. (2000b). Learning categories composed of varying instances: The effect of classification, inference and structural alignment. *Memory & Cognition, 28*(1), 64–78.

Yzerbyt, V., Rocher, S., & Schadron, G. (1997). Stereotypes as explanations: A subjective essentialistic view of group perception. In S. Russell, P. J. Oalkes, N. Ellmers, & S. A. Haslam (Eds.), *The social psychology of stereotyping and group life* (pp. 20–50). Oxford, UK: Blackwell Publishers.

CHAPTER 15

MANAGING STIGMA

Disidentification from the Academic Domain Among Members of Stigmatized Groups

Colette van Laar and Belle Derks

> *To give up pretensions is as blessed a relief as to get them gratified; and where disappointment is incessant and the struggle unending, this is what men will always do.*
>
> —James (1890, p. 311)

Motivation on a particular domain is high when individuals have some reasonable expectation of meeting their goal, and when they value that goal. When either expectation or value is at zero value, motivation to work towards the goal is absent (Atkinson, 1957; Atkinson & Birch, 1978; Pintrich & Schunk, 1996). Motivation tends to be high then in domains that we value. Self-evaluation is also dependent on achievements in domains that we value. As William James suggested above, one way to protect self-worth in the case of disappointing achievement in a particular domain is to forgo any pretensions that we have in that domain (James, 1890). Disidentifying from a domain occurs when the importance or value of a domain is reduced, and it is no longer a part, or it is a less central part, of one's self-definition. In the case of academic disidentification, it is the school, or more specifically, academic achievement that becomes less incorporated

Teaching, Learning, and Motivation in a Multicultural Context, pages 345–393
Copyright © 2003 by Information Age Publishing
All rights of reproduction in any form reserved.

into one's self-definition (Voelkl, 1996). The student does not value school, and may not feel like he or she belongs in school. This work has been discussed under various terms: school involvement, attachment, membership, engagement and commitment, or school dropout, attrition, disidentification, and alienation. Academic disidentification can be psychological (the student withdraws psychologically from academic achievement or school goals altogether), or physical, the student withdraws from school through truancy or dropping out. Disidentification may be accompanied by feelings of distrust and suspicion, or even anger and hostility towards the school and those associated with it. Moreover, although we will use the term "school," a substantial part of the research has looked at college withdrawal or dropout.

Researchers concerned with the value or importance attached to tasks or domains by individuals have also studied the concept of disidentification. In this framework, disidentification has been discussed as investment or involvement in a task or domain, as well as devaluation or disengagement. Also, various forms of disidentification have been distinguished: lower value or trust can be placed on performance feedback in a certain domain (often referred to as the discounting of feedback), feedback may be trusted but have no impact on self-views in that domain, or self-views in that domain may be impacted but have no effect on global self-views.

Whereas most write about the psychological movement *away* from a domain on which one has low status (a status relevant domain), others discuss how one may move *towards* alternative domains on which to base one's sense of self-worth. Moreover, a distinction can be made between temporary disidentification and more long-term or stable devaluing of the academic domain. Similarly, disidentification can be directed at specific aspects of a domain or more globally to the domain in general (see Mark & Folger, 1984). Domain disidentification can be primarily an individualistic strategy targeted to the improvement of personal identity, or a more collective strategy designed to improve the worth of a group. In both cases, however, the strategy is primarily cognitive, improving perceived but not actual worth. We will come back to these terms as we discuss the literature below. For ease of discussion, except when making a distinction between these terms, we will refer to the collection of these various processes as domain disidentification. This thus refers to the lower impact of performance feedback as well as the less value placed on a specific domain for global self-evaluation.

Although domain disidentification is an effective strategy to protect self-worth, it tends to undermine motivation in that domain. After all, the motive to maintain self-esteem is lost as a source of motivation when self-esteem is no longer dependent on outcomes in a particular domain. Domain disidentification is thus a topic that illustrates the sometimes competitive relationship between achievement and well-being. Domain disidentification is particularly costly when it occurs in domains that are highly valued in a society, such as doing well in school. In recent years, researchers studying ethnic minority achievement have become concerned that disidentification from the academic domain may be one strategy used by ethnic minority students who do not do well in school (Crocker & Major, 1989; Major, Spencer, Schmader, Wolfe, & Crocker, 1998; Osborne, 1995; Steele, 1992, 1997). Similarly, researchers studying the achievements of women and girls in math and science suggest that women may disidentify from these male-dominated fields (Quinn & Spencer, 2001; Spencer, Steele, & Quinn, 1999). When disidentification becomes a group phenomenon, it can reproduce systematic differences in achievements between groups that are not warranted by actual differences in potential. Domain disidentification may then itself reproduce the low status (Van Laar & Sidanius, 2001). A vicious cycle may result, in which existing low expectations, stereotypes, prejudice or discrimination lead a group to disidentify from a particular domain, lowering motivation and achievement, which is then interpreted as evidence for the group's lower ability (Crocker & Major, 1989; Crocker, Major, & Steele, 1998; Steele, 1992).

In this chapter we review work on domain disidentification from various theoretical angles: After a general section on disidentification and the self we review four areas of work relevant to domain disidentification. These come from the social psychological and from the educational literature. We begin with research on the self, self-evaluation and social comparison. Here we discuss how the self-system may use domain disidentification as part of its motive to protect and enhance the self. We make a distinction between specific and more global self-views, and discuss how comparisons with others can lead individuals to identify more or less with a particular domain. We also discuss work on relative deprivation that provides an interesting perspective on domain disidentification. Second, we turn to research on the self within the group from social identity theory. Research conducted in this framework shows that individuals are members of groups and use certain strategies in order to protect their social identities in these groups. One way to protect social identity is to disengage feelings of self-worth from domains in which the group does not do well. Educational research on motivation and achievement provides a third body of research. We review intrinsic and extrinsic motivation, and discuss how disidentification may develop with age. The stigma perspective provides a last body of research for this review. It is concerned with how members of groups that are devalued in a society have an extra difficult task in maintaining positive self-views. As a result they may develop certain strategies to escape the negative expectations, stereotypes and prejudice that they encounter. Disidentifying from domains in which the group has traditionally not done well, and selecting other domains on which to focus achievement efforts is one possible strategy. We also examine evidence for disidentification amongst members of ethnic minority groups and learning disabled children. As part of the review on stigma we discuss work on resistance cultures that suggests that members of low status groups may reject behaviors that would make them successful in school, as such behaviors are defined as 'selling out' their ethnic or socioeconomic group.

A review of the literature on domain disidentification provides theoretical and empirical support for the concept from various perspectives. In addition, the reviewed evidence allows us to describe various concepts of domain disidentification. We summarize what has been gained from the research in terms of the causes of domain disidentification, its mediators, who it affects, and what its consequences are. We also summarize the conditions that appear to moderate the occurrence of domain disidentification, how widespread it is thought to be, and of course, what may prevent it. Our own work suggests that there are various factors that will limit the use of domain disidentification as a general strategy. These factors include the social comparisons available in the social context, and social pressures in the environment more generally. Our review will end with a discussion of these findings. Let us start with a discussion of disidentification and the self.

DISIDENTIFICATION AND THE SELF

Theorists interested in motivation have long studied the self because of assumed links between self-perception and achievement behaviors. Motives to protect the self and to maintain a positive view of the self play a central role in the self-system. Both the social psychological and educational literatures offer evidence on the workings of the self system and its efforts to protect and enhance the self (Baumeister, 1998; Maslow, 1970; Taylor, 1991). Domain disidentification may be one result of such efforts. We begin by discussing literature on the structure of the self, and the link between global and specific self-views. Second, we review how social comparisons may affect tendencies to disidentify from a domain. Last, we review some research from the relative deprivation framework that reveals the conditions under which individuals with low status may devalue the possibility of achievement on a domain on which their group does not do well.

The Structure of the Self: The Role of Domain Importance in Specific and Global Self-Views

One of the sources of theoretical and empirical support for domain dis-identification comes from research on how the self protects itself from negative evaluation. Susan Harter developed one of the most widely accepted models of the self. Building upon the previous work of James (1890) and Rosenberg (1979), Harter (1986) specified a hierarchical model of self in which the self is a superordinate category under which subcategories of the self are organized, made up of various self-facets or domains. In such hierarchical models the strength of the relationship between specific and global aspects of self-worth depends on the value that the individual attaches to any specific component (for other hierarchical models of the self, see Marsh & Shavelson, 1985; Shavelson, Hubner, & Stanton, 1976). Harter has identified five primary domains in children's lives: academic competence, athletic competence, social acceptance, physical appearance, and behavioral conduct. In her model, she takes into account both the child's evaluation of each of these domains as well as the importance he or she attaches to that domain (Harter, 1986). Importance thus acts as a moderator of whether the child will suffer as a consequence of failing, or be happy when he or she succeeds. When children do less well in school, Harter suggests that they may discount the importance of that domain. Children may also disidentify from school for reasons not related to failure, such as finding little challenge in school, having serious social issues in their lives to contend with that override school interest, or having goals that are inconsistent with school achievement. Research has generally provided support for Harter's model across various cultures (Chan, 1997; Harter, 1999; Miller, 1998; Muldoon, 2000). In a typical study, Harter, Whitesell, and Junkin (1998) assessed perceptions of self-worth in various domains, in addition to importance ratings of each of these domains. They studied three groups of students: normally achieving, behaviorally disordered and learning disabled students. Harter et al. were particularly interested in the perceptions of self-worth in domains in which these children considered themselves inadequate. The results show that whereas students who discounted the importance of these domains had high self-worth, students who continued to consider these domains important suffered low self-worth. More generally, Harter has tended to find self-worth to be highly related to self-evaluations in domains considered important (correlations ranging from .67 to .70) and much less related to self-worth in domains considered to be unimportant (correlations ranging from .30 to .34) (Harter, 1993).

Whereas Harter has generally found strong support for the distinction between specific and global self-views, evidence for the key role of value or importance in determining self-worth has sometimes been more mixed (e.g., Hamid & Cheng, 1995; Hoge & McCarthy, 1984; Marsh, 1986; see Pelham & Swann, 1989 for a review). Both Marsh (1986; 1993a; 1993b), and Pelham and colleagues have taken up the challenge of finding support for the original Jamesian notion. They argue that the reason for the lack of evidence is that James' original formulation has not been appropriately investigated. Marsh (1993b) argues that it is not individuals' importance ratings that matter, but general or group importance ratings that determine self-worth. However, in two studies and an additional meta-analysis of eight existing studies, Pelham (1995b) was able to show that, although group ratings are important, individual importance ratings do contribute to self-esteem over and above group ratings. Pelham's conclusion is that people define and weigh their specific self-views relative to other people and relative to their other self-views (Pelham, 1995a). Moreover, Harter (1999) argues that a problem with much previous research is that it has tended to look at the role of importance in populations in which importance variability is restricted in range: that is, amongst individuals for whom the domain is likely to be of high importance. This is likely to lead to the underestimation of the role of importance (p. 150).

Various other self theorists also stress the importance of the value that individuals place on domain specific self-views in determining global self-worth. Tesser's model of self evaluation maintenance states that people behave in ways that maintain or increase their self-evaluation (Tesser, 1988). When the self is threatened by a negative comparison with another, individuals can lower the relevance of the dimension to their self-definition. Applying this model directly to school behavior, Tesser and Campbell (1982), argued that self-evaluation is dependent on three variables: one's relative level of performance in school, the relevance of school to one's self-definition, and the psychological closeness of a comparison to other classmates. This has been supported in various studies: For example, Tesser and Paulhus (1983) had male undergraduates working on tasks said to be valid indicators of a fictitious trait called "cognitive perceptual integration." They assessed the relevance of the trait to the student's self-definition using oral, written, and behavioral measures. Consistent with domain disidentification, they found that the lower participants' performance relative to others, the lower they judged the importance of the trait (also see Tesser & Campbell, 1980; Tesser, Millar, & Moore, 1988). Others have similarly suggested that individuals can alter the importance they attach to various domains: Steele maintains that people experiencing a threat to some self-relevant domain may try to reaffirm the self in a different identity domain (Liu & Steele, 1986; Spencer, Josephs, & Steele, 1993; Steele, 1988, 1992). Hence, after a failure, one may restore one's self-image by affirming important aspects of one's self—aspects that can be related or unrelated to the domain on which one failed.

Theorists concerned with the self and its global and specific components thus tend to find that individuals can compensate for failure in one domain by focusing on other domains. Self-evaluation is flexible in that the importance of specific domains can be altered to satisfy their needs for a positive self-view. Compensating for failure in one domain by increasing the value of another domain appears successful in preventing the impact of the failure experience on subsequent functioning.

Social Comparison on Important and Less Important Dimensions

Work on social comparison has emphasized that individuals may switch comparison dimensions in order to maintain positive self-worth. The main message of social comparison work is that one's assessments and satisfaction with oneself is determined by the comparison of one's outcomes, opinions and characteristics with those of others on important dimensions (Festinger, 1954). One implication of Festinger's social comparison theory is that once a dimension declines in importance, the comparison ceases to be important.

Although much of the work on social comparison has been concerned with the selection of comparison others, there has been some work on the selection of comparison dimensions (see e.g., Taylor, Wood, & Lichtman, 1983; Tesser & Campbell, 1980; Van Knippenberg, Wilke, & De Vries, 1981; Wood, 1989; Wood, Giordano Beech, & Ducharme, 1999). Tesser and Campbell (1980) had students take two tests together with a confederate. On one test the participant was outperformed by the confederate, and on the other the confederate and participant scored equally. Participants were then given the opportunity to choose on which task to continue working, and provided self-descriptions with respect to the domains in written and oral form. The results showed that participants' self-definition moved away from the domain on which the confederate outperformed them. They were less interested in working on this domain and considered this domain less important. Baumeister and Jones (1978) call this compensatory self-enhancement. This work suggests that individuals may selectively make comparisons on dimensions on which they are advantaged (see Wood, 1989 for a review). Such selection of favorable dimensions has been found with college students (Tesser & Campbell, 1980; Van Knippenberg et al., 1981), with boys building huts (Lemaine, 1974), and with individuals coping with breast cancer (Taylor et al., 1983). Individuals may not only select but may also create new dimensions on which to compare: Buunk and

Ybema (1995) showed that individuals coping with disability stress would devalue former dimensions of comparison and create new ones in order to protect their self-evaluation. Identification with a new comparison dimension may even allow individuals to maintain comparisons with others who outperform them (Wood et al., 1999).

Social comparison research therefore suggests that individuals may favor and select dimensions on which they compare favorably, and avoid dimensions on which the resulting comparisons are negative. The protection offered by these strategies is such that it may even allow individuals to continue to compare to others who outperform them on some self-relevant dimensions.

Reducing The Worth of Non-obtained Outcomes: Relative Deprivation and Dissonance

Research on reactions to non-obtained outcomes from various perspectives suggests that individuals may respond by reducing the value of the outcomes that were not obtained. Relative deprivation theorists maintain that one way individuals lacking a certain outcome can react is by denigrating their original goal (see also Klinger, 1975; Mark, 1985; Mark & Folger, 1984; Merton, 1957). Mark (1985, Study 1) had students being deprived of a desirable outcome by either fair or unfair procedures. Specifically, his participants took part in a class with a special "option" to serve as research assistants in an "interesting and important" study. Students deprived of the outcome by unfair means denigrated the desirable outcome relative to those withheld fairly from the outcome. Merton (1957) referred to this devaluation of a deprived object as "retreatism." Dissonance theory also suggests that reducing the importance of a non-obtained outcome should reduce distress (Festinger, 1957). Research on deprivation of outcomes has also identified conditions that increase the likelihood of domain disidentification: For example, Mark and Folger (1984) suggest that domain disidentification is especially likely to occur when low outcomes are perceived as controlled by others, or are perceived as justified (see Mark, 1985 for evidence; also see Wortman & Brehm, 1975). In both cases self-worth is restored, in the first case as one is not responsible for the outcome, and in the second case as one no longer cares about the outcomes. In contrast, perceiving control by the self over outcomes should lead to increased striving on the dimension, and thus prevent disidentification (Wortman & Brehm, 1975).

Research on being deprived of desirable outcomes therefore suggests that, to reduce distress, individuals may react to such situations by decreasing the value of the original goal. This is especially likely to occur when individuals perceive no personal control over the outcomes or when they perceive that the low outcomes as justified.

SOCIAL IDENTITY AND DOMAIN DISIDENTIFICATION

A large body of work on domain disidentification has been conducted in the framework of social identity theory (Tajfel & Turner, 1986). This theory addresses the role of the individual in the group—in particular the interplay between the personal and social (or group) oriented aspects of the self. Social identity theory suggests that comparing one's group to other groups can either bolster one's social identity or threaten it. Positive social identity will result from comparing one's group to groups that have lower status on relevant dimensions. However, a problematic situation arises when people are members of a group that has low status, as intergroup comparison on status relevant dimensions cannot result in a positive social identity. Social identity theory maintains that because of the threat of a negative social identity to the self, members of low status groups will try to attain positive social identity.

The theory proposes several strategies by which low status group members can reduce such threats to the self. One of these strategies is to try to gain individual higher status. Members of a low status group can attain higher status as individuals by trying to achieve higher levels on the status-defining dimension and joining higher status groups. Tajfel and Turner refer to this individual-level strategy as *individual mobility*. A second strategy that members of low status groups can use to reduce threat to the self is to try and attain higher status for the group as a whole. This group-level strategy is referred to as *social change*. When status structures are stable and have impermeable boundaries, it is, however, difficult for members of low status groups to change their individual or group status. In these situations, cognitive rather than behavioral strategies are used. These strategies are referred to as *social creativity* strategies (Ellemers & Van Knippenberg, 1997; Lemaine, 1974; Tajfel & Turner, 1986; Van Knippenberg, 1978; Van Knippenberg & Ellemers, 1993). Individuals can, for instance, restrict comparisons to ingroup members, thereby ignoring unfavorable comparisons with high status outgroup members. Another way to enhance social identity is to attribute negative outcomes externally. Low status group members can attribute negative outcomes of their group to prejudice, thereby removing any negative implications for self-evaluation. The group can also challenge the superiority of the outgroup and claim superiority instead for the own group (e.g., Black is beautiful). Lastly, and most relevant here, social identity theory suggests that low status group members may disidentify from domains on which the group has low status (status relevant domains) and select an alternative domain on which to base self-worth.

As in theories of the self reviewed earlier, social identity theory also warns of the dangers of domain disidentification for domain motivation. If members of ethnic minority groups disidentify with school in an effort to protect self-worth from negative comparisons with the majority group, then motivation to achieve in school will suffer, eventually reproducing lower achievement, and thus reproducing the status difference between the groups. As such, domain disidentification can reinforce the status hierarchy.

Evidence for Domain Disidentification From Research on Social Identity

Although social identity theory has generated a huge amount of research, research specifically examining disidentification from a status relevant domain and increased identification with an alternative domain is scarcer. Moreover, evidence for domain disidentification sometimes comes from social identity research on ingroup bias, rather than on research specifically targeted to examine domain disidentification. When we take this research together, there is quite some evidence that low status groups select *alternative* domains. However, social identity theory provides less evidence for the devaluation of the *status relevant* domain (Hinkle, Taylor, Fox Cardamone, & Ely, 1998).

One study that does provide evidence for the devaluation of the status relevant domain is by Wagner and colleagues (Wagner, Lampen, & Syllwasschy, 1986). They showed that law students who were told that they had lower status than students of economics in the domain of discussion ability, rated discussion ability of less importance to law students than law students who did not experience this identity threat. The lower importance rating of this domain is a clear instance of domain devaluation by members of a low status group. An interesting study by Van Knippenberg and Van Oers (1984) showed indications of domain disidentification in a natural intergroup setting consisting of two groups of nurses with educational backgrounds that differed in status. Whereas the nurses with higher education stressed the importance of theoretical insight, the less educated nurses accentuated the difference in practical skills and found this aspect more important. By de-emphasizing low status on the status relevant domain (educational background) and attaching more value to the dimension on which their ingroup outperformed the outgroup (practical skills), the less-educated nurses maintained positive social identity. Similarly, in our own research we have found that the status relevant domain becomes less central to self-definition when ingroup members are segregated from out-group members (Derks, Van Laar, & Wilke, 2001).

Most other studies, however, provide evidence for the increased identification with an alternative domain. Lemaine's studies on groups of children in summer camps showed the selection of alternative criteria as a reaction to low status (Lemaine, 1974; Lemaine, Kasterztein, & Personnaz, 1978). Two groups of children took part in a hut-building contest in the wood. When one group was disadvantaged in building materials, this group constructed a garden as an alternative criterion. They also tried to gain acceptance for this alternative criterion with the camp leaders. Thus, the children tried to improve their self-worth by inventing an alternative domain. The same effect was shown in a second study. Students who were asked to write an application letter and knew they were up against a student from a more reputable college or with more experience, emphasized their character and personality type in a second letter. They thus tried to find other criteria on which they hoped to positively distinguish themselves from the other student. Lemaine and colleagues (1978) also maintained that the selection of alternative dimensions was accompanied by the attachment of greater value to this new dimension. Lemaine did however not obtain direct evidence for this in the studies.

Research on ingroup bias also finds some evidence for the increased value placed on alternative domains. Studies by Ellemers, Van Rijswijk and colleagues (Ellemers & Van Rijswijk, 1997; Ellemers, Van Rijswijk, Roefs, & Simons, 1997) show that low status group members will search for alternative criteria on which to display ingroup favoritism, and tend to attach more value to these new dimensions than other individuals do. However, low status group members also continued to acknowledge that the status relevant domain is of primary importance (Ellemers et al., 1997). Jackson and colleagues manipulated low status by associating a negative trait (either egocentrism or subservience) with one group but not the other (Jackson, Sullivan, Harnish, & Hodge, 1996). When it was not possible to change their individual status, low status group members rated the negative characteristic as less negative. Also, bias in favor of the ingroup was found on alternative dimensions, indicating the search for alternative criteria when the status on a relevant domain is low. A second study supported the idea that the search for alternative dimensions and ingroup bias on these new dimensions is used only when status is low. A number of other studies have similarly found ingroup bias on alternative dimensions when social identity is threatened (Hinkle et al., 1998; see also Levin, 1996; Spears & Manstead, 1989, study 1). None of these studies, however, show that low status group members attach more value to these new dimensions as compared to the status relevant dimension. In each case low status group members indicated that they found the status relevant dimensions of more importance than the alternative dimensions.

In conclusion, whereas the research generated by social identity theory provides evidence for the selection of alternative criteria as a strategy to enhance the self, evidence for devaluation of the status relevant domain as a strategy remains elusive. Instead, low status group members tend to acknowledge their low status position on a status relevant domain. One reason why researchers may have failed to find evidence for domain disidentification on the status relevant domain may be because domain disidentification is a process that occurs largely below awareness, and thus cannot be measured with typical attitude scales. Stigma research has examined domain disidentification in more indirect ways and tends to find more evidence for this process, as we will see later. However, it may also be the case that the selection of alternative domains occurs more easily than disidentification from the status relevant domain: domain disidentification from the status relevant domain may be restricted by the realities of the intergroup situation. It is not easy to distance the self from domains considered valued and important by the surrounding social context. Let us now turn to some of the structural factors in the social context that impact the tendency to disidentify from a domain.

The Impact of Socio-structural Factors on the Tendency to Disidentify From a Domain

Social identity theory has been particularly concerned with the socio-structural aspects of a society that may influence self-protective strategies. According to this literature, socio-structural factors such as the permeability, stability and legitimacy of the status hierarchy affect how likely it is that a member of a low status group will disidentify from the status relevant domain, and select an alternative domain with which to identify. The research tends to suggest that (together with other cognitive social creativity strategies) domain disidentification is a last resort strategy used only when the status structure does not allow low status group members to actually *increase* their individual or group status.

Tajfel and Turner (1979) suggested that in the case of identity threats, individuals will first use individual strategies that enhance their personal status rather than collective strategies that attempt to enhance the status of the group. Taylor and McKirnan (1984) made similar predictions in their five-stage model of responses to intergroup inequality. According to these models, it is only when situational variables make use of individual mobility impossible that threatened individuals will use other strategies. Therefore, the socio-structural variables that prevent individual mobility tend to promote domain disidentification.

Numerous studies show that the tendency to use individual mobility is moderated by the *permeability* of the status structure, or the degree to which individuals can pass from one group to another (Ellemers, Doosje, Van Knippenberg, & Wilke, 1992; Ellemers, Van Knippenberg, De Vries, & Wilke, 1988; Ellemers, Van Knippenberg, & Wilke, 1990; Ellemers, Wilke, & Van Knippenberg, 1993). Thus, when a situation is permeable, individuals can pass from one group to another more easily than when group boundaries are impermeable. In contrast, when the status difference is perceived as impermeable, individuals tend to attempt to enhance the status of their group as a whole, or tend to use creative strategies that cognitively enhance their status, such as domain disidentification (Ellemers et al., 1990; Ellemers et al., 1993; also see Jackson et al., 1996). According to this research, then, domain disidentification is most likely to occur when members of low status groups perceive the status difference as impermeable. For example, ethnic minority students would be more likely to disidentify from the academic domain if they perceive that it will be difficult to improve their personal academic performance (see also Dweck & Leggett, 1988).

A second structural variable that moderates tendencies to disidentify from a domain is the *stability* of the status hierarchy (Ellemers, 1993; Ellemers et al., 1990; Tajfel, 1978, 1981; Van Knippenberg, 1984, 1989). Status structures vary in how fixed the status differences between the different groups are. Tajfel (1978) proposed that stable status structures make it almost impossible for low status group members to try to change the status of their group, leading them to use other strategies such as domain disidentification. This has been supported in studies by Ellemers and colleagues (Ellemers et al., 1990). When status structures are unstable, individuals tend to attempt to improve the status of their group, and have less need for cognitive self-enhancement strategies. Domain disidentification thus is more likely to occur in impermeable and stable group hierarchies. For example, women would be less likely to aspire to careers in the math's and sciences if they believe that the group difference in math performance between males and females is very stable. So whereas permeability refers to the possibility of one person moving between groups (but the status of the groups as a whole remaining constant), stability refers to the likelihood of change in the status of the group as a whole.

A third social structural variable that was proposed by Tajfel (1978) is the *legitimacy* of the status structure. A situation is legitimate when individuals believe that the status difference between groups is based on 'true' differences and not attributable to, for instance, unjust procedures. Studies indicate that domain disidentification is more likely to occur when individuals perceive the status difference as legitimate. For example, Ellemers and colleagues (Ellemers et al., 1993) found that when the status difference between the groups was legitimate, members of low status groups preferred to use an alternative criterion on which to compare groups rather than the status relevant criterion (see also Ellemers et al., 1990). Individuals cannot easily discard the information about their low status when they are in a situation in which group status appears to be legitimate. In these circumstances, the selection of an alternative domain is preferred over attempts to change individual or group status. It thus appears that it is only in status structures that are perceived as somewhat legitimate that disidentification from the status relevant domain, and increased identification with an alternative domain is likely to occur. Thus, ethnic minority students would be more likely to disidentify from the academic domain if they believe that the achievement gap between majority and minority students reflects real differences in aptitude between these students rather than lower access to resources or other disadvantage. Perceived legitimacy is thus one of the moderators of domain disidentification. However, we must note that it seems likely that long-term illegitimacy under stable circumstances would also lead to domain disidentification if individuals believe that there is no hope for a change in the illegitimate but stable status structure. We will come back to this point when we discuss research on domain disidentification from the stigma perspective.

Restrictions on Domain Disidentification in the Social Context

Although social structural factors provide the boundary conditions for self-protection strategies amongst low status group members, restrictions in the social context may further guide reactions of low status group members to low status. Various studies by social identity researchers suggest that although members of low status groups can be creative and flexible in their choices of self-protection, they are somewhat limited by factors in the social context. Thus they may find it difficult to avoid acknowledging the superiority of the outgroup on the status relevant dimension, but have more freedom on alternative dimensions. They may distinguish the self from the ingroup when the objective differences amongst ingroup members allow this, but be prevented from doing so when ingroup differences appear minimal. Third, members of low status groups may be restricted in their enhancement strategies when outgroup members are present, but be free and creative when they are not under the scrutiny of higher status outgroup members. We will discuss research evidence for each of these constraints in the social setting in turn.

Consensually Accepted Differences in Status as a Context Restriction

The impact of social reality constraints on the use of cognitive self-enhancing strategies is apparent in research by Ellemers and colleagues on ingroup bias (Ellemers et al., 1997). They investigated two natural groups (student associations) that differed in status on some valued domain. Relevant to our discussion are their conclusions about the use of ingroup bias by low status group members. Much research has found that group members tend to enhance their social identity by viewing their own group as better than other groups. Low status groups thus tend to show a bias towards the ingroup when they evaluate different groups in terms of performance (Brewer, 1979; Hinkle & Schopler, 1979; Messick & Mackie, 1989). Ingroup bias is a strategy that resembles domain disidentification in that low status group members search for alternative domains on which they believe that their ingroup is superior when performance on the status relevant dimension is objectively low.

Several studies have found that the use of undifferentiated ingroup bias, which involves favoring the ingroup on every possible dimension to enhance the self, is not always possible. Especially in situations in which the outgroup is clearly superior on the status relevant dimension, ingroup bias on this status relevant dimension will not be displayed. Ellemers and her colleagues (1997) found that when their group is low in status, group members display ingroup bias not on the status relevant dimension (the dimension on which the outgroup outperforms them), but instead on alternative dimensions. They did not discard the value of the status relevant domain, nor did they claim ingroup superiority on this domain. By preventing low status group members from claiming superiority on the status relevant domain, restrictions in the social context can therefore lead members of low status groups to shift their focus to alternative domains. Similar results have been found by Ellemers and Van Rijswijk (1997). They had participants work as a group on a "group creativity task" against another group. The outcome was manipulated such that the participants' group either outperformed (high status) or underperformed (low status) relative to the other group. When asked to rate the two groups on various characteristics, high status group members showed ingroup favoritism on the dimension on which they were tested, indicating that they believed their group to be better on this dimension, and the low status group acknowledged this. Members of this low status group did, however, show ingroup bias on an alternative dimension (one rating the "honesty" of members of each group) whereas the high status group did not differentiate between groups on this dimension. This research shows that social reality constraints lead low status group members to use other social creativity strategies, like the selection of alternative criteria, to bolster their social identity. Female students may thus be more likely to stress their superior verbal and social skills than attempt to challenge a consensually held view of higher math and science ability among males.

Intragroup Composition as a Contextual Restriction

Another social reality constraint was portrayed in two studies by Doosje, Spears and Koomen (1995). They investigated the use of intragroup variability judgments to deny unfavorable intergroup differences. Stressing the homogeneity or variability of the ingroup can serve as a self-enhancing strategy in that judging your own group as highly variable gives individuals a chance to portray themselves as having higher status than the average ingroup member. They thereby deny personal low status. However, studies indicate that low status group members are not able to stress the heterogeneity of their ingroup when social reality restricts them from claiming this (Doosje et al., 1995). Thus, if females are all perceived as very similar in visual spatial ability, it will be hard for an individual to claim high status for herself on that domain. Again, restrictions in the social context place constraints on the use of self-enhancing strategies.

Outgroup Presence as a Contextual Restriction

Research by Ellemers, Van Dyck, Hinckle, and Jacobs (2000) shows that the presence of outgroup members can also constrain the possibilities that low status group members have to protect the self. Thus, they may refrain from showing ingroup bias when the outgroup is present, but show the usual ingroup bias in situations in which scrutiny by outgroup members is absent. The presence of an outgroup audience thus places restrictions on the use of ingroup bias on the status defining domain (see also Barreto, 2000; Barreto, Spears, Ellemers, & Shahinper, 2001; Ellemers, Barreto, & Spears, 1999). We found further evidence for this in our own research (Derks et al., 2001). Specifically, Derks and colleagues showed that the presence of high status outgroup members can restrict low status group members from devaluing the status relevant domain. In this study, low status group members were either confronted with only ingroup members or with only high status outgroup members. In the outgroup condition, participants based their global self-esteem on the status relevant domain, indicating that domain disidentification had not taken place. However, in the ingroup condition participants no longer based their self-esteem on the status relevant domain, indicating that these participants had disidentified from the status relevant domain. It thus appears that segregation with ingroup members allows low status group members to use domain disidentification as a self-protective strategy. The presence of high status outgroup members, who value the domain and who base their self-esteem on that domain, prevents low status group members from discarding this domain as important for their self-esteem. Learning disabled students at integrated classrooms may thus be more likely to stress the value of academic performance than students in special education classes. Disidentification from academic domains will then be more likely to occur in segregated special education classes than in integrated classes.

In summary, whereas the social structural characteristics of a status hierarchy can provide the boundary conditions determining which strategies are available to members of a low status group to protect and enhance their social identity, constraints present in the social context can determine whether individuals will act on these strategies. These constraints can come in the form of stimuli that impose pressures, or prescribe certain norms or rules, that lead members of low status groups to use certain strategies over others. For instance, even when an individual perceives that individual mobility is possible, he or she may be restricted from valuing a domain that is devalued by the ingroup. We will return to the role of the ingroup when we discuss research from the stigma literature on domain disidentification as a group norm. Similarly, the presence of outgroup members who value a status relevant domain may make domain disidentification a less viable strategy.

The Role of Commitment to the Ingroup in Domain Disidentification

Another variable that influences the use of domain disidentification to protect the self is the degree of commitment an individual has to the low status group. Several studies on social creativity indicate that members of low status groups react differently depending on the degree of identification they feel with the ingroup (for a review see Ellemers, Spears, & Doosje, 2002). Research has found that whereas high identifiers tend to stay loyal to their group and try to change the status of their ingroup (either behaviorally or cognitively), low identifiers will tend to distance themselves from their ingroup in order to enhance their personal identity (Doosje, Ellemers, & Spears, 1999). Thus high identifiers tend to use collective self-enhancing strategies meant to improve the status of the group as a whole, while low identifiers are more interested in individualistic strategies. Domain disidentification can be either a collective or individualistic strategy, depending on whether the intention is to raise group or individual status.

Ellemers and Van Rijswijk found evidence for domain disidentification as a collective strategy (Ellemers & Van Rijswijk, 1997). Specifically, they found that members of the low status group who were highly identified with the group showed ingroup favoritism on alternative domains to enhance their identity when social reality restricted them from using ingroup bias on the status relevant dimension. Low identifying participants, however, did not differentiate between the two groups in performance on the alternative dimensions. Also, relative to low identifiers, high identifiers made more use of group level strategies by emphasizing the homogeneity of their group on the alternative dimension. Low identifiers, meanwhile, used individual self-enhancing strategies to protect their personal identity, stressing the heterogeneity of their group on the status relevant domain, in order to discard the relevance of the status information for the self. In the same vein we expect that disidentification of the status relevant domain will only be used as a collective strategy by high identifying individuals. High identifiers will try to cognitively alter the status position of their ingroup by looking for alternative dimensions on which positive intergroup comparisons can be made, whereas low identifiers will try to enhance their identity by distancing themselves from this group. Low identifying individuals may, however, individually disidentify from a domain on which their group does poorly in order to enhance their personal self-worth. As such, we would expect that ethnic minority students who are highly identified with their ethnic group would be more likely to disidentify from the academic domain and to stress the superiority of their group on alternative domains. Ethnic minority students who are less identified with their ethnic group would be less likely to disidentify from the academic domain to protect their ethnic group, but would consider such a possibility if it would allow them to distance themselves from the negative stereotype of their group.

In summary, group commitment can be an important factor in domain disidentification. Domain disidentification may be used as a collective strategy by highly identified members of the low status group in order to enhance social identity. Low identifying members of the low status group may, however, also use domain disidentification to protect their personal identity.

Social identity theory provides a clear theoretical framework for domain disidentification and the selection of alternative domains in response to self-threat. Threats can be perceived primarily as threats to the group, especially by high identifiers, or as threats to personal identity, in particular by low identifiers. Evidence for domain disidentification is strong for the selection and valuing of alternative domains. There is substantially less evidence for the abandonment of status relevant domains. A review of the factors that may moderate tendencies to disidentify suggests that constraints in the social setting may make it hard for members of low status groups to abandon the status relevant domain altogether. Such constraints may come in the form of objective consensual differences between the groups on this important and valued domain, and as a result of the presence of outgroup members who enforce the importance of the domain. Also, abandonment of the status relevant domain is a costly enterprise that over time may actually reproduce the status difference. The selection of an alternative domain in addition to the status relevant domain is, therefore, a more viable strategy. Nevertheless, our own research suggests that the abandonment of the status relevant domain may occur under specific circumstances, in particular when outgroup members are absent, such as in segregated situations, and when identification with the ingroup is high.

ACADEMIC MOTIVATION: DISIDENTIFICATION IN RESPONSE TO LOW PERFORMANCE

Whereas research on social identity theory has been conducted almost exclusively from a social psychological perspective, educational researchers have come to study domain disidentification as part of research on motivation. In particular, educational researchers have become interested in the reasons why students may withdraw from academic domains.

The importance of academic identification for engagement in school and academic achievement has been well established. Students who are disidentified with school are less prepared for class, participate less in class work and for shorter lengths of time, are less motivated, can be more verbally and physically abusive and less disciplined and attentive, attend school less often, and are more likely to drop out (Finn, 1993; Finn & Cox, 1992; Goodenow, 1993; Goodenow & Grady, 1993; Newmann, 1992; Pintrich & De Groot, 1990; Wehlage, Rutter, Smith, Lesko, & Fernandez, 1989). Similar relationships have been found in studies of college dropout (Astin, 1993; Pascarella, Terenzini, & Wolfle, 1986). These relationships between student involvement in school or college and academic achievement hold after controlling for ability measures, academic preparation, and other student input characteristics (Astin, 1993).

Whereas the importance of identification with school and the valuing of school for achievement has been well established, the variables that affect the importance or value that students attach to school have remained more uncertain. In fact, some argue that the value aspect has received relatively little attention relative to expectancy aspects of motivation (e.g., Brophy, 1999; Middleton & Toluk, 1999). In his leading article in the recent special issue of the Educational Psychologist on value, Brophy (1999) argues that much more attention should be paid to the value, interest and appreciation aspects of motivation. Similar arguments are made by Wigfield and Eccles (1992) who find evidence that the value attached to education is a much better predictor of long term engagement in academics than beliefs (or expectancies) about success in the academic domain. In fact, it appears that while expectancies are the best predictor of actual *achievement*, the value a student attaches to an academic domain is the best predictor of the *choices* a student makes (also see Chipman, Krantz, & Silver, 1992; Eccles, 1983; Meece, Wigfield, & Eccles, 1990; Wigfield & Eccles, 1992).

In response, Eccles and Wigfield have developed a comprehensive model of the value component in their expectancy-value framework of achievement motivation (Eccles & Wigfield, 1995; Wigfield & Eccles, 2000). They make a distinction between four types of value: valuing attainment in school or its subjects, having intrinsic interest in school, having extrinsic utility for school, and the cost involved in engagement in the academic domain or task. These four aspects are thought to operate together in determining the value that a student attaches to an academic domain or task. We will discuss in turn how academic disidentification appears to develop, and how it can be prevented through the encouragement of intrinsic task interest.

The Development of Academic Disidentification

A review of the literature by Finn (1989) suggests that withdrawal from school is a developmental process that can begin in the earliest school years. Following poor school performance, a pattern develops in which the students becomes increasingly less involved in various academic, social and sports activities at the school, culminating in a total withdrawal. Students no longer identify with the academic domain: they do not feel they belong in the school, and no longer value academic tasks (Finn, 1989; Voelkl, 1996). Belongingness refers to a sense of inclusion, acceptance and respect in school, whereas valuing represents the degree to which one finds academic activities important in their own right, for future goals, or for society (Osterman, 2000).

Eccles and colleagues tend to find that academic disidentification increases with age, with older children being less interested, attaching less importance, and valuing school subjects less than younger children (Wigfield, 1994; Wigfield & Eccles, 1992). A study by Eccles et al. (1984), for example, found a general developmental decline from third to tenth grade in the value placed by students on academic achievement. It appears these changes are due in part to a change in classroom environment, from a freer (elementary school) environment to more advanced school levels that are less trusting, more formal, controlling and evaluation prone. In these environments, grading standards are more salient, and social comparisons become more focused on ability. Moreover, these moves are also associated with the disruption of social networks that may make students less able to buffer threats. With age, students thus appear to move from an accepting environment in which each is an individual with particular strengths and weaknesses along many dimensions to one in which they are primarily graded along a single academic competence dimension. Another explanation for declines in the value students attach to academic subjects with age focuses on children's beliefs about ability. Dweck and colleagues have shown that as children get older they develop perceptions of ability as increasingly stable and unchangeable (Dweck & Leggett, 1988). As a result, poor performance may lead to a devaluation of the domain in order to protect self-evaluation. Consistent with these ideas, in the United States the greatest declines in the value attached to academic activities tend to occur with the move from the elementary to junior high school level (Eccles et al., 1984; Eccles et al., 1989; Wigfield, Eccles, Mac-Iver, Reuman, & Midgley, 1991). Disidentification of course does not occur for all students in all subjects—some studies show no decline in math for example, and others show increases in the value attached to English (see Pintrich & Schunk, 1996 for a review). In other social systems, changes in value attached to academic subjects will then be dependent on when the relevant changes in classroom structure and culture occur in their educational system. The role of beliefs about ability and the matching of school practices to the student is also revealed in research on intrinsic motivation. We will discuss this next.

Intrinsic Motivation and Academic Identification

Brophy maintains that the value aspect of motivation plays an especially important role (more so than the expectancy aspect) when a student is intrinsically motivated. Intrinsic motivation is viewed as an inner drive to action that is rewarding in and of itself. When an action is rewarding in and of itself, expectancies for success become much less important. However, Brophy argues that we know relatively little about how value originates, or how we may increase value. He suggests two characteristics of learning situations that should increase the value that students attach to a task or to learning more generally. He finds that students value domains or activities in which there is an optimal match between the task and the current characteristics of the student (see also Csikszentmihalyi, 1993), and activities or domains that students perceive as relevant for their personal identity or agenda (Brophy, 1999; also see Covington, 1999). When there is no match between the student and the domain or task, or when the student does not perceive the domain or task as relevant to his or her personal goals, he or she may disidentify with the task or domain. This is likely to occur if the domain or task is not familiar to the student, or is not in the student's developmental zone.

A number of researchers show that what is perceived as relevant, and thus what may be valued, can be dependent in part on group membership. This includes membership in cultural, gender or religious groups (Bergin, 1999; Brophy, 1999). Thus, girls may start to perceive math and science as not linked to their gender roles, and devalue, or disidentify with these subjects. Students who are members of ethnic or cultural groups that have historically not excelled in academic domains may disidentify from these domains (e.g., African Americans from academics altogether, boys from literature). Students that are disidentified from academic domains or tasks also tend to be members of groups that evidence lower achievement in these task or domains. Interestingly, while most consider it difficult for low achieving students to maintain intrinsic motivation, Covington (1999) shows that low achievement does not necessarily have to lead to low identification with a domain or task. He maintains that too often low identification does lead to low achievement because educational rewards are too extrinsic, and thus undermine intrinsic motivation. Also, rewards tend to be scarce and tend to be distributed among students in a zero-sum like manner, with rewards for one student meaning fewer rewards for other students (Covington, 1999). Students may become failure avoidant rather than success oriented, further undermining actual engagement in the task (Covington, 1999). Covington suggests that teachers should reinforce alternative rewards to achievement, such as reflection on learning, in an attempt to maintain students' identification with tasks or domains even in the case of low achievement. Also, Covington suggests that teachers should link what students are learning to their larger life or career goals (Covington, 1999). In this way, enthusiastic teachers are able to maintain positive attitudes towards learning even when students are disappointed with their own achievement. Similarly, Brophy (1999) suggests that teachers can model, coach, and "scaffold" enjoyment of the activity. When this is the case, then disappointing achievement does not hamper the interest or the value that the student attaches to the task or domain. Covington, Teel and colleagues have conducted a strong test of these ideas, reorganizing the reward structures of African American students in an inner city classroom (Covington & Teel, 1996; Teel, Debruin Parecki, & Covington, 1998). The students were given multiple performance opportunities, their responsibility and choice was increased, and grading became effort rather than outcome based. In addition, the cultural heritage of the students was validated as part of the regular classroom curriculum. Working in this manner with two different classes of students over a two year period, Teel et al. found that the majority of students who initially appeared to lack motivation began to exhibit higher levels of engagement, interest, and confidence. In addition, student effort increased, and their grades and grade aspirations improved.

In summary, the research on academic motivation and disidentification suggests that students maintain intrinsic interest in a task or domain when it matches their cognitive or developmental level, when it is perceived as relevant to self or group goals, and when external pressures such as scarce rewards do not undermine intrinsic motivation. When this is the case, low achievement in the domain need not undermine task or domain identification. The evidence indicates that students place increasingly less value in school as they attend longer. This appears to be due to a less effective match between student and school with increasing age, and due to students linking value with achievement: only when they do well do they value the task. Covington effectively argues that we need to encourage students to value school for other reasons than for attainment. Moreover, the evidence suggests that teachers can model, coach and scaffold students' behavior so as to encourage such task and domain identification through intrinsic task and domain interest.

GROUP DISADVANTAGE AND DOMAIN DISIDENTIFICATION

While the educational work focuses on the risks students from all backgrounds run when they experience disappointing achievement and perceive the academic domain as low in relevance, work on the effects of group disadvantage suggests that groups that have low status may be particularly at risk from academic disidentification. Much of this work derives from the recent stigma perspective.

The stigma perspective is a body of work focusing on the experience of individuals who are members of disadvantaged or stigmatized groups (Crocker & Major, 1989; Crocker et al., 1998; Heatherton, Kleck, Hebl, & Hull, 2000; Swim & Stangor, 1998). This work focuses on how the stigmatized understand and interpret their stigmatization, how they cope with it, and how it affects well-being, cognitive functioning, and interactions with others (Crocker et al., 1998). Working within a stigma framework, Crocker and Major (1989) suggested that one way in which members of devalued or stigmatized groups may protect their self-esteem from negative stereotypes and prejudice is by selectively devaluing domains in which their group fares poorly relative to other groups, and by selectively increasing the value of domains in which their group does well.

The stigmatized are more likely to experience negative and low outcomes than the nonstigmatized. This may be because the nature of the stigma makes success in a particular domain unlikely or impossible, as a result of prejudice and discrimination, or because stereotype threat interferes with their performance (Crocker et al., 1998; Steele & Aronson, 1995).

Stigmatized or devalued groups tend to be ethnic, cultural, religious or socioeconomic groups, often (but not always) numerical minority groups in their particular society. Such groups are found in most societies. Examples are African Americans in the United States, the Baraku in Japan, various immigrant groups in Northern Europe (e.g., Turkish, Moroccan, West Indian), Aboriginals in Australia, the Maoris of New Zealand, Sephardic Jews in Israel, and the Harijans of India (Ogbu, 1986; Sidanius & Pratto, 1999). Although much of the research has tended to focus on ethnic groups, African Americans in particular, other research has addressed women in male-dominated fields, such as math and science in which stereotypes hold them to be of lower ability (Eccles & Jacobs, 1987; Inzlicht & Ben Zeev, 2000; Oswald & Harvey, 2000–2001; Quinn & Spencer, 2001; Spencer et al., 1999). Also, there is some work on students with (learning) disabilities. The message of this research is that disidentification, or disengagement, may be one way in which members of stigmatized groups can protect their self-worth in the case of low expectations, or in the case of negative stereotypes, prejudice and discrimination.

We have already discussed how perceptions of failure may lead to disidentification. Here we will discuss how stereotype threat, or prejudice and discrimination may lead to domain disidentification. After we outline what theorists have said about the relationship between stigma and disidentification, we review the empirical evidence for a link between stigma and disidentification.

Stereotype Threat as a Precursor of Disidentification

As outlined in the theory of stereotype threat, experienced stereotype threat is assumed to be one major precursor of disengagement and disidentification (Crocker et al., 1998; Spencer et al., 1999; Steele, 1992, 1997, 1998). Stereotype threat occurs when a negative stereotype about a group to which one belongs becomes self-relevant, as a plausible interpretation for something one is doing or for an experience one is having (Steele, 1997 p. 616). Stereotype threat is thought to elicit anxiety and self-doubt, and evaluation anxiety. This anxiety may itself lead a person to disengage or disidentify from the domain (Chipman et al., 1992; Crocker et al., 1998; Osborne, 2000; Spencer et al., 1999; Steele, 1992; Steele, 1995; Steele & Aronson, 1995). The effect of stereotype threat is to lower performance, and lower performance can instigate domain disidentification.

Prejudice and Discrimination as Causes
of Domain Disidentification

More generally, research indicates that awareness of prejudice and discrimination may be a causal factor in the development of domain disidentification. Steele and colleagues have stressed that when members of stigmatized groups become aware that they are devalued in an academic context this can lead them to disengage their feelings of self-worth from academic achievement (Crocker et al., 1998). Furthermore, the stigmatized may show anticipatory disidentification because they are aware that members of their group often experience negative outcomes in a certain domain, or because they are aware that others are biased against them and that they therefore will not be given a fair chance to succeed (also see Allison, 1998; Crocker et al., 1998). Steele (1992) has shown that reducing racial stigma in an educational setting enhances the achievement of African American students. Alarmed by the performance of Black students at Berkeley, Professor Treisman developed the Mathematics Workshop Program based on group study of calculus concepts. The main part of the program was however the allaying of the racial vulnerabilities felt by these students (what Steele calls 'wise' schooling') by stressing their potential, and reinforcing this with challenging honors level work. In a very short time the students in the program were outperforming their White and Asian counterparts, and they graduated at comparable rates to the Berkeley average.

Students may disengage altogether from the academic domain, or may develop a distrust specifically of performance feedback when they realize that stereotypes, prejudice and discrimination make performance feedback less reliable (see Major, 1995 for evidence). Awareness of prejudice or discrimination may also lead more generally to disengagement from the opinions of others, or from the opinion of the dominant group in particular (Crocker et al., 1998; Major, 1995). Terrell and Terrell (1981) use the concept of cultural mistrust to refer to mistrust of the higher status, dominant group. They find evidence that Black students with high levels of cultural mistrust may disidentify from high status occupational domains (Terrell, Terrell, & Miller, 1993).

Evidence for Disidentification From Stigma Research

Does research conducted with members of stigmatized groups support the notion that stigma can lead to disidentification? Indirect evidence comes from research on achievement and self-esteem. Although African American students under-perform relative to White students, African

American students have consistently been found to evidence levels of self-esteem equal to or greater than White American students (Crocker & Major, 1989; Graham, 1994; Hoelter, 1983; Hughes & Demo, 1989; Porter & Washington, 1979; Rosenberg, 1979; Simmons, 1978; Wylie, 1979). It thus appears than Black students may be basing their sense of self-worth on domains other than academic achievement. In the early years of research on this topic, Rosenberg and Simmons (1971) hypothesized that school and work domains would be less salient in the global self-esteem of Blacks than of Whites as these are domains in which Whites dominate Blacks (also see Rosenberg, 1979). Their research supported this hypothesis. In two large studies of adolescents, Winston, Eccles and colleagues also found that the academic self-concept and achievement of African American students was not as highly linked to global self-esteem as was the case amongst White students (Winston, Eccles, Senior, & Vida, 1997). As the ability self-concepts and global self-esteem of these students were very positive despite poorer performance, the results suggest that they were discounting performance feedback as an indicator of their ability. Other researchers have found what appears to be higher (compensatory) self-esteem in other domains. For example, Hare and Castenell (1985) found Black students to have lower school achievement but higher peer group self-esteem, perhaps explaining their overall global self-esteem levels comparable to Whites (also see Hare, 1987; Heiss & Owens, 1972). Although we might then expect that members of stigmatized groups would place less value on education and educational achievement, and that this may be in part responsible for lower academic performance of African American students (McCarthy & Yancey, 1971), empirical evidence is mixed. Parents of African American children appear to value education as much as parents of White school children, and both Black and White children believe that a good education pays off (Mickelson, 1981; Steinberg, Dornbusch, & Brown, 1992). However, Steinberg and colleagues did find that Black students were less likely to believe that negative consequences would follow from *not* getting a good education. Also, although Mickelson (1990) found that Black and White students had equally positive abstract values towards education, the *concrete* attitudes towards education held by the Black students in her study were significantly less positive than those of White students. At the college level too, there is evidence pointing towards disidentification. Black college students tend to be less satisfied and more alienated than White students (Bennett & Okinaka, 1990; Dorsey & Jackson, 1995; Suen, 1983; Walden, 1994). Moreover, dissatisfaction and alienation tend to increase among Black students over the college years, while they decrease among White students (Bennett & Okinaka, 1990). Dissatisfaction and alienation appear particularly strong at historically White colleges, and less so at Historically Black colleges (Astin, 1993).

However, these studies tend to examine academic disidentification only indirectly. Osborne (1995) directly examined the evidence for a dissociation between academic performance and self-esteem using the National Education Longitudinal Study, a large national study of U.S. high school students. He found that during high school, the self-esteem of African American students became increasingly less related to academic performance, suggesting that African American students are devaluing the academic domain as a source of their self-esteem (Osborne, 1995, 1997a, 1997b). The effects were strongest among African American boys, but occurred to a lesser degree, and somewhat later, among African American girls as well. Meanwhile, the correlation between achievement and global self-esteem remained stable for White boys and girls. A further study showed no evidence of academic disidentification among Hispanic students (Osborne, 1997b). Major and colleagues have also found direct evidence for disidentification amongst Black college students: In one study Black and White students were given a standardized ability test followed by negative or positive performance feedback (Major et al., 1998). The feedback was followed by a self-esteem measure. Major and colleagues found that White students showed the expected response of high self-esteem following success and low self-esteem following failure. However, Black participants showed no reaction to the positive or negative feedback - their self-esteem was not responsive to either feedback. Study 2 showed that Black students were both chronically more disengaged from the intellectual domain than White students (on the Intellectual Orientation Inventory, see Major, 1995), and that racial priming led to a shorter-term situational disengagement. Major (1995) found disidentified and disengaged Black college students to have lower grade point averages, even when controlling for Scholastic Aptitude Test scores (SATs). Moreover, she found that Black students who were not doing so well in college had higher self-esteem as they were less invested in school, whereas Black students doing well in college showed higher self-esteem following high investment in school. There is also evidence that academic disidentification is influenced by perceiving discrimination and prejudice. Taylor and colleagues found that the more discrimination African American high school students perceived, the less important they considered academic achievement, and the less engaged they were in their school work (Taylor, Casten, Flickinger, Roberts, & Fulmore, 1994). The alternative process by which these students then maintain positive self-worth was not identified.

Many studies of domain disidentification have used existing low status or stigmatized groups. However, an experimental paradigm is also being developed to study the basic processes involved in disidentification with experimentally created, or minimal, low status groups (Major, Sciacchitano, & Crocker, 1993; Schmader & Major, 1999). Schmader and Major

(1999) showed that lower ingroup performance can lead members of stigmatized groups to disidentify from a domain (however, it can also increase it, see Major et al., 1993). Schmader and Major provided participants with positive or negative feedback about the performance of existing (gender) or experimentally created in- and outgroups. When the ingroup scored lower on the attribute, participants also believed that they personally were less good on the attribute, and this perception in part mediated the effects of group performance on the devaluation of the attribute. Studies by Major and colleagues (1998) provide evidence that features of the social context may play an important role in disengagement. They show that domain disidentification is particularly likely to occur in situations in which negative stereotypes, expectations of racial bias or expectations of poor performance are primed. Also, disidentification may become more chronic if prejudice and discrimination are a relatively stable feature of the surrounding environment (Major & Schmader, 1998). As a group, this evidence thus suggests that members of stigmatized groups may disidentify following lower performance by their group on the domain. The perception of unfair treatment may enhance disidentification.

Academic Disidentification Among Learning Disabled Students

Most research on the impact of low status on disidentification has focused on members of ethnic minority groups. Another group potentially at risk is students with learning disabilities. As these students too tend to underperform academically relative to other students, they may disidentify from the academic domain in order to protect the self from the negative comparison. Research tends to find that students with learning disabilities have more negative perceptions of their academic abilities, but not of their abilities in other domains such as athletics, social acceptance or physical appearance. Also, these students do not necessarily have lower global self-evaluation (see Clever, Bear, & Juvonen, 1992 for a review). In fact, it appears that the self-concept of only some students with learning disabilities suffers under their lower performance. One possible explanation for this is that many students with learning disabilities devalue the importance of the academic domain. In fact, some have suggested that to increase feelings of self-worth, professionals working with learning disabled students should encourage disidentification on domains in which these students are unable to compete (Mayberry, 1990).

Harter and colleagues have found some evidence for such disidentification in a study with normal, behaviorally disordered and learning disabled adolescents (Harter et al., 1998). They found that students better able to discount domains in which they did not do well had higher self-worth. Weisman (1998) similarly found that academic and global self-worth among learning disabled adult college students suffered over time as they were unable to discount the academic domain. However, not all the empirical evidence supports the importance of disidentification in protecting self-worth. In fact, researchers sometimes find that learning disabled children are well aware that they are less academically competent, do not disidentify from the academic domain, and yet maintain positive feelings about the self, often equal to those of normal achieving students (e.g., Clever et al., 1992; Kloomak & Cosden, 1994). For example, Clever and colleagues examined the self-perceptions of learning disabled, low achieving, and normal achieving students in an integrated classroom setting. They found that children with learning disabilities and children with low achievement had more negative perceptions of scholastic competence, but had equal perceptions of self-worth, despite the fact that they considered scholastic competence as important as the normal achieving children did. Various researchers point out that it may be difficult for these students to disidentify from a domain that is so highly valued by most (Clever et al., 1992; Harter, 1985). Nevertheless, why self-worth then does not suffer is unclear. Harter (1986) suggests that these children may be selecting a more specific lower status reference group with which to compare even when in an integrated setting (see also Crocker & Major, 1989; Tajfel & Turner, 1986). They may also be denying or distorting their performance, may be answering in a socially desirable manner, or be responding regarding their ideal versus actual self. Of course, without further evidence this remains an open question.

Disidentification as a Group Norm

Some research suggests that domain disidentification can become embedded in a peer culture. John Ogbu has been a major force in this research. Ogbu and colleagues suggest that Black students experience ambivalence with regard to academic achievement in response to long-term stigmatization on this domain (e.g., Crouch, 1999; Fordham & Ogbu, 1986; Ogbu, 1991, 1993, 1994). More generally, Ogbu and colleagues suggest that long-term stigmatization can result in "cultural inversion"—a tendency for minorities to regard certain forms of behavior as inappropriate for the ingroup as they are associated with the majority group (Ogbu, 1992). In the case of African Americans, for example, ingroup members who try to behave as White Americans, try to cross cultural boundaries or "act White" in forbidden domains face opposition from the ethnic group (Fordham & Ogbu, 1986). As a result, a norm can be transmitted to group members regarding disidentification from domains in which the group has low status, or domains perceived to be associated with the higher status group. This norm may also be enforced by pressure, and can result in the group rejecting those who resist domain disidentification. A number of other researchers have also suggested that protective disidentification can become a group norm, with students reacting to a shared sense of threat in a particular domain (Crocker et al., 1998; Steele, 1992).

In various studies, researchers have found support for such a process (Fordham & Ogbu, 1986; Gibson & Ogbu, 1991; Haw, 1991; Mickelson, 1981; Rovner, 1981; Solomon, 1992). Fordham and Ogbu showed that coping with the burden of "acting White" affected both high achieving and low achieving students in a Washington DC high school (Fordham & Ogbu, 1986). This resulted in more difficulty in accepting academic attitudes and practices, in less time spent on educational goals, and in strategies to camouflage academic pursuit and achievement. Often students would take up alternative "Black" domains such as athletic or team activities to mute perceptions of engagement in academics. High achieving students would clown around in order to withdraw attention from their academic pursuits. In a large study of high school students, Steinberg and colleagues found evidence that the absence of peer support for achievement among Black and Latino students undermines academic achievement, whereas among White and Asian students positive peer support for academic achievement tends to positively affect achievement (Steinberg et al., 1992).

The process of disidentification as a group norm has also received substantial criticism. The criticisms level themselves both at parts of the process outlined by Ogbu and colleagues (Kromhout & Vedder, 1996), and question the extensiveness of the phenomenon described (Cook & Ludwig, 1998). A number of researchers have found relatively little evidence for "acting White" effects (e.g., Bergin & Cooks, 1995; Spencer, Noll, Stoltzfus, & Harpalani, 2001). Others have found "acting White" effects under subpopulations of students (Collins Eaglin & Karabenick, 1993; Witherspoon, Speight, & Thomas, 1997), with specific groups of peers -such as peers outside the school setting (Datnow & Cooper, 1997), or in particular schools. Bergin and Cooks (1995) for example, suggest that "acting White" processes are more likely to get started in racially balanced schools in which there may be more racial polarization than in non-balanced schools. Sometimes academic disidentification is found but it does not seem to originate from or be enforced by the ethnic group. For example, Taylor and colleagues (Taylor et al., 1994) found that academic disidentification increased as awareness of discrimination increased, but actually decreased as students were more identified with their ethnic group. Last, students sometimes report being accused of "acting White" but deny that it affects achievement (Bergin & Cooks, 1996). Of course it is not clear that students have to be aware of the process for "acting White" to occur.

Regardless of the pervasiveness of the phenomena, we believe that the message from Ogbu and colleagues' research is a very valuable one in it's more abstract sense: that members of low status groups in a society may develop negative attitudes towards the status relevant domain as a result of long-term low outcomes on this domain, and low expectation of change. Experience with limited success in a domain, or with limited opportunity, prejudice and discrimination, can lead members of low status groups to disidentify from the domain that best represents their low status. Ogbu further suggests that these processes are especially likely to occur amongst minorities who are in the society involuntarily (caste-like, nonimmigrant minorities who have been denied assimilation). Whether the group entered the society voluntarily or not can be diagnostic (as it is for Black Americans), but may simply be a distal indicator of a more important variable: the relationship of the low status group to the dominant group and the status relevant domain. In our view, members of what were originally 'voluntary' minority groups in Ogbu's definition (Asian Americans, some Latinos), can become 'involuntary' minority groups when their low status in the society becomes more permanent and with less hope of change as it is for African Americans. Such groups may then begin to disidentify from domains in which their group is not doing well, or is experiencing negative stereotypes, prejudice and discrimination. We believe such processes are occurring with 'voluntary' minority groups in various countries: Examples are some groups of later generation Latinos in the United States (e.g., see Portes & MacLeod, 1996, 1999; Portes, Parker, & Cobas, 1980), and groups of Moroccan and Antillean boys in the Netherlands (Kromhout & Vedder, 1996). Viewed in this way, Ogbu's theory has much value. There is clearly a need for research that examines the conditions under which "acting White" effects, or disidentification from status relevant domains more generally, tend to occur and become group norms.

In summary, research on the relationship between stigma and domain disidentification suggests that stigma may instigate several processes that increase the likelihood of domain disidentification. On average, members of disadvantaged groups are lower achievers on the status relevant domain. To protect the self, they may disidentify from this domain. Their exposure to prejudice and discrimination may lead them to distrust performance feedback, or protectively disengage from status relevant domains altogether. They may also select alternative domains on which to base self-worth. Threats from existing stereotypes may reproduce lower achievement, and this lower achievement may itself lead to disidentification. Moreover, stereotype threat may provoke anxiety and thus encourage domain disidentification. The provocative research by Ogbu and colleagues suggests that domain disidentification may become a group norm, in which members of low status groups reinforce each other's disidentification, and may even pressure those who do not comply to disidentify. While the evidence for the extensiveness of this phenomenon is mixed, in our view the process itself is consistent with the theoretical literature.

SUMMARY

In this review, we have attempted to show that theory and research on domain disidentification can be found in quite divergent literatures. As a result, various concepts are used: domain disidentification, lowered investment, disengagement, and discounting, to name just a few. Distinctions are made between placing less value on performance feedback, devaluing a specific domain, and dissociating a particular domain from one's overall sense of self-worth. Moreover, disidentification can involve letting go of a status relevant domain as well as the selection of a new domain on which to base one's sense of self-worth. Such distinctions are important as these disidentification processes can occur independently from each other.

The reviewed literature tends to suggest that domain disidentification occurs primarily in response to a self-threat, usually low performance or status on a particular domain. Research shows that members of low status groups will choose other strategies to protect self worth, in particular attempts at individual mobility, or attempts to improve the group status, before resorting to cognitive strategies that leave the low status intact. Domain disidentification may be an individual strategy designed to restore personal self-worth, or a group strategy designed to protect collective self-worth. Lower group performance can then also trigger domain disidentification, as can low expectations for future performance. The reviewed literature suggests that individuals are particularly likely to disidentify when they perceive low control over outcomes. Similarly, low outcomes perceived as justified are likely to increase tendencies to disidentify. Nevertheless, the reviewed literature also shows that individuals experiencing unjustified low outcomes will disidentify if they have no hope that things will change. Also, research from the stigma perspective suggests that salient stereotypes, prejudice or discrimination may increase the likelihood that an individual will disengage his or her sense of self-worth from a status relevant domain, and choose an alternative domain on which the maintenance of positive self-worth is more easily accomplished.

Disidentification is likely to result in lower motivation and achievement on the status relevant domain. It can also result in lower trust of feedback on the domain, little response to low or high performance, the devaluing of the domain, as well as protective withdrawal from the situation, and devaluation of settings relevant for the domain. Research by Eccles and colleagues suggests that disidentification may be especially likely to affect the choices individuals make. Thus we might expect major or career decisions to be affected by disidentification. Achievement meanwhile appears to be more influenced by expectancies of future success.

The reviewed literature also suggests some conditions that may moderate the tendency to disidentify from a domain. Our own work suggests that the presence of outgroup members may make it difficult for members of a low status group to disidentify from a domain. The presence of ingroup members, and pressure from them, may make it easier and more likely that a status relevant domain is abandoned as a basis for self-worth. More generally, norms or pressures in the social context are likely to impact the possibilities members of low status groups have to disidentify. Any condition that increases threat is likely to increase tendencies toward disidentification: Thus when low status group members are highly identified with their group, and when the status difference is highly salient, they are more likely to feel a need to restore positive self-worth through disidentification. Moreover, the impossibility of future change is likely to increase tendencies to disidentify - thus status differences that are stable, legitimate and impermeable are likely to increase tendencies towards disidentification.

Disidentification can affect any individual facing a self-threat. However, it may be particularly likely to influence members of groups that have low status. Thus, members of ethnic or cultural minority groups, women in traditional male fields, and members of groups low in socioeconomic status may be particularly at risk of disidentification in domains in which they have traditionally underachieved. Students with learning disabilities may be at risk particularly in mainstream classrooms in which they are unable to restrict their social comparisons. Most of the evidence for disidentification has been found amongst groups that have long faced disadvantage, such as African American students in the United States. Nevertheless, members of lower status groups will never choose disidentification easily. Domain disidentification is a two edged sword, affording self-protection and enhancement at the cost of motivation and thus declining performance. Eventually, domain disidentification reproduces the group differences between the high and low status group.

Solutions for reducing domain disidentification can be found in changes in structure and in context. When status differences are perceived as legitimate, segregating low and high status groups away from each other may afford the best protection for self-worth. Thus students with learning disabilities may profit most from high quality separate schools targeting others with similar disabilities. When domain disidentification results from illegitimate low group status and little hope that there will be future increases in status, the solutions are clearly structural. More equal outcomes between the high and low status group will undo the need for domain disidentification. In the meantime, reducing negative stereotypes, and lessening prejudice and discrimination against the low status group will reduce the need for protective domain disidentification. Moreover, changes in context can be attempted in the meantime: The classroom emphasis can be moved from attainment to intrinsic task interest, and such changes are effective in maintaining intrinsic interest in the task and domain. Our own research suggests that an emphasis in the local environment on the value and importance of the academic domain is likely to reduce tendencies to disidentify. Also, it seems that the possibility of identification with an alternative domain in addition to the status relevant domain may lessen the need for disidentification from the status relevant domain.

Some New Directions

The above makes clear that there is now a relatively good understanding of what may cause disidentification. Several lines of evidence all suggest that disidentification may result when an individual performs less well than he or she would like, feels threatened, and wishes to restore positive feelings of self-worth. This may be particularly likely when this happens to a group with a history of low achievement in a setting that does not stress domain importance. Nevertheless, a review of the literature also suggests that despite the frequent occurrence of these conditions, domain disidentification does not always result. In fact, it often does not result. Our own interest then, is in what factors may moderate the tendency to disidentify. In our recent research we have been focusing on two factors: the salience of the difference between own and others' achievement, and restrictions in the social situation that may prevent disidentification despite threats to self-worth.

The Salience of the Difference Between Own and Others' Achievement

For the disidentification process to start, a self-threat has to be experienced. This usually comes in the form of a negative achievement comparison between the self and others. Despite objective differences between one's own achievement and that of others, such a threat may not always be subjectively experienced. Evidence from various sources suggests that individuals can choose the comparisons they make, but also that the social environment places restrictions on the social comparisons individuals can choose (e.g., Diener & Fujita, 1997; see Van Laar, Derks, & Van Tongeren, 2003 for a review). Such evidence can be found in the general social comparison literature (Hyman, 1942; Rogers, Smith, & Coleman, 1978; Verkuyten & De Jong, 1987; Wood, 1989), in research on the social comparison choices of learning disabled children more specifically (Harter, 1986), in literature on the self-concept (Major et al., 1993; Rosenberg, 1979), and in research on self-evaluation in education (Mac Iver, 1987).

In part, the salience of the difference between one's own and others achievement depends on the availability of others with whom to compare. Early findings from research we are currently conducting suggests that both ingroup and outgroup comparison may increase the likelihood of disidentification, but for different reasons. Comparisons with outgroup members should increase threat, and thus make disidentification more likely (e.g., Gibbons, Benbow, & Gerrard, 1994; see also Inzlicht & Ben Zeev, 2000; Steele, 1997). Much research suggests that comparisons with others doing better than the self is threatening (e.g., Bear, Clever, & Proctor, 1991; Gibbons & Gerrard, 1989; Reis, Gerrard, & Gibbons, 1993; Rosenberg & Simmons, 1971), and thus could increase domain disidentification (see also Browell, 1997; Dryler, 1999; Major & Schmader, 1998; Major et al., 1998). In a study with students attending mixed or separate schools, Lawrie and Brown showed, for example, that the presence of boys led girls to perceive traditional male school subjects as more male and more difficult (Lawrie & Brown, 1992). More generally, various studies on the frog pond effect have shown that students tend to see themselves as more or less competent depending on who is available in their local environment with whom they can compare (Davis, 1966; Marsh, 1990; Marsh, Chessor, Craven, & Roche, 1995; Marsh, Kong, & Hau, 2000; McFarland & Buehler, 1995; St. John, 1971). On the other hand, the safety of ingroup members may allow the individual or group to decide that a domain on which the group does not do well is not important, and may choose an alternative domain on which there is a better chance to show one's ability. Some desegregation research does suggests that segregated schools tend to foster lower aspirations and attainment (Wells & Crain, 1994). A recent study we conducted supported the idea that the presence of ingroup members may increase tendencies to disidentify (Derks et al., 2001). Specifically, it was only participants in the presence of ingroup members who disidentified from the status relevant domain, all participants in the presence of outgroup members continued to identify with the status relevant domain. Such findings would suggest that when members of stigmatized groups become segregated, they may be more likely to disidentify from the academic domain. This occurs when schools are ethnically segregated, when students with learning disabilities attend special as opposed to mainstream schools, and when girls and boys attend separate schools.

We are currently investigating the impact of such in- and outgroup comparison processes on disidentification and the selection of alternative domains. Another factor we are studying is the pressures and restrictions to disidentification offered by the surrounding context. We will discuss this next.

Environmental Restrictions on Tendencies to Disidentify

Whereas comparison with in- and outgroup members can make the status difference more or less salient, and thus influence tendencies to disidentify, the social environment may also restrict opportunities to disidentify (see Ellemers et al., 1999; Ellemers et al., 1997 for discussion of social reality restrictions more generally). In particular, the presence of outgroup members may make it more difficult for a member of a stigmatized group to disidentify from a domain considered valued and important by the higher status outgroup. Various authors have suggested that domains that are valued by a society or powerful group are difficult ones for individuals to discount. Rosenberg and Simmons (1971) maintain for example, that it may be easier for Black children than for White children to disidentify with school as the environments in which White children find themselves may stress the importance of academic diplomas and high grades more explicitly that the environments in which Black children find themselves. Research by Graham and colleagues suggests that having White friends may buffer Black children from disidentifying with school (Graham, Baker, & Wapner, 1984). Crocker and colleagues have suggested that girls may receive more support from their parents on domains on which they do not do well, and that this may prevent disidentification amongst girls more so than amongst boys (Crocker et al., 1998). More generally, researchers working in the area of domain importance have suggested that the importance an individual attaches to a domain is dependent in part on the value of that domain to the group or society at large (also see Clever et al., 1992; Crocker & Major, 1989; Harter, 1985; Pelham, 1995a, 1995b). In fact, Marsh suggests that the importance the group attaches to the domain better explains motivation than do individual importance ratings (e.g., Marsh, 1993b; but see Pelham, 1995a). In our own research we find that the presence of outgroup members may well prevent a low status group from disidentifying with a status relevant domain considered important and valued by the higher status outgroup (Derks et al., 2001). This research suggests that domain disidentification may be more likely in segregated than in integrated schools. Other research we have done suggests that whereas students may disidentify internally, they may well still show motivation to achieve because of external factors, such as teacher or parental pressure (Van Laar, Vedder, & Bemer, 2003). Again, this research suggests the important of external pressures in domain disidentification. We are continuing this research examining the impact of social and contextual pressures on domain disidentification.

In summary, our work has revealed some social structural factors (segregation, awareness of disadvantage, and environmental restrictions) that moderate tendencies to academically disidentify. Specifically, segregation may increase tendencies to disidentify when the student is aware that his or her group does not do well on the domain in question. Segregation may, however, lessen such tendencies when the segregation itself makes the difference in achievement less salient. Segregated schools that foster a sense of student efficacy can thus generate a pool of students highly identified with academic achievement, and with high expectancies and motivation. We hope that over time a better understanding of these processes can inform the debate on classrooms in various societies struggling with the difficulties of achieving optimal performance for heterogeneous groups of students. We need to understand what the advantages and disadvantaged of separate versus integrated classrooms are for the self-perceptions, achievements and aspirations of members of different gender, ethnic, and socio-economic groups. In the Netherlands, for example, school populations are tending to separate into ethnic minority and White populations, following the movements previously occurring in the United States. Also, a recent national education policy is sending students who previously attended special schools back to mainstream schools. Although this may increase performance, the research reviewed suggests that it also could increase negative comparisons. It is therefore important to identify which of these processes is more likely to occur. Similarly, the debate on how to get girls more interested in math and sciences has struggled with the issue of whether separating girls from boys may be one solution. Each of these policies has the potential of increasing disidentification with school amongst already challenged populations. A better understanding of the processes involved will help us provide policymakers with better answers to these social and educational issues.

REFERENCES

Allison, K. W. (1998). Stress and oppressed social category membership. In J. K. Swim & C. Stangor (Eds.), *Prejudice: The target's perspective* (pp. 145–170). San Diego, CA: Academic Press, Inc.

Astin, A. W. (1993). *What matters in college: Four critical years revisited.* San Francisco, CA: Jossey-Bas.

Atkinson, J. W. (1957). Motivational determinants of risk-taking behavior. *Psychological Review, 64*, 359–372.

Atkinson, J. W., & Birch, D. (1978). *Introduction to motivation* (2nd ed.). New York: Van Nostrand.

Barreto, M. (2000). *Identity and strategy in pro-group behaviour.* Free University Amsterdam, Amsterdam.

Barreto, M., Spears, R., Ellemers, N., & Shahinper, K. (2001, February). *Who wants to know? The effect of audience on identity expression among minority group members.* Paper presented at the Society for Personality and Social Psychology, San Antonio, Texas.

Baumeister, R. F. (1998). The self. In D. T. Gilbert & S. T. Fiske (Eds.), *The handbook of social psychology, Vol. 1 (4th ed.)* (pp. 680–740). New York: McGraw-Hill.

Baumeister, R. F., & Jones, E. E. (1978). When self-presentation is constrained by the target's knowledge: Consistency and compensation. *Journal of Personality and Social Psychology, 36*(6), 608–618.

Bear, G. G., Clever, A., & Proctor, W. A. (1991). Self-perceptions of nonhandicapped children and children with learning disabilities in integrated classes. *Journal of Special Education, 24*(4), 409–426.

Bennett, C., & Okinaka, A. M. (1990). Factors related to persistence among Asian, Black, Hispanic, and White undergraduates at a predominantly White university: Comparison between first and fourth year cohorts. *Urban Review, 22*(1), 33–60.

Bergin, D. A. (1999). Influences on classroom interest. *Educational Psychologist, 34*(2), 87–98.

Bergin, D. A., & Cooks, H. C. (1995, April). *"Acting White": Views of high school students in a scholarship incentive program.* Paper presented at the Annual Meeting of the American Educational Research Association, San Francisco, CA.

Bergin, D. A., & Cooks, H. C. (1996, June). *Fear of "Acting White" and perceptions of academic achievement.* Paper presented at the Society for Psychological Study of Social Issues, Ann Arbor, MI.

Brewer, M. B. (1979). In-group bias in the minimal intergroup situation: A cognitive-motivational analysis. *Psychological Bulletin, 86*(2), 307–324.

Brophy, J. (1999). Toward a model of the value aspects of motivation in education: Developing appreciation for particular learning domains and activities. *Educational Psychologist, 34*(2), 75–85.

Browell, E. P. (1997). *Self-concept of learning disabled students as a correlate of inclusion versus resource placement.* Unpublished Doctoral Dissertation, Texas Woman's University.

Buunk, B. P., & Ybema, J. F. (1995). Selective evaluation and coping with stress: Making one's situation cognitively more livable. *Journal of Applied Social Psychology, 25*(17), 1499–1517.

Chan, D. W. (1997). Self-concept domains and global self-worth among Chinese adolescents in Hong Kong. *Personality and Individual Differences, 22*(4), 511–520.

Chipman, S. F., Krantz, D. H., & Silver, R. (1992). Mathematics anxiety and science careers among able college women. *Psychological Science, 3*(5), 292–295.

Clever, A., Bear, G. C., & Juvonen, J. (1992). Discrepancies between competence and importance in self-perceptions of children in integrated classes. *Journal of Special Education, 26*(2), 125–138.

Collins Eaglin, J., & Karabenick, S. A. (1993, April). *Devaluing of academic success by African American students: On "acting White" and "selling out."* Paper presented at the Annual Meeting of the American Educational Research Association, Atlanta, GA.

Cook, P. J., & Ludwig, J. (1998). The burden of "acting White": Do Black adolescents disparage academic achievement? In C. P. M. Jencks (Ed.), *The Black White test score gap* (pp. 375–400). Washington, DC: Brookings Institution.

Covington, M. V. (1999). Caring about learning: The nature and nurturing of subject-matter appreciation. *Educational Psychologist, 34*(2), 127–136.

Covington, M. V., & Teel, K. M. (1996). *Overcoming student failure: Changing motives and incentives for learning.* Washington, DC: American Psychological Association.

Crocker, J., & Major, B. (1989). Social stigma and self-esteem: The self-protective properties of stigma. *Psychological Review, 96*(4), 608–630.

Crocker, J., Major, B., & Steele, C. (1998). Social stigma. In D. T. Gilbert & S. T. Fiske & G. Lindzey (Eds.), *The handbook of social psychology* (4th ed., Vol. 2, pp. 504–553): Boston, MA: Mcgraw-Hill.

Crouch, S. (1999). Being a dummy makes one a real person: The braining down of the education of African Americans. *Journal of Blacks in Higher Education, 24,* 103–105.

Csikszentmihalyi, M. (1993). *The evolving self: A psychology for the third millennium.* New York: Harper/Collins.

Datnow, A., & Cooper, R. (1997). Peer networks of African American students in independent schools: Affirming academic success and racial identity. *Journal of Negro Education, 66*(1), 56–72.

Davis, J. A. (1966). The campus as a frog pond: An application of the theory of relative deprivation to career decisions of college men. *American Journal of Sociology, 72*(1), 17–31.

Derks, B., Van Laar, C., & Wilke, H. (2001, February). *Domain change as a self-esteem enhancing strategy among members of low status groups.* Paper presented at the Society of Personality and Social Psychology, San Antonio, Texas.

Diener, E., & Fujita, F. (1997). Social comparisons and subjective well-being. In B. P. Buunk & F. X. Gibbons (Eds.), *Health, coping, and well being: Perspectives from social comparison theory* (pp. 329–357). Mahwah, NJ: Lawrence Erlbaum Associates.

Doosje, B., Ellemers, N., & Spears, R. (1999). Commitment and intergroup behavior. In N. Ellemers & R. Spears (Eds.), *Social identity: Context, commitment, content* (pp. 84–106). Oxford, England: Blackwell.

Doosje, B., Spears, R., & Koomen, W. (1995). When bad isn't all bad: Strategic use of sample information in generalization and stereotyping. *Journal of Personality and Social Psychology, 69*(4), 642–655.

Dorsey, M. S., & Jackson, A. P. (1995). Afro-American students' perceptions of factors affecting academic performance at a predominantly White school. *Western Journal of Black Studies, 19*(3), 189–195.

Dryler, H. (1999). The impact of school and classroom characteristics on educational choices by boys and girls: A multilevel analysis. *Acta Sociologica, 42*(4), 299–318.

Dweck, C. S., & Leggett, E. L. (1988). A social-cognitive approach to motivation and personality. *Psychological Review, 95*(2), 256–273.

Eccles, J., Midgley, C., & Adler, T. (1984). Grade-related changes in the school environment: Effects on achievement motivation. In J. Nicholls (Ed.), *The development of achievement motivation* (Vol. 3, pp. 282–331). Greenwich, CT: JAI Press.

Eccles, J. S. (1983). Expectancies, values, and academic behaviors. In J. T. Spence (Ed.), *Achievement and achievement motives.* (pp. 75–146). San Francisco, CA: Freeman.

Eccles, J. S., & Jacobs, J. E. (1987). No: Social forces shape math attitudes and performance. In M. R. Walsh (Ed.), *The psychology of women: Ongoing debates* (pp. 341–354). New Haven, CT: Yale University Press.

Eccles, J. S., & Wigfield, A. (1995). In the mind of the actor: The structure of adolescents' achievement task values and expectancy-related beliefs. *Personality and Social Psychology Bulletin, 21*(3), 215–225.

Eccles, J. S., Wigfield, A., Flanagan, C. A., Miller, C., Reuman, D., & Yee, D. (1989). Self-concepts, domain values, and self-esteem: Relations and changes at early adolescence. *Journal of Personality, 57*(2), 283–310.

Ellemers, N. (1993). The influence of socio-structural variables on identity management strategies. In W. Stroebe & M. Hewstone (Eds.), *European Review of Social Psychology* (Vol. 4, pp. 27–57): John Wiley & Sons Ltd.

Ellemers, N., Barreto, M., & Spears, R. (1999). Commitment and strategic responses to social context. In N. Ellemers & R. Spears (Eds.), *Social identity: Context, commitment, content* (pp. 127–146). Oxford, England: Blackwell Science Ltd.

Ellemers, N., Doosje, B., Van Knippenberg, A., & Wilke, H. (1992). Status protection in high status minority groups. *European Journal of Social Psychology, 22*(2), 123–140.

Ellemers, N., Spears, R., & Doosje, B. (2002). Self and social identity. *Annual Review of Psychology, 53*, 161–186.

Ellemers, N., van Dyck, C., Hinkle, S., & Jacobs, A. (2000). Intergroup differentiation in social context: Identity needs versus audience constraints. *Social Psychology Quarterly, 63*(1), 60–74.

Ellemers, N., & Van Knippenberg, A. (1997). Stereotyping in social context. In R. Spears & P. J. Oakes & N. Ellemers & S. A. Haslam (Eds.), *The social psychology of stereotyping and group life.* (pp. 208–235). Oxford, England: Blackwell Publishers, Inc.

Ellemers, N., Van Knippenberg, A., De Vries, N., & Wilke, H. (1988). Social identification and permeability of group boundaries. *European Journal of Social Psychology, 18*(6), 497–513.

Ellemers, N., Van Knippenberg, A., & Wilke, H. A. (1990). The influence of permeability of group boundaries and stability of group status on strategies of individual mobility and social change. *British Journal of Social Psychology, 29*(3), 233–246.

Ellemers, N., & Van Rijswijk, W. (1997). Identity needs versus social opportunities: The use of group-level and individual-level identity management strategies. *Social Psychology Quarterly, 60*(1), 52–65.

Ellemers, N., Van Rijswijk, W., Roefs, M., & Simons, C. (1997). Bias in intergroup perceptions: Balancing group identity with social reality. *Personality & Social Psychology Bulletin, 23*(2), 186–198.

Ellemers, N., Wilke, H., & Van Knippenberg, A. (1993). Effects of the legitimacy of low group or individual status on individual and collective status-enhancement strategies. *Journal of Personality and Social Psychology, 64*(5), 766–778.

Festinger, L. (1954). A theory of social comparison processes. *Human Relations, 7*, 117–140.

Festinger, L. (1957). *A theory of cognitive dissonance.* Evanston, Ill: Row Peterson.

Finn, J. D. (1989). Withdrawing from school. *Review of Educational Research, 59*(2), 117–142.

Finn, J. D. (1993). *School engagement and students at risk* (NCES–93–470). Washington, DC: National Center for Education Statistics.

Finn, J. D., & Cox, D. (1992). Participation and withdrawal among fourth-grade pupils. *American Educational Research Journal, 29*(1), 141–162.

Fordham, S., & Ogbu, J. U. (1986). Black students' school success: Coping with the "burden of acting White." *Urban Review, 18*(3), 176–206.

Gibbons, F. X., Benbow, C. P., & Gerrard, M. (1994). From top dog to bottom half: Social comparison strategies in response to poor performance. *Journal of Personality and Social Psychology, 67*(4), 638–652.

Gibbons, F. X., & Gerrard, M. (1989). Effects of upward and downward social comparison on mood states. *Journal of Social and Clinical Psychology, 8*(1), 14–31.

Gibson, M. A., & Ogbu, J. U. (Eds.). (1991). *Minority status and schooling: A comparative study of immigrant and involuntary minorities.* New York: Garland Publishing, Inc.

Goodenow, C. (1993). The psychological sense of school membership among adolescents: Scale development and educational correlates. *Psychology in the Schools, 30*(1), 79–90.

Goodenow, C., & Grady, K. E. (1993). The relationship of school belonging and friends' values to academic motivation among urban adolescent students. *Journal of Experimental Education, 62*(1), 60–71.

Graham, C., Baker, R. W., & Wapner, S. (1984). Prior interracial experience and Black student transition into predominantly White colleges. *Journal of Personality and Social Psychology, 47*(5), 1146–1154.

Graham, S. (1994). Motivation in African Americans. *Review of Educational Research, 64*(1), 55–117.

Hamid, P. N., & Cheng, C. (1995). Self-esteem and self-concept clarity in Chinese students. *Social Behavior and Personality, 23*(3), 273–284.

Hare, B. R. (1987). Structural inequality and the endangered status of Black youth. *Journal of Negro Education, 56*(1), 100–110.

Hare, B. R., & Castenell, L. A., Jr. (1985). No place to run, no place to hide: Comparative status and future prospects of black boys. In M. B. Spencer & G. K. Brookins (Eds.), *Beginnings: The social and affective development of black children. Child psychology* (pp. 201–214). Hillsdale, NJ: Lawrence Erlbaum.

Harter, S. (1985). *Manual for the self-perception profile for children.* Denver, CO: University of Denver.

Harter, S. (1986). Processes underlying the construction, maintenance and enhancement of the self-concept in children. In J. Suls & A. G. Greenwald (Eds.), *Psychological perspectives on the self* (Vol. 3, pp. 136–182). Hillsdale: Lawrence Erlbaum.

Harter, S. (1993). Causes and consequences of low self-esteem in children and adolescents. In R. F. Baumeister (Ed.), *Self esteem: The puzzle of low self regard.* (pp. 87–116). New York: Plenum Press.

Harter, S. (1999). *The construction of the self: A developmental perspective.* New York: The Guilford Press.

Harter, S., Whitesell, N. R., & Junkin, L. J. (1998). Similarities and differences in domain-specific and global self-evaluations of learning-disabled, behaviorally disordered, and normally achieving adolescents. *American Educational Research Journal, 35*(4), 653–680.

Haw, K. F. (1991). Interactions of gender and race-a problem for teachers? A review of the emerging literature. *Educational Research, 33*(1), 12–21.

Heatherton, T. F., Kleck, R. E., Hebl, M. R., & Hull, J. G. (Eds.). (2000). *The social psychology of stigma.* New York: The Guilford Press.

Heiss, J., & Owens, S. (1972). Self-evaluations of Blacks and Whites. *American Journal of Sociology, 78*(2), 360–370.

Hinkle, S., & Schopler, J. (1979). Ethnocentrism in the evaluation of group products. In W. Austin & S. Worchel (Eds.), *The social psychology of intergroup relations* (pp. 160–173). Monterey, CA: Brooks/Cole.

Hinkle, S., Taylor, L. A., Fox Cardamone, L., & Ely, P. G. (1998). Social identity and aspects of social creativity: Shifting to new dimensions of intergroup comparison. In S. Worchel & J. F. Morales (Eds.), *Social identity: International perspectives* (pp. 166–179). London, UK: Sage Publications.

Hoelter, J. W. (1983). Factorial invariance and self-esteem: Reassessing race and sex differences. *Social Forces, 61*(3), 834–846.

Hoge, D. R., & McCarthy, J. D. (1984). Influence of individual and group identity salience in the global self-esteem of youth. *Journal of Personality and Social Psychology, 47*(2), 403–414.

Hughes, M., & Demo, D. H. (1989). Self-perceptions of Black Americans: Self-esteem and personal efficacy. *American Journal of Sociology, 95*(1), 132–159.

Hyman, H. H. (1942). The psychology of status. *Archives of Psychology Columbia University*(269), 94.

Inzlicht, M., & Ben Zeev, T. (2000). A threatening intellectual environment: Why females are susceptible to experiencing problem-solving deficits in the presence of males. *Psychological Science, 11*(5), 365–371.

Jackson, L. A., Sullivan, L. A., Harnish, R., & Hodge, C. N. (1996). Achieving positive social identity: Social mobility, social creativity, and permeability of group boundaries. *Journal of Personality and Social Psychology, 70*(2), 241–254.

James, W. (1890). *The principles of psychology* (Vol. 1). New York: Henry Holt and Company.

Klinger, E. (1975). Consequences of commitment to and disengagement from incentives. *Psychological Review, 82*(1), 1–25.

Kloomak, S., & Cosden, M. (1994). Self-concept in children with learning disabilities: The relationship between global self-concept, academic "discounting," nonacademic self-concept, and perceived social support. *Learning Disability Quarterly, 17*(2), 140–153.

Kromhout, M., & Vedder, P. (1996). Cultural inversion in Afro-Caribbean children in the Netherlands. *Anthropology and Education Quarterly, 27*(4), 568–586.

Lawrie, L., & Brown, R. (1992). Sex stereotypes, school subject preferences and career aspirations as a function of single/mixed-sex schooling and presence/absence of an opposite sex sibling. *British Journal of Educational Psychology, 62*(1), 132–138.

Lemaine, G. (1974). Social differentiation and social originality. *European Journal of Social Psychology, 4*(1), 17–52.

Lemaine, G., Kasterztein, J., & Personnaz, B. (1978). Social differentiation. In H. Tajfel (Ed.), *Differentiation between social groups: Studies in the social psychology of intergroup relations* (pp. 269–300). London, UK: Academic Press.

Levin, S. (1996). *A social psychological approach to understanding intergroup attitudes in the United States and Israel.* Unpublished doctoral dissertation, University of California, Los Angeles.

Liu, T. J., & Steele, C. M. (1986). Attributional analysis as self-affirmation. *Journal of Personality and Social Psychology, 51*(3), 531–540.

Mac Iver, D. (1987). Classroom factors and student characteristics predicting students' use of achievement standards during ability self-assessment. *Child Development, 58*(5), 1258–1271.

Major, B. (1995, August). *Academic performance, self-esteem, and race: The role of disidentification.* Paper presented at the American Psychological Association Convention, New York.

Major, B., & Schmader, T. (1998). Coping with stigma through psychological disengagement. In J. K. Swim & C. Stangor (Eds.), *Prejudice: The target's perspective.* (pp. 219–241). San Diego, CA: Academic Press, Inc.

Major, B., Sciacchitano, A. M., & Crocker, J. (1993). In-group versus out-group comparisons and self-esteem. *Personality and Social Psychology Bulletin, 19*(6), 711–721.

Major, B., Spencer, S., Schmader, T., Wolfe, C., & Crocker, J. (1998). Coping with negative stereotypes about intellectual performance: The role of psychological disengagement. *Personality and Social Psychology Bulletin, 24*(1), 34–50.

Mark, M. M. (1985). Expectations, procedural justice, and alternative reactions to being deprived of a desired outcome. *Journal of Experimental Social Psychology, 21*(2), 114–137.

Mark, M. M., & Folger, R. (1984). Responses to relative deprivation: A conceptual framework. *Review of Personality and Social Psychology, 5,* 192–218.

Marsh, H. W. (1986). Global self-esteem: Its relation to specific facets of self-concept and their importance. *Journal of Personality and Social Psychology, 51*(6), 1224–1236.

Marsh, H. W. (1990). Influences of internal and external frames of reference on the formation of math and english self-concepts. *Journal of Educational Psychology, 82*(1), 107–116.

Marsh, H. W. (1993a). Academic self-concept: Theory, measurement, and research. In J. M. Suls (Ed.), *The self in social perspective. Psychological perspectives on the self* (Vol. 4, pp. 59–98). Hillsdale, NJ: Lawrence Erlbaum Associates, Inc.

Marsh, H. W. (1993b). Relations between global and specific domains of self: The importance of individual importance, certainty, and ideals. *Journal of Personality and Social Psychology, 65*(5), 975–992.

Marsh, H. W., Chessor, D., Craven, R., & Roche, L. (1995). The effect of gifted and talented programs on academic self-concept: The big fish strikes again. *American Educational Research Journal, 32*(2), 285–319.

Marsh, H. W., Kong, C. K., & Hau, K. T. (2000). Longitudinal multilevel models of the big-fish-little-pond effect on academic self-concept: Counterbalancing contrast and reflected-glory effects in Hong Kong schools. *Journal of Personality and Social Psychology, 78*(2), 337–349.

Marsh, H. W., & Shavelson, R. (1985). Self-concept: Its multifaceted, hierarchical structure. *Educational Psychologist, 20*(3), 107–123.

Maslow, A. H. (1970). *Motivation and personality* (2nd ed.). New York: Harper and Row.

Mayberry, W. (1990). Self-esteem in children: Considerations for measurement and intervention. *American Journal of Occupational Therapy, 44*(8), 729–734.

McCarthy, J. D., & Yancey, W. L. (1971). Uncle Tom and Mr. Charlie: Metaphysical pathos in the study of racism and personal disorganization. *American Journal of Sociology, 76*(4), 648–672.

McFarland, C., & Buehler, R. (1995). Collective self-esteem as a moderator of the frog-pond effect in reactions to performance feedback. *Journal of Personality and Social Psychology, 68*(6), 1055–1070.

Meece, J. L., Wigfield, A., & Eccles, J. S. (1990). Predictors of math anxiety and its influence on young adolescents' course enrollment intentions and performance in mathematics. *Journal of Educational Psychology, 82*(1), 60–70.

Merton, R. K. (1957). *Social theory and social structure* (Rev. ed.). New York: The Free Press.

Messick, D. M., & Mackie, D. M. (1989). Intergroup relations. *Annual Review of Psychology, 40*, 45–81.

Mickelson, R. A. (1981, April). *Black working class adolescents' attitudes toward academic achievement.* Paper presented at the Annual Meetings of the American Educational Research Association, Los Angeles, CA.

Mickelson, R. A. (1990). The attitude-achievement paradox among Black adolescents. *Sociology of Education, 63*(1), 44–61.

Middleton, J. A., & Toluk, Z. (1999). First steps in the development of an adaptive theory of motivation. *Educational Psychologist, 34*(2), 99–112.

Miller, H. M. (1998). *Perceived competence, social support, and global self-worth: A cross-cultural study at the Finnish elementary school level.* Unpublished Doctoral Dissertation, State University of New York at Albany.

Muldoon, O. T. (2000). Social group membership and self-perceptions in Northern Irish children: A longitudinal study. *British Journal of Developmental Psychology, 18*(1), 65–80.

Newmann, F. M. (1992). *Student engagement and achievement in American secondary schools.* New York: Teachers College Press.

Ogbu, J. U. (1986). Structural constrains in school desegregation. In J. Prager & D. Longshore & M. Seeman (Eds.), *School desegregation research: New directions in situational analysis.* New York: Plenum Press.

Ogbu, J. U. (1991). Minority coping responses and school experience. *Journal of Psychohistory, 18*(4), 433–456.

Ogbu, J. U. (1992). Understanding cultural diversity and learning. *Educational Researcher, 21*(8), 5–14.

Ogbu, J. U. (1993). Differences in cultural frame of reference. Special Issue: International roots of minority child development. *International Journal of Behavioral Development, 16*(3), 483–506.

Ogbu, J. U. (1994). From cultural differences to differences in cultural frame of reference. In P. M. Greenfield & R. R. Cocking (Eds.), *Cross-cultural roots of minority child development.* (pp. 365–391). Hillsdale, NJ: Lawrence Erlbaum.

Osborne, J. W. (1995). Academics, self-esteem, and race: A look at the underlying assumptions of the disidentification hypothesis. *Personality & Social Psychology Bulletin, 21*(5), 449–455.

Osborne, J. W. (1997a). Identification with academics and academic success among community college students. *Community College Review, 25*(1), 59–67.

Osborne, J. W. (1997b). Race and academic disidentification. *Journal of Educational Psychology, 89*(4), 728–735.

Osborne, J. W. (2000, April). *Testing stereotype threat: Does anxiety explain race and sex differences in achievement?* Paper presented at the Annual Meeting of the American Educational Research Association, New Orleans.

Osterman, K. F. (2000). Students' need for belonging in the school community. *Review of Educational Research, 70*(3), 323–367.

Oswald, D. L., & Harvey, R. D. (2000–2001). Hostile environments, stereotype threat, and math performance among undergraduate women. *Current Psychology: Developmental, Learning, Personality, Social, 19*(4), 338–356.

Pascarella, E. T., Terenzini, P. T., & Wolfle, L. M. (1986). Orientation to college and freshman year persistence/withdrawal decisions. *Journal of Higher Education, 57*(2), 155–175.

Pelham, B. W. (1995a). Further evidence for a Jamesian model of self-worth: Reply to Marsh (1995). *Journal of Personality and Social Psychology, 69*(6), 1161–1165.

Pelham, B. W. (1995b). Self-investment and self-esteem: Evidence for a Jamesian model of self-worth. *Journal of Personality and Social Psychology, 69*(6), 1141–1150.

Pelham, B. W., & Swann, W. B. (1989). From self-conceptions to self-worth: On the sources and structure of global self-esteem. *Journal of Personality and Social Psychology, 57*(4), 672–680.

Pintrich, P., & Schunk, D. (1996). *Motivation in education.* Englewood: Prentice Hall.

Pintrich, P. R., & De Groot, E. V. (1990). Motivational and self-regulated learning components of classroom academic performance. *Journal of Educational Psychology, 82*(1), 33–40.

Porter, J. R., & Washington, R. E. (1979). Black identity and self-esteem: A review of studies of Black self-concept, 1968–1978. *Annual Review of Sociology, 5,* 53–74.

Portes, A., & MacLeod, D. (1996). Educational progress of children of immigrants: The roles of class, ethnicity, and school context. *Sociology of Education, 69*(4), 255–275.

Portes, A., & MacLeod, D. (1999). Educating the second generation: Determinants of academic achievement among children of immigrants in the United States. *Journal of Ethnic and Migration Studies, 25*(3), 373–396.

Portes, A., Parker, R. N., & Cobas, J. A. (1980). Assimilation or consciousness: Perceptions of U.S. society among recent Latin American immigrants to the United States. *Social Forces, 59*(1), 200–224.

Quinn, D. M., & Spencer, S. J. (2001). The interference of stereotype threat with women's generation of mathematical problem-solving strategies. *Journal of Social Issues, 57*(1), 55–71.

Reis, T. J., Gerrard, M., & Gibbons, F. X. (1993). Social comparison and the pill: Reactions to upward and downward comparison of contraceptive behavior. *Personality and Social Psychology Bulletin, 19*(1), 13–20.

Rogers, C. M., Smith, M. D., & Coleman, J. M. (1978). Social comparison in the classroom: The relationship between academic achievement and self-concept. *Journal of Educational Psychology, 70*(1), 50–57.

Rosenberg, M. (1979). *Conceiving the self.* New York: Basic Books.

Rosenberg, M., & Simmons, R. G. (1971). *Black and White self-esteem: The urban school child.* Washington, DC: American Sociological Association.

Rovner, R. A. (1981). Ethno-cultural identity and self-esteem: A reapplication of self-attitude formation theories. *Human Relations, 34*(5), 427–434.

Schmader, T., & Major, B. (1999). The impact of ingroup vs outgroup performance on personal values. *Journal of Experimental Social Psychology, 35*(1), 47–67.

Shavelson, R. J., Hubner, J. J., & Stanton, G. C. (1976). Self-concept: Validation of construct interpretations. *Review of Educational Research, 46*(3), 407–441.

Sidanius, J., & Pratto, F. (1999). *Social dominance: An intergroup theory of social hierarchy and oppression.* New York: Cambridge University Press.

Simmons, R. G. (1978). Blacks and high self-esteem: A puzzle. *Social Psychology, 41*(1), 54–57.

Solomon, R. P. (1992). *Black resistance in high school: Forging a separatist culture.* Albany, NY: State University of New York Press.

Spears, R., & Manstead, A. S. (1989). The social context of stereotyping and differentiation. *European Journal of Social Psychology, 19*(2), 101–121.

Spencer, M. B., Noll, E., Stoltzfus, J., & Harpalani, V. (2001). Identity and school adjustment: Revisiting the "acting White" assumption. *Educational Psychologist, 36*(1), 21–30.

Spencer, S. J., Josephs, R. A., & Steele, C. M. (1993). Low self-esteem: The uphill struggle for self-integrity. In F. B. Roy (Ed.), *Self-esteem: The puzzle of low self-regard. Plenum series in social/clinical psychology.* (pp. 21–36). New York: Plenum Press.

Spencer, S. J., Steele, C. M., & Quinn, D. M. (1999). Stereotype threat and women's math performance. *Journal of Experimental Social Psychology, 35*(1), 4–28.

St. John, N. (1971). The elementary classroom as a frog pond: Self-concept, sense of control and social context. *Social Forces, 49*(4), 581–595.

Steele, C. M. (1988). The psychology of self-affirmation: Sustaining the integrity of the self. In B. Leonard (Ed.), *Advances in experimental social psychology* (Vol. 21, pp. 261–302). San Diego, CA: Academic Press, Inc.

Steele, C. M. (1992). Race and the schooling of black Americans. *The Atlantic Monthly, 269*(April), 68–78.

Steele, C. M. (1995). *A burden of suspicion: How stereotypes shape the intellectual identities and performance of women and African Americans* (Unpublished manuscript): Stanford University.

Steele, C. M. (1997). A threat in the air: How stereotypes shape intellectual identity and performance. *American Psychologist, 52*(6), 613–629.

Steele, C. M. (1998). Stereotyping and its threat are real. *American Psychologist, 53*(6), 680–681.

Steele, C. M., & Aronson, J. (1995). Stereotype threat and the intellectual test performance of African Americans. *Journal of Personality and Social Psychology, 69*(5), 797–811.

Steinberg, L., Dornbusch, S. M., & Brown, B. B. (1992). Ethnic differences in adolescent achievement: An ecological perspective. *American Psychologist, 47*(6), 723–729.

Suen, H. K. (1983). Alienation and attrition of Black college students on a predominantly White campus. *Journal of College Student Personnel, 24*(2), 117–121.

Swim, J. K., & Stangor, C. (Eds.). (1998). *Prejudice: The target's perspective.* San Diego, CA: Academic Press, Inc.

Tajfel, H. (1978). Social categorization, social identity and social comparison. In H. Tajfel (Ed.), *Differentiation between social groups: Studies in the social psychology of intergroup relations* (pp. 61–76). London: Academic Press.

Tajfel, H. (1981). Exit and voice in intergroup relations. In H. Tajfel (Ed.), *Human groups and social categories* (pp. 288–308). Cambridge, UK: Cambridge University Press.

Tajfel, H., & Turner, J. (1979). An integrative theory of intergroup conflict. In W. G. Austin & S. Worchel (Eds.), *The social psychology of intergroup relations.* Monterey: Brooks/Cole Publishing Company.

Tajfel, H., & Turner, J. C. (1986). The social identity theory of intergroup behavior. In S. Worchel & W. G. Austin (Eds.), *The psychology of intergroup relations.* Chicago: Nelson-Hall.

Taylor, D. M., & McKirnan, D. J. (1984). Theoretical contributions: A five-stage model of intergroup relations. *British Journal of Social Psychology, 23*(4), 291–300.

Taylor, R. D., Casten, R., Flickinger, S. M., Roberts, D., & Fulmore, C. D. (1994). Explaining the school performance of African-American adolescents. *Journal of Research on Adolescence, 4*(1), 21–44.

Taylor, S. E. (1991). Asymmetrical effects of positive and negative events: The mobilization-minimization hypothesis. *Psychological Bulletin, 110*(1), 67–85.

Taylor, S. E., Wood, J. V., & Lichtman, R. R. (1983). It could be worse: Selective evaluation as a response to victimization. *Journal of Social Issues, 39*(2), 19–40.

Teel, K. M., Debruin Parecki, A., & Covington, M. V. (1998). Teaching strategies that honor and motivate inner-city African-American students: A school/university collaboration. *Teaching and Teacher Education, 14*(5), 479–495.

Terrell, F., & Terrell, S. (1981). An inventory to measure cultural mistrust among Blacks. *Western Journal of Black Studies, 5*(3), 180–185.

Terrell, F., Terrell, S. L., & Miller, F. (1993). Level of cultural mistrust as a function of educational and occupational expectations among Black students. *Adolescence, 28*(111), 573–578.

Tesser, A. (1988). Toward a self-evaluation maintenance model of social behavior. In B. Leonard (Ed.), *Advances in experimental social psychology* (Vol. 21, pp. 181–227). San Diego, CA: Academic Press, Inc.

Tesser, A., & Campbell, J. (1980). Self-definition: The impact of the relative performance and similarity of others. *Social Psychology Quarterly, 43*(3), 341–346.

Tesser, A., & Campbell, J. (1982). A self-evaluation maintenance approach to school behavior. *Educational Psychologist, 17*(1), 1–12.

Tesser, A., Millar, M., & Moore, J. (1988). Some affective consequences of social comparison and reflection processes: The pain and pleasure of being close. *Journal of Personality and Social Psychology, 54*(1), 49–61.

Tesser, A., & Paulhus, D. (1983). The definition of self: Private and public self-evaluation management strategies. *Journal of Personality and Social Psychology, 44*(4), 672–682.

Van Knippenberg, A. (1978). Status differences, comparative relevance and intergroup differentiation. In H. Tajfel (Ed.), *Differentiation between social groups: Studies in the social psychology of intergroup relations.* (pp. 171–199). London, UK: Academic Press.

Van Knippenberg, A. (1984). Intergroup differences in group perceptions. In H. Tajfel (Ed.), *The social dimension: European developments in social psychology* (pp. 560–578). Cambridge, UK: Cambridge University Press.

Van Knippenberg, A. (1989). Strategies of identity management. In J. P. Van Oudenhoven & T. M. Willemsen (Eds.), *Ethnic minorities: Social psychological perspectives* (pp. 59–76). Amsterdam, the Netherlands: Swets & Zeitlinger.

Van Knippenberg, A., & Ellemers, N. (1993). Strategies in intergroup relations. In M. A. Hogg & D. Abrams (Eds.), *Group motivation: Social psychological perspectives.* (pp. 17–32). London, UK: Harvester Wheatsheaf.

Van Knippenberg, A., & Van Oers, H. (1984). Social identity and equity concerns in intergroup perceptions. Special Issue: Intergroup processes. *British Journal of Social Psychology, 23*(4), 351–361.

Van Knippenberg, A., Wilke, H., & De Vries, N. K. (1981). Social comparison on two dimensions. *European Journal of Social Psychology, 11*(3), 267–283.

Van Laar, C., Derks, B., & Van Tongeren, P. (2003). *Stigma and social comparison: Effects on self-evaluation and motivation* (Manuscript under review).

Van Laar, C., & Sidanius, J. (2001). Social status and the academic achievement gap: A social dominance perspective. *Social Psychology of Education*(4), 235–258.

Van Laar, C., Vedder, P., & Bemer, S. (2003). *Disidentification from school and academic achievement: Intrinsic and extrinsic motivation in ethnic minority groups* (Manuscript in preparation).

Verkuyten, M., & De Jong, W. (1987). Zelfwaardering en onderwijsleerprestaties van Turkse kinderen [Self-experience and educational achievement of Turkish children]. *Pedagogische Studien, 64*(12), 498–507.

Voelkl, K. E. (1996). Measuring students' identification with school. *Educational and Psychological Measurement, 56*(5), 760–770.

Wagner, U., Lampen, L., & Syllwasschy, J. (1986). In-group inferiority, social identity and out-group devaluation in a modified minimal group study. *British Journal of Social Psychology, 25*(1), 15–23.

Walden, C. (1994). The health status of African American college students: A literature review. *Journal of American College Health, 42*(5), 199–205.

Wehlage, G. G., Rutter, R. A., Smith, G. A., Lesko, N., & Fernandez, R. R. (1989). *Reducing the risk: Schools as communities of support.* New York: Falmer Press.

Weisman, N. C. (1998). *The self-concept of learning-disabled adults.* Unpublished Doctoral Dissertation, The Fielding Institute, US.

Wells, A. S., & Crain, R. L. (1994). Perpetuation theory and the long-term effects of school desegregation. *Review of Educational Research, 64*(4), 531–555.

Wigfield, A. (1994). Expectancy-value theory of achievement motivation: A developmental perspective. *Educational Psychology Review, 6*(1), 49–78.

Wigfield, A., & Eccles, J. S. (1992). The development of achievement task values: A theoretical analysis. *Developmental Review, 12*(3), 265–310.

Wigfield, A., & Eccles, J. S. (2000). Expectancy-value theory of achievement motivation. *Contemporary Educational Psychology, 25*(1), 68–81.

Wigfield, A., Eccles, J. S., Mac-Iver, D., Reuman, D. A., & Midgley, C. (1991). Transitions during early adolescence: Changes in children's domain-specific self-perceptions and general self-esteem across the transition to junior high school. *Developmental Psychology, 27*(4), 552–565.

Winston, C., Eccles, J. S., Senior, A. M., & Vida, M. (1997). The utility of expectancy/value and disidentification models for understanding ethnic group differences in academic performance and self-esteem. *Zeitschrift fur Paedagogische Psychologie, 11*(3–4), 177–186.

Witherspoon, K. M., Speight, S. L., & Thomas, A. J. (1997). Racial identity attitudes, school achievement, and academic self-efficacy among African American high school students. *Journal of Black Psychology, 23*(4), 344–357.

Wood, J. V. (1989). Theory and research concerning social comparisons of personal attributes. *Psychological Bulletin, 106*(2), 231–248.

Wood, J. V., Giordano Beech, M., & Ducharme, M. J. (1999). Compensating for failure through social comparison. *Personality and Social Psychology Bulletin, 25*(11), 1370–1386.

Wortman, C. B., & Brehm, J. W. (1975). Responses to uncontrollable outcomes: An integration of reactance theory and the learned helplessness model. In L. Berkowitz (Ed.), *Advances in experimental social psychology* (Vol. 8, pp. 277–336). New York: Academic Press.

Wylie, R. (1979). The self-concept: Theory and research on selected topics (Vol. 2). Lincoln, NE: University of Nebraska Press.

CHAPTER 16

ABOUT THE AUTHORS

Hector Betancourt completed his undergraduate education and professional training in psychology at the Universidad Católica de Chile, in 1976, and his Ph.D. in Social Psychology and Personality at the University of California, Los Angeles (UCLA), in 1983. Although most of his academic career has taken place in the United States, he has also taught, conducted research, and been a consultant on higher education and graduate training in psychology in a number of Latin American Countries. Currently, he is a Professor of Psychology at Loma Linda University, California, where he also holds a Senior Researcher position and has been Chair of the Department of Psychology. His research contributions and interests include the study of culture in psychology, and the role of culture in psychological processes, interpersonal and intergroup behavior (e.g., conflict, conflict resolution, and violence), as well as health behavior. He has been active in organized psychology and served in a number of leadership positions. For example, he has served as president of the Society for the Study of Peace, Conflict, and Violence, the Peace Psychology Division of APA, and is currently a member of the National Steering Committee of Psychologists for Social Responsibility. At the international level, he has been Secretary General of the Interamerican Society of Psychology and is currently serving as a Vice President and a Board member, representing the United States and Canada. He has also served in the editorial board of a number of national and international journals, such as, *Journal of Personality and Social Psychology, Peace and Conflict, Psicologia Contemporanea* (Mexico), *Psykhe* (Chile), *Revista de Psicologia Social* (Spain), and *Interdiciplinaria* (Argentina).

Teaching, Learning, and Motivation in a Multicultural Context, pages 395–399
Copyright © 2003 by Information Age Publishing
All rights of reproduction in any form reserved.

Monique Boekaerts is a professor at the Center for the study of Education and Instruction, Leiden University, the Netherlands. Monique Boekaert's interest lies in research and design of innovation strategy that would guide behavioral change processes in teachers, students and curriculum designers in the participating schools. Currently together with her students she is engaged in many related research including : task specific cognitive and affective processes, self-regulation and external regulation, the effect of instruction on self-actualization and social interaction, management of multiple goals. Monique Boekaerts has held many important national and international offices, including the following positions: Chair of the Department of Educationel Sciences (Nijmegen University, 1985–1990), Dean of the School of Educational Sciences (Nijmegen University, 1988–1990), Chair of the Research Committee of the Faculty of Social Sciences (Leiden, 1998–2001), Member of the Executive Committee of the European Association for Research on Learning and Instruction (1991–1993), Chair of the Center for the Study of Education and Instruction (Leiden, 1992–present), Project director of the research program: Self-Regulated Learning (1992–present), Program chair of the undergraduate program (Psych. Ed, 1992–present), Secretary-Treasurer of the Division of Educational, Instructional and School Psychology of the International Association of Applied Psychology (1990–1994), President-elect of the Division of Educational, Instructional and School Psychology of the International Association of Applied Psychology (1994–1998), President-elect of the European Association of Learning and Instruction (1997–1999), President of Division 5 of the International Association of Applied Psychology (IAAP) (1998–2002), President of the European Association for Research on Learning and Instruction (EARLI) (1999–2001), Member of the board of the International Academy of Education (2002–present), Member of the Quality Audit for Educational Research, appointed by the Dutch Royal Academy of Sciences (1990–1994).

Márta Fülöp is a senior research fellow at the Institute for Psychology of the Hungarian Academy of Sciences, Budapest and a Szechenyi Professor at the Department of Psychology of the University of Szeged, Hungary. In 1996–1997 she was a fellow of Japan Foundation and carried out research at the Tohoku Fukushi University in Sendai, Japan. In 1997–1998 she was a Lindzey Fellow in the Center for Advanced Study in the Behavioral Sciences, Stanford University. She has been doing extensive research on students' and teachers' concepts of competition in different cultures.

Sandra Graham is a Professor in the Department of Education at UCLA. She received her BA from Barnard College, an MA in History from Columbia University, and her PhD in Education from UCLA. Her major research interests include the study of academic motivation, peer aggression, and juvenile delinquency, particularly in African American children and adolescents. Professor Graham has published widely in developmental, social, and educational psychology journals. She currently is Principal Investigator on grants from the National Science Foundation, and the W. T. Grant Foundation. She also is the recipient of an Independent Scientist Award, funded by the National Institute of Mental Health. She is a former recipient of the Early Contribution Award from Division 15 (Educational Psychology) of the American Psychological Association and a former Fellow at the Center for Advanced Study in the Behavioral Sciences, Stanford, California. Among her professional activities, Professor Graham is an Associate Editor of *Developmental Psychology*, a member of the National Research Council Panel on Juvenile Crime, Prevention, and Control, and a member of the MacArthur Foundation Network on Adolescent

Kit-Tai Hau is Professor and Chair of the Educational Psychology Department, The Chinese University of Hong Kong. His research centers around motivation, structural equation modeling, psychometrics and suicide.

Rumjahn Hoosain is a Professor of Psychology at the University of Hong Kong. His interests are in cognitive psychology, including psychological aspects of the Chinese language, bilingualism, and the learning of language.

Dennis McInerney is a Professor in the School of Psychology at the University of Western Sydney. His research specializations are motivation and learning in cross-cultural contexts, multicultural education, and instrument design and validation in cross-cultural contexts.

Chit-Kwong Kong is a part-time Lecturer in the Faculty of Education at the Chinese University of Hong Kong. His research interests include self-concept, motivation, structural equation modeling, and multilevel analysis.

Valentina McInerney is an Associate Professor in the School of Psychology at the University of Western Sydney. Her research specializations are multicultural education, and information technology in education.

Herbert W. Marsh is Professor of Education and Director of the SELF Research Centre at the University of Western Sydney, located in Campbelltown, Australia. His professional interests center around self-concept research, student evaluations of teaching, confirmatory factor analysis, and research design.

Ference Marton is a professor at the Department of Education of the University of Gothenburg, Sweden. He spent 3 years at the University of Hong Kong as a Distinguished Visiting Professor (1998–2002). He specializes on human learning and is founder of Phenomenography the research program which aims at the study of the qualitively different ways in which people experience the world around them. He has especially studied how learning and related phenomena are made sense of in different cultures. Most recently he has carried out such studies with indigenous students in Australia and with Chinese students in Hong Kong and Shanghai. He has written: Marton, F & Booth, S. (1997) *Learning and Awareness.* Mahwah: Lawrence Erlbaum

Paul R. Pintrich is Professor of Education and Psychology and Chair of the Combined Program in Education and Psychology at The University of Michigan, Ann Arbor. He also has served as the Associate Dean for Research for the School of Education at Michigan. His research focuses on the development of motivation, epistemological thinking, and self-regulated learning in adolescence. He has published over 100 articles, book chapters and books including co-authoring or co-editing 8 books. He is the past editor of the American Psychology Association journal for Division 15–Educational Psychology, *Educational Psychologist.* His research has been funded by the National Science Foundation (NSF), the Office of Educational Research and Improvement (OERI) in the Department of Education, the Spencer Foundation, and the Kellogg Foundation. He is a Fellow of the American Psychological Association and has been a National Academy of Education Spencer Fellow. Along with his co-author Barbara Hofer, he won the 1999 Best Research Review Article Award from the American Educational Research Association for an article on epistemological thinking that appeared in *Review of Educational Research.* He is currently President-Elect of Division 5–Educational and Instructional Psychology for the International Association of Applied Psychology and President for Division 15–Educational Psychology for the American Psychological Association. He also has won the Class of 1923 Award from the College of Literature, Science, and Arts and the School of Education at The University of Michigan for excellence in undergraduate teaching.

Farideh Salili is an Honorary Professor at the Department of Psychology, the University of Hong Kong. She served as the Director of the Educational Psychology Programs in the Department of Psychology until 2001. She is currently a Professor in the Behavioral Science Unit of the Department of Community Medicine at the University of Hong Kong. Her research interest lies in cross-cultural differences in student motivation and has published widely in that area.

David Watkins is a Reader in Education at the University of Hong Kong. He has published widely in the areas of student learning, self-esteem, and the evaluation of university teaching based on research in Australia and a number of Asian and African countries.

Akane Zusho is currently a doctoral candidate in the Combined Program in Educational Psychology at the University of Michigan, Ann Arbor. She received her B.A. in psychology and her M.A. in developmental psychology, both from the University of Michigan. Her research interests include the interplay of culture and motivation, as well as achievement motivation and self-regulated learning of ethnic minority adolescents.

Gangaw Zaw is a graduate student in Clinical Psychology at Loma Linda University, Loma Linda, California. She is currently a Research Assistant in the Department of Psychology's Laboratory for Culture and Interpersonal-Intergroup Processes. Her research focuses on the role of culture and psychological factors in conflict resolution styles. Her experience includes involvement in basic mediation training for small disputes and family/divorce mediation in community dispute resolution centers. As an undergraduate student at California Polytechnic State University, Pomona, she participated in the project leading to the publication of Key Terms in Multicultural Psychology.

INDEX

A

Academic achievement, 91, 268–269
  favorable/unfavorable task apprais-
    als, 18–22
  folk theory of success, 293–294, 296,
    299, 311
  self-esteem and, 371
Academic disidentification, 345–346,
  364–365
  learning disabled students, 372–373
  low performance and, 363–365
Academic motivation, 102–106; *see also*
  Motivation
  disidentification and low perfor-
    mance, 363–365
  Eccles and Wigfield model, 364
  identification and intrinsic motiva-
    tion, 365–367
Academic motivation training, 93,
  95–96
Accreditation process, 227
Acculturation, 44
Achievement goal theory, 47–48
Action research, 253–254
African American students, 369–374
Aggression, 91
Alexander, P. A., 149–150
American Association for Higher Edu-
  cation (AAHE), 234
American Custom Complex, 38–41

American Society for the Study of
  Higher Education (ASSHE), 230
Anti-racism education programs, 196
Appraisal model, 21–22
Arbitration, 70
Arnow, J., 71, 74
Asian Americans, 45–47, 49, 53
  cultural capital of, 291
  educational achievement of,
    290–293
Assimilation effects, 133–134
Association of Universities and Colleges of Canada (AUCC), 230
At-risk youth, school-based intervention, 91–92
  academic motivation and training,
    93, 95–96, 102–103
  costs vs. benefits of, 113–114
  cumulative folders assessment,
    108–109
  curriculum intervention, 96–98
  implication for design, 110–111
  laboratory analogue task, 103–106
  outcome measures, 98
  overview of, 92–95
  results of, 98–99
  sample attrition, 97–98
  selecting participants, 97
  social skills training, 92–96, 99–102
  summary of intervention effects,
    109–110